CAREER OPPORTUNITIES

IN THE

SPORTS

INDUSTRY

SECOND EDITION

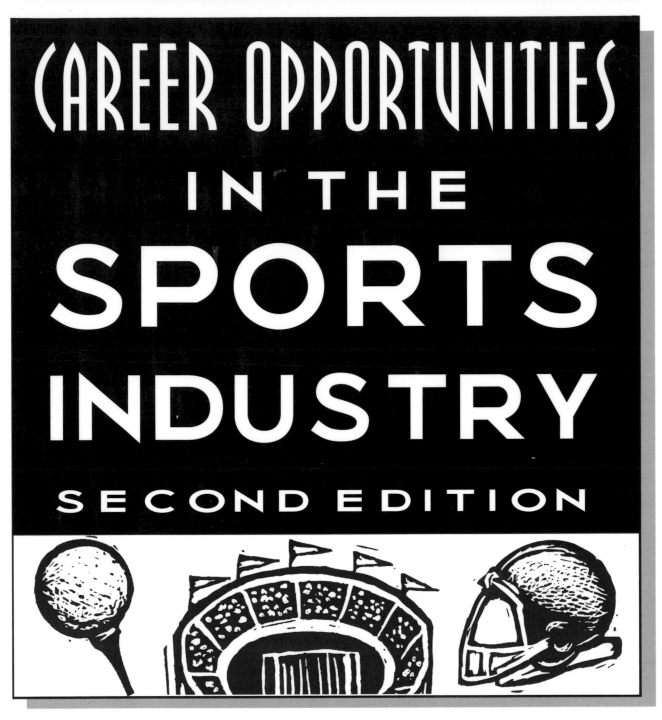

**A Comprehensive Guide to Exciting Careers
Open to You in Sports**

◆ Indispensable and Realistic Information on More
Than 70 Specific Jobs

◆ Details on Salaries, Skill Requirements, Advancement
Prospects, Trade Associations, Special Opportunities
and Much More

SHELLY FIELD

CAREER OPPORTUNITIES IN THE SPORTS INDUSTRY

Second Edition

SHELLY FIELD

Checkmark Books™
An imprint of Facts On File, Inc.

*This book is dedicated to my parents, Ed and Selma,
and my sisters, Jessica and Debbie,
for their continuing support,
guidance, and love.*

CAREER OPPORTUNITIES IN THE SPORTS INDUSTRY, Second Edition

Copyright © 1999 by Shelly Field

Checkmark Books
An imprint of Facts On File, Inc.
11 Penn Plaza
New York NY 10001

Library of Congress Cataloging-in-Publication Data

Field, Shelly.
    Career opportunities in the sports industry : a comprehensive
guide to the exciting careers open to you in sports or sports-
related fields : indispensable information on 73 specific jobs /
Shelly Field. — 2nd ed.
        p.   cm.
    Includes bibliographical references (p.   ) and index.
    ISBN 0-8160-3794-9 (hardcover). — ISBN 0-8160-3795-7 (pbk.)
    1. Sports—Vocational guidance—United States.   I. Title.
GV734.F545   1999
796'.023'73—dc21   98-16483

Checkmark Books are available at special discounts when purchased in bulk
quantities for businesses, associations, institutions, or sales promotions. Please call
our Special Sales Department in New York at 212/967-8800 or 800/322-8755.

You can find Facts On File on the World Wide Web at http://www.factsonfile.com

Printed in the United States of America

VB FOF 10 9 8 7 6 5 4 3 2 1
    (pbk) 10 9 8 7 6 5 4 3 2 1

This book is printed on acid-free paper.

CONTENTS

HOW TO USE THIS BOOK

Purpose

In the years since this book was first written in 1991, the sports industry has exploded. It is a booming business and many job seekers want a piece of the action.

Thousands of people are currently working in the sports arena and many more want to enter but have no idea how to go about getting a job in the field. They have no concept of where to locate the career opportunities or the training required to be successful in their quest.

This book was written for everyone who aspires to work in the sports industry but does not know how to get into it. The 73 jobs discussed in this book include careers not only in professional athletics but also in the business end of the industry, education, officiating, sales, recreation, fitness, and many more.

The sports industry holds opportunities for a great variety of people with many different talents. It needs athletes, secretaries, receptionists, salespeople, publicists, trainers, business managers, scouts, statisticians, coaches, teachers, referees, judges, store managers, health and fitness personnel, nutritionists, and more. The key to locating a job is to develop your skills and use them to get you in the door of the sports field of your choice. Once you have accomplished this, you have a good chance of climbing the career ladder.

Read through the book and determine what you are qualified for or interested in, or how you can obtain training in the field you want to enter. You can then work toward getting in an interesting, exciting and financially rewarding job in the sports industry.

Sources of Information

Information for this book was obtained through interviews, questionnaires, and a variety of books, magazines, newsletters, television and radio programs, college catalogs, etc. Some information came through personal experience working in the industry. Other data were obtained from friends and business associates in various areas of the sports industry.

Among the people interviewed were men and women in all aspects of sports. These include individuals working in business and administration, amateur and professional athletics, colleges, newspapers, magazines, radio and television stations, health and fitness clubs, spas, racetracks, and sports medicine clinics. Also interviewed were agents, managers, publicists, team managers, owners and employees, physical therapists, nutritionists, coaches, referees, and judges. Professional sports teams were contacted, as well as schools, colleges, personnel offices, unions, trade associations, etc.

All information in this newly revised edition has been updated.

Organization of Material

Career Opportunities in the Sports Industry is divided into 11 general employment sections. These sections are: Professional Athletes; Career Opportunities with Professional Sports Teams; Career Opportunities in Sports Business and Administration; Career Opportunities in Coaching and Education; Career Opportunities in Officiating; Career Opportunities in Sports Journalism; Career Opportunities in Recreation and Fitness; Career Opportunities in Boxing and Wrestling; Career Opportunities in Racing; Career Opportunities in Wholesaling and Retailing; and Career Opportunities in Sports Medicine. Within each of these sections are descriptions of individual careers.

There are two parts to each job classification. The first part offers job information in a chart form. The second part presents information in a narrative text. In addition to the basic career description, you will find additional information on unions and associations as well as tips for entry.

This edition features an expanded appendix. Nineteen updated appendices are offered to help locate information you might want or need to get started looking for a job in the field. Names and addresses are included so that you know who and where to send your résumés to. You can also use these to assist you in locating internships or obtaining general information about a sports-related job.

These appendices include college and university degree programs for sports administration and physical education; programs in sports officiating; workshops, seminars and symposiums; trade associations and unions; professional sports teams; collegiate athletic conferences; boxing and wrestling promoters; and cable and network television sports departments. A bibliography of sports-related books and periodicals and a glossary are also included.

Whether you choose to be a professional athlete, a sports official, a general manager of a sports team, sports reporter, or a sports store manager, your job can be both exciting and fulfilling. Your career in the sports industry is waiting for you. You just have to go after it! Persevere and you will make it!

Shelly Field

ACKNOWLEDGMENTS

I thank every individual, team, company, corporation, agency, association, and union that provided information, assistance, and encouragement in the development of this book and its previous edition.

I acknowledge with appreciation my editors, Nicole Bowen and Jim Chambers, for their help and encouragement. I also must thank Kate Kelly, who as my initial editor provided the original impetus for this book, and Neal Maillet, another editor of this project. I gratefully acknowledge Matthew E. Strong for his sports expertise and guidance through the development and writing of this work. I could not have successfully completed this book without the assistance of Ed and Selma Field. Others whose help was invaluable include the American Football Coaches Association; American Hockey League; American League; Jim Baker, Deputy Director of Operations, Major League Soccer; Dave Barnett; Dan Barrett; Ryan Barrett; Allan Barrish; Mistie Bass; Eugene Blabey, WVOS Radio; Al Buongiorne, Supervisor of Driver/Training Licensing for United States Trotting Association; Sue Cabot; Anthony Cellini; Dr. Jessica L. Cohen; Norman Cohen; Community General Hospital, Harris, N.Y.; Jan Cornelius; Crawford Memorial Library Staff; Meike Cryan; Elias Sports Bureau; Lisa Estrada, Coordinator/Director, Los Angeles Laker Girls; Ernest Evans; Eddie Ferenz, Philadelphia Phillies Traveling Secretary; Field Associates, Ltd.; Deborah K. Field, Esq.; Finkelstein Memorial Library Staff; Pat Flemming, MSG Sports; Paul Francis, Jr., Executive Director, International Association of Approved Basketball Officials; Clark Gaines, Regional Director, National Football League Players Association; John Gatto; Shelia Gatto; George Glantzis; Kaytee Glantzis; Sam Goldych; Mary Griffin, Account Executive, Rhulen Markel Insurance Agency; Gail Haberle; Kent Hastings, North American Judges and Stewards Association; Darren Hawks, NBA Media Relations; Larry Hazzard, Commissioner, New Jersey Athletic Commission; Allan Henry, Coordinator of Tennis Teacher Development, United States Professional Tennis Association; Hermann Memorial Library Staff; Tom Hoover, New York State Athletic Commission; Jay Horowitz, New York Yankees; Jimmy "Handyman" Jones; Joan Howard; Gerry Hunsicker, Director of Minor League Operations, New York Mets; Al "Flap" Ingber, Apollo Plaza; International Association of Approved Basketball Officials; International Boxing Federation; Roland Johnson, Director of Scouts, New York Mets; Ben Kaplan; Don King Enterprises; Mark Levin, National Football League Research; Los Angeles Lakers; Los Angeles Laker Girls; Joe McIlvaine, V.P. of Baseball Operations, New York Mets; Darcy Maccarone, MSG Sports; Major Indoor Soccer League; John Manzi, Monticello Raceway; Larry Miller, Racing Secretary, Monticello Raceway; MSG Sports; Monticello Central High School Guidance Department; Monticello Central School High School Library Staff; Monticello Central School Middle School Library Staff; Monticello Raceway; Edward P. Marion, Executive Director of the Professional Football Referees Association; Werner Mendel, New Age Health Spa; Mike Moore, National Association of Professional Baseball Leagues; Sharon Morris; National Association of Professional Baseball Leagues; National Basketball Association; National Football League; National Football League Players Association; National Hockey League; National League; New Jersey Athletic Commission; New York Mets; New York State Athletic Commission; New York Yankees; North American Judges and Stewards Association; Dorsey J. Parker, Assistant Public Relations Director, National League; Philadelphia Phillies; Professional Football Referees Association; Mel Pulliam, American Football Coaches Association; Ramapo Catskill Library System; Doug Richards; Ross Richardson, Director of Administration, New York Yankees; Bob Rosen, Statistician, Elias Sports Bureau; Eva Shain, Professional Boxing Judge; Frank Shain, Professional Ring Announcer; Laura Solomon; Bob Sparks, National Association of Professional Baseball Leagues; Marjorie Snyder, Director of Resources, Women's Sports Foundation; Ron Scott Stevens, Promoter—Matchmaker; Thrall Library Staff; Mary Ann Toomey, Apollo Plaza; Marie Tremper; United States Professional Tennis Association; United States Trotting Association; Carol Williams; Chet Williams; John Williams; Mike Wimer, Public Relations Assistant, Major Indoor Soccer League; WNBA; The Women's Sports Foundation; and WVOS Radio.

My thanks also to the many people, companies, and organizations that provided material for this book and wish to remain anonymous.

INTRODUCTION

The sports industry is highly lucrative. It has become a multi-billion-dollar business. Thousands of people work in the various facets of the industry. One of them can be you.

Almost any talent you have can be applied to obtaining a job in the sports industry. The possibilities are endless. You can be anything from a professional athlete to the general manager of a sports team; a coach, gym teacher, referee, secretary, or receptionist in a major sports team organization office. If you prefer, your job in the field of sports can be that of a physical therapist, sports journalist, commentator, or television anchor person. You might want to become a boxing judge, a retail sports shop sales clerk, or a manufacturer's representative for athletic equipment.

The world of sports is all-encompassing. Every time you exercise, attend a baseball game, watch a tennis tournament, play golf, or put on a pair of running shoes, you are dealing with an aspect of the sports industry.

As you read the various sections in this book, searching to find the job you have always dreamed about, keep in mind that there are many ways to break into the sports industry. I have given you some guidelines. You have to do the rest.

Within each section of this book you will find all the information necessary to acquaint you with most of the important jobs in sports. A key to the organization of each entry follows:

Alternate Titles

Many jobs in sports have alternate titles. The duties these jobs consist of are similar; only the names are different. The job title may vary from sport to sport and from team to team.

Career Ladder

The career ladder illustrates a typical career path. Remember that in the sports industry there are no set rules. Advancement may occur in almost any manner.

Position Description

Every effort has been made to give well-rounded job descriptions. Keep in mind that no two jobs are structured exactly the same, therefore, no two positions will be precisely the same. For example, teams might have various supervisors doing the same type of job or might eliminate certain positions entirely.

Salary Range

Salary ranges for the 73 job titles in the book are as accurate as possible. Salaries for jobs in the sports industry reflect many variables. These include the specific sport an individual is working in as well as his or her experience, responsibilities, and position. Earnings also are dependent on the specific team an individual is working for, as well as its prestige and popularity. Geographic location is also a significant factor effecting salary ranges.

Employment Prospects

If you choose a job that has an EXCELLENT, GOOD, or FAIR rating, you are lucky. You will have an easier time finding employment. If, however, you would like to work at a job that has a POOR rating, don't despair. The rating means only that it is difficult to obtain a job—not that finding one is totally impossible.

Advancement Prospects

Try to be as cooperative and helpful as possible in the workplace. Don't attempt to see how little work you can do. Be enthusiastic, energetic, and outgoing. Go the step that no one expects. Learn as much as you can. When a job advancement possibility opens up, make sure that you're prepared to take advantage of it.

Education and Training

Although this book cites only the minimum training and educational requirements for a particular job, this doesn't mean that you should limit yourself to them. Try to get the best training and education possible. A college degree does not guarantee a job in the sports industry, but it will provide a person with more choices within it. Education and training also encompass courses, seminars, programs, on-the-job training, internships, apprenticeships, and learning from others.

Experience/Skills/Personality Traits

These requirements will differ from job to job. However, whichever job you want to work at, you will probably need a lot of perseverance and fortitude. There is a great deal of competition in all facets of the sports industry.

Become the best at what you intend to do. If you are interested in becoming a professional athlete, you will need to have the talent. If you are seeking a position working with a professional team in an administrative capacity, you will have to have good communications skills.

Contacts are important when searching for a job in any industry, and the sports field is no exception. Make as many contacts as you can. They may prove invaluable in getting your career started and helping you to advance in it.

Best Geographic Location

Jobs in the sports industry are located throughout the country. Opportunities may be found in cities hosting major league, minor league, or collegiate sports teams.

Opportunities in sports-oriented journalism, television, and radio may be located both in large metropolitan areas and small rural towns. The same is true of jobs in retailing, wholesaling, education, fitness, recreation, and sports medicine. Those interested in becoming professional athletes might have to relocate to areas where sports teams or events are headquartered.

Unions/Associations

Unions and trade associations offer valuable help in obtaining career guidance, support, and personal contacts. They may also offer training, continuing education, scholarships, fellowships, seminars, and other beneficial programs.

Tips for Entry

Use this section for ideas on how to get a job and gain entry into the areas in which you are interested. When applying for any job always be as professional as possible. Dress neatly and conservatively. Don't wear sneakers. Don't chew gum. Don't smoke. Don't wear heavy perfume or men's cologne. Always have a few copies of your résumé with you. These, too, should look neat and professional. Have them typed and presented well, checked and rechecked for grammar, spelling, and content.

The ability to go on-line, whether from your home computer or one in a school or public library, puts you at a great advantage. You can obtain information about teams, sports, and industry news. Many sports teams, sports-oriented programs,

No matter what aspect of the sports industry piques your interest, become computer literate. It is always a plus.

newspapers, and magazines now feature web sites that may be helpful in your quest for that perfect job. Additionally, there are myriad job and career sites online offering information on getting a job, as well as specific jobs that may be available.

If you aspire to become a professional athlete, get the best training you can. Refine your skills and techniques. Talk with your coaches and instructors and ask for help. Most people are glad to provide it.

Use every contact you have. If you are lucky enough to know someone who can help you obtain a job, accept his or her assistance. You'll have to prove yourself at the interview and on the job. Nobody can do that for you. The last piece of advice in this section is to be on time for everything. This includes job interviews, phone calls, work, meetings, sending letters, etc. Habitual lateness will certainly have a negative effect on your prospects for career advancement.

Do not be afraid to pursue your dream job. You can have a career that will enable you to get up each morning happy that you are going to work. The sports industry can be both glamorous, exciting, and financially rewarding. Don't get discouraged during your job-hunting period. Every person does not secure the first job he or she applies for. You may have to pay your dues in the minor leagues. You may have to knock on a lot of doors, send out a lot of résumés, and apply for a lot of jobs you don't get, but eventually you can find the job of your dreams.

You have already taken the first step by picking up this book. Have fun reading it. Use it. It will help you find a career that you will truly love. Good luck!

CAREER OPPORTUNITIES FOR PROFESSIONAL ATHLETES

PROFESSIONAL BASEBALL PLAYER

CAREER PROFILE

Duties: Playing baseball professionally; training; keeping in shape.

Alternate Title(s):   Ball Player; Player; Baseball Player

Salary Range: $14,000 to $12,000,000+

Employment Prospects: Poor

Best Geographical Location(s) for Position: Cities hosting professional ball clubs.

Prerequisites:

Education or Training—No formal educational requirement.

Experience—Experience playing baseball necessary.

Special Skills and Personality Traits—Talented in the sport; love of baseball; team player; motivated; ability to travel; ability to deal with stress.

CAREER LADDER

```
┌─────────────────────────────────┐
│   Professional Baseball Player  │
│              with               │
│     Major League Ball Club      │
└─────────────────────────────────┘

┌─────────────────────────────────┐
│   Professional Baseball Player  │
│              with               │
│       Minor League Team         │
└─────────────────────────────────┘

┌─────────────────────────────────┐
│                                 │
│     Amateur Baseball Player     │
│                                 │
└─────────────────────────────────┘
```

Position Description

It is the dream of many youngsters to grow up and play professional baseball. Most go on to other careers and forget their childhood dream. Some lucky young men (there are currently no successful professional leagues for women), however, get the opportunity to pursue their dream and become Professional Baseball Players.

The road to becoming a Pro Ball Player is not easy. There are many pitfalls along the way. Competition is stiff in this industry. A lot of hard work is involved not only in becoming a Pro Player, but in staying in the pros as well. It is a long climb up the career ladder from an amateur baseball player to a Pro in the major leagues, but for those who love the sport, it is well worth it.

An individual usually begins his career by playing amateur baseball. He might be on a school, civic, nonprofit, or community team. Someone notices that he has more talent than the rest of the team members. It might be a coach, a physical education teacher, or someone just watching the game. Sometimes the individual begins to emerge as a star of the team. Over a period of time, a number of people will see a special talent in the player, a talent that the other athletes do not appear to possess.

By the time the individual reaches high school, it will be evident that he can play better than others on the team. He might have excellent pitching skills or be a harder hitter.

The next step toward becoming a Baseball Player entails getting the attention of someone in the pros to determine if the talent is really there. This process can be handled in a number of different ways. The individual's coach or another interested person may contact a professional team or a scout. The individual might contact these people himself. Also, some scouts travel throughout the country searching for talented young men who want to become Professional Ball Players. Besides holding tryouts, they may visit schools, colleges, and other locations to talk to coaches, teachers, and players.

As noted previously, competition in this profession is fierce. Scouts may see hundreds of young men playing the game before they find one individual whom they feel will make it in the pros. When the scout does locate a talented player, he or she will bring him to the attention of a member of the baseball club, such as the director of minor league operations or the head scout.

The Scout will then talk to the athlete and his family about the possibility of signing a contract to work with the team. In order to make an offer more acceptable, they may offer the athlete a full or partial scholarship to a college he would like to attend. A contract must then be negotiated and signed.

Athletes who are in college and want to turn pro may sign up for the draft. The draft is a system where teams get to choose athletes from a list of players who want to become professionals. The first team to choose from the list is the one that placed last in standings during the year. The next team to choose is the one that placed next to last, and so on. The team that won the championship gets last choice. If a team wants certain players who have already been chosen, the team may trade other players for them.

Baseball clubs have four different classes or levels of teams. The first three are called minor league clubs. They consist of the A team or rookie team; the AA team; the AAA, or "Triple A," team; and the major league club. While there are no hard-and-fast rules regarding which level club the novice Professional Baseball Player is assigned to, usually he begins to play with the rookie team. If, however, the individual is extremely talented, he might be assigned to play with any level.

Each major league ball club has a number of minor league affiliates. Therefore, if a Player is under contract to the New York Mets, he might be working with the Jackson Mets, the Mets AA team.

While in the minor leagues, Baseball Players are trained to refine their skills while competing with other teams of the same stature. Players are expected to attend spring training and any other mandatory and regular training sessions.

After a season, if the Player is ready, he may move up from the rookie team to the AA team. After another, he may be assigned to play in the Triple A club. What every Professional Ball Player aspires to is an assignment to play on a major league team. This is extremely difficult and does not happen to every Player. Many Players stay in the minor leagues for their entire career. It is important to remember that Players in the major league club may also be reassigned back to one of the minor league teams. As noted previously, there is no set rule for the level a Pro Ball Player may be assigned to play.

Those playing in the minor leagues will not get even a fraction of the recognition or financial compensation that athletes in the major leagues do. These Players travel in buses from one area to another competing in games. Usually they do not stay in the most prestigious hotels or eat at the better restaurants. They do have the opportunity to learn and gain experience.

Every Ball Player hopes eventually to be assigned to work in the major league team. During this period, he will be earning an excellent income for his efforts as well as gaining recognition as a Player. He may stay at this level for one or more years depending on his skills and talent.

Baseball Players must concern themselves with injuries that might prevent them from working or force them into early retirement. They must also worry about staying on top. At any time during their contract with one of the teams, the Pro Ball Player may be traded to another team. While this may not bother some people, to others, the rejection can be an emotional strain.

Many major league Ball Players work under tremendous stress and pressure for additional reasons. They must constantly stay at the top. Games or entire tournaments may depend on the actions of an individual, which adds to the stress level.

It is important to remember that individuals choosing baseball as a career will not have a choice of cities where they will be headquartered. They must move to the area where the team they are working with is located. Players also must travel extensively to away games during the playing season.

For most Players who make it to the major leagues, a career as a Professional Baseball Player is a dream come true. Many feel it is especially exciting to have thousands of fans cheering for them while they are working at a vocation that most people consider an avocation.

Salaries

Salaries for Pro Baseball Players vary greatly depending on the individual, his prestige, and the level he is playing at. Individuals may earn from $14,000 and up working in the minor leagues. Some Pro Ball Players in the major leagues command salaries of $2,000,000 to $12,000,000 plus.

Employment Prospects

Employment prospects are poor for those aspiring to be Pro Baseball Players. Competition is keen. If individuals have talent, however, they can make it in this profession.

While major league teams are located in major cities throughout the country, many minor league clubs are found in smaller cities.

Advancement Prospects

Advancement prospects for a Pro Player are largely dependent on the individual's skills, talents, drive, and determination. It takes hard work to train and play in this sport. Those who show they can do it and are good at what they do will move up. Advancement for Pro Players means that they move up a level in the types of clubs they play with. A rookie advances by moving to a team in the AA or AAA level. Each club has teams in each level. If a player shows potential, he will be moved to a higher level team to play. All Players hope to advance to an assignment to a major league team. Majors league Players can advance their careers by improving their performance and command higher and higher salaries.

Education and Training

There are no formal educational requirements for Professional Ball Players. This is not to say that Ball Players are not educated. Many Players have college degrees from prestigious schools.

Individuals must be trained in the sport. Most formal training is obtained once the Player is under contract with a team, although Players who play ball in college may also obtain experience comparable to the minor leagues. During this period players are trained by team coaches, trainers, and support staff to shape their talent and refine their skills.

Experience/Skills/Personality Traits

Professional Baseball Players must love the sport. They should understand the rules, regulations, and policies of baseball. Individuals must be talented and skillful. It is useful for them to be team players and get along well with others.

The Players should be physically fit and energetic. They need to be motivated and confident as well as have the persistence, drive, and determination necessary to work their way to the top of the profession.

Individuals must be flexible in the geographic area they will have to live in during the playing season. Ball Players must also not mind traveling. They must also have the ability to deal with the stress and pressure that comes from working in this profession. Individuals who make it to the top must also be able to deal with the fame that usually follows.

A good sense of business is useful. While most individuals have someone to represent them, it is helpful to have a working knowledge of the business end of the industry.

Unions/Associations

Professional Ball Players belong to the a professional organization called the Association of Professional Ball Players of America (APBPA). They may also be members of the Major League Ball Players Association (MLBPA). These organizations work on behalf of Ball Players to provide better conditions and also negotiate other parts of their contracts.

Tips for Entry

1. If you really want to become a Pro Baseball Player, you must practice and play at every opportunity.
2. If someone offers you constructive criticism, take it and try to improve your skills.
3. Try to find someone, such as a coach or a physical education teacher, who can help you in your career. If such people feel that you are talented, ask if they can contact a scout or a major league team recruitment official on your behalf.
4. If you cannot find anyone to act on your behalf, you might want to contact the recruitment office of one of the ball clubs. Tell them about yourself and learn what you should do to help your career progress.
5. If you or others feel that you have the talent, persevere. This is a difficult career to enter, but it can be done.

PROFESSIONAL BASKETBALL PLAYER

CAREER PROFILE

Duties: Playing basketball for a professional sports team.

Alternate Title(s): Pro Player; Pro Basketball Player

Salary Range: $242,000 to $20,000,000+

Employment Prospects: Poor

Best Geographical Location(s) for Position: Cities hosting professional basketball teams.

Prerequisites:

Education or Training—No formal educational requirement; however, most players do attend college.

Experience—Experience playing amateur basketball necessary.

Special Skills and Personality Traits—Excellent physical condition; energetic; fast; talented in skills and techniques of basketball; love of game.

CAREER LADDER

```
┌─────────────────────────────────┐
│          Superstar              │
│ Professional Basketball Player  │
└─────────────────────────────────┘

┌─────────────────────────────────┐
│         Professional            │
│     Basketball Player           │
└─────────────────────────────────┘

┌─────────────────────────────────┐
│     Amatur or Scholastic        │
│      Basketball Player          │
└─────────────────────────────────┘
```

Position Description

For those who enjoy shooting baskets as a form a recreation, it is often hard to believe that there are actually people who get paid to do just that. Professional Basketball Players have the job of playing basketball for professional teams and earning a living at the game. Today, women as well as men can play professionally.

Most Basketball Players began shooting baskets while they were youngsters. Basketball was their choice when it came to sports. Many played on their junior and varsity high school basketball teams. During this time, coaches, college scouts, and members of college alumni programs watched the young players. By the time they were juniors in high school, many potential Professional Basketball Players had been contacted by colleges or their representatives about the possibility of attending their school and playing on their basketball team.

Scouts and coaches look for a number of things. A very tall, athletic individual will usually catch their eye. There are, however, a number of shorter players. Those who score a lot of points on the court will generate the same interest. Scouts and other personnel may visit in person or obtain information from high school coaches, friends, acquaintances, or by reading sports articles in local newspapers.

Some students who appear to be very talented at the game are contacted by more than one college. Individuals must decide which college they want to attend. For many students, the decision is based not only on the academic standards of the school, but on the prestige of the school's basketball team. Strict regulations forbid scouts from offering and students from accepting incentives such as cars, money, and so on in order to attend a certain school and play on its basketball team.

Once a student is playing for a college team, he or she is usually not allowed to participate in the National Basketball Association (NBA) draft until graduation. However, there are some exceptions to the rule. For example, an exception might be granted if an individual could prove that staying in school was a financial hardship.

A good number of Professional Basketball Players go through the draft system. Individuals who intend to turn professional sign up to participate in the draft. Teams have the option of choosing their players from the draft.

Other players who do not make it through the draft system and are not chosen can become free agents. These individuals usually hire an agent to represent them. The agent "shops around" for a team for the individual to play with. If the Player is talented and has a good record, he may be asked to go to a preliminary camp to see if his skills can be refined. If the camp visit works out satisfactorily, the individual becomes a member of the team.

Professional Basketball Players train at camps before the basketball season starts. Most basketball training camps and clinics start in the early fall. Individuals then play for the season, which begins in November and lasts about seven months.

Individuals must learn and adhere to the rules, regulations, and policies of the game. Individuals play either defensively or offensively, depending on their skills.

One of the best things about playing professional basketball is that it is always played on an inside court. Unlike players in baseball or football, Basketball Players do not have to concern themselves with the weather. It can be raining or snowing outside, but inside the weather is always perfect.

In addition to training, practicing, and playing games, Players may be expected to perform in exhibitions. They may participate for nonprofit causes or act as spokespeople for issues that are of concern to them individually or to the team.

Pro Players who make a name for themselves and perform well on the court may also be asked to endorse products in commercials or advertisements. Some Pro Players work with clothing or sports shoe companies developing lines of clothing and sneakers. Others endorse food products or sports-related products.

Individuals who are under contract to a team have to live in the area where the team is headquartered at least during the season. Professional Players train long hours. They must always stay in good physical shape. An injury to any part of the body could cut their career short. Professional Players must also continue to perform well in order to remain successful in their career.

Salaries

Earnings of Professional Basketball Players vary greatly depending on a number of factors. These include the team the individual is playing for as well as his experience level, skills, talents, and popularity.

The annual salary for an individual who has just been picked from the draft currently runs from a minimum of $242,000 to a maximum of $2,473,000. The minimum annual salary for a player chosen in the first-round of draft choices, or the first 29, is currently $494,000.

From that point on, Professional Basketball Players can negotiate contracts that pay upward into the millions. Basketball does, however, have a cap on salaries. This means that the team organization can spend only a certain amount of money for all their members. They can split the dollar amount any way they want but cannot go over the limit.

The average Professional Basketball Player earns a salary of approximately $2,300,000. There are some Players who are big draws and have negotiated multimillion dollar contracts of $20 million or more annually.

It should be noted that these figures are for men playing in the NBA. Women playing professionally, have considerably lower salaries.

Both men and women playing professional basketball can also earn millions of dollars in endorsements for various products such as shoes, clothing, toys, etc.

Employment Prospects

Employment prospects for Pro Basketball Players are poor. Each team only hires 12 players, and there are only a limited number of teams.

Some individuals who are talented but have not been able to find a position playing with the NBA have been fortunate to find work with other leagues, such as the Continental Basketball Association (CBA) or leagues that play in other countries.

As noted, women now also have the opportunity to play professionally for the WNBA.

Advancement Prospects

Advancement prospects for Professional Basketball Players are difficult to determine. Some individuals become superstars during their participation in the sport, while others are forgotten after their stint with a team. Advancement for Pro Basketball Players depends largely on their skills, talent, determination, popularity, and drive. Individuals who have those traits may become superstar Players demanding high earnings. They may also market themselves and obtain lucrative product endorsements.

Education and Training

There are no educational requirements for Professional Basketball Players. However, most individuals are graduates of the college they played for during their amateur days. Majors vary depending on the individual interests of the players.

Experience/Skills/Personality Traits

The majority of Pro Basketball Players are at least six feet tall. Most are taller. There are exceptions, but these are limited. Individuals must be in excellent physical condition.

Pro Players should be very talented in the techniques and skills of the game. Being a team player is most helpful. As the individual will spend so much time on the court, a love of the game is necessary.

Unions/Associations

Individuals playing for teams in the National Basketball Association (NBA) are members of the NBA Players Association (NBAPA). This organization works on behalf of the Players in the NBA.

Women play for teams in the WNBA.

Tips for Entry
1. Attend basketball clinics, camps, seminars, and workshops to perfect and refine your skills.
2. Play every chance you get and practice as much as possible.
3. Talk to your coaches and physical education teachers about your aspirations and see if they can help or offer any advice.

PROFESSIONAL FOOTBALL PLAYER

CAREER PROFILE

Duties: Playing football on a professional team.

Alternate Title(s):   Athlete; Pro Football Player

Salary Range: $131,000 to $8,400,000+

Employment Prospects: Poor

Best Geographical Location(s) for Position: Cities hosting professional football teams.

Prerequisites:
Education or Training—Football training.
Experience—Experience playing amateur/collegiate football necessary.
Special Skills and Personality Traits—Love of the sport; talented in skills and techniques of football; physically fit; aggressive; competitive; large and muscular body type.

CAREER LADDER

```
┌────────────────────────────────┐
│   Professional Football Player │
│        with the Ability to     │
│      Command Large Salary      │
└────────────────────────────────┘

┌────────────────────────────────┐
│   Professional Football Player │
└────────────────────────────────┘

┌────────────────────────────────┐
│        Amateur/College         │
│        Football Player         │
└────────────────────────────────┘
```

Position Description

Football is one of the most popular sports today. Millions view professional football games on television and in person. Tickets to the annual Superbowl are coveted.

Professional Football Players usually start their careers playing touch football as youngsters. (There are no female professional football leagues.) As they grow older they may try out for their junior high or high school team. Over time many individuals develop sufficient talent to obtain athletic scholarships to colleges that seek them out to play on their teams. Other individuals enroll in military academies and play on armed services teams.

Members of college teams generally must have at least a minimum passing grade to stay on the team. In addition to playing in games, schools that put a great deal of emphasis on their football program train their team members extensively in the sport. Athletes then have opportunities to refine their skills and learn everything there is to know about the game. They practice constantly. Players attend clinics and seminars to help them improve their skills and techniques until they are as close to perfect as possible.

Games and competitions help individuals hone their skills. Most colleges have tournaments against others schools. Some colleges belong to national collegiate conferences that organize tournaments.

Many college football games are televised by local, regional, and/or network television. This helps to bring the talented Players to the attention of pro teams. Scouts also travel to the various colleges seeking the very best players. When individuals decide to turn professional, they sign up for a draft. This system gives professional teams the opportunity to choose new players from people who are still amateurs. Only 336 players are chosen from the draft each year. Players who are not drafted may become free agents and market themselves to any of the National Football League (NFL) teams. Others may try to become members of teams in the Canadian Football League (CFL).

Those who are lucky enough to be chosen will play professional football. Professional Football Players do not start right in playing with the team. Athletes attend training camps, which are usually held during the summer months. During this time they attend lectures and practice. They also compete against internal teams as they get ready for the football season. Individuals are assigned to do a specific job as part of the team. They may play offensively or defensively, depending on their skills.

Professional Football Players work actively for about six months of the year, during the football season. Individuals must constantly stay in shape, train, and exhibit talent or they will not be successful and their contracts may not be renewed. Players must move, at least during the season, to the area where the team is located. They must also travel to games held away from the home base.

The careers of Pro Football Players may be cut short due to injuries. Players who make it to the top, however, try to keep that worry in the back of their mind. What they try to concentrate on is the thought of being on a team that not only plays in the Superbowl, but wins it as well.

Salaries

Salaries for Professional Football Players vary greatly depending on the individual and his skills, talent, experience, prestige, and popularity.

The minimum annual salary any team can pay a Professional Player is $131,000. Earnings go up considerably for those in demand. Professional Football Players may work out any financial contract that they can with their team. Some players have earnings in the millions. Individuals may earn extra money by endorsing products or landing acting roles in television or the movies.

Employment Prospects

Employment prospects are poor for those aspiring to be Professional Football Players. However, talented individuals can make it into the pros if they show promise on their college team and stimulate interest in themselves by the professional teams.

Football Players who are still in college or getting ready to graduate who want to turn pro sign up to become part of the football draft. Professional teams send scouts around prior to the draft to determine who would be an asset to their team. Individuals then wait to be chosen. As noted previously, Players can also become free agents and market themselves to teams.

Advancement Prospects

Professional Football Players strive to be the best in the profession. Advancement prospects are determined mainly by the skills, talent, determination, and drive of the individual athlete. If he constantly performs well, other teams will want him under contract. When a demand is created, an individual's worth rises. He can then negotiate large salary contracts. The highlight of many Professional Football Players' careers is being a member of a winning Superbowl team.

Individuals who become major football stars may also advance their careers by obtaining endorsements and movie and television deals.

Education and Training

Many professional athletes in other sports, such as baseball or boxing, come directly out of high school. Pro Football Players, however, usually stay amateur until they graduate from a four-year college.

Pro Football Players may have degrees in any subject. A Pro Football Player needs a good education to fall back on in case he is injured or cannot play for other reasons.

It is important for aspiring Football Players to attend a college or university that has a strong football program. In this way, they can make sure they obtain the necessary training, experience, and exposure to be picked up by one of the pro teams.

Experience/Skills/Personality Traits

Usually Professional Football Players have played the game from the time they were youngsters. Individuals move up the ranks from high school through college and then to the professional level. Most people in this sport have a genuine love for the game.

A Professional Football Player, of course, must be extremely talented in the skills of the sport. Individuals must learn to be team players and to follow the rules of the game.

Football Players must be physically fit. Individuals should be competitive and aggressive. Most Football Players have large and muscular builds.

Because of the great number of injuries incurred when playing the game, the average playing life of a Football Player is only three and a half years. Players must be able to work with the knowledge that they may be injured at any time and that their career can be cut short.

Unions/Associations

Professional Football Players with the National Football League are members of the NFL Players Association. The NFLPA helps players maintain good working conditions and better contract negotiations. Individuals playing in Canada may be members of the Canadian Football League (CFL).

Tips for Entry

1. If you are interested in becoming a Professional Football Player, it is imperative to be on your college team. If you want to make it to the pros, you should try to attend a college that places a heavy emphasis on its football program.
2. Showing promise on a college team is one way to open the door to being successful as a pro.
3. Talk to your high school or college coach about your aspirations and ask for advice.
4. Keep yourself in good physical condition. You won't be able to play at all if you aren't.
5. Learn as much as you can about the sport. In addition to knowing the rules, regulations, and policies, read about its history, other players, teams, and so on.

PROFESSIONAL HOCKEY PLAYER

CAREER PROFILE

Duties: Playing hockey for a professional sports team.

Alternate Title(s):   Pro Hockey Player

Salary Range: $25,000 to $8,000,000+

Employment Prospects: Poor

Best Geographical Location(s) for Position: Cities hosting professional hockey teams.

Prerequisites:

Education or Training—No educational requirement.

Experience—Experience playing amateur hockey necessary.

Special Skills and Personality Traits—Knowledge of rules and regulations of professional hockey; ability to ice skate; hockey skills; physically fit; competitive; aggressive.

CAREER LADDER

```
┌─────────────────────────────────────┐
│     Major League Hockey Player       │
└─────────────────────────────────────┘

┌─────────────────────────────────────┐
│     Minor League Hockey Player       │
└─────────────────────────────────────┘

┌─────────────────────────────────────┐
│      Amateur Hockey Player           │
│              or                      │
│      College Hockey Player           │
└─────────────────────────────────────┘
```

Position Description

Professional hockey is played on a special ice-skating rink that is surrounded by protective walls. Two teams compete against each other with both trying to place a hockey puck into the opponent's goal area. The Hockey Player plays the game while wearing ice skates. Teams are comprised of six players each. Hockey Players may hold offensive, defensive, or goalie positions. (Professional hockey currently has no women players.)

There is a great deal of teamwork involved in this sport. The game is classified as a contact sport much like football. While trying to make goals, players block those of the opposing side with their bodies. They may block another player with either their shoulders or hips.

Players must wear uniforms that include protective gear with shoulder pads, hip pads, helmets, and so on, similar to football players. They must be in top physical form or they will not be able to endure this sport.

Officials and referees in the game call fouls or penalties. Penalties can be called if a player holds on to the the puck too long, blocks another player illegally, fights, or breaks any of the rules or regulations of the game. Penalties differ depending on the seriousness of the infraction. They can run the gamut of removing a player from the team for a few minutes to removing him for the entire game.

Hockey Players can turn pro after graduating from high school or may remain amateurs while they are attending

college. Those who turn pro right after high school often play in the minor leagues to gain experience. Individuals who attend or want to attend college may take part in the National Hockey League (NHL) draft. Players may be drafted before they attend college with the understanding that the team has an option on them after they graduate college. Individuals may also play college hockey and then take part in the draft.

Another path that aspiring Pro Hockey Players may take is to try to locate a team to play with outside of the United States. While they will usually not earn as much, many Players feel the experience and exposure will be worth it.

Individuals train during the fall. The regular playing season begins in October and continues through March. NHL playoffs for the Stanley Cup begin in late March or early April and go through May. Individuals who want to become Pro Players may have to relocate, at least for the playing season, to the team's home base. Players are expected to play in home games as well as travel to games held away from home.

Salaries

Salaries for Pro Hockey Players vary greatly. Factors determining earnings include whether the individual is playing in the minor leagues or with a major league team and its geographic location. Other factors include the player's experience, expertise, skill in the game, and popularity. Individuals playing with minor league teams in this country may earn from

$25,000 to $50,000. Players in the major leagues have salaries ranging from $150,000 to $8,000,000. Most Hockey Players average $200,000 to $350,000 for the season.

Individuals who make a name for themselves and are popular with fans may also earn extra money endorsing products, appearing in commercials, and acting or making cameo appearances in movies or television.

Employment Prospects

Employment prospects for Professional Hockey Players are poor. Competition is tough for athletes in all sports, and hockey is no exception. However, as in all other sports, individuals who are extremely talented and skillful at hockey and have a great deal of drive and determination can break in.

Opportunities to play hockey may be located in the United States and Canada as well as Europe.

Advancement Prospects

Many Hockey Players advance their careers by moving from the minor leagues to the majors. Individuals may also climb the career ladder by landing a contract with a more prestigious team or by staying with the same team but commanding and receiving contracts for higher yearly earnings.

Advancement as an athlete in this sport, as in most others, depends on skills, talent, drive, and determination. The top spot a Pro Hockey Player can strive for is to be a member of the team that wins the Stanley Cup. Winning the Stanley Cup is to hockey what winning the World Series is to baseball.

Education and Training

There is no formal educational requirement to become a Pro Hockey Player. Some Players turn professional after finishing high school and others become Pros after college.

Individuals must, however, be able to skate expertly and know the skills and techniques of the sport. Much of top-notch talent comes from playing hockey and getting experience in the game at an early age. Many Pro Hockey Players refined their skills while playing on college teams.

Experience/Skills/Personality Traits

Pro Hockey Players must be extremely skillful in the sport. Individuals must also be excellent ice skaters. They must know how to play well as well as know all the rules, regulations, and policies of the game. Successful Hockey Players have usually had a great deal of experience playing the game. Many started as young boys and became more experienced and skillful playing against others with the same interest.

Pro Players need to be competitive and aggressive. They should be team players. Individuals should have a lot of drive, determination, and and perseverance if they want to make it in this sport. Pro Players need to be physically fit and have a lot of stamina.

Unions/Associations

Individuals playing for the National Hockey League are members of the NHL Players' Association (NHLPA). Those playing for other leagues are usually members of their players' associations.

Tips for Entry

1. Learn how to skate well. Take lessons to help you improve.
2. Talk to a coach or physical education teacher about your aspirations. Ask for advice.
3. Find an amateur hockey league to play with. If you are serious about this profession, you must start playing as young as you can and practice as much as possible.
4. Look for a college that offers hockey as one of its team sports. This will be a good way to refine your skills. Play in competition for the opportunity of being seen by scouts looking for talented individuals who are interested in turning pro.
5. Consider attending a hockey camp. These are usually held in the summer and can help you improve your skills and techniques.

PROFESSIONAL BOXER

CAREER PROFILE

Duties: Fighting in boxing bouts; learning and developing boxing skills.

Alternate Title(s):   Fighter; Pugilist

Salary Range: $200 to millions depending on individual's success

Employment Prospects: Good

Best Geographical Location(s) for Position: Any location hosting boxing shows offers possibilities; Atlantic City, Las Vegas, and New York City are boxing capitals.

Prerequisites:
Education or Training—Training in boxing skills.
Experience—Experience as amateur boxer.
Special Skills and Personality Traits—Boxing skills; drive; determination; physically fit; patience; perseverance.

CAREER LADDER

Champion or World-Class Boxer or Boxer Fighting More Prestigious Opponents

Professional Boxer

Amateur Boxer

Position Description

In the last few years, boxing has become a multimillion-dollar business. Network and cable television stations pay huge amounts of money to obtain television rights to top fights. Promoters are paying extraordinary sums of money for the opportunity to stage fights.

Great numbers of fans pay fees to watch fights on pay-for-view stations. These fights are not televised on regular TV. Others pay admission to arenas, clubs, and bars to see fights on giant screens. Some boxing enthusiasts may pay up to $2,500 or more for a ringside seat at a championship event.

The sport of boxing has turned into an entertainment extravaganza. A number of the stars of the ring, the Boxers themselves, are also beginning to command purses in the multimillion-dollar range. It is no wonder then that so many young men want to become Professional Fighters. Boxing opens up opportunities of fame and fortune that most people can only dream about. While boxing is a male-dominated sport, women are now participating in it.

Those who aspire to be Professional Boxers start off as amateurs. During this time, the individual learns the rules and regulations of the game, such as round length, time between rounds, which blows are legal and illegal, and so on. The Boxer must also learn how to use all of the equipment in the gym to get into top physical condition. The Fighter may run, jump rope, use the heavy bag, punching bag, pads, perform aerobics exercises, and so on. Fighters who are not in perfect physical shape will not be able to perform well in the ring.

The Fighter must learn all the basic forms, styles, and blows used in boxing and to know when to use which blows. The Boxer must also be familiar with the defenses that can be used in the ring. Some Boxers instinctively know when to throw a left hook and when to throw a right uppercut. Others must work on skills to make them instinctive.

Amateur Boxers compete in competitions and tournaments gaining experience and skills against opponents in the ring. When they or their trainer feel they are ready, the individuals turn professional.

Fighters are classified in categories by their weight. Fighters must "make," or be, this weight at the official weigh-in to fight in the category.

Managers of Professional Boxers try to obtain matches for their fighters with opponents of equal size, weight, and with an equal amount of experience and skill. An individual just starting out, usually has a match with another Fighter in the same weight category who either is just starting out or has had only two or three previous fights.

Pro Boxers move ahead in their career trying to advance to a level where they can become Champions or World-Class Fighters. Depending on their skills, determination, drive, and the people working with them, they may fight only a few times or a great many times before achieving this goal.

As Boxers become more proficient and successful, they begin to receive more money to fight. They also may be rated by one of the boxing organizations that sanction fights. This is important because it helps them obtain opportunities to fight for championships. As individuals go through their career, they obtain a record of wins, losses, knockouts (KOs), and draws.

Fighters are usually licensed to fight by state athletic commissions. Either they are licensed by their own state, or they may receive a temporary permit from the state they are fighting in. Individuals are examined by a physician before a fight to make sure that they are physically fit to fight.

Boxers must travel often to other states or abroad to fight. Usually they are reimbursed for travel, room and board, and training expenses.

Boxers are expected to train, stay in good physical condition, and fight regularly. Most individuals have a manager who takes care of business, obtains fights, and watches out for the Boxer's interests. The manager receives a percentage of the Boxer's earnings in return for his or her services.

The Boxer has a trainer who usually works in his corner during a professional fight. As the Boxer becomes more successful, others are added to the team. These people might include promoters, attorneys, and publicists.

Although some individuals in their late thirties and early forties are still fighting, most Boxers retire at an earlier age. While they are pursuing their career, fighters must dedicate their life to boxing. Those who are successful can look forward to fame, fortune, and travel.

Salaries

Earnings vary enormously for Boxers, depending on their status and prestige in the boxing world. The money paid to Boxers for fighting is called a purse. There are Professional Fighters who receive a $200 purse for a bout; others receive multimillion-dollar purses.

Amateurs do not get paid. They fight in competitions to obtain experience in the ring and upgrade their status as fighters.

Professional Fighters beginning their careers may fight a four-round bout and receive $200 to $400. As they journey up the career ladder, individuals may earn $1,000 to $50,000 or more. Fighters on championship undercards (meaning they are not the main event) or those appearing on televised events may have larger purses. Individuals who can attract a great deal of publicity and large audiences, such as Champions, command the biggest purses of all. They may also receive percentages of money earned from ticket sales, promotional packages, television rights, and so on. Boxers may also be compensated very well for endorsing products and appearing in advertisements, on television shows, and in movies.

Employment Prospects

Prospects for individuals who want to be Boxers are excellent. Almost any healthy individual who wants to fight and is not afraid to get into the ring can become a Fighter. The problem is that many people want to become a Boxer in theory, but do not really want to fight.

A great many people decide that they want to be Boxers, find a gym, train, learn the skills, get in the ring with an opponent, and find that they never want to do it again. Individuals who have had training and experience in the ring and determine that they want to be involved professionally can turn pro. Individuals may fight on any type of fight card, or program, from small clubs to large arenas. If they are just starting out, they usually fight on the undercard of a main event. As the individual's career progresses, it is hoped that his position on the card will go up. All Fighters aspire to be the main attraction in a championship event.

Advancement Prospects

All Fighters begin their careers as amateurs. If they show promise, Boxers are entered into amateur competitions and tournaments, such as the Golden Gloves. When they are ready, they may move on to either the Olympics or turn pro. Many champions have come out of both the Golden Gloves and the Olympics.

Advancement prospects differ from person to person depending on a number of factors. These include how good a fighter the individual is, connections in the boxing industry, drive, determination, skill, and luck. Some individuals have become Champions in as little as nine pro fights. Others have fought 100 times and still are at the same level. For example, some Fighters stay at the club level for their entire career. They fight in bouts on boxing shows and make a living but never really advance their career.

Others may move from the amateurs to the pros and quickly catch the eye of a promoter, moving up to become a World-Class Fighter. With more and more fights being televised, it is easier than ever for talented individuals to be seen by promoters, managers, or other industry people.

Education and Training

There is no formal educational requirement for Boxers. Fighters may have diverse educational backgrounds. Some individuals do not have a high school diploma, others are college graduates.

There is also no formal training program for Boxers. Most individuals begin their careers working out and training in gyms or youth programs. They are trained by either staff trainers or private trainers who feel that they show potential. Individuals usually train daily to become Professional Boxers. They may perform a variety of exercises and activities to become conditioned as well as to learn to skills and rules of the sport.

Experience/Skills/Personality Traits

Boxers need to be healthy and in good physical shape. They must want to fight in order to become successful. If an individual has drive and determination, he can learn the skills that are needed. Fighters who want to make it to the top must make a commitment to the sport. They will have to train hard daily. Individuals must live a healthy life-style, sleeping enough, eating nutritiously, and avoiding drugs and alcohol.

The Fighter should be able to take instruction and constructive criticism. Self-confidence, motivation, and the ability to deal with fear is necessary. A desire to be in the ring is mandatory. Patience and perseverance are helpful in attaining success.

Unions/Associations

Fighters living and/or fighting in states hosting athletic commissions must usually be associated with those organizations. In many states, the Fighter must be licensed to fight through state athletic commissions.

Fighters may also be associated with any number of organizations and trade associations or sanctioning organizations dedicated to the profession. These may include the International Boxing Federation (IBF), the International Boxing Association (IBA), the World Boxing Association (WBA), the World Boxing Organization (WBO), the World Boxing Federation (WBF), the International Boxing Hall of Fame (IBHF), the International Veteran Boxers Association (IVBA), or the National Veteran Boxers Association (NVBA).

Tips for Entry

1. Look for local gyms that train Boxers and spend some time in them.
2. Watch the various trainers, Fighters, managers, and so on. Talk to them and tell them you are interested in becoming a Boxer. Ask for advice and recommendations for a trainer or a program to become involved in.
3. Many Police Athletic Leagues (PAL), newspapers, boys' clubs, radio and television stations, and youth or community organizations sponsor boxing programs. These groups will help amateur Boxers begin their careers in the sport.
4. Contact your state's athletic commission if you have any questions about how to proceed or to check out credentials, qualifications, and reputations of trainers, managers, and so on. In states that have athletic commissions, these people usually must be licensed.
5. Read all you can about boxing. There are books and magazines about the history, skills, amateurs, professionals, current news, and so on. Learn as much as you can.
6. Contact trade associations to find out if they are holding seminars, workshops, or other meetings.

PROFESSIONAL SOCCER PLAYER

CAREER PROFILE

Duties: Playing either the indoor or outdoor variety of soccer professionally.

Alternate Title(s): None

Salary Range: $20,000 to $6,000,000

Employment Prospects: Poor

Best Geographical Location(s) for Position: Areas hosting professional soccer teams.

Prerequisites:

Education or Training—No educational requirement; training in the sport of soccer.

Experience—Experience as an amateur.

Special Skills and Personality Traits—Complete knowledge of soccer rules and regulations; skilled in techniques of the sport; good one-on-one skills; team player; agile; quick reflexes; physically fit.

CAREER LADDER

```
┌─────────────────────────────┐
│  Professional Soccer Player │
│     Earning Top Money       │
│  Playing for a League Abroad│
└─────────────────────────────┘

┌─────────────────────────────┐
│  Professional Soccer Player │
└─────────────────────────────┘

┌─────────────────────────────┐
│   Amateur Soccer Player     │
│            or               │
│   Semipro Soccer Player     │
└─────────────────────────────┘
```

Position Description

Many people in the United States became aware of soccer when Brazilian superstar Pélé signed a major money deal with the Cosmos, an American soccer team. For a sport to be financially viable today, it must be televised. Only very recently has soccer been able to capture the American public's sports imagination; for example, major games of the 1998 World Cup were aired on a major U.S. television network. Slowly, professional soccer is becoming a spectators sport in the United States.

Professional soccer is extremely popular overseas where live attendance makes it financially profitable. However, as the game is played extensively on the amateur and collegiate level here, there are athletes who turn pro in the sport in the United States. Some individuals get amateur training here and then seek work abroad. And now some are even finding profitable work without leaving home. Those who play soccer in other countries can become major sports superstars. They also reap the rewards of huge salaries that players in this country do not receive.

There are two varieties of soccer. One is played outdoors on a soccer field and the other indoors in an arena.

Professional Soccer Players begin their careers as amateurs. Many play in amateur youth leagues. Some gain experience playing on the high school level. In this country, most indi-viduals begin by playing outdoor soccer and then make the transition to the indoor variety.

Teams recruit players in two ways. One is through the draft system. In the draft, amateur players who want to turn professional sign up to participate. The teams may then choose the players they want. The draft is for both high school and college seniors. Teams also conduct tryouts for those who do not take part in the draft.

Once a Soccer Player is chosen to play on a team, he attends training and practice sessions. If the Player shows that he will be an asset to the team, he is asked to stay. If not, he is let go.

Soccer Players who show great talent and skill in the sport may be lucky enough to be sought out by an international team. This is difficult, however, because of the intense competition. If an individual is chosen to be a member of an international team, he will have to relocate out of the country, at least for the playing season.

Salaries

Salaries for Professional Soccer Players in the United States are quite low in comparison to earnings in other professional sports. Individuals may have annual earnings ranging from $20,000 to $150,000. The median salary for the Pro Soccer Player in the United States is $50,000. Individuals may earn more if they locate a position playing soccer for an overseas league. There are some players who have earnings up to $6,000,000, but these are the exception.

Employment Prospects

Employment prospects are poor. There are only a limited number of teams to work with in this country. Many individuals try to obtain contracts with overseas leagues where more opportunities exist to play professionally.

Advancement Prospects

Advancement prospects are poor for Pro Soccer Players. Individuals may climb the career ladder by having a lot of talent and skill in the game. They will then be able to command the top salaries in the sport.

Other individuals who may be playing with a semipro league may advance their career by obtaining contracts with a professional team.

Still others climb the career ladder by going abroad to play with a foreign league.

Education and Training

There are no educational requirements to become a Professional Soccer Player. It is necessary, however, to be trained in the sport. Many individuals obtain this training by playing collegiate and amateur soccer while in college.

Those attending colleges hosting major soccer teams may have a better chance to refine their skills and techniques. They may also have a better opportunity to be seen playing the game.

Experience/Skills/Personality Traits

Professional Soccer Players usually have obtained experience in the sport by playing on high school or college teams. Some may have gained experience by playing with a semiprofessional team before turning pro.

Individuals must have a full knowledge of the rules and regulations of soccer. They must be skilled in the techniques of the sport. Players should have good one-on-one skills and be team players.

To play the game successfully, Professional Soccer Players need quick reflexes and should be agile. Individuals should also be in excellent physical shape.

Unions/Associations

Professional Soccer Players may be members of Major League Soccer or other professional leagues.

Tips for Entry

1. Since competition is so intense in for this sport, you must be very talented. Play the game as often as possible. The more experience you have, the better your chances of being chosen to be a team member.
2. Learn to play soccer both indoors and outside. Understanding the different rules for the game will provide you with a well-rounded training.
3. Try to attend a college that puts a heavy emphasis on its soccer team.
4. Consider attending a soccer camp to help refine your skills.
5. Contact the teams in the various soccer leagues to find out when they are holding tryouts. You can find the addresses in Appendixes XIII and XIV.

CAREER OPPORTUNITIES WITH PROFESSIONAL SPORTS TEAMS

TEAM GENERAL MANAGER

CAREER PROFILE

Duties: Handling day-to-day activities of team; developing a successful, popular team; hiring and firing personnel.

Alternate Title(s): GM; Business Manager

Salary Range: $22,000 to $1,000,000+

Employment Prospects: Fair

Best Geographical Location(s) for Position: Cities hosting professional sports teams.

Prerequisites:

Education or Training—College degree preferred for most jobs.

Experience—Business and/or marketing experience helpful.

Special Skills and Personality Traits—Understanding of specific sport; business and marketing skills; articulate; negotiation skills; energetic.

CAREER LADDER

```
┌─────────────────────────────────┐
│      General Manager with       │
│      More Prestigious Team       │
└─────────────────────────────────┘

┌─────────────────────────────────┐
│      Team General Manager        │
└─────────────────────────────────┘

┌─────────────────────────────────┐
│       Business Manager           │
│      or Marketing Director       │
│  with Knowledge of Sports Industry │
└─────────────────────────────────┘
```

Position Description

All professional sports teams have General Managers. The General Manager of a professional sports team has an extremely important job. He or she is responsible for handling all of the day-to-day details of the team. The individual in this position has a lot of power and prestige. If things are going right for the team, the GM receives a share of the credit. If things do not go right for the team, the GM is often blamed and his or her position may be terminated.

It is important to remember that the sports industry is a multibillion-dollar business. Many of the qualifications required in any of the sports administration positions are similar to those that are important in any successful business venture. Responsibilities of the General Manager of a professional sports team are also much the same as they would be for any individual running a multibillion-dollar business.

Professional sports Team General Managers may work in any sport. The most common of these are basketball, baseball, football, soccer, and hockey. The GM may work with any of the major league teams or may work with various levels of minor league teams. The GM will have varied duties depending on the size and prestige of the specific team.

His or her main function is to oversee all functions of the team's activities. Individuals working with smaller teams or those at various levels may be responsible for the actual day-to-day, operational function. These duties might include operating the concessions and hiring the ticket takers, ushers, and other box office personnel. The GM might be responsible for all the publicity, press, and marketing of the team.

General Managers of larger, more prestigious major league teams usually are responsible for recommending, hiring, and supervising people to attend to these jobs. The extent of this hiring depends on how much leeway the team owner gives the Manager. A good GM surrounds him- or herself with the best people possible. This helps make the team a success, and the success will rub off on the GM.

The General Manager, for example, may recommend the hiring of the club secretary, assistant manager, marketing people, publicity people, trainers, and so on. The individual is also responsible for putting together a winning team. He or she may recommend the trading and drafting of team members. It is important that the GM stay up to date on the activities and background of all players in the sport. He or she needs almost a second sense regarding players and personnel.

The General Manager may decide, with the owner, salaries for team members and support personnel. As athletes become more and more popular and valuable, their salaries escalate.

The General Manager must help develop a team that is not only popular but also regularly draws fans to their events. Keeping the stadiums filled is important to professional sports teams. Popularity means money in the teams' pockets. It means the games will be sold out and good marketing prospects. It also means that successful television and radio contracts may be negotiated.

It is up to the General Manager to see that everything regarding the team and its organization is operating properly and efficiently. He or she must oversee everything, from the ticket takers and ushers to the moneymaking concessions, and must supervise all segments of all departments including the equipment manager, the players, publicity people, advertising, promotion and marketing, and anything and everything else relating to the team.

Depending on the team, the General Manager works closely with the owner and business manager. In some cases, when the GM works for a smaller minor league team, he or she might be called the business manager.

The General Manager must make sure that everything done by any member of the team and/or the support personnel works to make the team a success. The GM is directly responsible to the team owner. He or she works long hours trying to build a popular, successful team.

Salaries

Salaries for Team General Managers will vary depending on the sport, the team, its size and prestige, and the individual's expertise and experience.

Salaries can range from $22,000 to $50,000 plus for those working with minor league teams. Salaries for General Managers working for larger or major league teams may go to $1,000,000 plus.

Employment Prospects

Employment prospects are fair for individuals willing to start working for lower salaries in the minor leagues. Some General Managers were athletes prior to obtaining this job. Most people, however, obtain this type of job by being familiar with business operations.

Advancement Prospects

A professional sports Team General Manager can advance his or her career by obtaining a position with another more prestigious team. To do this the individual must prove him- or herself thoroughly and build a track record of success. A great deal of this is determined by not only the individual's abilities but his or her drive to succeed.

Another way that a Team General Manager can advance his or her career is by building a team that emerges as a championship team. This usually makes the individual more valuable as a GM and increases his or her value both in prestige

and money. This could happen, for example, if an individual is working with a baseball team that isn't expected to win in its league. The team surprises everyone and not only makes it to finals but wins the big game.

Education and Training

Some individuals have become Team General Managers without a college degree. However, competition is so fierce for these jobs that a good education is extremely helpful.

Individuals aspiring to this type of career could major in sports or athletic administration. This relatively new degree is growing in popularity in colleges throughout the country. (A list of colleges and universities offering these degrees is in Appendix I.)

Other educational possibilities for General Manager positions might include majors in business or business administration, journalism, communications, or law. Seminars and other courses in sports administration, business, promotion, marketing, and publicity are also helpful.

Experience/Skills/Personality Traits

The General Manager of a professional sports team needs a complete understanding of the sport he or she is working with. Enjoying the specific sport is certainly helpful. The individual literally sleeps, eats, and lives the sport.

Good communications skills are necessary. The GM should be articulate in his or her speech and mannerisms. The ability to successfully negotiate is essential. A solid business background is also required. An eye for both marketing and business will boost the GM's opportunities for success.

The General Manager should have a lot of stamina and energy. He or she will be working long hours. The ability to deal with stress and tension is vital. The GM's job has more than its share of these tensions.

The individual should possess a great deal of self-confidence and be able to make sound decisions and judgments quickly. He or she also should be able to handle many details at one time without getting flustered.

Unions/Associations

There is no specific trade association for Team General Managers. Individuals may, however, belong to any number of professional trade associations related directly to their sports.

Tips for Entry

1. To become a Team General Manager, you will need to have a lot of luck, a great track record, and have to be in the right place at the right time. Be prepared.
2. Consider attending a college that offers a degree in sports administration. This will not only give you the training required but will help you make important contacts.

3. Attend seminars and workshops in sports management, business, marketing, and publicity.
4. Join sports-oriented trade associations and organizations. These groups will provide you with professional guidance and training, and help you make needed contacts.
5. If you are still in college, try to obtain an internship with a professional sports team. This too will provide you with a wealth of training and contracts.
6. Offer to manage an amateur or school sports team. This will help provide you with needed experience.
7. Apply for an office or clerical job with a professional team. This will get your foot in the door. Learn as you earn. Keep your ears open for new opportunities within the organization.

BUSINESS MANAGER/ PROFESSIONAL SPORTS TEAM

CAREER PROFILE

Duties: Handling business of team; obtaining bids for goods and services; making sure contracts are signed; dealing with problems of the team and its members.

Alternate Title(s): None

Salary Range: $23,000 to $750,000+

Employment Prospects: Fair

Best Geographical Location(s) for Position: Cities hosting many professional sports teams.

Prerequisites:

Education or Training—Four-year college degree required or preferred for most positions.

Experience—Experience working in business management situations helpful.

Special Skills and Personality Traits—Organized; business skills; administrative skills; articulate; good communications skills; detail oriented; ability to solve problems.

CAREER LADDER

```
┌─────────────────────────────────┐
│       Business Manager          │
│   for More Prestigous Team      │
│            or                   │
│    Team General Manager         │
└─────────────────────────────────┘

┌─────────────────────────────────┐
│       Business Manager          │
└─────────────────────────────────┘

┌─────────────────────────────────┐
│   Assistant Business Manager    │
└─────────────────────────────────┘
```

Position Description

The Business Manager of a professional sports team has many responsibilities. He or she works with the team general manager handling financial and business matters. In some professional teams, the Business Manager may also take on the duties of the general manager. Professional teams are structured in different ways. The Business Manager's duties depend on the specific structure of each team.

The Business Manager generally is responsible for handling the business of the team. He or she is, for example, required to make sure that there are signed contracts on file for every aspect and function of the team. These include contracts for athletes, coaches, trainers, as well as those for concessionaires, food service companies, rentals, and so on. If contracts are not signed, the Business Manager must contact the appropriate department or person to have them signed.

The Business Manager is responsible for obtaining bids for services used by the team. He or she may send out letters or make calls to advise suppliers that the team is seeking certain services. In this way, team management can be assured that the team obtains the best prices for required services. The

individual may seek bids for things such as food service catering for the team and its support staff, hotels, motels, transportation, insurance, laundry service, and the like. Once the Business Manager has decided on the most effective and economical supply company to use, he or she contacts the company and has contracts drawn up. After services have been rendered, the individual is responsible for obtaining bills and invoices, approving them, and making sure they are paid in a timely fashion.

In the same vein, the Business Manager may also be required to obtain bids for products used by the team, including office supplies, office equipment, training supplies and equipment, and other things. He or she always tries to find the most cost-effective companies to do the best job. The individual must get to know the various companies and their reputations. An organization that performs services late might be the least expensive but is not practical to use.

The Business Manager may be responsible for handling employment applications. After reviewing them, he or she may either distribute them to the appropriate department or personally respond. In teams that do not have a personnel director, the

Business Manager may be responsible for handling advertising to fill positions as well as for conducting interviews.

Other personnel duties might include dealing with staff problems, responding to questions, and handling suggestions. The Business Manager must listen to individual problems and determine how to handle each. In some cases, the Business Manager deals with the difficulties personally. In other instances, he or she sends the individual to the appropriate person in the organization.

Dealing with general problems and complaints of patrons, fans, staff, associates, or others within or surrounding the team may also be one of the Business Manager's functions. He or she may be required to investigate problems which have been reported to him or her, and seek solutions or pass the responsibility on to the appropriate staff member.

Another function of the Business Manager may be to work with the stadium or arena hosting the team's events. The Business Manager must schedule the stadium when required for games, tournaments, or practice sessions. He or she might also schedule the use of rooms in the stadium for business meetings or other team events.

The Business Manager is required to keep track of all bills, invoices, charges, and so on, as well as all services rendered and products purchased. He or she must keep accurate records. In teams with larger business organizations, the Business Manager assigns duties to other staff members. In smaller organizations, he or she is responsible for handling all details.

In some teams, the Business Manager is in charge of collecting daily or weekly expenses and bills from personnel. The individual reviews, records, and sends them to the payroll department before filing them.

The individual works closely with the traveling secretary to work out travel arrangements for the team when it is playing away from the home base. Hotels, motels, transportation, food service, and so on must all be planned out before a team leaves home. The Business Manager may obtain bids on these services, recommend companies, hotels, bus lines, or other services, send out the actual contracts, and arrange for payments.

The Business Manager may be required to handle payroll responsibilities or may work with other departments, such as the comptroller, on the fiscal matters.

Depending on the specific team, sport, and organization, the Business Manager may also be responsible for arranging for training camps, rookie camps, drafts, and other meetings. The individual must oversee all the team's business, making sure that nothing is overlooked. The job is a great deal of work and responsibility. Most Professional Sports Team Business Managers, however, do not seem to mind the 10- to 14-hour work days.

Salaries

Salaries for Team Business Managers vary depending on the sport, the team, its size and prestige, and the individual's expertise and experience.

Salaries can range from $23,000 to $60,000 plus for those working with minor league teams. Salaries for Business Managers working for larger or major league teams may go to $750,000 plus.

Employment Prospects

Employment prospects are fair for those aspiring to be Business Managers for Professional Sports Teams. Individuals may, however, have to work for smaller, less well-known teams in order to gain some experience.

Those seeking to find jobs as Business Managers with major league teams will find it difficult to break into the field without some experience and a track record of success.

Advancement Prospects

A Business Manager working for a professional sports team may advance his or her career by obtaining a job with a more prestigious team. This will result in higher earnings and more responsibilities.

The individual may also climb the career ladder by becoming a team general manager.

Education and Training

A four-year college degree is preferred or recommended for most positions, although educational requirements may vary from job to job. Some professional teams do hire Business Managers without formal education but with on-the-job experience instead. Former athletes or support personnel are in this category.

Good choices for college majors might include business, business administration, sports administration, marketing, and liberal arts. Other educational possibilities may include majors in journalism, communications, and law. Seminars and courses in sports administration, business, promotion, and marketing will also be helpful.

Experience/Skills/Personality Traits

A Team Business Manager has to be highly organized and be able to deal with many projects at the same time. He or she must not get flustered. The Business Manager must be able to deal with the stress and tension on the job.

The more the individual knows about business, administration, and the sports industry, the better he or she will fare in obtaining and keeping this type of position. He or she should be poised and articulate with good communication skills.

The Business Manager must be good at dealing with people in a variety of situations. He or she must have the ability to solve problems and the foresight to try to avoid them. The individual should be self-confident and able to make sound decisions and judgments quickly.

Unions/Associations

There is no specific trade association for Professional Sports Team Business Managers. Individuals may, however, belong to any number of professional trade associations that are related directly to their sport.

Tips for Entry

1. Consider attending a college that offers a degree in sports administration. This will not only give you the training required but will help you make important contacts within the sports industry.
2. Attend seminars and workshops in sports management, business, and marketing.
3. If you are still in college, try to obtain an internship with a professional sports team. This too will provide you with a wealth of training and contracts.
4. Offer to be the Business Manager for a school sports team. This will help provide you with experience.
5. Send your résumé and a cover letter to professional sports teams inquiring about openings. Ask that your résumé be kept on file if there are no current openings. You might not get the job as Business Manager, but you might find an assistant's position open.

DIRECTOR OF BASEBALL OPERATIONS

CAREER PROFILE

Duties: Coordinating the scouting, signing, and development of athletes for a baseball team.

Alternate Title(s): Vice President of Baseball Operations

Salary Range: $50,000 to $500,000+

Employment Prospects: Poor

Best Geographical Location(s) for Position: Cities hosting major league baseball teams.

Prerequisites:

Education or Training—No formal educational requirement for most positions; four-year college degree may be preferred.

Experience—Experience in game of baseball as athlete, scout, coach, trainer, and so on.

Special Skills and Personality Traits—Love of baseball; good with people; empathy; understanding; communications skills; ability to predict and project athletic talent.

CAREER LADDER

```
┌─────────────────────────────┐
│   Team General Manager,     │
│      Executive V.P.,        │
│           or                │
│       Team Owner            │
└─────────────────────────────┘

┌─────────────────────────────┐
│ Director of Baseball Operations │
└─────────────────────────────┘

┌─────────────────────────────┐
│    Former Ball Player,      │
│       Scout, Coach,         │
│           or                │
│  Minor League Team Manager  │
└─────────────────────────────┘
```

Position Description

The Director of Baseball Operations is responsible for coordinating the scouting, signing, and development of athletes for a baseball team. His or her contact with the athlete runs from the time a ball player is located by a scout, through his arrival on the team and entire stay.

The person, often called the Vice President of Baseball Operations, is an integral force in the success of a team. He or she works on the personnel side of the team attempting to obtain the best possible athletes.

The goal of the Director of Baseball Operations is to secure athletes from the draft of high school seniors, junior college students, and juniors and seniors in four-year colleges. In drafting athletes at this stage, a lot of prediction and projection is required. It is often hard to tell how an athlete's skills and techniques can and will be developed.

The main function of Director of Baseball Operation is to take an athlete from high school or college into the rookie leagues and through the ranks until the player is ready for the major league. In the process, he or she may be traded and other athletes selected for the team.

There are four different levels of baseball ranging from the rookies or class A team, to AA, AAA, and the major leagues.

The Director of Baseball Operations is responsible for drafting and recruiting talent from high schools, junior colleges, and colleges. The individual works with scouts across the country and visits schools and colleges to try to locate the talent. He or she is also responsible for evaluating talented athletes that scouts have located.

When an athlete shows promise, the Director is responsible for trying to recruit him and getting him to sign a contract. In order to make an offer more attractive, the Director of Baseball Operations may offer a bonus to the player on signing. Bonuses might include additional monies and/or full college scholarships.

The Director of Baseball Operations determines which team the athlete will play with. As a rule, newer athletes are assigned to the rookie team first. After training and experience they move up the ranks of AA, AAA, and then, possibly, the major league team.

The Director is responsible for overseeing the development process of all the team's athletes. He or she help take an athlete's raw talent, develop it, and bring out skills and techniques so that he will be ready to move up to play in the major leagues.

In some circumstances, the Director may feel that an athlete should be traded. This is a difficult situation for all concerned. The Director must explain the trade to the athlete and hope it is a good decision for the team. If, after the athlete has been traded, the individual turns out to be a superstar for a competing team, the Director may receive a lot of flack from upper management and from the fans. This type of job can have a lot of pressure. Other people frequently offer opinions to the Director on what he or she should not have done. This may happen in draft choices as well as trades. The Director will, however, be praised when he or she makes a good decision regarding team personnel.

The Director of Baseball Operations travels extensively. When not actively scouting, recruiting, and signing athletes, he or she often visits the affiliated minor league ball clubs. The Director may attend practice sessions or actual games. He or she talks with the athletes and makes sure that they are progressing satisfactorily. When not on the road, the Director is at home games for the major league team.

The Director of Baseball Operations usually supervises a number of other individuals, including the director of scouting, the director of minor league operations, and all the minor league managers.

Most Directors of Baseball Operations are very satisfied with their position. Many dreamed of working in baseball from the time they were youngsters. Now they can work at something they love.

Salaries

Earnings for a Director of Baseball Operations can vary dramatically. Variables may include the specific team and the experience and responsibilities of the individual. Annual salaries can range from $50,000 to $500,000 plus.

Employment Prospects

Employment prospects are poor for individuals aspiring to be a Director of Baseball Operations. There are only a certain number of teams that offer such jobs. Additionally, people who are already in this position do not move out of it rapidly.

Individuals who are interested in this type of job may seek positions working in other sports. They must, however, know a great deal about any other sport in which they expect to participate.

Advancement Prospects

The Director of Baseball Operations is one of the top-ranking jobs in the sport. Individuals may advance their careers by becoming a team general manager, executive vice president, owner, or commissioner, but at this level prospects are limited. Most people who make it to this level of baseball are extremely satisfied with their position.

Education and Training

While there is no formal educational requirement for this job, competition is fierce. Often the most qualified person gets the position. A college degree will help prepare an individual

aspiring to be the Director of Baseball Operations for this position and for others he or she will have before and after.

Sports administration is one of the best possibilities as a college major. Individuals might also take courses in sports studies, communications, English, psychology, public relations, marketing, and business.

Experience/Skills/Personality Traits

The Director of Baseball Operations must be knowledgeable about all aspects of the sport. To be successful and happy, he or she must love baseball. This job entails almost constant contact with the sport. Long hours are spent traveling, talking, and thinking baseball.

There are numerous career paths leading to this job. Some individuals were former ball players, scouts, or coaches. Others were team managers.

One of the most important attributes for a person in this position is the ability to deal with people well. The individual should be empathetic, understanding, and a good listener.

The Director of Baseball Operations needs good communications skills. He or she should be articulate and poised. An ability to write and a command of the English language are also necessary.

The ability to be a good judge of character and talent is essential in this field. The individual is responsible for meeting people who have raw, untapped talent. He or she must be able to judge not only if they are talented but if they have what it takes to make it playing professional ball.

The Director of Baseball Operations should not mind traveling. He or she might be on the road in various capacities for over half the year.

At times the Director of Baseball Operations may feel that everyone is pulling him or her in different directions. For example, when the Director makes a decision about a trade, others may not agree. The individual must be confident in his or her decisions. He or she must also have the ability to work under pressure in stressful situations.

Unions/Associations

There is no bargaining union for an individual employed as a Director of Baseball Operations, nor is there a specific trade association for people in this position. Individuals do, however, work closely with the players' union.

Tips for Entry

1. Be prepared to start at the bottom of the career ladder. The major problem in obtaining any job in professional baseball is entering the field. After you get in, you will have an easier time moving up the ladder. Try to locate a position in any capacity to help you get your foot in the door. Even if you have a four-year college degree, you may have to work in the mail room, as a clerk, or as a secretary. Once on the job, you will be able to move up as

you learn and you will be on the spot when openings occur.

2. Try to obtain an internship with a professional sports team. Write to each team and inquire about the possibilities. This will help you gain hands-on experience and provide an avenue to make contacts.

3. Attend a college with a sports administration program. Many of these schools work directly with professional sports teams. Internships with the teams are available through cooperative programs.

4. Similar jobs are often available in other sports. If you are interested, contact other types of professional teams.

DIRECTOR OF MINOR LEAGUE OPERATIONS

CAREER PROFILE

Duties: Overseeing a baseball team's minor league operations; acting as liaison between minor league affiliates and major league club.

Alternate Title(s):   Minor League Director

Salary Range: $35,000 to $250,000+

Employment Prospects: Poor

Best Geographical Location(s) for Position: Cities hosting major league ball clubs.

Prerequisites:

Education or Training—No formal educational requirement for some positions; some clubs may prefer a four-year college degree.

Experience—Experience in some facet of baseball required.

Special Skills and Personality Traits—Familiarity with baseball; management and business skills; articulate; detail oriented; ability to work under stress; multilingual.

CAREER LADDER

```
┌─────────────────────────────────┐
│         Major League            │
│    Team General Manager         │
└─────────────────────────────────┘

┌─────────────────────────────────┐
│ Director of Minor League Operations │
└─────────────────────────────────┘

┌─────────────────────────────────┐
│     Other Position in Baseball  │
│     such as Player, Coach,      │
│     Manager of Minor League     │
│         Team, etc.              │
└─────────────────────────────────┘
```

Position Description

The Director of Minor League Operations oversees a baseball team's minor league operation. The job is much like that of the team general manager. The Director of Minor League Operations may have varied duties depending on the specific team and its requirements.

The individual is responsible for all of the ball club's minor league teams. He or she acts as a liaison between the minor league affiliates and the major league club. Much of the Director's job is administrative.

Minor league teams are often owned by private individuals and work under the auspices of the major league team. The Director of Minor League Operations must make sure that everything that the minor league club requires is available. For example, he or she must ensure that each team has adequate and satisfactory playing facilities.

The Director oversees the spring training of the minor league clubs. The individual checks into the housing, transportation, special foods, and so on needed by the team members. He or she also is responsible for ordering equipment required

for the training camps and making sure it arrives on time and is in the correct location.

The Director of Minor League Operations is often responsible for hiring staff members necessary for the training and development of the team members. These people might include trainers, coaches, and others.

Another function of the individual is to oversee the movement of the players in the minor leagues. The Director of this department must know the strengths and weakness of each player in his or her clubs. He or she uses this information to determine where each athlete will play. There are different levels of teams in each league, ranging from A to AAA and up to the majors. The Director of Minor League Operations must decide which players belong in which league and what position they are best suited for.

One of the purposes of the minor league teams is to help develop and train talented athletes to play in the major leagues. The Director of Minor League Operations is responsible for handling problems with the players' development. Some athletes may, for example, require more individualized training or coaching. The Director must see to it that these situations are handled and taken care of in a timely fashion.

The Director may recommend the trading and drafting of team members. He or she works with the league's scouts in locating talent that will be an asset to the ball club. Depending on the specific position, the individual may recommend salaries for the team and its support personnel. He or she is also involved with contract negotiations.

In most cases, the Director of Minor League Operations works closely with the team's owner, business manager, and director of baseball operations. Sometimes the individual also assumes some of the duties of a business manager for the minor league clubs.

The Director of Minor League Operations uses his or her skills to ensure that the minor league teams are successful. He or she also works toward helping the athletes in the minor league system move up the ranks to the major league.

Depending on the situation, the individual may be directly responsible to the team owner or to the general manager.

Salaries

Salaries vary greatly for this position, depending on the specific duties, experience, and responsibilities of the Director of Minor League Operations. Individuals may earn from $35,000 to $250,000 plus annually.

Employment Prospects

Employment prospects are poor. Only a limited number of teams in the country have this type of position, and competition is stiff. Those aspiring to become a Director of Minor League Operations may have more opportunities once they get their foot in the door of a professional sports team.

Advancement Prospects

Advancement prospects are poor for a sports team's Director of Minor League Operations. The next step up the ladder for most people in this profession would be to become a team general manager. However, as there is no one career path in the sports industry, individuals may also advance their careers in other jobs that have higher salaries and more prestige.

Education and Training

While there is no formal educational requirement for this position, as noted previously, competition is fierce. Individuals who have the opportunity to obtain a college degree would be wise to take advantage of it.

Good majors might include business or sports administration. Classes, seminars, and workshops in business administration, management, sports administration, sports studies, and similar areas will prove useful.

Trade associations and organizations governing the sport may also provide valuable training.

Experience/Skills/Personality Traits

The Director of Minor League Operations needs to be familiar with almost every aspect of the sport. Individuals may have served in a number of different positions prior to obtaining the job of Director of Minor League Operations, from playing athletes to coaches or scouts.

Management and business skills are imperative in this position. The ability to successfully negotiate is essential. The individual must also be detail oriented. He or she is responsible for overseeing many ball clubs with a variety of different problems.

The Director of Minor League Operations should be articulate with good communications skills, both verbal and written. As many players now are coming from other countries, the ability to speak languages other than English is helpful. He or she must be self-confident and have the ability to make decisions and judgments quickly and efficiently.

The Director should have a lot of stamina and energy. He or she works long hours. An ability to deal with problems without becoming flustered is necessary as is the ability to deal well with stress and tension.

Unions/Associations

There is no specific trade association for the Director of Minor League Operations. The team the individual works for may belong to the National Association of Professional Baseball Leagues (NAPBL) or the International League of Professional Baseball Clubs (ILPBC).

Tips for Entry

1. The baseball commissioner's office offers training programs for those in the field of baseball. If you are interested in working in any facet of the sport, try to get involved with this program.
2. If you have not yet chosen a college, consider one that offers courses in sports administration. These courses are aimed at people interested in sports careers. Colleges with these majors also often offer internship programs with major sports teams.
3. If your college does not get offer internships, you might want to contact the major sports teams yourself to see if you can work out an internship on your own.
4. Consider a clerical position or one as an administrative assistant with a professional sports team. It is an opportunity to learn the about the industry. As an added bonus, you will know when there are openings to apply for.
5. Get the best training you can in the management and business fields. These areas will prove useful when applying for a job as well as after obtaining one.
6. Send your résumé and a cover letter to each of the ball clubs you are interested in working with and inquire about assistant positions.

PROFESSIONAL SCOUT

CAREER PROFILE

Duties: Finding outstanding athletes for professional sports teams; evaluating athletes.

Alternate Title(s):   Scout; Talent Scout

Salary Range: $20,000 to $100,000+

Employment Prospects: Fair

Best Geographical Location(s) for Position: Positions located throughout the country.

Prerequisites:

Education or Training—No formal education requirement for most positions.

Experience—Experience as scout, athlete, coach, etc., preferred.

Special Skills and Personality Traits—Ability to evaluate athletes; persuasive; communications skills; articulate; multilingual.

CAREER LADDER

```
┌─────────────────────────────────┐
│   Professional Scout for        │
│   More Prestigious Team          │
│            or                    │
│   Team Scouting Director         │
└─────────────────────────────────┘

┌─────────────────────────────────┐
│                                 │
│     Professional Scout          │
│                                 │
└─────────────────────────────────┘

┌─────────────────────────────────┐
│   Athlete, Coach, Trainer,      │
│            or                    │
│     Assistant Scout             │
└─────────────────────────────────┘
```

Position Description

Professional Scouts work for professional sports teams. They are responsible for finding talented athletes to play for their teams. These individuals usually specialize in a specific sport, such as baseball, football, hockey, basketball, or soccer.

A Professional Scout does a great deal of traveling. The individual must constantly be on the lookout for promising new talent. He or she may travel the country from coast to coast and abroad to seek out these people.

Scouts find promising athletes in a variety of ways. Word of mouth is one method. Someone might know the Scout and call to discuss a promising new prospect. The Scout may visit colleges and talk with coaches. The individual may also see potential professional athletes on televised amateur games or in live tournaments and other sports events.

Depending on the situation, the Scout may be responsible for actually signing an athlete or may just bring him or her to the attention of the team management. Some Scouts are authorized to negotiate and offer financial packages. Other Scouts are responsible for calling the team general manager or coach to make arrangements to bring the parties together for negotiation.

The Scout must evaluate possible new athletes for teams. To do this, the individual may talk to the athletes' former and current coaches, trainers, and others. He or she also watches the individual in practice as well as in actual game competitions. The Scout may have a checklist of elements to look for. These things might include the athlete's talent, how he or she takes coaching instruction, interaction with the other members of the team, personal ego, and so on. Even though an athlete might be the best player in the world, the player will have little value if he or she does not cooperate with other members of the team. Scouts may also be interested in an athlete's psychological as well as physical makeup.

Some Scouts have other functions. For example, a Scout may be responsible for finding out which members of other professional teams are looking for a change. The Scout would then have to relevant information about these players, such as any injuries the athletes have had, difficulties with team members, and so on.

Some Professional Scouts are responsible for watching the members of other teams to determine the competition's strengths and weaknesses.

The individual may be expected make recommendations for both current and future athlete procurement. The Scout is required to report all his or her activities to the team's general manager or head coach. He or she keeps the appropriate individual abreast of the status of all potential athletes. The Scout also reports on all geographic areas, specific games, tournaments, schools, and events visited on behalf of the team as well as coaches and other people he or she has talked with.

The Scout's work day is not the normal nine to five. The individual may be on the road traveling for a few days, weeks, or months until his or her mission is completed. The Scout is directly responsible to either the team's general manager or the head coach, depending on the specific situation.

Salaries

Salaries are dependent on the specific organization the individual Scout is working for. Earnings may also depend on the individual's experience and track record in the field.

Scouts may earn from $20,000 to $65,000 plus. Individuals working for major league teams may have annual salaries of $100,000 and more.

Employment Prospects

Employment prospects are fair for Professional Scouts and growing increasingly better. Almost every professional team has at least a couple of Scouts on their payroll. Most major teams employ a large number. Some teams employ 20 to 25 full-time scouts in addition to a number of part-timers.

Employment may be found throughout the country in cities hosting professional sports teams. Positions may also be located with scouting pools and independent scouting agencies.

Advancement Prospects

Advancement prospects are fair for Scouts because the demand for fresh, talented athletes continues to grow. Individuals may climb the career ladder by locating a position with a more prestigious team. Others may advance by becoming a team's scout director.

Education and Training

While there may be no formal education requirement for many Professional Scout positions, a four-year college degree may prove useful. Individuals should consider attending a college that offers a degree in physical education, sports administration, or sports studies. These colleges will help the individual get a well-rounded education in addition to providing useful contacts and career guidance.

Many claim that an individual must have scouting in his or her blood to succeed. They feel the talent cannot be learned. Others feel that any individual with a complete understanding of a specific sport can gain sufficient experience.

Experience/Skills/Personality Traits

Many Professional Scouts began their career as part-timers who worked full-time jobs in other professions. Other individuals were former athletes, coaches, or trainers. Scouts may come from all walks of life. What they have in common,

however, is a complete understanding of the sport and an innate sense and ability to locate raw talent.

One of the most important qualifications a Professional Scout can have is the talent to evaluate athletes before they are superstars. This is difficult but can be attained with experience and background knowledge.

Professional Scouts should be personable, enthusiastic, and persuasive. After a Scout finds a talented athlete, he or she must be able to talk to the person and offer encouragement about the decision to sign up with the team.

The Scout must also be sympathetic and empathetic. At times, he or she may have to tell an athlete that he or she is not good enough to be signed to the team. This is a difficult situation for most people.

Professional Scouts need to have good communications skills. They should be articulate communicators and they should also maintain a professional appearance. As many players are now coming from other countries, the ability to speak languages other than English is helpful.

A Professional Scout needs to be able to keep a confidence on many levels. When the individual finally finds a potential athlete, he or she must not discuss publicly the subject until the person is signed with the team. If news gets out that a team is considering a specific athlete, other teams might step in and bid for the athlete.

Unions/Associations

Professional Scouts who work in the major leagues may belong to athletic organizations and associations relevant to the particular sport they are working with.

Tips for Entry

1. Attend a college offering degrees in sports administration studies or physical education. Many of these schools have intern programs with professional sports teams. See if you can be assigned to this area. Hands-on experience in school will be useful in obtaining a job later.
2. If your college does not offer internships, write to professional teams and ask about the possibilities of internship. There may not be any financial compensation, but the experience could pay off later with job possibilities.
3. Talk to coaches in colleges. Many will have any contacts with professional teams.
4. Read the sports news regularly as well as periodicals specific to the sport you are interested in. This will give you a good insight into the sports industry.
5. Try to find out when Scouts will be visiting your college or high school. See if you can arrange a meeting to talk about their career and any advice they can offer you.

MARKETING DIRECTOR/ PROFESSIONAL SPORTS TEAM

CAREER PROFILE

Duties: Developing marketing plans and campaigns for sports team; implementing campaigns; creating new markets; licensing team's name, likeness, and logo to other companies.

Alternate Title(s): Director of Marketing

Salary Range: $25,000 to $150,000+

Employment Prospects: Poor

Best Geographical Location(s) for Position: Cities hosting professional sports teams.

Prerequisites:

Education or Training—Four-year college degree required.

Experience—Marketing, promotion, public relations, or advertising experience needed.

Special Skills and Personality Traits—Creative; marketing skills; communications skills; articulate; writing skills; ambitious; aggressive; motivated; detail oriented.

CAREER LADDER

```
┌─────────────────────────────┐
│    Marketing Director with   │
│    More Prestigious Team     │
└─────────────────────────────┘

┌─────────────────────────────┐
│      Marketing Director      │
└─────────────────────────────┘

┌─────────────────────────────┐
│     Marketing Assistant      │
└─────────────────────────────┘
```

Position Description

The Marketing Director of a professional sports team is responsible for developing techniques of marketing a team, its name, and players' personalities. He or she may handle this in a variety of ways. The more successful and popular the team is, the easier the Marketing Directors job ultimately will be.

The individual is responsible for developing the concepts and campaigns that will decide how the team is to be marketed. In a sports team, the marketing department works in conjunction with the promotion, advertising, and public relations departments.

The Marketing Director decides how much and what type of advertising, promotion, public relations, and sales support will be most effective. He or she must develop sound, effective techniques to market both the team and its products.

Working with the promotion director, the individual might develop contests, promotions, giveaway programs, and so on. The Marketing Director constantly strives to expand and open up new markets. For example, the Director may find that offering a senior citizen's discount during afternoon games will help open up a new market. He or she might also find that reducing admission for adults bringing in children under 12 might also reach a different market. Everything the Marketing Director does is designed to bring more people to the stadium and to make the team popular and exciting. It helps, of course, if the team is currently on a winning streak.

All marketing techniques are not accomplished in the stadium. The individual may develop personal appearance tours for the athletes, booking them as guests on television and radio shows or at autograph sessions in local malls. The Marketing Director may also arrange interviews with the press.

One of the important functions of the Marketing Director is to sell licenses to companies or organizations so that they can make licensed team products. In order to be sold legally, such products as mugs, glasses, T-shirts, hats, dolls, and so on bearing the team's name and logo must all be licensed.

The individual must decide which companies will be allowed to produce products to sell with the team logo emblazoned on them. He or she must also determine what companies will be associated with the team name.

Once permission is given to use the team logo, the Marketing Director makes sure that contracts are signed. He or she may also determine how the team will be compensated for the use of its name and/or logo. The team might receive a percentage of profits from each item sold or a flat fee for licensing.

The Marketing Director must plan, coordinate, and implement of all the team's marketing goals and objectives. He or she is expected to organize projects and become involved in promotions. Depending on the size of the marketing department, the individual may be responsible for everything or may assign duties to others working in the department.

The Marketing Director may be expected to write marketing campaign preliminary proposals or outlines for review by team management. The individual may also be responsible for writing memos or other informational data to keep other departments aware of the new marketing plans and campaigns that are undertaken.

The Marketing Director may be responsible for researching facts and data or may assign this task to an assistant. The individual might need demographic information about potential purchasers of team-licensed products, fans, patrons, and so on. He or she may also be interested in evaluating the effectiveness of certain advertising and promotions.

The Marketing Director may be required to write, design, or develop sales promotion letters or direct mail pieces in order to initiate new concepts, attract new fans, secure group sales, or reach other patron markets.

Where there is no director of public relations, the Marketing Director may be responsible for the preparation of promotional brochures, press releases, or newsletters. He or she may also be expected to attend trade shows and conventions on behalf of the team.

The Marketing Director works normal business hours most of the time but may have to work overtime on projects, special events, and promotions. He or she may spend a great deal of time working weekends or in the evenings when games, tournaments, and promotions are taking place.

Salaries

Salaries for Marketing Directors depend on a number of variables. These include the specific team the individual is working for and its prestige in the marketplace and media. Other factors affecting salaries are the individual's experience, responsibilities, and duties.

Earnings can range from $25,000 to $150,000 plus for a Marketing Director with a lot of experience, a great deal of responsibility, and working for a team that has a high visibility.

Employment Prospects

Employment prospects are poor for Marketing Directors of professional sports teams. Competition is fierce for these positions. There are only a limited number of professional teams, and once an individual obtains a job, he or she does not usually move on unless a better job opens up.

Advancement Prospects

Advancement prospects are dependent on the individual and his or her skills, drive, and determination. Those who are aggressive and productive will move up the career ladder.

One of the most common career paths for individuals in this field is to advance their career by moving into a similar position with a larger, more prestigious team.

Education and Training

A good education is necessary for individuals aspiring to be Marketing Directors of professional sports teams. A four-year college degree is the minimum requirement. Good choices for majors include marketing, public relations, communications, journalism, English, liberal arts, business, and sports administration.

Workshops and seminars in publicity and marketing will also prove useful.

Experience/Skills/Personality Traits

The Marketing Director of a professional sports team needs to be creative and innovative. He or she should have excellent communication skills.

The ability to write well is essential. The individual should have a good command of the English language, spelling, and word usage. He or she must understand and have skills in marketing, public relations, and advertising.

The Marketing Director should be ambitious, aggressive, highly motivated, and energetic. He or she should be able to work under stress, handling many details and a variety of projects at one time.

Unions/Associations

There are no specific associations for Marketing Directors of Professional Sports Teams. Individuals may belong to trade associations relevant to the particular sport. They may also join general marketing, public relations, advertising, or promotion organizations, such as the American Marketing Association (AMA), the Association of National Advertisers (ANA), the Business/Professional Advertising Association (BPAA), the American Advertising Federation (AAF), Women In Communications (WIC), or the Public Relations Society of America (PRSA).

Tips for Entry

1. Try to find an internship with a professional sports team's marketing department. You probably will have to do a lot of clerical work, but it will be worth the experience. These opportunities are often located through your college placement office or directly through the team.

2. If you can get your foot into the door, it may be easier to move up the career ladder. A job as an assistant, trainee, or clerk in the marketing office will help you accomplish this. Once you are in, volunteer to do extra projects. Keep your eyes and ears open and learn as much as possible.

3. Consider obtaining some experience in a marketing field outside of the sports world. Send your résumé and cover letter to marketing firms or departments of stores, businesses, associations, and so on. If you learn the skills you will be able to work anyplace in any field.

4. Attend workshops and seminars in marketing, promotion, public relations, and sports administration. These will help give you additional expertise on subjects as well as giving you a good opportunity to make contacts.

5. Send your résumé and a cover letter to professional sports teams inquiring about openings in the marketing department.

6. Job openings may be located on the Internet. Search popular career and job sites as well as others such as sports, sports teams, etc.

MARKETING ASSISTANT/ PROFESSIONAL SPORTS TEAM

CAREER PROFILE

Duties: Assisting marketing director accomplish duties; helping develop campaigns; performing clerical and secretarial duties.

Alternate Title(s): Assistant

Salary Range: $20,000 to $40,000+

Employment Prospects: Fair

Best Geographical Location(s) for Position: Cities hosting professional sports teams.

Prerequisites:

Education or Training—Minimum of four-year college degree.

Experience—Experience in marketing, public relations, and promotion preferred but may not be required.

Special Skills and Personality Traits—Articulate; good writing skills; clerical and secretarial abilities; good communications skills; creative; marketing skills; aggressive; enthusiastic; ambitious; detail oriented.

CAREER LADDER

```
┌─────────────────────────────────┐
│      Marketing Director         │
└─────────────────────────────────┘


┌─────────────────────────────────┐
│      Marketing Assistant        │
└─────────────────────────────────┘


┌─────────────────────────────────┐
│ Marketing or Public Relations Intern │
│              or                 │
│          Entry Level            │
└─────────────────────────────────┘
```

Position Description

The Marketing Assistant working in a sports team assists the marketing director accomplish his or her duties. Depending on the individual's experience level, he or she may be responsible for a wide range of functions, from performing secretarial or clerical duties to assisting with the development of the team's marketing plan.

The Sports Team's Marketing Assistant may help the director of the department develop and implement concepts and campaigns. The marketing department of a sports team works with the ticket sales, promotion, advertising, and public relations departments.

In teams with smaller budgets, such as a team with low visibility, one individual and an Assistant might be responsible not only for the marketing but also for the promotion, advertising, and public relations departments. While this type of job usually pays considerably less, the Assistant has the opportunity to work in all facets of marketing and will receive a well-rounded training.

The Marketing Assistant also works with the marketing director in the planning and coordination of all the team's marketing goals and objectives. If the individual has sufficient experience and expertise, he or she may be expected to help plan and organize projects and become involved in promotions. If the Assistant is just a beginner, he or she takes on more clerical types of duties. The Assistant may be responsible for typing letters, reports, proposals, and memos. He or she may be required to make phone calls, answer the telephone, and take messages on behalf of the marketing director.

The Marketing Assistant may be expected to help coordinate and implement special events, promotions, and other programs that have been developed in the department. The individual often is responsible for working with other departments to ensure that marketing efforts and projects run smoothly.

The individual may develop or assist in the development and writing of sales promotion letters, direct mail pieces, brochures, press releases, and newsletters to help market the team. These might be used, for example, to attract new fans, patrons, or licensees interested in using team logos.

The Marketing Assistant may be responsible for helping the director handle the licensing of the team's name, logo, and likeness. He or she may be expected to field calls from potential companies interested in using the team's logo, do research on them, and send them information regarding the process. The individual may arrange meetings between the marketing director and interested companies to finalize agreements.

The Marketing Assistant is directly responsible to the team's marketing director. He or she works long hours, attending to regular business as well as working overtime during games, tournaments, championships, projects, special events, and promotions.

Salaries

A Marketing Assistant working for a professional sports team can earn between $20,000 and $40,000 plus annually. Salaries vary depending on the specific team and the individual's responsibilities, functions, duties, and experience level.

Individuals with little or no experience in the field, or those working for sports teams with minimal popularity and visibility, average salaries on the low end of the scale. Marketing Assistants with more experience, greater responsibility, and working for teams with higher visibility may average annual earnings on the higher end of the salary scale.

Employment Prospects

Employment prospects are fair for Marketing Assistants willing to work in the marketing departments of lesser-known professional teams. Job opportunities occur less frequently for individuals aspiring to work for major league teams.

Advancement Prospects

Advancement prospects are fair for Marketing Assistants. Individuals must work hard, be aggressive, driven, and highly motivated. The Marketing Assistant can take a number of different paths in career advancement. The individual may locate a similar position with a more prestigious team. This usually results in additional responsibilities and higher earnings. He or she may also climb the career ladder by landing a position as a professional sports team's marketing manager or director. If the Marketing Assistant has a thorough knowledge of marketing, public relations, promotion, and advertising, he or she might also move on to become the director or manager of any of those departments.

Education and Training

Competition is fierce in all facets of the sports industry. Those with the best education have the most opportunities both to obtain a position and be successful at it.

Most professional sports teams require that Marketing Assistants have at least a four-year college degree. Good choices for majors include marketing, public relations, advertising, business administration, liberal arts, communications, or sports administration.

Some colleges offer sports administration degrees. An advantage in going to such a college is that these colleges often work with professional sports teams to obtain on-the-job train-

ing programs for their students. This helps when trying to obtain internships in the industry.

Experience/Skills/Personality Traits

It is not necessary to know everything about sports to be a Marketing Assistant for a pro team. It does help, however, to have a general knowledge about the sport the team is associated with.

The Marketing Assistant should be articulate and have excellent communication skills. The ability to write well is necessary. The Marketing Assistant should have a good command of the English language and be able to spell well. Creativity in writing, speaking, and in developing ideas and concepts is helpful.

Those who want to succeed in this profession should be enthusiastic, ambitious, aggressive, highly motivated, and energetic. Marketing Assistants should be detail oriented with the ability to handle many details and a variety of projects at one time without getting flustered.

The Marketing Assistant should be able to perform clerical and secretarial duties, such as typing, filing, and handling phone calls. The ability to work on word processors or computers is a plus.

Unions/Associations

Marketing Assistants working for professional sports teams do not belong to any specific trade association. Individuals may be members of a number of marketing, advertising, or public relations trade associations, such as the American Marketing Association (AMA), the Association of National Advertisers (ANA), the Business/Professional Advertising Association (BPAA), the American Advertising Federation (AAF), Women In Communications (WIC), or the Public Relations Society of America (PRSA). Individuals may also be members of organizations geared specifically toward the sport they are working with.

Tips for Entry

1. Send your résumé and cover letter to professional sports teams. Inquire about openings in the marketing department. Addresses of a number of pro teams are given in the Appendixes to help get you started.
2. Join trade associations. They offer continuing education, seminars, and internships. Attend their meetings. They will help you make valuable contacts.
3. Look for marketing seminars offered throughout the country. These will have educational value as well as offer the opportunity to make contacts.
4. Try to obtain an internship with a professional sports team. Many schools work with pro teams with their internship programs. If yours does not, contact teams directly to inquire about internship possibilities.
5. Job openings may be located on the Internet. Search popular career and job sites as well as others such as sports, sports teams, etc.

PROMOTION DIRECTOR/ PROFESSIONAL SPORTS TEAM

CAREER PROFILE

Duties: Setting up promotions for sports team; developing ideas to help sell seats in stadiums; arranging for personal appearances of team athletes.

Alternate Title(s):   Promotion Manager; Director of Promotion

Salary Range: $20,000 to $125,000+

Employment Prospects: Poor

Best Geographical Location(s) for Position: Cities hosting professional sports teams.

Prerequisites:

Education or Training—No educational requirement. College degree or background may be preferred.

Experience—Experience working in promotion, publicity, or public relations helpful but not always necessary.

Special Skills and Personality Traits—Knowledge of promotion; creative; good writing skills; free to travel; articulate; ability to deal with a variety of people; energetic; organized; capable of dealing with many projects at one time.

CAREER LADDER

```
┌─────────────────────────────────────┐
│      Team General Manager,           │
│       Promotion Director,            │
│       or Marketing Director          │
│   for Larger, More Prestigious Team  │
└─────────────────────────────────────┘

┌─────────────────────────────────────┐
│        Promotion Manager            │
└─────────────────────────────────────┘

┌─────────────────────────────────────┐
│       Press Agent, Publicist,        │
│                or                    │
│          Sports Writer               │
└─────────────────────────────────────┘
```

Position Description

The Promotion Director working for a professional sports team is responsible for handling all of the promotions and special events used to help bring the team to the attention of the public and make them more prestigious and popular. A sports team makes money and a profit by having fans come see the games. Through various promotions, the Promotion Director attempts to find ways to keep stadium seats filled.

The Promotion Director may have varied responsibilities, depending on the size of the team organization. In smaller organizations, the individual may be responsible for the team's public relations, publicity, and promotion. In larger organizations, such as major league teams, the individual usually is responsible for supervising publicists, public relations, and the promotions themselves. Depending on the staff size, he or she may work alone or may supervise one or two promotion representatives.

While a great many promotions occur during the game season, many take place throughout the year. Just because the team is not playing does not mean that the individual can stop developing and implementing promotional ideas.

The Promotion Director may come up with almost any type of promotion to boost ticket sales. For example, he or she might set up a promotion in a shopping mall where the team athletes sign autographs, take photos, and give out team memorabilia.

At times, he or she may arrange for the athletes to appear on television and radio talk, news, and variety shows. The Promotion Director might also set up personal appearances for athletes at nonprofit events. In many instances, the Promotion Director responds to the needs of charities and other nonprofit groups by arranging a variety of activities. He or she may have team athletes play in celebrity baseball or basketball games. The individual might set up hospital and prison appearances and the like. This type of event not only keeps the team in the public eye, but also is good public relations.

Depending on the sport, the Promotion Director might arrange for a number of team members to visit a Little League game or a Special Olympics event.

The Promotion Director is responsible for developing or working with fan associations, which in turn keep people interested in the team. He or she may have a fan appreciation day where fans receive lower-priced tickets, team memorabilia, and photos.

The Promotion Director is responsible for developing team-related giveaways, such as team hats, jackets, or T-shirts. He or she may also be in charge of coming up with merchandising ideas for items to sell that will keep the team's name in the public eye on a more consistent basis.

On occasion, the Promotion Director develops contests to promote the team. These contests may or may not run in conjunction with other tie-in companies. His or her main goal is to keep coming up with new and unique ideas to help make people know and like the team enough to spend money on stadium tickets.

The individual in this position works under constant pressure. His or her job performance is measured by the number of people buying ticket seats. The Promotion Director works long hours, both in the office and while at home trying to develop effective promotions and ideas. He or she also is usually on hand for all team games and events.

Depending on the team and the particular situation, the individual is responsible to the team manager or owner.

Salaries

Annual earnings for Promotion Directors of professional sports teams can range from $20,000 to $125,000 plus bonuses. The salaries vary greatly depending on a number of factors, including the sport, type of league involved, and the prestige, popularity, and success of the team with which the individual is working. Other variables include the individual's experience level and responsibilities.

Individuals working in this position often receive additional incentives or bonuses for filling stadium seats.

Employment Prospects

Employment prospects are poor for those seeking this position in a professional team. While most teams have a Promotion Director, he or she is usually is hired from within the organization.

An individual may find it easier to enter the field by seeking work with a minor league or lesser-known team as a publicist. Then after obtaining some experience and proving him- or herself, the individual should seek employment with a major league team. People who have made contacts with others in sports teams as interns or trainees will have an easier time in their job hunt.

Advancement Prospects

Once they get their first job, advancement prospects are fair for Promotion Directors. While there is no set way for an individual to climb the career ladder in this field, one path is to become the team's general manager. Team owners often feel that if an individual can fill the stadium seats with fans fairly constantly, he or she would be a good general manager. Another way for a Promotion Director to move up the career ladder is to become a Promotion Director with a more popular, prestigious team. There are some individuals who advance their career by becoming a team Marketing Director.

Education and Training

While it is not imperative for Promotion Directors to hold college degrees, the education and training often helps. The best choice for a major for those seeking entry in this field is one in sports administration. Colleges offering this major usually assist students in obtaining some type of internship, which will in turn help the individual get his or her foot in the door with a sports team.

Other majors that might be useful include business, advertising, marketing, or public relations.

Experience/Skills/Personality Traits

Promotion Directors need to be creative people. They must be able to see unique ways to promote the team as a whole as well as its individual players.

The Promotion Director of a sports team should be articulate with good communication skills, both verbal and written. The individual should be personable and easy to talk to. He or she deals with members of the team, management, and media. It is also important that the Promotion Director know how to follow through on projects so that they get done from beginning to end.

The individual should be energetic, because during promotions he or she works long hours. The Promotion Director must know how to arrange priorities and deal with them in a logical order and be able to assign tasks to others.

Unions/Associations

There are no unions or trade associations that Promotion Directors working in sports must belong to. Depending on what type of experience he or she entered the job with, however, the individual may belong to the National Sportscasters and Sportswriters Association (NSSA), the Public Relations Society of America (PRSA), Women In Communications (WIC), or the National Federation of Press Women (NFPW).

Tips for Entry

1. Try to get involved with an internship or training program with a major sports team. These can be located

through colleges with sports administration programs or by directly contacting teams.

2. Promotion is promotion. If you know the basics and you are creative, you can promote anything in any area. Get experience in promotion and publicity even if it is not working in the sports industry. For example, you might work with a public relations firm, a publicist, an advertising agency, or the like.

3. Consider working as a sports writer or reporter for your school or local newspaper. This will help you make valuable contacts with those in the sports industry.

4. Try to work with a sports team in any capacity. Money should not be the most important factor at this point in your career. The experience will pay off financially later.

PUBLIC RELATIONS DIRECTOR/ PROFESSIONAL SPORTS TEAM

CAREER PROFILE

Duties: Handling the functions of the public relations department; supervising team publicists; handling special requests by fans or patrons; developing biographies, press kits, press releases, articles, etc.; dealing with the media.

Alternate Title(s): Director of Public Relations; Public Relations Manager; PR Director; Director of PR

Salary Range: $40,000 to $125,000+

Employment Prospects: Poor

Best Geographical Location(s) for Position: Cities hosting professional sports teams.

Prerequisites:
Education or Training—Four-year college degree required.
Experience—Experience working as publicist, sports information director, or sport journalist required.
Special Skills and Personality Traits—Public relations skills; writing skills; energetic; communication skills; creative; innovative; personable.

CAREER LADDER

```
┌─────────────────────────────────────┐
│    Public Relations Director         │
│    for More Prestigious Team         │
│              or                      │
│  Director of Marketing or Promotion  │
└─────────────────────────────────────┘

┌─────────────────────────────────────┐
│    Public Relations Director         │
│    Professional Sports Team          │
└─────────────────────────────────────┘

┌─────────────────────────────────────┐
│       Sports Team Publicist          │
│              or                      │
│  College Sports Information Director  │
└─────────────────────────────────────┘
```

Position Description

The Public Relations Director of a professional sports team is the individual in charge of the department dealing with the public. This means that the PR Director is responsible for handling the press, media, and public information.

In some organizations, the public relations department is large and the PR Director has team publicists working under him or her. In other teams, the individual is required to take charge of all duties. Responsibilities vary depending on the size of the department and the specific team. The individual may function in a number of different areas, including public relations, publicity, promotion, and/or marketing.

It is important to a team's management to keep the public informed and satisfied with the team. The PR Director is responsible for handling all problems that arise regarding the public. These difficulties can include anything from an unhappy fan to a patron who did not like the way a stadium employee dealt with a situation. The individual may answer letters and/or phone calls regarding problems and all types of situations.

The Public Relations Director may deal with usual fan requests, such as wanting to know how to obtain photographs of the team or of individual athletes, autographs, biographical information, game schedules, and so on. The individual may take care of these projects, or assign an assistant, intern, or trainee to them.

Special requests of fans and patrons are always routed to the Public Relations Director. For example, the PR Director may be contacted by the family or friends of a 100-year-old fan to inquire if it would be possible to have a birthday card signed by the team. He or she may be called by a family member or physician to have a terminally ill child visited by a team member who may be the child's idol.

Some Public Relations Directors also organize team or individual athlete fan clubs. They may be responsible for developing the entire fan club or merely provide materials, such as biographies, press kits, and so on, to others who organize and run the clubs.

The Director of Public Relations is ultimately responsible for all publicity functions of the team. He or she may perform publicity tasks personally or supervise team publicists. The individual is responsible for developing and writing regular and special news announcements, press releases, feature stories, and articles.

The individual works with local, regional, and national media in print and broadcast press. He or she answers requests for interviews, photographs, and information as well as conducts press conferences about special events. The PR Director might even make suggestions for photo opportunities or feature stories to members of the media.

The PR Director is responsible for biographies, press kits, player rosters, stock photographs, statistical information, and other promotional and press information. He or she may also be responsible for producing media guides, daily programs, team newsletters, and other publications.

When team games are televised, especially those airing nationally, the PR Director may be responsible for providing clips of prior games for promotional purposes or clips of current games to news or sports directors.

Many professional sports teams have a promotion department. In those that do not, the PR Director may be required to handle promotional functions, including the development and implementation of ideas and campaigns. In teams with promotional departments, he or she may be responsible for publicizing the promotions.

The Public Relations Director may be required to handle community service projects, such as providing speakers to local groups, bestowing awards to local dignitaries and other honorees, becoming involved in community projects, and the like.

The Public Relations Director in a professional sports team works long hours, often late at night and on weekends. He or she may be responsible to the team's marketing director, general manager, or owner, depending on the structure of the organization.

Salaries

Salaries for Public Relations Directors working for professional sports teams can vary greatly from job to job depending on a number of factors. These include the sport and the prestige of the specific team the individual is working for. Earnings also vary depending on the responsibilities, duties, qualifications, and experience level of the individual. Salaries range from $40,000 to $125,000 plus, with those on the lower end going to individuals working with lesser-known teams.

Employment Prospects

Employment prospects are poor for those aspiring to be Public Relations Directors of professional sports teams. Competition is fierce for these positions. It is more difficult to

obtain positions with major leagues and prestigious teams than with lesser-known and minor league teams.

Advancement Prospects

Advancement prospects are fair for the Director of Public Relations of a professional sports team. Individuals can take a number of different paths to climb the career ladder.

The PR Director may find a similar position with a more prestigious team. This will result in increased responsibilities and higher earnings. He or she may also become the director of marketing or promotion.

Education and Training

A minimum of a four-year college degree is necessary for most positions as Director of Public Relations for a professional sports team. Good choices for majors include public relations, communications, journalism, English, liberal arts, marketing, or business or sports administration.

Extra classes or seminars in writing, sports administration, marketing, public relations, and journalism can also be useful.

Experience/Skills/Personality Traits

Some Public Relations Directors working in professional sports teams may have worked with the same or another team as a publicist or as a college sports information director before landing their current position. Others worked in journalism as sports reporters in either the print or broadcasting fields. Some individuals obtained experience handling public relations, publicity, or marketing in other fields before entering the sports industry.

Successful PR Directors are creative, innovative people. They are articulate and well groomed. Individuals must have good communications skills and be comfortable speaking on the phone or in person to large and small groups.

The PR Director should know enough about the sport to speak and write intelligently about it. A great many individuals are or become ardent fans of the sport and team they work with. The Director must be capable of planning and executing all public relations skills.

The PR Director must be able to communicate on all levels. He or she should be able to develop and write factual, concise, and interesting letters, press releases, copy, and feature stories.

Individuals should be energetic and be able to work on countless projects at the same time without becoming flustered. Supervisory skills may also be required.

Public Relations Directors working for sports teams should be persuasive and personable. They should not only be able to deal well with people, but enjoy it. This includes the general public as well as the media.

Unions/Associations

The Director of Public Relations working for a professional sports team is not usually a member of any union or bargaining association. Individuals in this field may belong to a number of trade associations that provide educational and professional guidance as well as bring people with similar careers together. These might include the National Sportscasters and Sportswriters Association (NSSA), the Public Relations Society of America (PRSA), Women In Communications (WIC) and the National Federation of Press Women (NFPW). Individuals might also be members of organizations specific to the sport they are working in.

Tips for Entry

1. Join trade associations and attend their meetings, seminars, and conventions. This is a good way to obtain some extra continuing education as well as to make important contacts.

2. Try to locate an internship in the public relations, promotion, or marketing department of a professional sports team. This will help you gain hands-on experience and get your foot in the door. Contact professional sports teams or see if your college sponsors an internship program.

3. Another good way of getting your foot in the door is to locate a job as an assistant or trainee in the PR department of a professional sports team. Write or call and inquire.

4. If you have some public relations experience, send your résumé and a cover letter to the various professional teams. Ask that your résumé be kept on file if there are no current job openings.

5. Get as much experience writing as possible. Think about writing a sports column or being a sports reporter for your school or local newspaper.

PROFESSIONAL SPORTS TEAM PUBLICIST

CAREER PROFILE

Duties: Creating public interest in team and players; creating publicity; preparing and writing press releases, press kits, informational sheets, and yearbooks; dealing with the media.

Alternate Title(s):   Sports Publicist; Team Publicist; Publicist

Salary Range: $20,000 to $100,000+

Employment Prospects: Fair

Best Geographical Location(s) for Position: Cities hosting professional sports teams.

Prerequisites:

Education or Training—Four-year college degree required.

Experience—Sports writer or reporter or experience in college sports information preferred.

Special Skills and Personality Traits—Understanding of the specific sport; public relations skills; good writing skills; articulate; ability to deal with media; energetic; ability to deal with many projects.

CAREER LADDER

```
┌──────────────────────────────────────┐
│      Professional Sports Publicist    │
│       for More Prestigious Team        │
│                  or                    │
│          Individual Athlete            │
└──────────────────────────────────────┘
```

```
┌──────────────────────────────────────┐
│     Professional Sports Publicist      │
└──────────────────────────────────────┘
```

```
┌──────────────────────────────────────┐
│      Sports Information Director        │
│                  or                    │
│        Sports Writer or Reporter        │
└──────────────────────────────────────┘
```

Position Description

A Professional Sports Team Publicist has an interesting job. The individual's main function is to publicize a professional team and its players. This creates public interest, which in turn makes people want to attend games and fill up stadiums and arenas. With the current interest in televised sports, increased popularity of a team or an athlete also means that the ownership can get more money and better deals for televised events.

The Publicist in this field might work with professional teams in any sport, including hockey, baseball, basketball, jai alai, soccer, football, or others. He or she might work with the major or minor leagues. In order to be effective in the job, it is important that the individual have an understanding of the sport in which he or she works.

The professional sports industry is a major force in the entertainment world. The Professional Sports Team Publicist works with the sports news media daily. The individual deals with newspapers, magazines, television, cable networks, and radio stations. On the professional level, the Sports Team Publicist works with local, regional, and national media.

He or she knows the sport editors and calls to inform them of new deals being made by the team, new players, coaches, owners, managers, and so on. The Professional Sports Team Publicist frequently receives calls from the sports media asking specific questions or to request interviews with the players, coaches, trainers, or management.

The Professional Sports Team Publicist or Team Publicist, as he or she might be referred to, is responsible for setting up schedules of appearances for team members, coaches, managements, and owners. This could be for paid appearances or for appearances for nonprofit groups and charities. For example, a popular team member might be the national chairperson for an organization against teenage alcohol and drug abuse.

Professional teams receive many requests for public appearances, for either single athletes or the entire team. The Publicist has to decide which appearances to accept and which ones to reject. He or she must then write letters of regret with explanations that do not antagonize anyone to those requests that were not accepted.

The Team Publicist arranges guest appearances on television and radio talk, variety, news, and sports shows for team members as well as print interviews. He or she also develops feature story ideas for both sports editors and the general media.

The Publicist must know everything that is happening, ranging from dates of games and scores to players' injuries. The individual prepares press releases on a regular basis with this information. When major events are occurring within the team, he or she may write releases more frequently. These press releases will be sent to sports media from a prepared media list.

The individual also prepares statistical informational sheets, injury data, and the like regularly. He or she is responsible for interviewing players, managers, coaches, and owners to obtain information for biographies, team yearbooks, press kits, and game programs.

The Sports Publicist arranges and conducts press conferences. Major leagues usually hold more conferences than minor leagues. The individual may present press conferences weekly or even more frequently if a major event is taking place, such as a major trade or the signing of a popular athlete.

The Sports Publicist is available for the media at games as well as at practice sessions. He or she must arrange for press passes, press credentials, and seating for members of the media. The individual also arranges locker room interviews. He or she is responsible for passing out press kits, biographies, and releases to press people at this time.

If the team the individual works for is traveling to another city, the Sports Publicist phones media in that city to arrange interviews, appearances, and press conferences. The Sports Publicist might also travel to the city ahead of time and take care of these tasks in person. In this manner, he or she gets to know the sports press from the other cities.

The individual in this job socializes frequently with sports writers and reporters. He or she attends sports-related and social functions on behalf of the team. The Sports Team Publicist is always looking for a way to publicize his or her team and its members.

The Sports Team Publicist works long hours and many weekends. Activities sometimes slow down slightly during the sport's off season. The individual in this position may be responsible to the team owners, general manager, or public relations director.

Salaries

Salaries vary from job to job depending on the team the individual works for. Salaries can range from $20,000 to $100,000 plus.

Variables include the sport, type of league the individual works with, and the team's popularity and success. Earnings also depend on the individual's experience level and responsibilities.

Individuals who work for minor league teams earn salaries ranging from the low teens to the middle twenties. Those working for major league teams earn from $40,000 to $100,000 plus.

Employment Prospects

Employment prospects are fair for Professional Sports Team Publicists. Some teams have a Professional Sports Team Publicist and an Assistant Publicist or a number of assistants. Individuals may have more luck finding jobs in the minor leagues and with lesser known teams.

Advancement Prospects

Advancement prospects for Professional Team Publicists are good once an individual has held a job in this profession. The Team Publicist may go on to work for another team in the sports industry or an individual athlete, or may go into sports marketing and endorsements. The individual might also start his or her own public relations or publicity company or find a job in a top agency. He or she might also become a press agent for people in other facets of the entertainment industry.

Things can change overnight in the sports industry. An individual may be working for a team that isn't very well known or doesn't have a lot of prestige. If the team wins unexpectedly, all of a sudden it might become popular, making the Team Publicist position even more valuable.

Education and Training

The Team Publicist usually must have a four-year college degree. The exception to this might be an individual who was a former professional athlete who has an understanding of sports, public relations, and publicity from working in the industry.

The Sports Team Publicist will find courses and seminars in public relations, publicity, marketing, journalism, English, writing, media exposure, sports studies, and physical education useful.

Experience/Skills/Personality Traits

Professional Sports Team Publicists usually have had previous experience with the media. They often were sports writers or reporters themselves. Some individuals in this position worked as college sports information directors before holding a job in professional sports.

The Team Publicist must have a total understanding of the sport, the players, and the industry. He or she must also have a full working knowledge of how to use public relations and publicity tactics to promote the team. The individual should be a good writer with the ability to turn out factual, concise, and interesting press releases, biographies, yearbooks, and the like.

The ability to communicate well and speak articulately is essential. The individual must be comfortable speaking to large groups. He or she may often conduct press conferences.

The Team Publicist should be personable. Sports writers and reporters must like the individual and feel comfortable talking to him or her. A good working relationship between the Team Publicist and the sports media is necessary.

The individual must be energetic. He or she must be able to work long hours, handle many details, and work on many different projects at one time.

Unions/Associations

The Professional Sports Team Publicist does not belong to any union. However, he or she may belong to a number of trade associations, including the National Sportscasters and Sports-writers Association (NSSA), the Public Relations Society of America (PRSA), Women In Communications (WIC) and the National Federation of Press Women (NFPW).

Tips for Entry

1. Consider a summer or part-time job as a sports reporter for a local newspaper.
2. Work on your college newspaper. It is important to gain as much experience as possible writing.
3. Work in your college sports information office as an assistant or aide. This will give you a good overview of the job on an amateur level.
4. The Professional Sports Team Publicist often has a number of assistants or trainees working with him or her doing the leg work and clerical work. Try to locate one of these positions.
5. An internship or summer job in the sports department of a local television station would also prove helpful. You will learn how sports reporters work and make some valuable contacts.
6. Job sites and professional sports team web pages may list job openings.

TICKET MANAGER

CAREER PROFILE

Duties: Handling ticket sales; keeping track of seats sold; arranging for group ticket sales; dealing with fans' and patrons' ticket and seat problems.

Alternate Title(s): Box Office Manager

Salary Range: $20,000 to $70,000+

Employment Prospects: Fair

Best Geographical Location(s) for Position: Cities hosting professional sports teams; those with arenas and stadiums.

Prerequisites:

Education or Training—Some positions prefer a four-year college degree; others require a high school diploma.
Experience—Experience working in box office, ticket office, etc.
Special Skills and Personality Traits—Detail oriented; highly organized; bookkeeping skills; computer skills; math skills; ability to get along well with people; ability to communicate calmly.

CAREER LADDER

```
┌─────────────────────────────────────┐
│          Ticket Manager             │
│            for More                 │
│ Prestigious Team in Larger Facility │
└─────────────────────────────────────┘

┌─────────────────────────────────────┐
│          Ticket Manager             │
└─────────────────────────────────────┘

┌─────────────────────────────────────┐
│          Ticket Clerk,              │
│         Assistant Ticket,           │
│               or                    │
│        Box Office Manager           │
└─────────────────────────────────────┘
```

Position Description

Sports teams earn money for their owners in a number of ways. One method of obtaining income is selling television and cable rights to their games. Another income producer is selling items or licensing products emblazed with team logos. Still another important source of income for most sports teams are sales of tickets to their games.

The Ticket Manager is in charge of the department that handles ticket sales for scheduled team games. He or she has varied duties depending on the prestige and popularity of the team and the size of the ticket office.

Minor league teams and those with less fan drawing power may have one individual in charge of ticket sales. He or she has the title Ticket Manager and is responsible for everything that occurs in the ticket office. Major league and other highly visible sports teams with a large fan following may have many people working in their ticket offices. In these instances the Ticket Manager oversees an entire office and staff.

An important function of the Ticket Manager is handling season ticket sales and fan seating requests. When the Ticket Manager receives requests for season tickets, he or she sends information to patrons on prices and available seat selections. The individual is responsible for compiling lists of season ticket holders and keeping the list up to date and in order. As many patrons purchase season tickets year after year, the Ticket Manager may also be responsible for communicating with fans and for regularly sending out brochures or flyers to them. He or she must keep track of every ticket subscription sold and the boxes or seats reserved.

Most stadiums have scheduled hours that patrons can purchase tickets prior to a game. If the individual is working a one-person ticket office, he or she is required to sell tickets personally. If the operation is larger, the Ticket Manager assigns sales duties to staff members working in the office. These individuals are responsible for selling the actual tickets, obtaining payment, and assigning seats.

The Ticket Manager must be aware of the various sections in the stadium and the pricing fees for tickets for each of these sections. In most stadiums the Ticket Manager has a layout chart of the seats. He or she marks off seats as they are purchased by fans. In some stadiums this chart is on a computer. In this manner, the Ticket Manager can see at a glance which seats are available and their location.

The Ticket Manager is also responsible for selling tickets the night or day of the event. Even if the individual is not personally selling the tickets, he or she generally is at the stadium for each game.

Handling group ticket sales is another function of the Ticket Manager. The individual is responsible for telling groups what the discounted price of tickets will be if they purchase them in blocks. He or she is also expected to arrange for the blocks of seats.

There is no room for error in the ticket office. All tickets must be accounted for. The Ticket Manager must keep track of each ticket sold by number and the payment received. Computerized ticket machines have made this task easier.

Individuals must be aware of how to put credit card purchases through the system and how to authorize ticket sales made by check. The Ticket Manager must also know how to spot counterfeit tickets.

The Ticket Manager is responsible for holding and dispersing tickets to fans who have purchased them prior to a game but have not picked them up. Another duty of the individual may be to give out complimentary tickets or passes that have been issued by team management, players, public relations, publicity, or marketing departments. These are often left at a "will call" window.

Ticket Managers must also deal with fans and patrons who have problems with their tickets and seating. These individuals might include people who have purchased tickets prior to the event and lost them, patrons who do not like the position of seats, or those who want to move to a different seat for other reasons. The Ticket Manager must remain calm and in control at all times and try to keep the fans as satisfied as possible.

Individuals in this position may be responsible to the business manager, comptroller, or general manager, depending on the structure of the particular team.

Salaries

Earnings for Ticket Managers can vary greatly. Variables include the responsibilities and experience of the individual, the size of the stadium, and the prestige of the team. While some stadiums can seat 1,500 people, others have seating capacities of over 100,000. Ticket Managers responsible for ticket control in the 100,000-seater earn more than individuals handling smaller stadiums.

Ticket Managers working in smaller stadiums may earn $20,000 per year, while individuals handling many responsibilities in larger stadiums may earn $70,000 plus.

Employment Prospects

Employment prospects are fair for Ticket Managers. Individuals may work for teams in a variety of sports. While positions may be located throughout the country, the prospects usually are better in cities hosting a large number of professional sports teams and having a number of stadiums.

Individuals may find employment working for professional major league teams, minor leagues, or colleges.

Advancement Prospects

There is no individual career path for Ticket Managers. The best prospects for advancement are for the person to locate a position with additional responsibilities and with a more prestigious team. This usually results in higher earnings.

Education and Training

As in many sports industry positions, educational requirements vary. Some positions may require an individual to have a four-year college degree. Others may require only some college experience. Still others may offer positions to individuals with a high school diploma and prior experience working in a box or ticket office.

Experience/Skills/Personality Traits

A Ticket Manager must be a highly organized individual. He or she should be able to deal with many details at the same time. The Ticket Manager needs to be able to keep accurate records.

Bookkeeping and math skills are mandatory. A good memory is essential. As many box offices are now becoming computerized, it would be in the individual's best interests to have computer skills.

The Ticket Manager should have both verbal and written communications skills. He or she should also be a people person. At times the individual will have to deal with patrons who are unhappy with their seats or the prices. He or she should have the ability to remain cool and calm and be able to resolve disputes.

An ability to supervise and work well with others is necessary in this position.

Unions/Associations

There are no specific trade associations for Ticket Managers working with sports teams. Individuals may be members of organizations relevant to the particular sport they are working with.

Tips for Entry

1. Consider a summer or part-time job in a movie or theater ticket office. This will help you gain on the job experience.
2. Make sure that you have computer training and know how to work and feel comfortable with computer systems. Many offices are automated. Computer literacy gives you an extra edge in the job market.

3. You may be able to gain experience in your college's activities or athletic department. See if you can locate a position working in the box office, doing clerical work in the activities office, or selling tickets to entertainment or sporting events.

4. Expect to start at the bottom of the career ladder in a professional sports team's box office. Take a job selling tickets to get your foot in the door. Learn as much as you can and wait for your opportunity to climb the career ladder.

5. Jobs in the box office may be advertised in the newspapers display or classified section in cities hosting arenas and domes. Look under heading classifications of "Box Office," "Tickets," "Sports," "Athletic Events," "Stadiums," or "Entertainment."

6. Call or write the personnel office of professional sports teams and inquire about openings in the box office or ticket department. Send your résumé and a cover letter requesting that it be held if there are no immediate openings.

7. Many professional sports teams offer internship programs. Request an assignment in ticket sales or the box office.

8. Search the Internet for job openings. Look on popular career and job sites as well as sites hosted by sports teams.

TRAVELING SECRETARY/ PROFESSIONAL SPORTS TEAM

CAREER PROFILE

Duties: Making travel arrangements for a professional sports team; moving the team around the country; dealing with crises and problems on the road; handling business affairs on the road.

Alternate Title(s): Road Manager; Road Secretary

Salary Range: $28,000 to $125,000+

Employment Prospects: Poor

Best Geographical Location(s) for Position: Cities hosting professional sports teams.

Prerequisites:

Education or Training—No educational requirement for some positions; others require or prefer college background or degree.

Experience—Experience working with either professional sports teams or travel helpful but not always necessary.

Special Skills and Personality Traits—Free to travel; enjoy traveling; articulate; ability to deal with a variety of people; energetic; organized; capable of dealing with many projects at one time; basic understanding of travel industry.

CAREER LADDER

```
┌─────────────────────────────────┐
│   Traveling Secretary           │
│   for More Prestigious Team,     │
│   Team Business Manager          │
│           or                     │
│   Other Administrative Position  │
└─────────────────────────────────┘

┌─────────────────────────────────┐
│      Traveling Secretary         │
└─────────────────────────────────┘

┌─────────────────────────────────┐
│   Traveling Secretary Intern     │
│           or                     │
│      Professional Athlete        │
│           or                     │
│     Travel Agent or Escort       │
└─────────────────────────────────┘
```

Position Description

The Traveling Secretary working for a professional sports team is responsible for handling the operational details of the team when it is on the road. The individual makes sure that team members are as comfortable as possible and that their basic needs are met.

The Traveling Secretary is responsible for making travel arrangements for the team when it is on the road to other locations to play games. The individual is in charge of booking or chartering all buses, planes, and cars for the team. This includes transportation to get the players from a stadium to the airport, from the airport to the stadium, and to and from hotels. The Traveling Secretary either charters planes or books blocks of seats on commercial flights for the team. At times the individual also arranges for cars, limousines, or any other transportation needed to get players from point A to point B.

The Traveling Secretary must negotiate the best possible prices for the transportation as well as for hotels, motels, restaurants, and so on. He or she often must obtain price quotes from a number of different companies and is responsible for choosing the best one.

Another responsibility of the Traveling Secretary is to make sure that the entire team knows the correct meeting times and places for travel. He or she may fill in forms or write letters or memos to alert team members of the dates, times, and locations of bus and plane travel.

The individual is ultimately responsible for making sure that the all team members get where they are supposed to be on time with as little trouble as possible. For example, the Traveling Secretary is in charge of taking the team by bus to the airport so that they can fly to their destination. He or she is responsible for making sure that all their luggage gets on the plane. When the team arrives at the destination, the Traveling Secretary once again makes sure a bus is waiting to take the team either to the stadium or to the hotel. Once again, he or she must make sure that luggage gets off the plane and goes to the correct place.

The individual is responsible for making sure that each team member is assigned a hotel or motel room. He or she usually also makes arrangements for meals as well as distributes meal money to the team members.

The Traveling Secretary handles some of the work even before the team leaves town. A successful Traveling Secretary checks on details ahead of time, confirming that buses, planes, restaurants, and hotels are available at the right time. He or she must also be able to deal with a crisis when it occurs. The individual must know what to do if a plane is late, luggage is lost, or hotel rooms are not available. He or she must also be able to deal with players who are late and miss planes or any other unexpected circumstance.

The Traveling Secretary goes with the team to all out-of-town games and to spring training sessions. He or she is responsible for moving the team throughout the country. In some situations, the individual also has additional responsibilities, such as managing the club house or working with the teams ticket operation or sales campaign.

Depending on the situation and the team, the Traveling Secretary is usually responsible to either the team manager or the owner.

Hours are long. When the team travels, the individual works 24 hours a day. The job of Traveling Secretary can be rather stressful due to last-minute travel changes, people missing flights, and the like. Some people thrive on the excitement. Individuals have the opportunity of being with a sports team at all times, traveling around the country and seeing all the games of their favorite sport.

Salaries

Annual earnings for Traveling Secretaries can range from $28,000 to $125,000 plus benefit packages. The salaries vary greatly depending on a number of factors. These include the sport, type of league involved, and the prestige, popularity, and success of the team with which the individual is working. Other variables include the individual's experience level and responsibilities.

Employment Prospects

Employment prospects are poor. There is little turnover in this position. Once someone obtains a job, he or she seems to keep it for a long time.

While every sports team that moves around needs someone to make travel arrangements, many teams do not have an individual on staff with the job title Traveling Secretary. In many teams, the team managers, administrative assistants, or secretaries handle this job.

Most Traveling Secretary positions are held by those working in professional baseball. This is because teams in this sport move around the country more frequently and for longer periods of time than in other sports. As there are only 26 major league teams, jobs are quite limited.

Individuals may find it easier to break into this type of position working with smaller teams or minor leagues where they might also have additional responsibilities. In this way, they can obtain the needed experience as well as make important contacts.

Advancement Prospects

Advancement prospects are fair for the Traveling Secretary once he or she obtains a job. He or she may climb the career ladder by obtaining a position with a more prestigious team. Other Traveling Secretaries advance their careers by becoming a team's business manager or moving into another administrative position.

As in all jobs in the professional sports industry, it is difficult to determine the exact path of a career ladder. Depending on an individual's luck, perseverance, and qualifications, a Traveling Secretary can move to almost any position in a sports team once he or she gets a foot in the door.

Education and Training

Education and training for those seeking positions as Traveling Secretaries differ. While it is not essential to hold a college degree, it certainly can't hurt. Competition is keen in the sports industry, and the better educated an individual is, the better his or her chances of success.

The best choice for a major for those seeking entry in this field is one in sports administration. Other majors that might be useful include business, hotel management or administration, and training in the travel industry.

Experience/Skills/Personality Traits

One of the most important traits for the Traveling Secretary to possess is the freedom and ability to travel. This is not the type of job for people who can't leave their home base or their family for extended periods of time. The individual must also enjoy traveling. The amount of time spent away from home usually depends on the sport. For example, Traveling Secretaries in the sport of baseball are probably away from home for longer periods of time than are those who work in football. It depends on the amount of time the team travels to other cities to play.

The individual should be personable and easy to talk to. He or she must deal with members of the team, management, and media as well as with people from hotels, motels, airlines, restaurants, and so on. Many people come to the Traveling Secretary with a variety of problems that they are having while on the road. These might be travel-related problems or those arising from being under pressure and away from home. The

Traveling Secretary must be able to discuss the problems and try to come up with effective solutions.

The Traveling Secretary should be articulate with good communications skills. He or she will be talking to different people, making travel arrangements, and dealing with crises on the road.

The individual should have a command of math, good interpersonal skills, and understand the art of negotiation. He or she should know how to read maps, airline schedules, rental agreements, and have a basic understanding of the travel industry.

The Traveling Secretary must be very energetic. At times, he or she works long hours. When on the road, the individual is on call 24 hours a day. The Traveling Secretary must know how to arrange priorities and deal with them in a logical order.

The Traveling Secretary needs to be extremely organized and able to handle many varied details at one time. He or she must be able to remain unflustered even when a crisis arises.

Unions/Associations

There are no unions or trade associations that the Traveling Secretary working in sports must belong to.

Tips for Entry

1. Look for an internship or training program. These can be located through colleges with sports administration programs or by contacting teams directly.
2. Get experience making travel arrangements by getting a summer or part-time job with a travel agency.
3. Consider working as a travel escort or tour director for a tour group. It is important to obtain as much experience working with people and arranging travel plans as possible.
4. Volunteer to do the travel arrangements for an amateur or school sports team, local theater group, or band.
5. Try to work with a sports team in any capacity. Experience and contacts are very important in making it in this industry.

EQUIPMENT MANAGER

CAREER PROFILE

Duties: Keeping equipment clean and repaired; transporting and securing the team's equipment when moving from game to game.

Alternate Title(s): None

Salary Range: $18,000 to $45,000+

Employment Prospects: Fair

Best Geographical Location(s) for Position: Cities hosting sports teams.

Prerequisites:

Education or Training—No formal educational requirement for most positions.

Experience—Experience handling and repairing equipment specific to the sport.

Special Skills and Personality Traits—Ability to make minor equipment repairs; dependability; reliability; knowledge of sports equipment; detail oriented.

CAREER LADDER

```
┌─────────────────────────────┐
│     Equipment Manager       │
│            for              │
│   More Prestigious Team     │
└─────────────────────────────┘

┌─────────────────────────────┐
│     Equipment Manager       │
└─────────────────────────────┘

┌─────────────────────────────┐
│ Assistant Equipment Manager,│
│     Equipment Staffer,      │
│             or              │
│  Athlete or Support Person  │
└─────────────────────────────┘
```

Position Description

The team Equipment Manager is responsible for making sure that all the team's playing equipment is in shape and in proper working order. This type of position offers an individual who loves a specific sport but doesn't play well enough to become a star athlete the opportunity to feel like one of the team. He or she is required to attend practice sessions, games, and tournaments. If the team travels, the individual travels with them.

Before each game or practice session, the Equipment Manager is responsible for getting together all the equipment the athletes need to play. Equipment varies from sport to sport. The individual must check all the equipment and make sure that it is clean, in good shape, and ready for play.

If pieces of equipment are broken, the individual is responsible for either repairing them or making sure that they are repaired. If something is in poor condition and cannot be fixed, the Equipment Manager must replace it. Depending on the specific situation, he or she may just be responsible for reporting that a particular piece needs replacing or may be personally responsible for ordering or purchasing. The individual must be sure that the repair or replacement is made in time for practice and games.

During the games and/or practice sessions, if something breaks, the Equipment Manager is responsible for fixing it on the spot or having a substitute on hand. The Equipment Manager hands out equipment to team members and coaches before each game or practice session. It is his or her duty to reclaim the equipment after each event. At this time, the Equipment Manager checks everything for wear and tear and determines how to handle any problems that may have developed.

The Equipment Manager is responsible for packing, transporting, and securing all equipment. When the team goes on the road for an "away" game, he or she travels with them carrying out the duties of the job. It is especially important for the team when it is away from home base that the Equipment Manager do his or her job professionally and correctly. It is often extremely difficult to obtain needed equipment in unfamiliar surroundings.

The Equipment Manager may deal with everyone related to the team, including athletes and support personnel. When anyone needs a specific piece of equipment or something needs repairing, he or she relies on the Equipment Manager. Depending on the specific situation, he or she may work alone or may supervise assistants and other equipment staffers.

Equipment Managers work during all games and practice sessions as well as before and after each event collecting, cleaning, repairing, transporting, and securing all of the team's equipment. Individuals in this position may be responsible to the owner, general manager, field manager, or head coach.

Salaries

Earnings for Equipment Managers vary greatly depending on a number of variables. These include the specific team that the individual works for and its prestige and status. Other variables include the specific duties of the individual and his or her experience in the field.

As a rule, Equipment Managers working with professional teams earn more than those working with amateur and scholastic teams. Salaries for this position can run from $18,000 to $45,000 or more annually.

Employment Prospects

Employment prospects are fair for individuals willing to begin their careers as Equipment Managers with smaller, less-prestigious teams. Opportunities occur less frequently for individuals seeking positions with better-known teams.

Employment possibilities may be located throughout the country with pro, semipro, amateur, and scholastic teams. Equipment Managers may have to relocate in order to find an opening in this field.

Advancement Prospects

Equipment Managers who want to climb the career ladder can usually advance by locating a similar position with a larger, more prestigious team. This, in turn, leads to higher earnings. Advancement prospects are determined by the drive and determination of the individual as well as his or her aptitude for the job. Some individuals advance their career by moving into other areas of sports administration.

Education and Training

There are no educational requirements for the vast majority of Equipment Manager positions. This is not to say that a college background is not useful, as it provides a solid education and an opportunity to make needed contacts. In addition, individuals may find college helpful in case they want to move into other facets of sports administration.

Experience/Skills/Personality Traits

A number of Equipment Managers landed their positions after actively playing on the team as an athlete. After retirement or injuries, the individual stayed with the team. Some Equipment Managers have worked themselves up from assistant equipment manager or other equipment staffer positions. Other Equipment Managers have had experience with the sport on a different level, such as coaching, training, or offici-

ating. Still others have worked as sales representatives for sporting goods companies or as sales people in retail shops.

Equipment Managers should have a complete understanding of the sport that they work with. Individuals also need a thorough working knowledge of all the equipment used in the particular sport and how it is used. It is essential that the individual know how to make at least minor repairs on the equipment used in the sport. The Equipment Manager should be reliable. When equipment is not in working condition, he or she must take care of the problem in a timely fashion.

The individual should also be detail oriented. He or she is responsible for making sure that all equipment is where it should be when it is required. The Equipment Manager must be able to know exactly what equipment is needed and how it is going to be packed and transported to the destination.

The Equipment Manager must also have the freedom to travel. He or she accompanies the team when it plays games away from their home turf.

Unions/Associations

Equipment Managers may belong to the Equipment Managers Association (EMA). This organization offers career guidance and support to individuals in this profession at both the amateur/scholastic level and in the pros. Individuals may also belong to organizations and trade associations directly related to the sport they are working with.

Tips for Entry

1. Volunteer to act as the Equipment Manager for one of your school's athletic teams. This is good experience and looks great on your résumé.
2. Consider attending a college offering a major in sports administration. These colleges usually provide internships that will help get your foot into the door of a professional team.
3. Learn everything you can about the particular sport you are interested in. Know the game, the rules, regulations, and, of course, the equipment required.
4. Try to locate internships or part-time jobs with sports teams, on the amateur level or in the pros. It doesn't matter if you can't find one in the specific sport that you're interested in. The important thing is to get experience and make contacts. Remember . . . always to try to obtain letters of recommendation from the teams you work with.
5. Join relevant trade associations and attend their meetings. These too will help you make valuable contacts.
6. Consider getting a summer or part-time job in a sporting equipment shop. This will help familiarize you with sporting equipment.
7. Hang around sports teams, both the athletes and the support personnel. Get to know people. It's another way to make contacts.

INTERN/PROFESSIONAL SPORTS TEAM

CAREER PROFILE

Duties: Working with a professional sports team to learn skills, get experience, and make contacts.

Alternate Title(s): Trainee

Salary Range: $0 to $350 a week

Employment Prospects: Fair

Best Geographical Location(s) for Position: Internships located throughout the country in cities that host professional sports teams.

Prerequisites:

Education or Training—Undergraduate or graduate college student.

Experience—College course work in subjects relevant to position the individual hopes to pursue or in sports administration.

Special Skills and Personality Traits—Eagerness; aggressiveness; desire to work in sports industry; good student; writing skills; communications skills; articulate; creative; innovative.

CAREER LADDER

```
┌─────────────────────────────────┐
│            Position             │
│  with Professional Sports Team  │
└─────────────────────────────────┘

┌─────────────────────────────────┐
│             Intern              │
└─────────────────────────────────┘

┌─────────────────────────────────┐
│          Entry Level            │
│              or                 │
│         College Student         │
└─────────────────────────────────┘
```

Position Description

Most professional teams in baseball, football, hockey, basketball, and the like have Interns working with the team. An Intern works directly with a sports team, learning the business by gaining hands-on experience.

The individual obtains the necessary skills so that after graduation from college, he or she will be ready to enter the sports industry. The Intern is involved in actual work situations.

The Intern may work in just one specific area or may float from department to department in the team management. The individual may be assigned to or ask to work in various departments, including public relations, marketing, general management, equipment management, promotion, business, and player development.

The Intern's responsibilities vary depending on the specific internship program, the team, and the department he or she is working in. Most Interns work full time for a specified period, usually from six weeks to a school semester. In other situations, the Intern works during the specific team's season.

In most instances, professional teams find their Interns through colleges and universities that offer sports administration degrees. Part of the requirements necessary to graduate usually includes working as an Intern for a sports team or league.

Duties of the Intern depend on the department that they are assigned to. In some programs, the Interns are responsible for taking part in discussion groups, attending seminars, and completing specific projects as well as working with the team. In others, the individual is just required to fulfill his or her job-related functions. If the Intern is using the program to get school credit, he or she may be required to write a paper or do a project relating to the internship.

Interns learn how to perform tasks by actually doing them. He or she may start out with messenger duties, doing photocopying, collating, and the like. At the beginning, it might seem that working as an Intern for a sports teams is similar to performing the duties of glorified secretary. However, interning gives the individual needed experience in the field and a feel for how the entire industry works. As Interns learn more, they are usually allowed more leeway in their work activities.

One of the most important reasons to become an Intern is to get a foot in the door of the sports industry and make valuable contacts. A good number of Interns are hired after graduation by the team that they interned with.

Hours are usually long for Interns. The Intern who volunteers to do more than is asked is usually the one who is offered a job later. The more an Intern learns at this stage of his or her career, the better.

Interns are usually responsible to the head of the department they are working with. In other situations, a college faculty member may be responsible for Interns. The Intern often meets with supervisors to discuss problems and potential solutions of the job.

The whole idea of the internship program is to give the individual an overview of the sports industry and help him or her gain on-the-job experience. The Intern must grab every opportunity to learn as much as possible about the industry from experienced people who are working in the field.

Salaries

Compensation for Interns is usually low, if there is any monetary payment at all. Most Interns work for professional sports teams as a way of gaining experience, making important contacts, and fulfilling college requirements. College credit is often offered for the experience.

The Interns who do get paid may make a flat rate, such as $600 to $1,000, for the length of the internship. Others may be paid minimum wages or salaries up to approximately $350 weekly.

Employment Prospects

Employment prospects are fair for individuals who want to pursue internships with professional sports teams. While anyone can apply for an internship, most internships with major professional sports teams are given out through colleges that have sports administration degrees.

Advancement Prospects

Advancement prospects are good for Interns. Individuals who have successfully gone through intern programs usually have an easier time finding employment after graduation. Individuals who are eager to learn, aggressive, and helpful are often be asked to return to the team after graduation. Other individuals find that with this added experience, coupled with contacts made during the internship, they have an easier time getting interviews and finding positions.

Education and Training

Interns working for sports teams are usually college students who are pursuing a career in the sports industry. Majors will differ depending on the specific career choice. For example, an individual hoping to get into the publicity, promotion, or public relations field might have a major in public relations, English, or liberal arts. An individual hoping to be in some facet of the sports administration field might major in one of the sports administration programs currently being offered at colleges throughout the country.

Experience/Skills/Personality Traits

One of the main reasons an Intern works for a sports team is to gain a degree of experience. He or she should learn as much as possible while on the job. This often means that the individual will be asked to perform menial or repetitive tasks. However, the experience value of this type of position is well worth the effort put in. Interns should be willing to do that extra amount of work without complaining.

The individual should be bright, aggressive, and articulate. He or she should have the ability to communicate well both verbally and on paper. The ability to follow instructions is imperative.

Unions/Associations

There are no specific unions or associations for Interns working with sports teams.

Tips for Entry

1. Write to professional sports teams and inquire about internships. Most have intern programs set up. In others you may have to create a position.
2. Start putting together a portfolio of your work. This will show initiative and illustrate your talents. For example, if you want to work in public relations, keep copies of all your press releases. If you are interested in box office management or promotion, volunteer your talents for school programs and build a portfolio of success stories.
3. Try to attend a college that has a sports administration or sports managment program. Recruiters frequently visit these colleges, which have cooperative programs with professional sports teams.
4. Obtain letters of recommendations from professors and employers. These are a good addition to your résumé.
5. Internship programs are often available for minority students. If you are in this category, use them to your advantage.

CHEERLEADER/ PROFESSIONAL SPORTS TEAM

CAREER PROFILE

Duties: Entertaining fans during halftime or other breaks; cheering for team; exciting fans who are watching the game; performing at special promotions and appearances.

Alternate Title(s): None

Salary Range: $35 to $100+ per game; individuals may earn extra money for performing at special promotions and shows

Employment Prospects: Poor.

Best Geographical Location(s) for Position: Cities hosting professional sports teams.

Prerequisites:

Education or Training—No formal educational requirement; dance training or the equivalent is necessary.

Experience—Experience performing in front of people helpful but not always necessary.

Special Skills and Personality Traits—Good dance skills; comfortable performing in front of groups of people; energetic; enthusiastic; physically fit; well groomed; ability to follow dance routines.

CAREER LADDER

```
┌─────────────────────────────┐
│       Choreographer,        │
│   Director, or Coordinator  │
│       of Cheerleaders       │
└─────────────────────────────┘

┌─────────────────────────────┐
│        Cheerleader          │
└─────────────────────────────┘

┌─────────────────────────────┐
│          Dancer             │
└─────────────────────────────┘
```

Position Description

Cheerleaders for professional sports teams are individuals who cheer the team on and help excite the fans who have come to see a game or are watching it on television. The main function of Cheerleaders is to entertain the fans with routines during breaks in the game. Individuals may perform during quarter breaks, halftimes, and time-outs. As a rule, Cheerleaders for professional sports teams are women. They usually perform with basketball and football teams.

Cheerleaders audition for spots on the squad. There is a great deal of competition for these positions. Depending on the specific team, there may be hundreds of applicants for each spot. For example, when the Los Angeles Lakers hold auditions for their cheerleaders, the Laker Girls, up to 600 women try out for the 15 openings.

Application procedures vary from team to team. Most include filling out a written application and résumé as well as

an in-depth interview. All applicants must audition. Usually individuals audition first in groups. Then as the competitors are weeded out, they may also audition on their own. Auditions may take one or more days to complete.

The lucky individuals who are chosen to be Cheerleaders will attend orientation sessions where they learn what is expected of them. This includes information on rules, regulations, and policies that they must adhere to in order to stay a member of the cheerleading team. At this time, Cheerleaders also find out when they are expected at practice sessions and receive a schedule of games where they will be appearing.

Cheerleaders work hard learning the routines that have been choreographed for them. They may practice two or three times a week for three or four hours a session. The Cheerleaders must work together as a team to make everything run smoothly and for routines to appear perfect.

Individuals must be in good physical shape and well groomed at all times. They must look good out on the field. Cheerleaders are expected to perform at all games. They may put on shows anytime there is a game in their home stadium. Usually these occur during breaks in the game, such as halftimes.

Cheerleaders from some teams may also perform at other times. They may put on shows for charities, nonprofit events, public service, or television shows. Some teams like to showcase their Cheerleaders in an effort to publicize and promote the team and for other public relations reasons.

Most individuals who aspire to be Cheerleaders for professional sports teams do so for the excitement and the exposure. A number love the sport and want to be involved in the industry. Many hope that this exposure will lead to other jobs in the entertainment world, including dancing, singing, modeling, or acting in television, movies, or the theater.

There is a constant turnover of people in this profession. In some teams individuals may have to try out for the season every year. In others, those who were members of the team and who performed well are asked back.

Cheerleaders are responsible to the coordinator or director in charge of the cheerleading team.

Salaries

It should be noted that cheerleading for a professional team is a part-time profession. Earnings for Cheerleaders vary from $35 to $100 plus per game depending on the team. Cheerleaders may earn additional money when performing in special appearances and promotions.

Generally, individuals feel that the experience and exposure gained is well worth the limited monetary returns.

Employment Prospects

Employment prospects are poor for individuals aspiring to be Cheerleaders for major league professional sports teams. Competition is keen. Cheerleaders usually have to audition every season. Individuals might find it easier to get their foot into the door by becoming a Cheerleader for a minor league team.

Advancement Prospects

Advancement prospects vary from individual to individual. Climbing the career ladder within the organization generally means becoming the director, coordinator, or choreographer of Cheerleaders.

Cheerleaders working with major league teams may get a great deal of recognition and move on to other areas of the entertainment industry. Many hope to be offered parts in television shows, movies, or commercials.

Others work with the team for a year or two and never get involved in anything else in the entertainment or sports indus-

try. As most individuals who become Cheerleaders are dancers, many go on to other dancing roles.

Education and Training

Educational requirements vary depending on the team. Most major league teams interview individuals extensively before signing them up to be Cheerleaders. A college degree is not usually required. However, as noted previously, this is usually a part-time position. Educational requirements, therefore, depend on the individual's other occupation.

Cheerleaders do need training in dance skills. This may or may not be formal training.

Experience/Skills/Personality Traits

As a rule, Cheerleaders are required to have extensive dance experience. The amount of experience differs with each team. Some teams require a minimum of eight years of dance experience.

Individuals must be able to follow, imitate, and remember dance routines. Knowledge of choreography may be useful.

Individuals should be energetic and physically fit. They need to be well groomed and have pleasing appearances. Cheerleaders should be personable. They should be have bubbly, exciting, and enthusiastic personalities. They need to be able to excite fans and entertain them.

Cheerleaders should be comfortable performing in front of large audiences. Individuals represent the team when they are working as well as when they are off the field. They should know how to carry themselves. Good verbal communications are imperative.

Unions/Associations

There is no specific trade association for Cheerleaders working with professional sports teams. Individuals may belong to associations related to various forms of dancing or choreography.

Tips for Entry

1. Take as many types of dance, aerobics, and choreography classes and workshops as you can. This will get you used to following other people's routines.
2. Watch the routines of dancers and cheerleaders and try to follow them. Then practice as much as you can.
3. Contact professional sports teams to find out whom you need to talk to or when they will be holding auditions for cheerleaders.
4. Bring a résumé with you to auditions as well as an 8 by 10-inch glossy photograph of yourself if you have one. Remember to find out ahead of time what to wear or bring to the audition.
5. Most professional sports teams require their Cheerleaders to be at least 18 years old.
6. Persevere. If you do not make the cheerleading squad the first time, you can try again next year.

CAREER OPPORTUNITIES IN SPORTS BUSINESS AND ADMINISTRATION

PROFESSIONAL SPORTS AGENT

CAREER PROFILE

Duties: Acting on behalf of athlete, sports official, or coach; securing best possible financial deals for clients; obtaining endorsements.

Alternate Title(s): Representative

Salary Range: Difficult to determine earnings

Employment Prospects: Fair

Best Geographical Location(s) for Position: Major entertainmnent capitals such as New York and Los Angeles.

Prerequisites:

Education or Training—Four-year college degree in business, accounting, or sports administration; law degree helpful.

Experience—Experience working in business or sports administration situations.

Special Skills and Personality Traits—Negotiating skills; sales ability; aggressiveness; ability to work under stressful conditions.

CAREER LADDER

```
┌─────────────────────────────────────┐
│  Agent with More Prestigious Clients │
└─────────────────────────────────────┘

┌─────────────────────────────────────┐
│     Professional Sports Agent        │
└─────────────────────────────────────┘

┌─────────────────────────────────────┐
│        Lawyer, Accountant,           │
│        Business Manager,             │
│        Sports Administrator          │
└─────────────────────────────────────┘
```

Position Description

A Professional Sports Agent works on behalf of professional athletes much as a booking agent works with entertainers. The individual in this position acts as an athlete's representative. When Agents work for athletes in this capacity, the athlete is called the client. The Agent tries to secure the best possible financial and benefit package for his or her client.

The Professional Sports Agent may function in a number of different ways for his or her client. To begin with, the Agent must locate a team for the client to work with. Usually by the time an athlete acquires an Agent, at least one if not more teams are bidding for the athlete's services.

Almost everyone is aware of athletes who receive huge salaries and contracts. These million-dollar salaries are usually the result of an Agent's work. The Agent acts as an intermediary and negotiator between the athlete and the team owner or general manager. He or she negotiates the best possible salary and contract for the athlete.

Some athletes retain their Agent to do other types of work. For example, the individual may also act as a financial Agent. He or she may recommend various investments to the athlete in order to help the individual build a solid financial base and secure tax advantages.

Agents may also locate product endorsements for their clients. Product endorsements mean that the athlete appears in an advertisement or commercial or endorses a product or service for a company. Many people respect the ideas and opinions of their sports idols. Obtaining a sports superstar's endorsement can mean an increase in product sales. As a result, the business of endorsements can be quite lucrative for the athlete. A part of the Agent's duties in this area is to make sure that the products endorsed will not harm the athlete's image but fit in with it. For example, most athletes will not endorse any brand of cigarette. It would ruin their health-conscious, athletic image.

Sports Agents may work for a variety of clients. They may, for instance, represent athletes, sports officials, coaches, managers, and members of sports-oriented organizations and trade associations. Most Sports Agents have more than one client. Agents must be sure, however, that they do not represent conflicting parties. Agents may also work with law firms, business management companies, certified public accountants, and management firms that specialize in sports.

Most athletes who have attained superstar status find that an Agent can represent them better than they themselves can. Agents who have both law and accounting backgrounds are familiar with contracts, legal problems, laws, and tax implications.

Sports Agents often do a great deal of socializing within the sports industry. Through these activities, they can keep up with the sports scene. Sports Agents do not work a nine-to-five day. They may go into the office early in the morning and stay late attending meetings and negotiating sessions.

Sports Agents are usually responsible directly to their clients. If the Agent is working for a firm, he or she may be responsible to the company's owner, manager, or director.

Salaries

It is difficult to determine salaries for Sports Agents. Most are paid on a percentage basis—usually a percentage of the client's income. Depending on the specific arrangement, the Agent may obtain a percentage of salary alone or of all monies generated. The individual might receive a percentage of monies earned from endorsements, autobiographies, investments, and the like.

Percentages too vary from Agent to Agent. Rates may range from 5% to 20%; most individuals receive an average of 10%.

Some Sports Agents working for companies or firms receive a set salary or a salary plus either a commission from all clients they bring in to the agency or a percentage of monies earned by specific clients.

Successful Agents may have earnings ranging from $200,000 to $750,000 and more. It must be kept in mind that many major athletes currently receive multimillion-dollar contracts for their services. Ten percent of this amount can make a Sports Agent rich.

Employment Prospects

Individuals who aspire to be Sports Agents and who are highly qualified through a solid educational background will have a fair chance at locating a position. Although jobs may be located throughout the country, the best bet for finding a position of this type is in the major entertainment capitals, such as New York or Los Angeles.

Individuals may find a position with a law firm that specializes in the representation of athletes, a talent agency that has star athletes among its clients, or a business management firm.

Aspiring Agents may also find their own clients and be self-employed, running their own agency.

Advancement Prospects

Advancement prospects are fair for individuals who have a lot of drive, determination, and skill. Agents climb the career ladder by obtaining either more clients or more prestigious ones. Those who build a track record for themselves by negotiating better contracts or endorsements will find clients coming to them.

Education and Training

The most successful Agents in the sports field are those who have prepared themselves thoroughly for the job. An undergraduate college background is necessary. Graduate work, such as law school, will help immensely. Good majors include accounting, business, or sports administration. A law degree is even better.

Seminars and workshops in different facets of sports administration, business, and entertainment law can be useful.

Experience/Skills/Personality Traits

Professional Sports Agents must be excellent negotiators. Much of the job revolves around negotiation. Sales ability is another good attribute. The individual in effect is selling his or her client's services, talent, and image.

Most Agents are aggressive in a nonthreatening way. They must work constantly to obtain more money for their clients, better contracts, endorsements, and the like.

Agents should be able to work under extreme pressure and deal well with stress. Many clients have big egos and think they are worth more money than they receive. The Agent must be able to work under these conditions and still keep plugging away.

Unions/Associations

There are no specific trade associations for Sports Agents. Depending on their background, individuals may belong to either law and/or accounting organizations, which will provide seminars and professional guidance.

Tips for Entry

1. Try to obtain an internship working with a professional team in any administrative capacity. This will help you get hands-on experience in the field and make important contacts.
2. See if you can find a part-time or summer job working with a Professional Sports Agent. It doesn't matter if the financial compensation is limited. The experience will be worth it.
3. If you can't locate a Sports Agent, consider working with a booking agent, a business manager, or literary agent. Working with individuals whose job it is to sell someone else's talents will give you an idea of how the business works.
4. Attend relevant workshops and seminars. These will give you needed training and help you make contacts.

SPORTS STATISTICIAN

CAREER PROFILE

Duties: Collecting, analyzing, and interpreting sports data.

Alternate Title(s):   None

Salary Range: $19,000 to $95,000+

Employment Prospects: Poor

Best Geographical Location(s) for Position: Cities hosting professional sports teams.

Prerequisites:
Education or Training—Minimum of two-year degree.
Experience—Experience working with computers.
Special Skills and Personality Traits—Computer capable; knowledge of specific sport; arithmetic and math skills; analytical mind.

CAREER LADDER

```
┌─────────────────────────────┐
│      Statistician in        │
│  More Prestigious Team or    │
│   Statistical Organization  │
└─────────────────────────────┘

┌─────────────────────────────┐
│        Statistician         │
└─────────────────────────────┘

┌─────────────────────────────┐
│  Computer Programmer or Analyst │
│            and              │
│         Sports Fan          │
└─────────────────────────────┘
```

Position Description

A Sports Statistician collects data and analyzes and interprets it. The Statistician's job is to count how many times something takes place and keep track of all the figures. While the actual job has been around for some time, it is becoming more visible with the emergence of computers.

Anyone who has watched an athletic event on television has probably seen the work of Statisticians. Baseball box scores are an example of statistics gathered by a Statistician. The number of punches a fighter throws at an opponent and the number that have landed are examples of boxing statistics.

Many commentators and announcers use these statistics, or "stats," when discussing the progress of a particular game. As an event progresses, the Statistician updates the game statistics and the various players' activities.

Statisticians may have varied duties depending on their specific work situation. At the bottom work level, the Statistician gathers raw data. He or she may then move up the career ladder and program the data into a computer or analyze it.

Statisticians working for a sports team or a private sports statistics bureau may gather information and figures on each player in a game as well as for the entire team. This information may then be fed to the announcer who is commenting on the game. Statistics may also be given to the press and the rest of the media. This is how most daily newspapers get the statistical data they print about games. Information may also be given to fans in game programs.

The Statistician also gathers statistics for the entire playing season. This information may be used in a number of ways. The publicity department may use the data in a media book for fans and the press. The information may also be used to determine the value of each player. This is important in deciding who might be traded and what kind of financial contract an athlete should be awarded.

The player relations committee uses statistical analysis to determine what skills a team will lose if a certain player is traded. This analysis also helps determine what playing assets a team will receive if it signs a new athlete.

As noted previously, most of the professional Sports Statistician's work is done on computers. The Statistician must know what to look for in the game and then must know how to input the information into the computer. He or she may then analyze this data.

Football statistics are compiled and analyzed to ascertain the statistics for each league for the year. Boxing Statisticians may show the stats of a fighter throwing hundreds of punches in a bout but landing only a small percentage of punches. In the same vein, a baseball Statistician may show one player hitting the ball a great number of times but never getting a run. Another ball player may have fewer hits but ones that are more important to the game.

Statisticians are used for a variety of reasons. Some coaches feel that being aware of statistical information can help team members play better. Knowing a competitor's statistics can help them plan offense and defense. Fans are also interested in the numbers and like to know much of the trivia that goes with the game.

Individuals may work directly for sports teams, for television or radio stations or wire services, or for private statistician organizations. Sports Statisticians may work in almost any sport—baseball, football, hockey, boxing, basketball, and others.

Statisticians usually specialize in one or two sports. Individuals must have a complete knowledge of the sport that they will be gathering and compiling statistics in.

Statisticians working with sports teams are usually part of the publicity department. Those working for private companies may work with sports writers, announcers, or directly with professional teams.

Salaries

Salaries for Statisticians may range from $19,000 to $95,000 plus depending on a number of factors. Variables include the type of organization the individual works for, its prestige, size, and location. Other variables include the duties, skills, and experience level of the Statistician.

Generally, those who are responsible for just gathering the raw data for statistics are paid less than those who do the computer programming and analysis.

Employment Prospects

Employment prospects are limited for full-time Sports Statisticians. Individuals may find work with professional teams, semiprofessional teams, television or radio stations, wire services, or private sports statistical organizations.

Positions with network television and radio stations are usually located in cities where the networks are headquartered, such as New York or Los Angeles. Smaller cities offer opportunities for local or regional broadcasting.

Advancement Prospects

Advancement for a Statistician may mean he or she locates a similar position with a more prestigious team or private statistical organization. This is often difficult, but not impossible. Individuals must exhibit a great deal of skill, drive, and determination to move ahead and be successful in this profession.

Some Statisticians advance their careers by locating a position in sports-oriented public relations, publicity, journalism, or broadcasting. Becoming a Statistician may give them entree into that field.

Education and Training

Most Statisticians are required to have at least a two-year degree. Many positions require a four-year college degree.

Good course choices for those aspiring to be Statisticians are math, computer science, and technology. Classes in various sports studies may also be helpful.

Those who wish to advance their career into another field may be wise to take communications courses, English, journalism, public relations, and sports administration.

Experience/Skills/Personality Traits

To be successful today, Sports Statisticians need to have a total working knowledge of computers. Individuals should know how to perform data entry as well as how to program and analyze data.

Statisticians should have analytical minds. Individuals need to have good math and arithmetic skills. The ability to add a list of numbers quickly and accurately is essential.

A knowledge and understanding of the sport that the individual is working in is necessary. Statisticians who are experts in more than one sport may find additional opportunities for work.

Unions/Associations

There is no specific trade association for Sports Statisticians. Individuals may, however, belong to organizations specific to the sport and situation they are working in. For example, Statisticians working in the baseball field may belong to the Baseball Writers Association of America (BBWAA). Other individuals may belong to the National Sportscasters and Sportswriters Association (NSSA), the Professional Football Writers of America (PFWA), the Professional Hockey Writers' Association (PHWA), or any other relevant organization.

Tips for Entry

1. Practice doing stats for your school sports teams. It will give you good hands-on experience.
2. Take as many computer courses as you can. This will help you get a step ahead of others competing for jobs.
3. Know everything there is to know about the sport you want to work in. Read books and periodicals about the game, its history, rules, and regulations.
4. Send your résumé to sports teams, wire services, and professional sports teams. Ask that it be kept on file if there are no current openings. Keep checking back. Don't wait for them to call you.
5. Job openings may be advertised in the classified section of newspapers in areas hosting professional sports teams. Look under headings such as "Professional Sports Team," "Pro Sports Team," "Sports," or "Statistician."

SPORTS INDUSTRY PUBLICIST

CAREER PROFILE

Duties: Creating positive, exciting image for athletes; developing and writing press releases, press kits, informational sheets, and feature stories; handling media.

Alternate Title(s):   Sports Publicist; Publicist; Sports-Oriented Publicist.

Salary Range: $20,000 to $150,000+

Employment Prospects: Fair

Best Geographical Location(s) for Position: Large cities hosting many professional sports teams and athletic events.

Prerequisites:

Education or Training—Four-year college degree required for most positions.

Experience—Public relations, publicity, or journalism experience preferred.

Special Skills and Personality Traits—Public relations skills; communications skills; articulate; creative; detail oriented.

CAREER LADDER

```
┌─────────────────────────────────────┐
│     Sports Industry Publicist        │
│   with More Prestigious Clients      │
└─────────────────────────────────────┘

┌─────────────────────────────────────┐
│     Sports Industry Publicist        │
└─────────────────────────────────────┘

┌─────────────────────────────────────┐
│     Publicist in Other Field,        │
│            Journalist                │
│               or                     │
│             Intern                   │
└─────────────────────────────────────┘
```

Position Description

The main function of a Publicist specializing in the sports industry is to create a positive, exciting image for an individual athlete, team, or sports-related event. The Publicist must create and develop methods to get the client's name better known and keep the individual's image in the spotlight.

A growing number of athletes in a variety of sports have become superstars. While this is due in part to their athletic talents, an exciting, diversified image is a great help. There have always been a few sports figures capable of drawing a great deal of recognition. Today the number is increasing. Part of this fame and superstardom may be attributed to an athlete's Publicist.

A Publicist in the sports industry may work for a public relations or publicity firm specializing in sports figures or an entertainment-oriented firm that handles sports stars. Individuals may also be self-employed and have one or more sports-oriented clients.

Professional athletes use the services of a private Publicist or publicity firm for a number of reasons. Individuals who are part of a team often want more publicity centered on them, and this requires more attention than they can obtain from the team publicist. Another reason for personal publicity may be that athletes who are recognized personalities can demand higher salaries. They may also be picked up to do lucrative advertising product endorsements or might even diversify into acting.

After obtaining a client one of the first things the Publicist does is to determine with the individual what type of image he or she would like to attain. The Publicist must also learn about the public's current perception of the client. The individual can then work on developing strategies and a publicity campaign to achieve the goals set forth.

Most Publicists try to keep their client's name and face in front of the public in a positive manner and as often as possible. Since the athlete may be visible only from an athletic standpoint, the Publicist has to come up with other interesting ways to have his or her client viewed.

This can be achieved in any of a number of ways, depending on the creativity of the Publicist. Publicists use promotions and publicity campaigns to attract attention. They may, for example, have the athlete appointed as the national chairperson of a major charity event. They may exploit a budding dating relationship between an athlete and another superstar. They constantly try to develop ideas to help bring the athlete's face and image to the attention of the media and public. This creates public interest in the athlete and helps push him or her to superstardom.

The professional sports industry is a major force in the entertainment world. As a result, the media usually follow stories and news developments about athletes.

The Publicist working in the sports industry works with the sports news media, advising them of new developments in the athlete's career. He or she also deals with newspapers and magazine editors and producers and reporters for television, cable, and radio stations outside the sports industry.

The Publicist arranges guest appearances on television and radio talk, variety, news, and sports shows for clients as well as print interviews. He or she also develops feature story ideas for both sports editors and the general media. When the Sports Industry Publicist sets up appearances and interviews for clients, he or she often accompanies them.

Sports Industry Publicists frequently receive calls from the sports media asking specific questions or requesting interviews with the athlete. If the athlete has already attained superstar status, the Publicist acts as a buffer between the individual and the media. He or she decides which interviews will be beneficial and which will not.

The Publicist also determines which public appearances the client will accept and which to reject. In rejecting requests, he or she must write letters of regret with explanations that do not antagonize anyone.

Another function of the Publicist is to write and develop press releases, biographies, informational sheets, and press kits, on a variety of subjects and then send them to the media from a prepared media list. This list includes names and addresses of editors, writers, producers, etc. in both the general press and sports-oriented media.

The Sports Publicist also arranges and conducts press conferences when important events are occurring in the athlete's life. He or she must be sure to schedule these conferences only when special events are occurring. If not, the press will not attend after the first conference. The individual may also arrange for press passes, press credentials, and seating for members of the media when the athlete is playing.

Publicists work long hours. Most of the time their job does not stop when they leave the office. They often think about campaign strategies and new ideas for clients, even at home. Individuals may also have late meetings and attend weekend and evening events. The Publicist may be responsible to his or her supervisor or directly to the client, depending on the situation.

Salaries

Salaries for Sports Industry Publicists vary greatly depending on a number of variables. These include the type of job setting the individual is working in and his or her experience level and responsibilities. Earnings may also depend on the specific clients and their publicity needs.

Salaries can range from $20,000 to $150,000 plus. Individuals with limited experience earn between $20,000 and $30,000. Those who have a proven track record and a great deal of responsibility have salaries ranging from $30,000 to $75,000. Publicists working with one or more superstar clients can earn $150,000 and more a year.

Employment Prospects

Employment prospects are fair for Sports Industry Publicists. Individuals may work for athletes in any sport. They may work on their own or for sports-oriented public relations and publicity firms. Publicists may also be retained to handle the publicity for sports-related events. Positions may be located throughout the country. Individuals do, however, have an easier time in larger cities hosting many different sports teams and events.

Advancement Prospects

Advancement prospects for Sports Industry Publicists are fair. An individual can advance his or her career in this profession by obtaining more prestigious clients. Publicists who are creative and build their clients' image will have no problem advancing.

Some Publicists working for firms may climb the career ladder by opening their own firm. This move means that the individual has to obtain his or her own clients.

Should the athlete a Publicist is working with become an overnight superstar as a result of unexpectedly winning a tournament or championship, the Publicist's image is boosted along with the athlete's.

Education and Training

Individuals aspiring to work as Sports Industry Publicists should obtain a minimum of a four-year college degree. Good choices for majors include public relations, marketing, English, liberal arts, communications, journalism, or sports administration.

Additional courses, workshops and seminars in writing, marketing, media exposure, publicity, public relations and sports marketing are also be useful.

Experience/Skills/Personality Traits

Publicists working in the sports industry may have worked in public relations or publicity or marketing in other fields prior to attaining their current job. Individuals might also have worked as journalists in either broadcast or print media. Others interned or had assistant positions working with full-fledged Sports Publicists, public relations firms, or professional teams.

The Sports Industry Publicist should have at least a basic understanding of the sport that the client plays and the industry. This will make it easier to talk and write about the field.

The Publicist must have excellent writing skills. He or she needs to be able to write creative, factual, concise, and interesting press releases, biographies, fact sheets, and feature stories. The individual needs to be able to implement a full range of public relations and publicity tactics to promote his or her clients.

Creative people usually make the most successful Publicists. There are hundreds of Publicists pushing their clients. The ones who develop creative strategies and campaigns are the ones who get the press.

The Publicist needs the ability to communicate well verbally. He or she must be as comfortable speaking to a large group of people as he or she is speaking to one person on the phone.

Publicists need to be nonthreateningly aggressive and persuasive. Individuals should also be likable and personable. Reporters and journalist should be comfortable talking to the Publicist. The better the relationship that the Publicist has developed with the media, the more press he or she will be able to obtain for a client.

Sports Industry Publicists must be detail oriented. They work on a great many projects at one time. Individuals also need the ability to deal with celebrities without being starstruck.

Unions/Associations

Sports Industry Publicists may belong to a number of trade associations that provide education, training, and professional guidance. These might include National Sportscasters and Sportswriters Association (NSSA), the Public Relations Society of America (PRSA), Women In Communications (WIC) and the National Federation of Press Women (NFPW). Individuals may also belong to organizations that are specific to their sport's clients.

Tips for Entry

1. Work on your school newspaper to get experience writing.
2. Contact public relations firms for summer or part-time jobs. Hands-on experience will be helpful for the training aspect and look good on your résumé.
3. Try to locate an internship with a professional sports team or a public relations firm specializing in entertainment or sports industry PR.
4. Consider a summer or part-time job as a sports reporter for a local newspaper. Obtain as much experience writing as you can.
5. Join trade associations and attend their meetings. They will help you make valuable contacts and may offer assistance locating a job.
6. Openings may be advertised in the classified section of newspapers in areas hosting professional sports teams.
7. Job openings may be located online via the Internet. Check out any of the major career sites on the web. Type in keywords such as "sports" and "sports publicist."

ACCOUNT EXECUTIVE FOR SPECIAL-RISK INSURANCE/ SPORTS, ATHLETICS, AND RECREATION

CAREER PROFILE

Duties: Writing special-risk policies for health clubs, spas, gymnastics schools, karate and judo schools, exercise clubs, athletes, sports complexes, etc.; pricing policies; typing policies; answering phone calls; providing insurance certificates.

Alternate Title(s): Assistant to Producer

Salary Range: $18,000 to $36,000+

Employment Prospects: Fair

Best Geographical Location(s) for Position: Positions may be located throughout the country.

Prerequisites:

Education or Training—High school diploma minimum requirement; some positions may require college background or diploma; licensing may be required in some states.

Experience—Experience in insurance helpful.

Special Skills and Personality Traits—Knowledge of insurance industry; knowledge of athletics, sports, and/or recreational clubs or schools; selling skills; pleasant personality; communications skills; phone skills.

CAREER LADDER

```
┌─────────────────────────────────────┐
│            Producer                  │
│     in Special Risk Insurance        │
└─────────────────────────────────────┘

┌─────────────────────────────────────┐
│        Account Executive             │
│    for Special-Risk Insurance        │
│       in Sports or Athletics         │
└─────────────────────────────────────┘

┌─────────────────────────────────────┐
│   Secretary to Account Executive     │
│                or                    │
│        Account Executive             │
│   in Other Facet of Insurance Industry│
└─────────────────────────────────────┘
```

Position Description

Every company that opens for business stands the risk of having people injure themselves while on their property. Most companies buy liability and/or comprehensive insurance policies to make sure they are covered financially in case of an accident. Sports facilities, such as exercise clubs, spas, gymnastic schools, health clubs, dance and exercise schools, need insurance too. In most instances, insurance on these types of facilities are called special-risk policies. Other special-risk policies in sports may be written for sports teams, individual athletes, athletic events, sports arenas, and coliseums.

The person who helps sell and write this type of insurance is called the Account Executive. He or she works in the special-risk division of an insurance agency. This division may specialize specifically in the sports industry or may handle a variety of special-risk needs, depending on the size of the organization.

The Account Executive works with an individual called the producer. Together the two will "write" insurance policies. Special-risk policies may be purchased for a number of different reasons. Facilities such as health clubs, exercise or dance schools, and the like may buy property and casualty insurance. This means that the facility is covered for liability and related coverage in case of an accident or injury that was either directly or indirectly their fault. Having coverage means that if an accident occurs, the policy pays for costs incurred as a result of the accident. Professional sports teams may buy an insurance policy for their players in case they are injured, incapacitated, or die. Sports complexes may buy a special policy for an outdoor event in case it rains. Organizations running golf tournaments with large prizes, such as a new car for making a "hole in one," may even purchase a special policy that covers costs if a player actually does make the hole in one. The policy pays for the car if the prize is won.

When an individual needs this type of policy, he or she calls an insurance agency that handles special-risk policies. The Account Executive talks with the individual, asks questions regarding the requirements of the policy, and secures information about the facility, athlete, or event being covered. The Account Executive may also ask the person to fill in forms or questionnaires in order to acquire as much information as possible.

The Account Executive and/or the producer then work on pricing the policy. This may be done in a number of ways depending on the situation, including using a percentage of gross sales and square footage of a facility. In special-risk policies for athletes, factors determining the price or premium might include the athlete's earnings, health, and duties within the scope of his or her job. The Account Executive and/or producer may then used published rates or simplified rates to calculate the cost of a policy. This price, which is called a premium, is then quoted to the individual. Premiums on high-risk policies can be expensive, depending on the specific risk involved. In insurance, the word *risk* refers to the probability that an accident or injury might occur as well as what the costs to take care of it if it did occur would be.

The Account Executive may have other duties and responsibilities, depending on the specific job. He or she is expected to answer phone calls and talk to new customers as well as established accounts. The individual is responsible for pricing policies, either with the producer or on his or her own, depending on the structure of the company and the Account Executive's experience. The Account Executive is required to type new price quotes for customers and renew quotes as they come due.

One of the functions of the Account Executive is to talk to customers and answer questions. Customers may want explanations of why the premium is priced the way it is, what they are covered for, or how to handle a claim. Account Executives therefore must understand as much as possible about the policy and what is being insured.

Most Account Executives working in this field generally learn as they go from their superiors. Knowledge of health clubs, gymnastic schools, exercise clubs, karate schools, spas, or whatever facet of the recreation or sports industry the individual is working with is essential.

As the Account Executive gains experience and knowledge in both the sports field and the insurance industry, he or she learns more about pricing policies, special risks, and how to make sound judgments.

The Account Executive is called upon when customers need endorsements or additions to their policies. These endorsements may be required for any number of reasons where additional risks might be added to current policies. Additions may include the installation of new equipment, such as a swimming pool, or a major event being planned. The Account Executive also is expected to supply customers with certifi-cates proving that they are insured. These may be necessary before a spa, club, or school opens up or before tickets can be sold to an event.

The Account Executive usually has normal working hours. He or she may work overtime when projects and special work must be completed. The individual usually is directly responsible to the producer he or she works with.

Salaries

Salaries for Account Executives working in special-risk situations vary depending on their experience level, responsibilities, drive, and determination. In addition to the regular salaries, many individuals earn bonuses when they bring in extra clients or write policies above those that they are expected to handle. Annual earnings can range from $18,000 to $36,000 plus.

Employment Prospects

Employment prospects in special-risk insurance in the sports, athletic, and recreational fields are fair and are improving every day. With more health and fitness clubs opening around the country as well as schools specializing in gymnastics, judo, karate, and the like, there will be a greater need for insurance. Athletes are also receiving record salaries and teams need to protect their investments.

Individuals may have to relocate in order to find a company handling special-risk sports insurance.

Advancement Prospects

Advancement prospects are good for individuals who are experienced and learn the business. The next step up the career ladder for most individuals is to become an insurance producer.

Individuals may stay in the facet of the industry handling special-risk policies in the sports, recreation, and athletic fields or may move into selling policies in unrelated areas.

Education and Training

Educational requirements vary from job to job and state to state. A high school diploma is the minimum requirement in most jobs. Some positions may require a college background or degree.

Depending on the specific state requirements and the individual's duties, he or she may also be required to obtain an insurance agent's license or insurance broker's license. These are obtained by completing educational requirements from an approved insurance school. In some situations, continuing education, workshops, and seminars may also be necessary.

Experience/Skills/Personality Traits

The individual in this type of job must be familiar with the insurance business. Most, but not all, individuals working in special-risk insurance have had experience in other facets of the industry. Knowledge of the sports, fitness, and health industries is also useful. For example, an individual who must quote a price on a policy for a health club will be able to do a better job if he or she knows the types of accidents that can occur in that type of facility.

Account Executives must be personable, pleasant, and easy to talk with. They need sales skills. What they do, in essence, after pricing a policy is sell it. A customer who feels more comfortable with the person he or she is talking to is more likely to purchase a policy with the company.

Communications skills, both verbal and written, are necessary. The Account Executive also should have good phone skills. A great deal of his or her work is done via the telephone.

Typing and/or word processing skills are other important skills for the Account Executive. The individual should be detail oriented and be able to deal with many different projects without getting flustered.

Unions/Associations

There are no trade associations specific to Account Executives handling special-risk insurance in the sports, recreation, and athletic fields. Individuals may, however, be members of groups such as the National Health Club Association (NHCA) and/or national and state insurance associations.

Tips for Entry

1. If you are still in school, consider a part-time or summer job working in an insurance agency. It doesn't matter what department you work in as long as you obtain experience.
2. Contact your state to find out what type of licensing requirements are required for agents and brokers in your area.
3. Talk to your local insurance agent to find out if he or she can recommend a company that handles special risk policies in the sports industry.
4. Insurance agencies may advertise openings in the newspaper's classified or display section. While the position may not be in special-risk policies, it may give you valuable experience and the opportunity to make important contacts. Look under heading classification of "Insurance," "Selling," "Special Risk," "Brokers," or "Agents."
5. Many insurance agencies have their own training programs. This will help you get your foot in the door of the insurance industry. You can then move on to special-risk departments.
6. Job possibilities may be located online via the Internet. Check out the major career and job sites on the web to get started on your search. Type in keywords or categories such as "insurance," "sports," or "athletics."

SPORTS EVENT COORDINATOR

CAREER PROFILE

Duties: Handling the logistics necessary to put together a sporting event; overseeing details of a sporting event.

Alternate Title(s): Event Coordinator

Salary Range: $24,000 to $90,000+

Employment Prospects: Fair

Best Geographical Location(s) for Position: Areas hosting many facilities, such as arenas, stadiums, coliseums.

Prerequisites:

Education or Training—Four-year college degree required for most positions.

Experience—Experience in event coordination, publicity, public relations, or marketing helpful.

Special Skills and Personality Traits—Detail oriented; organized; good written and verbal communications skills; ability to foresee problems; coordination and planning skills.

CAREER LADDER

```
┌─────────────────────────────────────┐
│     Sports Event Coordinator         │
│  at Larger, More Prestigious Facility│
└─────────────────────────────────────┘

┌─────────────────────────────────────┐
│     Sports Event Coordinator         │
└─────────────────────────────────────┘

┌─────────────────────────────────────┐
│           Publicist,                 │
│  Special Event Coordinator, Intern,  │
│              or                      │
│         College Student              │
└─────────────────────────────────────┘
```

Position Description

The Olympic Games, the Superbowl, and the World Series are major events in the world of sports. Other popular events might include the Kentucky Derby or a major heavyweight championship fight. These events are not thrown together haphazardly. Each detail is worked out ahead of time to make sure things will go smoothly. The individual hired to do this is called the Sports Event Coordinator.

Sports Event Coordinators handle the logistics necessary when putting together a sporting event. Their main function is to oversee all the details that make the show a success.

Some Sports Events Coordinators work directly for the facility. Others are employed by promoters. They may work in a variety of situations and facilities from arenas, auditoriums, stadiums, and coliseums to hotels and resorts.

Many facilities hold diverse events on their premises throughout the year, including concerts, ballets, operas, symphonies, circuses, trade shows and conventions, and sporting events. Each type of show requires special considerations to ensure that it will be successful. Individuals may be responsible just for the coordination of sporting events or may be expected to handle the coordination of all events hosted in the specific arena or venue. Duties vary depending on the situation in which each individual works.

The Sports Event Coordinator may specialize in the coordination of programs in one specific sport or many. Opportunities might include coordination of amateur, scholastic, or professional events in tennis, bowling, or golf tournaments, marathons, dog or cat shows, boxing or wrestling events, or auto or motorcycle racing. Other opportunities might occur in baseball, hockey, football, soccer, basketball, and swimming.

One of the first things the Sports Event Coordinator must do is determine the scope of the event. He or she must find out how popular a program might be and the intended audience. If the Coordinator is working in a facility that regularly holds such events, this will be easier. Football and baseball stadiums, for example, usually have an idea which games are going to be well attended before the event. The individual must know ahead of time if the facility will be large enough to handle the intended crowd. If it is not, he or she may be expected to search for a larger arena.

Once this has been accomplished, the individual must develop a plan of action. He or she works with the promoter, box office and ticket manager, public relations and marketing people, security, staff members, judges, officials, and others. The Coordinator may meet with the various department heads or directors to find out what possible problems might occur and how to head them off.

For some events that are bigger than usual, more rest room facilities, security, and food concessions than are normally required may have to be added. The individual must constantly try to foresee problems and situations that might occur and deal with them ahead of time. In this manner, things will probably go smoothly the day of the event.

The Coordinator is responsible for making sure that there is sufficient parking for the anticipated crowd. He or she may also develop routes to assist fans enter and exit the stadium. While doing this, the Coordinator may work with the local police department and local media advising them of crowd situations, potential traffic tie-ups and the like.

Depending on the particular situation, the Sports Event Coordinator may be expected to monitor what people in other departments are doing. He or she may supervise the public relations, advertising, and marketing efforts as well as work with the media. At times, the individual may function as a public relations person. He or she may call the media and arrange interviews, articles, feature stories, photo opportunities, and broadcasts. The Coordinator may have to set up and execute press conferences, cocktail parties, luncheons, and dinners. In other situations, the Coordinator may act as an intermediary between all the departments to make sure everything that is supposed to get done is completed.

The Coordinator may have additional duties depending on the specific event he or she is working with. For example, the Event Coordinator in a major boxing show is often responsible for making sure that a number of sets of new boxing gloves are delivered to the stadium. He or she must also make sure that a regulation scale is available at the prefight weigh-in. Those coordinating marathons must deal with the details of getting runners their identifying numbers, starting the race, checkpoints, finish lines, winners, and prizes. Those working in tennis may be responsible for officials, seating arrangements, and opponents. Each sport has its own set of special details to contend with.

In some cases, the Coordinator may be expected to handle transportation, food, and accommodations for athletes, officials, support staff, and other members of the production team. He or she is responsible for checking out all the little details that make the difference in a successful event and an unsuccessful one.

The individual may be expected to review what might be considered small things, such as checking on the temperature of the arenas and/or the playing or competing area. While this might seem insignificant to some, a playing area that is too hot or too cold may dramatically affect the way a team plays. The Coordinator may also be responsible for making sure that there are a sufficient number of dressing rooms for the competitors and staff members and that they are properly equipped.

If the event is to be televised, the Coordinator works with the television production people, helping them to set up cameras, obtain the proper electric, lighting, and sound. He or she may or may not be responsible for coordinating any interviews or other media opportunities.

The Coordinator may be responsible for checking to see that the correct medical personnel and equipment are on hand and that all personnel are stationed in the correct locations. The individual is expected to do the same with the security people.

One of the most important functions of the Sports Event Coordinator is dealing with problems as they occur. Problems might arise at any time, from the inception of the idea of the promotion through the conclusion of the event. The individual must be able to deal with a variety of situations in a calm, cool, and collected manner.

This is an idea type of situation for individuals who both are capable and enjoy taking control of a situation. The Coordinator works with a sporting event from the very beginning to the very end. Hours are long in this type of job. The Sports Event Coordinator is expected to be present at all events. In addition to regular daytime hours, individuals may work in the evenings and on weekends.

The individual is often judged by his or her last event. If it is a success, the Coordinator is deemed successful; if it is a failure, so may be the Coordinator in the eyes of his or her superiors. The Sports Event Coordinator may be responsible to the promoter, facility general manager, or owner, depending on the structure of organization.

Salaries

Earnings for Sports Event Coordinators vary from job to job depending on a number of factors. These include the geographic location of the arena, its prestige, and the type of events presented. Other variables may include whether the individual is working directly for the arena or for a promoter and his or her responsibilities and experience level.

Sports Event Coordinators have salaries ranging from $24,000 to $90,000 plus depending on the specific job. Individuals just starting out with little experience or those working for smaller arenas are on the lower end of the pay scale. Those working in more prestigious venues or for promoters of major events are on the higher end.

Employment Prospects

Employment prospects are fair for individuals willing to start in this profession in smaller facilities. Jobs may be located throughout the country in arenas, stadiums, auditoriums, and coliseums. Positions may also be located at larger hotels and resorts that regularly host sporting events. Sports promoters may offer other employment possibilities.

Advancement Prospects

Advancement prospects depend on the individual's drive, determination, and how well he or she handles the job. Those who coordinate events that run smoothly and successfully will climb the career ladder by locating similar positions at facilities hosting more prestigious events.

Education and Training

A minimum of a four-year college degree is required for most positions in facilities. Good choices for majors include sports administration or management, business administration, communications, marketing, or public relations.

Jobs with sports promoters may have varied educational requirements, ranging from a high school diploma up to a college degree.

Experience/Skills/Personality Traits

The first and foremost skill a Sports Event Coordinator must have is the ability to handle many details at one time. He or she must also be totally organized. The individual should have the ability to supervise others and delegate responsibility.

The Coordinator needs to be articulate and have good verbal communication skills. He or she needs to be able to deal with a variety of people on different levels. The individual must know how to write well and have a good grasp of the English language.

Event Coordinators need to have an understanding of the event or sport they are working with. The ability to foresee problems and deal with them is necessary. Individuals should have excellent planning and coordinating skills. A knowledge of public relations, marketing, and business will be useful.

Experience in publicity, special-event promotion, marketing, and public relations is useful in helping the individual not only obtain a job but to be successful. This experience may result from an internship in the sports industry or from working in either a related or an unrelated field.

Unions/Associations

Sports Event Coordinators may belong to associations and organizations that are directly related to the sport or sports in which they are working. These might include the National Association of Athletic Marketing and Development Directors (NAAMDD). Individuals might also belong to trade associations, such as the Public Relations Society of America (PRSA). These organizations may offer ideas, seminars, guidance, trade journals, and professional support.

Tips for Entry

1. Try to locate an internship in a major sports facility. This will help you obtain hands-on experience and offer you an opportunity to make important contacts.
2. Take courses and workshops in event coordination, sports marketing, and public relations. These will give you continued education in the field and ways of making contacts.
3. Send a letter with your résumé to the personnel directors of facilities requesting an interview. Ask that your résumé be kept on file even if a position is not currently available.
4. Obtain experience by volunteering to coordinate sports programs and events for your school.
5. Positions may be advertised in the classified or display sections of newspapers. Look under the heading classifications of "Sports," "Athletics," "Facilities," "Coordination," or "Coordinator."
6. You might also locate openings via the Internet. Check out the major career and job sites on the web to get started on your search. Type in keywords such as "sports," "athletic events," or "event coordination."

SPORTS INFORMATION DIRECTOR/ COLLEGE, UNIVERSITY

CAREER PROFILE

Duties: Publicizing team and players; writing press releases; providing media with information about team; responding to media questions; preparing biographies, press kits, and yearbooks; arranging press conferences and press briefings.

Alternate Title(s): Collegiate Sports Information Direction Director; Sports Information Manager

Salary Range: $24,000 to $48,000

Employment Prospects: Fair

Best Geographical Location(s) for Positions: Positions located throughout the country; areas that have colleges and universities with large sports teams hold the most opportunities.

Prerequisites:
Education or Training—Four-year college degree required for most positions.
Experience—Writing experience preferred.
Special Skills and Personality Traits—Good writing skills; personable; articulate; knowledge of sports; ability to deal with media.

CAREER LADDER

```
┌─────────────────────────────────────────┐
│  Sports Information Director in Larger,  │
│      more Prestigious Institution        │
│                   or                     │
│  Professional Sports Team Publicist      │
└─────────────────────────────────────────┘

┌─────────────────────────────────────────┐
│      Sports Information Director          │
└─────────────────────────────────────────┘

┌─────────────────────────────────────────┐
│     Sports Information Assistant,         │
│     Public Relations, Media,             │
│                   or                     │
│        Journalism Position               │
│                   or                     │
│           Entry Level                    │
└─────────────────────────────────────────┘
```

Position Description

The Sports Information Director works with collegiate athletic teams publicizing both the team and its players. The individual may work with one particular sports team or may be required to handle the press and publicity functions for all sports played at the college.

The Sports Information Director has a number of different writing responsibilities. He or she is required to write press releases on a variety of subjects. These might include upcoming games, new additions to the team, coaches, interesting stories on players, and the like. The Sports Information Director may also be required to send scores of games to the media. At times, the individual writes feature stories and articles for use by either the general media or specialized publications.

The Sports Information Director sends press releases, scores, and feature stories to all local media, including newspapers, magazines, other written publications, and television and radio stations. He or she is expected to look for additional avenues to distribute this information. If the individual is working with a school whose team merits regional or national publicity, he or she also sends information to sports editors in these areas. He or she might also send press releases to media in a player's hometown.

The Sports Information Director is responsible for interviewing each athlete and coach in order to prepare biographies about the players, the team, and the coaches. Depending on the size of the school and its emphasis on sports, this information may be be put together like a press kit in a folder, as a press guide in a booklet, or in the form of a yearbook. It may also contain statistics and records about the team, photographs of the players, coaches, and so on. The information is valuable to the Sports Information Director when writing press releases and feature stories or when answering media questions.

The Sports Information Director may be expected either to take photographs or arrange for a professional photographer. This depends on the size and budget of the college. Photos of single players and of players together as a team are needed. Game photos might also be required. If the individual is working in a situation where media coverage includes television, he or she might also arrange for video clips of the team.

The Sports Information Director is responsible for arranging, coordinating, and implementing press conferences and press briefings. Depending on the situation, these might be either formal affairs or informal events. The individual calls, sends, or delivers invitations to media informing them of the time, date, and location of the conference as well as the reason. Press conferences may be held for a number of reasons. A valuable new player might have transferred to the school and its team, a player might have been injured during a game and is hospitalized, or a new coach from a prestigious school might have been hired. There must be a real reason for a press conference. Otherwise, the next time one is scheduled, the media might not show up.

The Sports Information Director's relationship with the media is important. A good working relationship with these people helps make his or her job easier and more effective. The individual usually gets to know the sports reporters, editors, and journalists. Many areas have collegiate sports reporters or sports sections devoted entirely to the collegiate scene.

If the Sports Information Director has a good, honest relationship with the media, when the team needs some publicity, he or she can just pick up a phone. Conversely, the sports media people frequently need a story and should feel comfortable calling the Sports Information Director to suggest one.

The individual is responsible for responding to inquiries from the general public and the media. In some situations the Sports Information Director cannot answer a specific question at a given time or must say "No comment." This might be because of a delicate situation or a promise of confidentiality. The individual must explain the situation to the media without breaking confidentiality and while keeping the relationship in tact.

The individual is responsible for collecting articles, newspaper and magazine clippings, and stories about the team. Copies of radio or television stories might also be collected. He or she may perform this function, assign the task to an assistant, or hire a media clipping service.

The Sports Information Director is especially busy on days of games. He or she must make sure that the press received passes to get in, are seated in good seats, and receive the latest press information. The individual also answers any questions they might have.

The Sports Information Director also sees to it that any school or local dignitaries have received complimentary passes and arranges for their seating. After the game, he or she may arrange a press conference.

The individual in this job works long hours, often at night and on weekends. The Sports Information Director is usually expected to attend all team games. Depending on the structure of the school, he or she may be responsible to the sports director, the athletic director, or the president of the college.

Salaries

Salaries for Sports Information Directors vary greatly depending on a number of variables, including the size of the college or university, its enrollment, budget, and the amount of emphasis the school puts on sports. Compensation also is dependent on the experience level of the individual and his or her responsibilities.

Salaries can range from $24,000 to $48,000 or more annually for full-time Sports Information Directors. Those working in smaller schools or those with limited experience receive earnings on the lower end of the scale. Individuals working in large colleges and universities with major sports programs earn the higher salaries.

Employment Prospects

Larger schools may employ more than one individual in the Sports Information Department. A college may hire one director and an assistant director. Schools may also hire a Sports Information Director for football, one for basketball, and one for other sports.

Smaller schools usually have only one Sports Information Director. In very small colleges, the position may be only part time. Some small colleges don't employ anyone for this job, instead assigning the task to the college public affairs or public relations office. Other schools leave the sports information functions to the coaches.

Individuals who are willing to relocate to find a position, to work in a small school, or to take a part-time position have fair employment prospects.

Advancement Prospects

Advancement prospects vary depending on how the individual wants to climb the career ladder. He or she may find a position as a Sports Information Director in a larger, more prestigious school. This will result in increased earnings, responsibilities, and visibility.

The Sports Information Director might climb the career ladder by locating a position with a professional team. He or she might also work in public relations or publicity in another industry.

Education and Training

While there are rare cases of a high school graduate getting this job, the majority of these positions require a four-year college degree. In order to be prepared for a position as a Sports Information Director, the individual should take courses in public relations, publicity, marketing, journalism, English, writing, sports studies, and physical education.

A number of seminars available throughout the country on obtaining publicity, writing press releases, and securing media exposure would also prove useful.

Experience/Skills/Personality Traits

The individual in this type of job must enjoy sports. He or she has to watch games, work with coaches, and interact with players. It is also useful if the Sports Information Director has a knowledge of the various sports he or she is publicizing.

The Sports Information Director needs the ability to write well. He or she prepares press releases, booklets, leaflets, biographies, and feature stories. A good grasp of the English language is needed as is good spelling, word usage, and grammar.

The individual should be energetic. He or she works long hours. The Director should also be personable and enjoy dealing with people.

The Sports Information Director needs to be articulate with the ability to communicate well. A pleasant phone manner is essential. The ability to speak before groups of people is often necessary.

The individual should be able to work on many different projects at once and deal with details without getting flustered. He or she should have or be able to develop a good working relationship with the media.

Unions/Associations

The Sports Information Director working in a college or university does not belong to any union. He or she does, however, usually belong to a number of trade associations that provide forums for those in the same industry. The best known in this field is the College Sports Information Directors of America. The Sports Information Director might also be a member of the National Sportscasters and Sportswriters Association.

Individuals might also be members of a number of other public relations trade associations, including the Public Relations Society of America (PRSA), Women In Communications (WIC), and the National Federation of Press Women (NFPW).

Tips for Entry

1. Get experience working with the media. Volunteer to do publicity for a nonprofit group.
2. Consider a summer or part-time job writing for a newspaper.
3. If your school doesn't have a Sports Information Department, offer to do publicity on school sports teams. See if you can write a column for your school or local paper on the college sports scene.
4. If your school does have this department, see if you can become an intern, trainee, an aide, assistant, or typist. Working in this department in any capacity will give you valuable hands-on experience and be useful for your résumé.
5. Join trade associations. Attend their meetings and subscribe to trade journals. These organizations will keep you abreast of trends in the industry.
6. Jobs may be advertised in the classified section of newspapers in areas where colleges with major athletic departments are located.
7. Positions might also be found on the web sites of colleges and universities with major athletic departments or via a search through an on-line career or job site.

ATHLETIC PROGRAM FUND RAISING AND DEVELOPMENT DIRECTOR

CAREER PROFILE

Duties: Raising funds for college athletic department to support intercollegiate sports programs; creating and developing fund-raising programs; implementing programs; cultivating potential donors.

Alternate Title(s): Athletic Development Director; Director of Athletic Fund Raising

Salary Range: 19,000 to $60,000

Employment Prospects: Fair

Best Geographical Location(s) for Position: Positions may be located throughout the country.

Prerequisites:

Education or Training—Four-year college degree preferred for most positions.

Experience—Experience in fund raising may be preferred.

Special Skills and Personality Traits—Good interpersonal skills; aggressive; organizational skills; communications skills; creativity; interest in intercollegiate sports programs.

CAREER LADDER

```
┌─────────────────────────────────────┐
│  Athletic Department Fund Raising    │
│    and Development Director at        │
│        Larger College with            │
│   More Prestigious Sports Program     │
└─────────────────────────────────────┘

┌─────────────────────────────────────┐
│   Athletic Program Fund Raising       │
│               and                     │
│        Development Director           │
└─────────────────────────────────────┘

┌─────────────────────────────────────┐
│          Fund Raising,                │
│       Public Relations, or            │
│        Marketing Assistant            │
│               or                      │
│          College Student              │
└─────────────────────────────────────┘
```

Position Description

Running a college's athletic program is expensive. There are a number of ways a school can pay for their programs. Most schools charge for tickets to intercollegiate events. Funds from these programs, however, usually do not go very far if the school does not have a major facility to house events. Some colleges make money for their athletic programs by selling television rights to their games. Still others hire individuals to raise funds. The person in this position is called the Athletic Program Fund Raising and Development Director.

The individual's main function is to raise money for the college's athletic department and its programs. While this is not an easy job because so many organizations vie for funds from the public, many people take a special interest in their college's intercollegiate athletic program.

Responsibilities in this type of job vary from position to position. The main goal at most schools is to raise sufficient income to fund not only the current athletic programs but future ones as well.

The Athletic Program Fund Raising and Development Director is responsible for developing programs that raise funds to keep the institution's athletic programs solvent. The individual is expected to find ways to raise money not only for large capital campaigns, such as new buildings, but also for other programs of the department, such as athletic scholarships.

The Director has to create and develop these programs and is responsible for their implementation. Programs to raise money differ from college to college, depending on the emphasis the administration and boards place on their athletic department.

Some Athletic Program Fund Raising and Development Directors run special events or organize huge annual fundraising dinners, auctions, and dances to raise money. They may also develop and implement annual giving or sustaining campaigns. Most Athletic Program Fund Raising and Development Directors look for benefactors from within their alumni and school booster clubs.

In many instances, the Athletic Program Fund Raising Director works alongside the colleges' director of development. In other cases, the individual may be responsible for all fund-raising and development activities at the school.

The individual may also work with other departments to help attain athletic program fund-raising goals. For example, he or she might also deal with the public relations or public information department.

The Athletic Program Fund Raising and Development Director may be responsible for finding volunteers to help do the "leg work," or the running around necessary to make a project successful. The individual, for example, may organize a phone-a-thon where he or she can use volunteers to phone alumni and request donations.

The Athletic Program Fund Raising and Development Director is responsible for cultivating potential donors. To do this, he or she might attend luncheons, dinners, meetings, parties, and other affairs on behalf of the athletic department. The Director may also be expected to speak to groups of people about the athletic programs and department.

The Athletic Program Fund Raising and Development Director seeks annual gifts and endowments from individuals and corporations and tries to locate sponsorship for various projects the athletic department hopes to undertake. The individual might try to locate corporations willing to donate a number of athletic scholarships every year so that the college can obtain talented athletes to attend the school.

The Director is expected to handle a great deal of paperwork. This could include reports describing the progress of varied fund-raising projects, press releases, and publicity programs to promote other fund-raising events. Other writing responsibilities may include creating direct mail pieces, advertising copy, fliers, fund raising letters, invitations, speeches, and brochures.

The individual is responsible for keeping accurate records of donor activities and resource development. He or she may also develop and write newsletters advising patrons of new athletic programs undertaken at the school, athletic events, new athletes, coaches, and the like.

The Athletic Program Fund Raising and Development Director works long hours finding ways to keep the athletic program at the college running not only for the present but in the future as well. He or she works closely with the school's athletic director, coaches, and athletes.

The Athletic Program Fund Raising and Development Director is expected to attend to day-to-day office activities and social obligations to cultivate potential donors. The individual must also be familiar with everything that happening in the athletic department.

Salaries

Annual earnings for Athletic Program Fund Raising and Development Director can range from $19,000 to $60,000, depending on a number of factors. These include the experience of the individual and his or her responsibilities. Other variables affecting salaries include the school's size, location, prestige, and the emphasis it puts on its athletic program.

Employment Prospects

Employment prospects are fair for college Athletic Program Fund Raising and Development Directors. As money gets tighter, more colleges will begin to hire people for these positions.

Individuals, however, may have to relocate to find a position. Small colleges usually do not hire a special person for this job. Instead they rely on the services of the college's director of development. Those aspiring to become an Athletic Program Fund Raising and Development Director must locate schools that emphasize intercollegiate sports programs.

Advancement Prospects

Advancement prospects for Athletic Program Fund Raising and Development Directors are fair. Individuals can climb the career ladder by locating positions in larger schools with more prestigious athletic programs. Some individuals advance their career by moving into corporate fund raising.

Education and Training

Most positions for Athletic Program Fund Raising and Development Directors require a four-year college degree. Good choices for majors include marketing, public relations, sports administration, communications, or liberal arts.

Seminars and symposiums on fund raising, development, and marketing will be useful.

Experience/Skills/Personality Traits

For some people, the job of Athletic Program Fund Raising and Development Director is an entry-level position. Other individuals worked previously in public relations, fund raising, development, or marketing at amateur, collegiate, or professional sports or in another industry entirely.

Athletic Program Fund Raising and Development Directors should be fairly aggressive and have good organizational skills. Individuals in this position must also have good interpersonal skills and the ability to deal well with volunteers.

Athletic Program Fund Raising and Development Directors need good verbal and written communications skills. Creativity is helpful in developing fund-raising letters, brochures, and mailings. The Athletic Program Fund Raising and Development Director should also be capable of keeping accurate financial records and be adept at working with figures.

Individuals should have an interest in intercollegiate sports as well as an understanding of them. A great deal of their success in raising funds will come from talking to others interested in the same sporting subjects.

Unions/Associations

There is no specific organization that Athletic Program Fund Raising and Development Directors must belong to. Individuals may, however, be members of the National Society of Fund Raising Executives (NFRE).

Tips for Entry

1. Join a couple of nonprofit organizations with causes you are interested in. Volunteer to be on the fund-raising committee. This will provide useful experience and be important for your résumé.
2. If you are still in college, volunteer to do fund raising for your school's athletic program.
3. Look for internships with either a college athletic program or a nonprofit organization. The internship will give you valuable hands-on experience and offer you the opportunity to make valuable contacts.
4. You might consider sending a copy of your résumé and a short cover letter to a number of colleges with strong athletic programs.
5. College placement offices often know of openings

CAREER OPPORTUNITIES IN COACHING AND EDUCATION

COACH OR MANAGER/ PROFESSIONAL SPORTS TEAM

CAREER PROFILE

Duties: Coaching professional sports team; training and motivating players; devising strategies and developing game tactics.

Alternate Title(s): Coach; Head Coach

Salary Range: $35,000 to $1,500,000+

Employment Prospects: Poor

Best Geographical Location(s) for Position: Cities hosting professional sports teams.

Prerequisites:

Education or Training—Four-year college degree helpful but not required.

Experience—Experience coaching necessary.

Special Skills and Personality Traits—Good coaching skills; knowledge of the sport; communications skills; ability to deal with stress and work under pressure; motivation; supervisory skills.

CAREER LADDER

```
┌─────────────────────────────────────┐
│         Head Coach/Manager           │
└─────────────────────────────────────┘

┌─────────────────────────────────────┐
│    Coach/Professional Sports Team    │
└─────────────────────────────────────┘

┌─────────────────────────────────────┐
│ Assistant Coach/Professional Sports Team │
│                  or                  │
│            College Coach             │
│                  or                  │
│   Manager/Coach/Minor League Team    │
└─────────────────────────────────────┘
```

Position Description

The Coach or Manager working with a professional sports team has an important job. He or she is greatly responsible for the way a professional team plays for the season. The Coach at the pro level has one main function: to train, motivate, and work with team members to help them compete at the highest level.

Professional teams usually have a number of Coaches, although each has only one Head Coach. Baseball teams typically have a Manager who heads the team and a number of Coaches who function as assistants. The exact number depends on the specific sport and team. All Coaches work together trying to get their team prepared to play competitively for the season.

Depending on the specific sport, there may be a number of different types of Coaches working with the team. In addition to the Head Coach or Manager there will be assistants, strength coaches, pitching coaches, athletic trainers, and so on. The Coach works with other team personnel in his or her job. Coaches may work in any professional sport, including baseball, basketball, hockey, soccer, and football.

Professional Coaches do not have to coach more than one sport or more than one team. Their only responsibility is to the one team they have been hired to work with.

Coaches working with pros also do not have to teach players basic skills. By the time athletes make it to the pros, they are usually exceptionally talented players. Most are the cream of the crop in the particular sport they are competing at. Depending on the sport, individuals will come to the team through drafts, agents, and scouts. While the Coach is not solely responsible for choosing team members, his or her input is expected.

The Head Coach or Manager for the pro team is responsible for scheduling practice sessions and meetings. He or she is responsible for determining how frequently practices are held and the duration of each. Practices are devoted to refining the skills of both individual athletes and the team as a whole.

Coaches involved with pro sports must devise strategies and develop game tactics. They discuss team strategies and how they will be implemented. They also talk about problems with the way the team plays and potential solutions. In some instances, Coaches may use visuals to help train the players.

They may view videotapes of their own games, practice sessions, or even games of the competition.

Coaches must motivate their players and teach them how to play as a team. They must make their players aware of the best ways to play the game as well as the route to winning.

The Head Coach or Manager attends all of his or her team's games, at home or away. During a game, he or she may change strategies, give signals, and call time-outs to talk to team members. He or she must be aware of everything that is happening in the game. The Coach or Manager may also decide who will play during a certain portion of the game and which players will go in as substitutes. He or she must know the strengths and weaknesses of all the team's players in order to determine which athlete should be out on the field or on the court when.

Before a game and during halftimes, the Coach or Managers usually gives pep talks to the team and may offer advice to athletes regarding playing tactics. After a game, a Coach offers suggestions for the next competition.

In many instances, the Head Coach or Manager is expected to regulate the actions of the team members when they are not in actual playing situations. The team management or the individual Coach may have rules and regulations regarding what the athletes can and cannot do on their off time. For example, team members may have curfews when in training and during the playing season. Sports teams expect their athletes to refrain from substance abuse. The Manager or Coach can keep an athlete who fails to adhere to the rules from playing in a game or penalize him or her in some other manner.

Coaches work long hours preparing the team for competitions. In addition to attending the team's games and regular training sessions, Coaches must be at all practice sessions and training camps.

Coaches work closely with all members of the team and the organization. They are usually responsible to the team's general manager. Winning a game means that the individual's job is secure for the moment. Losing a game means the Coach or Manager could be replaced.

For Coaches who attain this level in the sport, there is usually a great deal of professional satisfaction, a lot of glamour working with high-visibility professional teams, and major financial remuneration.

Salaries

Coaches working on the pro level have a wide salary range. Earnings can vary from $35,000 for one Coach to $1,500,000 plus for others. Earnings depend on a number of variables including the individual's qualifications, experience, and responsibilities. Other influencing factors include the specific sport he or she is coaching as well as the prestige of the team.

Employment Prospects

Employment prospects are poor for Coaches or Managers aspiring to work with pro teams. There are only a limited

number of professional teams in any specific sport. However, individuals who have made a name for themselves coaching on the college level may be able to break in.

Individuals may find opportunities with minor league teams as well as major league teams.

Advancement Prospects

Advancement prospects for Coaches working in the professional leagues depend greatly on the performance of the individual. If he or she has built up a team dramatically, or if the team has won a number of competitions, the individual may climb the career ladder rapidly. Advancement prospects also are determined by the sport and the level at which the individual is currently in his or her career. If, for example, the Coach is working with a prestigious team, career advancement might include a major financial contract.

An individual working with a minor league team may move up to coach a major league team. Individuals may also become team managers.

Education and Training

As a great many individuals work their way through the college and university ranks, most individuals have a four-year college degree. However, *all* Coaches have a degree. A degree is useful not only when the individual is on the job, but in case he or she moves on to other careers after coaching.

Individuals often participate in coaching seminars, workshops, and symposiums in their specific sport through trade associations and other organizations.

Experience/Skills/Personality Traits

Pro Coaches should have a complete understanding of the sport that they are working with. Many individuals in this profession were former athletes or college coaches. Most Coaches in the pros held assistant coach positions before becoming a Head Coach. Most baseball Managers are former players, minor league managers, or major league coaches.

Especially at the pro level, Coaches must be able to motivate their team. The Coach must also be able to get the athletes to pull together and work as a team. This is often difficult to do when athletes begin to shine on their own as the team superstar. It is, however, a necessary task. Individuals must have excellent communications skills in order to explain styles and techniques.

Coaches should be calm individuals. Getting excited, yelling, and screaming does not serve any purpose. They must be able to deal well with people on all levels, from the owner of the team and players to the referee on the playing field.

The Head Coach or Manager works with a staff of assistants. He or she must therefore have have supervisory skills. The individual must also be extremely organized and detail oriented.

It is important for the Coach working in the pros to be able to work with pressure and stress. He or she must constantly deal with the possibility that the team may lose. There is not a great deal of job stability for pro Coaches. If the team is winning, everyone is happy. If the team loses more than once, management often puts the blame on the Coach. He or she can be replaced at any time.

Unions/Associations

Coaches may belong to trade associations and other organizations relevant to the sport they coach. These associations offer professional guidance, support, training, and education.

Tips for Entry

1. Positions for Coaches working in the professional leagues are very rarely advertised in newspapers or trade journals. These are the kind of jobs you have to be at the right place at the right time for.
2. If you aspire to be a Coach for a pro team, you should first make a name for yourself either as an athlete or as a coach for a university or college hosting prestigious sports programs and teams. Once you have the educational background you need, try to obtain a position coaching for a college team and work your way up from there. You must rise in the ranks to become a Coach in the pros.
3. Get experience coaching by volunteering to coach local youth teams.
4. Another way to obtain experience coaching is by getting a summer job as a sports counselor or coach at a camp.

COACH/COLLEGE, UNIVERSITY

Duties: Coaching college athletic teams; choosing team members; developing game strategies.

Alternate Title(s): Head Coach; Assistant Coach

Salary Range: $20,000 to $400,000+

Employment Prospects: Good

Best Geographical Location(s) for Position: Positions may be located throughout the country.

Prerequisites:

Education or Training—Minimum of four-year college degree required for most positions.
Experience—Experience as athlete helpful but not always necessary.
Special Skills and Personality Traits—Knowledge of sports; teaching and coaching skills; physically fit; ability to motivate; detail oriented.

```
┌─────────────────────────────────┐
│         Coach at More           │
│ Prestigious College or University │
│              or                 │
│   Coach for Professional Team   │
└─────────────────────────────────┘

┌─────────────────────────────────┐
│    Coach College, University    │
└─────────────────────────────────┘

┌─────────────────────────────────┐
│       Assistant Coach,          │
│       College Athlete,          │
│              or                 │
│       High School Coach         │
└─────────────────────────────────┘
```

Position Description

The Coach of a college or university is responsible for coaching one or more of the school's sports teams. In larger colleges the individual may coach one specific sport. In smaller schools he or she may be required to coach all sports. Coaches have varied duties depending on the school they are working at, the size of the athletic department, and the emphasis put on the sports program.

Coaches are ultimately responsible for getting athletic teams ready to play competitively in games, tournaments, and championships. One of the main duties of the Coach is to put together a team of the best athletes available in the specific sport. He or she runs tryout sessions at the beginning of each season and invites the outstanding and most promising athletes to be part of the team.

In some situations, the Coach recruits, students to play on the team from within the school. He or she may also have the responsibility of scouting high schools throughout the country to recruit athletes for the college team who are especially talented in a sport. The Coach may work with the college and offer young men and women athletic scholarships in an effort to entice them to attend and play on the school's teams. In larger schools the individual may pass this responsibility on to an assistant coach.

Once the athletes have all tried out, the Coach must choose the players of the team. The individual must evaluate each athlete's assets, drawbacks, and skills to determine who will be of greatest value to the team. He or she may do the evaluations alone, or may work with other coaches, instructors, and college personnel. The Coach then decides the position each athlete is best suited for.

The Coach sets times for the team to have practice sessions and meetings. He or she must determine how frequent practices will be and the duration of each session. Practices are devoted to developing the skills of both individual athletes and the team as a whole.

The individual discusses team strategies and methods of implementation. He or she also talks about any problems with the way the team plays and potential solutions.

The Coach works with other personnel in his or her college and opposing schools to schedule games, meets, tournaments, and championships. He or she is responsible for putting scheduled events on the calendar and notifying team members and others of the dates. The individual may also be responsible for scheduling practice areas, gym space, and transportation when games are played away from home base.

Coaches must motivate their players and teach them how to play as a team. They must make their players aware of the best techniques to play the game, the route to winning, and the rules of good sportsmanship.

In some colleges, the Coach might have additional duties. He or she may work as a physical education instructor. In this position, he or she is responsible for teaching duties as well. The Coach may be required to develop budgets, order equipment, keep it repaired and accounted for, and so on.

The Coach generally attends all of his or her team's games, at home or away. He or she is the leader of the team. During a game, the Coach may change strategies, give signals, and call time-outs to talk with team members. He or she must be aware of everything that is happening.

Before a game and during halftimes, the Coach usually gives pep talks to the team and may offer advice to athletes regarding playing tactics. After a game, the Coach offers suggestions for improvement that might be helpful for the next game.

Athletes often look upon the Coach as a good friend, teacher, or father or mother figure. Many athletes go to their Coach with athletic and personal problems. He or she works long hours, preparing the team for potential victories, attending games, and dealing with members of the team, faculty, and administration. Losing a game is an indication that the Coach has to work a bit harder with the team. Winning an important tournament or championship generally gives the individual a great deal of satisfaction.

Salaries

Coaches' salaries vary widely depending on a number of variables, including the size, location, and prestige of the college or university and its emphasis on sports and athletic programs. Earnings are also dependent on the qualifications, experience, responsibilities, and duties of the individual. Salaries may range from $20,000 to $400,000 plus for coaches working in colleges and universities. Coaches may also receive liberal fringe benefit packages.

Earnings of individuals coaching in small two-year schools or those with limited experience are on the lower end of the scale. Coaches working in large universities with strong emphasis on sports programs, such as those that belong to the National Collegiate Athletic Association (NCAA), receive higher earnings. These schools often derive large amounts of money from selling television rights to their games. They therefore can afford to pay Coaches higher salaries.

Employment Prospects

Employment prospects are good for Coaches working in colleges and universities. Positions may be located throughout the country. Individuals may, however, have to relocate to find a suitable position.

Coaches may work in junior colleges, community colleges, state schools, and private colleges and universities. Prospects become more difficult for those aspiring to Coach for NCAA (National Collegiate Athletic Association) college teams.

Advancement Prospects

Advancement prospects differ widely for Coaches depending on a number of variables. The most prominent factor to consider is the level the Coach is currently at in his or her career. Other factors include the drive and determination of the individual and his or her coaching skills and contacts in the field.

College Coaches climb the career ladder by obtaining a similar position in a larger, more prestigious school. Coaches working in small junior or community colleges have the best advancement prospects. Individuals may also move up the next rung on the career ladder by locating a position as an assistant coach in a larger school.

The most coveted positions in amateur coaching are found in colleges that are members of the NCAA. These schools put a great deal of emphasis on sports activities and their sports teams. As noted previously, individuals in these positions usually receive higher salaries than other collegiate coaches. As games are televised, the Coach gets a lot of exposure, which helps when trying to advance into the pros.

Education and Training

As a rule, colleges require their Coaches to have at least a four-year college degree. A graduate degree is helpful. One of the best choices for a major is physical education. The only exception to this rule may be as well-known professional athlete who has turned to coaching as a career.

Courses, workshops, and symposiums in coaching, sports, administration, and so on are useful.

Experience/Skills/Personality Traits

College Coaches need complete understanding of the sport (or sports) that they are coaching. Many individuals in this profession were college athletes prior to their entry in this career.

Coaches should be in good physical shape. They should also be able to provide information about health, nutrition, and fitness to their team. This is especially important now, when alcohol and drug abuse is so widespread.

A Coach should be able to motivate the athletes both individually and as a group. He or she is responsible for the athletes pulling together and working as a team. The Coach should be the type of person the team could look up to as a leader.

He or she needs the ability to deal with a variety of people in all situations. It is important that the Coach keep a level head and remain calm at all times.

The individual in this position must be able to handle many details at once. If the Coach is working with a staff, he or she must also have supervisory skills.

Unions/Associations

Coaches may belong to trade associations and other organizations relevant to the sport or sports they coach. These associations offer professional guidance, support, training and education.

Some of these might include the American Baseball Coaches Association (ABCA), the American Football Coaches Association (AFCA), the American Hockey Coaches Association (AHCA), the American Swimming Coaches Association (ASCA), the College Swimming Coaches Association of America (CSCA), the Intercollegiate Tennis Coaches Association (ITCA), the National Association of Collegiate Gymnastics Coaches (NACGC), and the National Interscholastic Swimming Coaches Association of America (NISCA).

Others might be the National Soccer Coaches Association of America (NSCA), the National Wrestling Coaches Association (NWCA), the United States Cross Country Coaches Association (USCCCA), the United States Women's Track Coaches Association (USWTCA), the Women Basketball Coaches Association (WBCA), and the various National Collegiate Athletic Association Coaches Associations (NCAACA).

Tips for Entry

1. Volunteer to coach local youth teams, such as Little League.
2. Consider a summer job as a sports counselor or coach at a camp.
3. Job openings may be advertised in the display or classified sections of newspapers. Look under heading classifications of "Coaching," "College," "Sports," "Athletics," or "Teaching."
4. Positions may also be advertised in trade journals.
5. Keep in close touch with your college's placement office. They are often advised of job openings.
6. State schools may publish lists of job opportunities in special bulletins. Write and inquire.
7. Join trade associations. These organizations provide a wealth of information for additional training as well as career guidance.
8. Search the major job and career sites on-line to see if there are openings in this field. There are also a number of sports sites on the web hosting jobs in sports.

COACH/HIGH SCHOOL

CAREER PROFILE

Duties: Coaching one or more of a high school's athletic teams; choosing team members; developing game strategies; teaching physical education.

Alternate Title(s): Head Coach

Salary Range: $20,000 to $70,000+

Employment Prospects: Good

Best Geographical Location(s) for Position: Positions located throughout the country.

Prerequisites:

Education or Training—Minimum of a four-year college degree required for most positions.
Experience—Student teaching experience may be required.
Special Skills and Personality Traits—Teaching and coaching skills; enjoy working with young adults; ability to motivate; understanding; personable.

CAREER LADDER

```
┌─────────────────────────────────┐
│   Coach in Larger High School   │
│               or                │
│  School with More Prestigious   │
│        Sports Program           │
└─────────────────────────────────┘

┌─────────────────────────────────┐
│        Coach/High School        │
└─────────────────────────────────┘

┌─────────────────────────────────┐
│   Physical Education Teacher    │
│               or                │
│         Student Teacher         │
└─────────────────────────────────┘
```

Position Description

A high school's Coach is often credited with the school's winning teams. Coaches working in high schools are responsible for coaching one or more of the school's sports teams. In larger schools the individual may coach one specific sport. In smaller schools, he or she may be required to coach all sports. These may include basketball, hockey, skiing, football, wrestling, soccer, and swimming, depending on the school's sports programs. High School Coaches are usually part of the teaching staff of the school.

Coaches working in secondary or high schools may work at public, private, or parochial institutions. They have varied duties depending on the school and the size of the athletic department. In many high schools Coaches are also responsible for teaching physical education classes. They may also teach health or other related courses.

In larger schools hosting many different types of sports programs, it is unrealistic to believe that a single individual has sufficient time to coach all the teams. Therefore, the Head Coach often has to locate additional suitable Coaches. He or she is then responsible for supervising the athletic teams and the other Coaches.

A team's Coach is the person responsible for getting the entire team ready to play competitively in games, tournaments,

and championships. He or she is responsible for putting together each team with the best athletes available in the school. The Head Coach works with the athletic director, head of the department, principal, and/or superintendent developing the athletic programs and deciding which sports the school actively participates in.

At the beginning of each school year, the Coach schedules tryout sessions for the specific sports. He or she may put announcements in the school paper, on the bulletin board, or in the gym. He or she may also personally invite athletes who show promise in selected sports to the tryouts.

The Head Coach and other school Coaches choose the members of the various teams once the athletes have all tried out. After the team members have been notified, practice sessions are scheduled. During these sessions, the Coach determines the positions each athlete is best suited for. The Coach informs team members of times and duration of practices. He or she also is responsible for letting team members know the rules, regulations, and policies of the school.

One of the main functions of the High School Coach is to help athletes develop their skills. He or she is also responsible for helping the members learn about good sportsmanship and teamwork.

The Coach must develop game strategies and methods for integrating them into the team. He or she also discusses problems with team plays and offer solutions.

In some situations, the Head Coach may be responsible for scheduling games, meets, tournaments, and championships with coaches from other schools. In other instances, this may be handled by the athletic director, head of the department, or other school personnel. The Head Coach is responsible for putting these athletic events on. No matter who sets up the programs, the Coach is responsible for making sure that his or her team is aware in advance of the event scheduled.

The Coach is also responsible for arranging for practice areas, gym space, and transportation when games are played away from the home school. He or she may also be required to plan for locker rooms or meals for competing teams coming to play at the school.

In addition to teaching skills and developing strategies, the Coach must be able to motivate his or her team and teach them how to work together. He or she must often offer words of praise and encouragement.

Depending on the specific responsibilities of the individual, he or she may be required to develop budgets, order equipment, keep it in repair, and so on. The Coach is responsible for making sure that the gym and all playing and athletic areas are neat, clean, and safe. If there is a problem, he or she must call a school maintenance person to deal with the difficulty.

The Coach attends all of his or her team's games, at home or away. team members often look to their Coach, as the leader of the team, for guidance. During a game, the Coach may change strategies, give signals, and call time-outs to talk to team members. He or she must be aware of everything that is happening.

Before a game and during halftimes, he or she usually gives pep talks to the team and may advise athletes on playing tactics. After a game, the Coach offers a review and suggestions for the next game.

Coaches are aware that a player with problems can affect an entire team. Team members usually have great respect for High School Coaches. Team members often come to the Coach with both personal and athletic problems. The Coach's door must always be open to talk to a team member.

An important function of a High School Coach is to help students with athletic talent attain sports scholarships. To do this, he or she may call or write a recommendation to colleges offering these programs for school athletes. During the course of his or her work, the High School Coach may also contact professional sports teams and organizations to evaluate the talent of specific athletes.

After long hours of training, practice, and motivation, every Coach gets an enormous amount of pleasure seeing his or her team win. It is also gratifying to know he or she helped an athlete become a major force in a collegiate sports team or a superstar professional athlete.

Salaries

The salaries of High School Coaches can vary greatly. The reasons include the size, geographic location, and type of school the Coach is working at as well as the school's emphasis on sports and athletic programs. Coaches working in public schools may receive different salaries from their counterparts in private or parochial institutions.

Earnings for Coaches are also dependent on their qualifications, educational background, experience, responsibilities, and duties. They may be employed as physical education teachers and also be responsible for all coaching duties.

Salaries may range from $20,000 to $70,000 plus for individuals working in high schools. The higher earnings are usually awarded to Coaches with a great deal of experience and responsibilities and who work in large cities.

Employment Prospects

Employment prospects are good for Coaches working in high schools. Positions may be located throughout the country. Coaches may work in public, private, or parochial schools. Individuals with the most opportunities are those who have highly diversified talents and who coach a variety of subjects. In a great many high schools, coaches also must teach physical education. Some schools may offer part-time coaching positions.

Advancement Prospects

Advancement prospects are fair for High School Coaches. Most Coaches advance their careers in ways similar to other school teachers.

Individuals may move up the career ladder in a number of ways. The first is to locate a job in a more prestigious school or district that puts a strong emphasis on the sports programs. This will lead to higher earnings and greater job prestige for the individual.

Another method of career advancement occurs when an individual obtains additional education or gains seniority. In many school systems, compensation is directly related to the amount of education an individual has and the number of years he or she has been working.

Coaches who consistently have winning teams are also in demand in school systems that emphasize their sports programs.

Education and Training

High School Coaches working full time in most school systems are required to have minimum of a four-year college degree. A master's degree may be required for some positions. One of the best choices for a major is physical education. As most High School Coaches are part of the teaching staff, education degrees are usually mandatory.

Courses, workshops, and symposiums in coaching, sports, and administration are useful.

Experience/Skills/Personality Traits

As noted previously, High School Coaches are usually part of the teaching staff. As a result, most have had experience with student teaching prior to a job appointment.

High School Coaches should enjoy working with young adults. Teaching and coaching skills are necessary. A complete knowledge and understanding of the sport (or sports) being coached is necessary. Coaches must be positive and able to motivate others. Teaching the skills of a sport is one part of the job; getting a team to implement the skills is another.

Coaches should be personable, understanding, and likable. They should be leaders whom team members can look up to.

First aid skills are helpful for Coaches in case of injuries or emergencies in the gym, practice area, or games.

Unions/Associations

Coaches working in high school settings may be members of local or national teachers' unions, depending on the school. Two of the largest of these bargaining unions are the National Educators Association (NEA) and the National Federation of Teachers (NFT). Organizations such as these work on behalf of teachers to help them obtain benefits, better working conditions, and higher salaries.

Coaches may also belong to any number of sports associations offering seminars, conferences, booklets, and career guidance. Some of these might include the American Baseball Coaches Association (ABCA), the American Football Coaches Association (AFCA), the American Hockey Coaches Association (AHCA), the American Swimming Coaches Association (ASCA), the National Federation Interscholastic Coaches Association (NFICA), and the National Interscholastic Swimming Coaches Association of America (NISCA).

Others might be the National Soccer Coaches Association of America (NSCA), the National Wrestling Coaches Association (NWCA), the National Youth Sports Coaches Association (NYSCA), the United States Cross Country Coaches Association (USCCCA), the United States Women's Track Coaches Association (USWTCA), and the Women's Basketball Coaches Association (WBCA).

Tips for Entry

1. Jobs openings for High School Coaches are often advertised in the display or classified sections of newspapers. Look under heading classification of "Coaching," "Sports," "Athletics," or "Teaching."
2. Many schools are now hiring Coaches for summer programs. This is a good way to obtain experience and get your foot in the door of a school system.
3. Volunteer to coach local youth teams, such as Little League teams.
4. Consider a summer job as a sports counselor or coach at a camp.
5. Coaching positions may also be advertised in trade journals.
6. Keep in close touch with your college's placement office. They are often advised of openings.
7. Send your résumé and a cover letter to schools. Ask that your résumé be kept on file if no opening is currently available.
8. Join trade associations. Trade journals usually offer career guidance, and the association meetings will help you make important contacts.
9. Search Internet job web sites for possible openings.

ATHLETIC DIRECTOR—EDUCATION

CAREER PROFILE

Duties: Supervising, developing, and administering a school's athletic programs and sports department; coordinating and supervising physical education teachers, instructors, and coaches.

Alternate Title(s): Director of Physical Education; AD

Salary Range: $20,000 to $85,000+

Employment Prospects: Good

Best Geographical Location(s) for Position: Positions available throughout the country.

Prerequisites:

Education or Training—Minimum of a four-year college degree; graduate degree may be preferred.

Experience—Experience teaching physical education, coaching, etc., usually preferred.

Special Skills and Personality Traits—Supervisory skills; administrative capabilities; good written and verbal communication skills; knowledge of preparation of annual budgets and reports; excellent interpersonal skills; keen interest in sports and athletics; enjoy working with youth.

CAREER LADDER

```
┌─────────────────────────────────────┐
│         Athletic Director           │
│  in Larger, More Prestigious School │
│                 or                  │
│      Other Supervisory Position     │
└─────────────────────────────────────┘

┌─────────────────────────────────────┐
│         Athletic Director           │
└─────────────────────────────────────┘

┌─────────────────────────────────────┐
│    Physical Education Teacher,      │
│      Retired Pro Athlete,           │
│                 or                  │
│       Sports Administrator          │
└─────────────────────────────────────┘
```

Position Description

The Athletic Director working in an educational setting has varied responsibilities depending on his or her situation. The individual is ultimately responsible for running the school system's athletic and sports programs.

Much of the work of the Athletic Director is supervisory and administrative. The individual works with other administrative personnel in the school system to plan and execute as broad a program as possible. His or her goal is to provide a full physical education program for all students in the school.

One of the main responsibilities of the Athletic Director is to develop, administer, and supervise the entire curriculum of physical education for the school or district, depending on the situation.

He or she assists in the recruiting, interviewing, and recommending of qualified people to work in the athletic department. The Athletic Director also is responsible for both supervising and evaluating people on the athletic staff. In certain positions, the individual is in charge of the orientation of the athletic staff and their in-service education.

The Athletic Director is responsible for coordinating and supervising the various physical education teachers, instructors, and coaches as well as all the teams and sports.

Depending on the situation, the Athletic Director is responsible for preparing the physical education budget for supplies. He or she either specifies requirements for the purchase of the supplies and equipment or supervises an individual in the department who handles this job. Once equipment and supplies are purchased, the Athletic Director is responsible for making sure that the supplies arrive in good shape or are replaced.

The Athletic Director is responsible for appraising, previewing, and recommending new materials and textbooks for use within the physical education department. He or she is required to work with the staff promoting the various physical fitness programs in the school as well as developing new upgraded programs. At times, the individual reviews and evaluates the programs that currently exist in the school.

The Athletic Director often meets with the school superintendent or director to inform him or her of the progress of the physical education and sports programs and recommend necessary changes.

The individual advises the superintendent if and when the school needs new facilities, such as athletic fields or tennis courts. He or she also must work with building and grounds personnel and other staff when assigning the physical education facilities for extracurricular use. The Athletic Director is responsible for the total organization and scheduling of all interscholastic athletic activities.

At the same time, he or she fosters good school-community relations by making sure that the community is aware of the accomplishments of the various school teams. This might include calling the press about winning teams or assigning someone to take care of this particular duty.

An important part of the job of the Athletic Director is to individualize physical education activities for students who have special needs and talents. For example, the AD might set up special competitions for students who are physically or mentally handicapped.

During competitions and games with other schools, the Athletic Director is responsible for arranging transportation for the home team to other schools. When another team comes to compete at his or her school, the AD must make arrangements for their needs, such as providing lockers, refreshments, and so on.

The individual must see to it that all insurance programs that cover school athletes or athletic programs are provided and administered. The Athletic Director must cooperate with school nurses, physicians, and office personnel to make sure that all reports are filed and claims made. He or she must make sure that all school athletes take physical exams before they participate in sports programs.

The Athletic Director either personally keeps records or assigns someone to the task of recording the results of all contests, competitions, awards, and scholarships. At intervals, he or she is usually required to plan and supervise recognition programs for outstanding school athletes.

The Athletic Director is in charge of directing all in-school and extracurricular sports and athletic programs. He or she attempts to obtain support from both the school athletic teams and nonparticipanting sports fans. The individual is also required, at times, to present programs to local community groups.

The Athletic Director works long hours. He or she often develops programs or attends school events after normal school hours and on weekends.

In smaller schools, the Athletic Director may also teach physical education and/or coach one or more sports. In larger schools, the individual does not have any teaching or coaching responsibilities, which frees up his or her time to administer programs.

Depending on the specific situation, the Athletic Director is responsible to either the school superintendent or the school director.

Salaries

Annual earnings for Athletic Directors working in education vary greatly depending on a number of factors. These include the size and location of the school the individual is working for, whether it is a private or public school, and the school's emphasis on sports programs. Compensation is also dependent on the experience level, responsibilities, and duties of the Athletic Director.

Salaries can start at $20,000 in a small private school system or may go up to $75,000 plus annually in large schools that put a great emphasis on their school's sports program.

Employment Prospects

Employment prospects are good for Athletic Directors. Individuals must, however, be willing to relocate to areas that need people in this position.

Jobs are available throughout the country in a variety of school systems. Individuals may look in both the public and private sector for employment.

Advancement Prospects

Advancement prospects are fair for Athletic Directors working in education. Individuals can move up the career ladder by obtaining a similar position in a larger school system with a more prestigious sports program. This will, in turn, usually lead to higher earnings.

Depending on the professional goals of the individual, he or she may also move into other supervisory positions in the school system or may move into a similar position in a large college.

Education and Training

Athletic Directors working in education require a minimum of a four-year college degree. Most positions require a graduate degree. Depending on the school system and the state in which the individual plans on working, the Athletic Director usually needs to major in education and/or physical education. He or she may also be required to take classes in administration.

Experience/Skills/Personality Traits

Athletic Directors need supervisory and administrative skills. Individuals in this type of position should be able to prepare budgets and schedules and know how to keep to them.

The Athletic Director needs excellent interpersonal skills. He or she will be dealing with other school personnel, students, and parents. Good communication skills, both written and verbal, are necessary.

Individuals should have a keen interest in physical education and athletics and enjoy working with youth. They should, furthermore, be energetic and enthusiastic.

Athletic Directors working in an educational settings usually need experience in teaching. However, this is not always true. Often, private schools do not require experience in the educational field; instead they opt for expertise in sports and/or administration.

Unions/Associations

Athletic Directors who started out as teachers or instructors or currently teach may belong to a union, such as the American Federation of Teachers, which negotiates on behalf of teachers. Others who work in private schools may not.

Individuals may belong to various local groups or associations related to sports they may coach. They may also be involved with the American Alliance for Health, Physical Education, Recreation and Dance.

Tips for Entry

1. Get experience by volunteering to run local sports programs for area youth.

2. Consider working as a recreation director or assistant in a summer program in your area.

3. Work with local Little League teams. The experience will be helpful later in your career and look good on your résumé.

4. Positions as Athletic Directors are often advertised in local newspaper display and classified sections. Look under heading classifications of "Education," "Athletics," and "Sports."

5. Jobs may also be advertised in educational magazines and journals.

6. Try to attend a school with a sports management or administration program. These schools offer help in job placement.

7. Search the major career and job sites on-line. You might find openings advertised. Keywords might include "education," "athletic director," or "sports."

PHYSICAL EDUCATION INSTRUCTOR/COLLEGE

CAREER PROFILE

Duties: Instructing college classes in sports, athletics, and physical education; evaluating students' progress.

Alternate Title(s): Gym Teacher; Phys. Ed. Instructor; Phys. Ed. Teacher; Professor; Coach

Salary Range: $23,000 to $70,000+

Employment Prospects: Good

Best Geographical Location(s) for Position: Positions may be located throughout the country.

Prerequisites:

Education or Training—Minimum of a four-year college degree; positions in many colleges require graduate work.

Experience—Experience teaching, coaching, or involvement with sports helpful.

Special Skills and Personality Traits—Enjoys sports and athletics; likes working with young adults; teaching skills; communications skills; knowledge of rules, regulations, and policies in sports; patience; motivation.

CAREER LADDER

```
┌─────────────────────────────────────────┐
│      Physical Education Instructor       │
│    at Larger, More Prestigous College    │
│                   or                     │
│            Department Head               │
│                   or                     │
│   Athletic Director or Assistant Director│
└─────────────────────────────────────────┘
```

```
┌─────────────────────────────────────────┐
│          Physical Education              │
│          Instructor/College              │
└─────────────────────────────────────────┘
```

```
┌─────────────────────────────────────────┐
│  High School Physical Education Teacher, │
│            College Student,              │
│                   or                     │
│            Graduate Student              │
└─────────────────────────────────────────┘
```

Position Description

Physical Education Instructors working in schools of higher education may work in junior, community, or four-year colleges and universities. They may work in private institutions or state or public schools. Responsibilities vary with the specific job. Instructors may also be called Teachers, Coaches, or Professors.

Individuals may teach required physical education classes to college students as well as elective subjects. Most colleges now provide a tremendous variety of courses for students to select from in order to fulfill their physical education requirements. Thus those who teach college physical education now may have the opportunity to teach and participate in some of their favorite sports.

Individuals may instruct classes in almost any sport, including archery, badminton, bowling, tennis, racquetball, golf, wrestling, swimming, boxing, aerobics, dance, and exercise, to name a few. Instructors may also teach team sport classes.

Individuals may have mixed classes or may be responsible solely for classes for women or men. Unlike teaching in elementary or secondary schools, those working in most college situations usually do not decide what types of sports should be taught. Rather, individuals are assigned specific courses to teach. They must then determine how to teach each course. Instructors may spend an entire semester teaching a specific class in one sport.

In some states there are minimum, state-mandated physical education and fitness requirements that must be followed. An example of this might be a state university that requires that students be capable of passing a basic swimming test before graduation. In these situations, the Instructor may be expected to help students attain this goal. This may include teaching classes in the subject as well as giving private instruction to students who require it.

Depending on the type and level of class that an individual is teaching, he or she may have to individualize the training. In a beginning golf course, all students would probably be on the same level of expertise. However, in an intermediate tennis course, for example, students may be at a number of different levels. The Teacher may be expected to give one-on-one instruction. Instructors must be adept at working with individuals of all levels of skill, even if they are in the same class.

Physical Education Instructors working on the college level may have a variety of students, including some who are taking classes just to meet graduation requirements and others who are taking electives because they like to be involved in sports. Some students may also be heavily involved with the college's athletic programs.

Instructors must help the students set realistic goals and help them attain them. Many college Instructors are responsible for assisting a student who has the ability to turn professional. The Instructor might contact scouts, professional teams, or other useful people to achieve this goal.

Depending on the size of the college's sports department, the Physical Education Instructor may also have coaching duties. He or she may be expected to put together one or all of the college's sports teams in addition to coaching them throughout the playing season.

The individual is required to handle paperwork, including grading exams and other student work. He or she is expected to evaluate student progress in classes and assign a mark. In some colleges, this may be a letter or number grade. In others, it may be a pass or fail evaluation.

The Phys. Ed. Instructor is also responsible for reporting any accidents that occur in the gym or during games. He or she may be required to fill in insurance reports and forms about the accident. The individual may also be responsible for making sure that any required medical forms are filled in for students in his or her classes.

The Instructor is expected to keep the gym, lockers rooms, and other sports-oriented areas safe, neat, and in working order. If equipment needs to be fixed or replaced, he or she must report the problem to the head of the department or maintenance and make sure it is taken care of.

College Instructors may teach during the regular school season or work throughout the year. Hours may vary depending on teaching schedules. Instructors are expected to prepare for classes and teach as well as schedule regular hours to meet with students. Individuals also have to attend college faculty meetings. If they are involved in coaching or working with students participating in tournaments, games, or competitions, Instructors are also expected to attend these events.

Physical Education Instructors usually are responsible to either the head of the department or the athletic director, depending on the structure of the school.

Salaries

Earnings for Physical Education Instructors working on the college level vary greatly depending on a number of factors. These include the specific college, its geographic location, and the emphasis it puts on its athletic and sports programs. Other variables include the individual's education, responsibilities, skills, and his or her seniority.

Salaries can range from $23,000 to $70,000 plus. Compensation is usually augmented by liberal fringe benefit packages. Those working at two-year schools with little or no experience earn salaries on the bottom end of the scale. Individuals working at schools with prestigious athletic programs earn salaries toward the top.

Employment Prospects

Employment prospects are good for Physical Education Instructors on the college level. Individuals may find it easier to break into the profession by locating a position in a two-year school. While individuals may have to move to other areas to locate specific jobs, employment may be found in almost every area in the country.

Most colleges, even small ones, have more than one Physical Education Instructor. Many, especially those that put a great deal of emphasis on their sports and athletic program, have much larger departments.

Advancement Prospects

Advancement prospects are fair for Physical Education Instructors on a college level. Individuals might advance their careers by locating a position at a larger or more prestigious college or university. This usually results in increased earnings.

Some Phys. Ed. Instructors climb the career ladder by becoming head of the department, assistant athletic director, or athletic director at either his or her school or at another institution. Others advance by becoming coaches for more prestigious schools.

Education and Training

A minimum of a four-year college degree is required to teach in any college. However, most four-year colleges and universities require a master's degree or a doctorate. The most common degree for this type of position is one in physical education.

Experience/Skills/Personality Traits

College Physical Education Instructors should enjoy working with adults. They should also like sports, athletics, and teaching. Most Instructors are sports fans.

Some Instructors have taught in high schools prior to obtaining a college-level job. Others landed their position after graduate school. Some individuals working in two-year schools located their job after graduating from a four-year school with a degree in physical education.

Individuals should have a knowledge of sports and athletics. While they need not be star athletes, they should know the rules, regulations, and skills of the sports they will be teaching.

Having expertise in one if not more sports is necessary. The more the individual knows about specific sports or athletics, the easier he or she will find a job.

Instructors should be able to teach on a number of different levels of expertise. Patience and motivation are useful skills for those aspiring to be successful at their job.

The Phys. Ed. Instructor should have good communications skills. He or she must be able to explain directions, rules, and regulations to students. Writing skills are necessary for handling paperwork connected with the job.

Unions/Associations

Physical Education Instructors may belong to a bargaining union that helps them obtain better benefits, working conditions, and salaries. This depends on the specific school and position.

College Instructors may be members of organizations specific to the sports they are teaching or any number of other sports associations that offer seminars, conferences, booklets, and career guidance.

The college or university that the individual works for may also belong to the National Association of Collegiate Directors of Athletics (NACDA), the National Association of Intercollegiate Athletics (NAIA), the National Collegiate Athletic Association (NCCA), the National Junior College Athletic Association (NJCAA), or any of the collegiate conference organizations.

Tips for Entry

1. Keep in touch with your college's placement office. These offices receive notices of other colleges that need to hire instructors.
2. Certain employment agencies specialize in locating positions for people in education. Check these out. They are usually located in major cities. Keep in mind that some agencies charge the employer a fee to find a suitable employee, while others charge the employee. Make sure you find out costs in advance.
3. Positions in education are often advertised in the display or classified section of the newspaper. Look under heading classifications of "College," "University," "Community College," "Junior College," "Instructor," "Physical Education," "Gym," "Teacher," "Professor," or the names of specific sports such as "Tennis Instructor," "Golf Instructor," and so on.
4. Get letters of recommendation from several of your professors at college.
5. Many state colleges have newsletters advising people of openings within the system. Contact state colleges to look into this.
6. It is sometimes easier to get your foot in the door by teaching at a local college part time. You then have experience on your résumé that may make it easier to obtain a full-time job.
7. Check out on-line job and career sites to see if there are any advertised openings. Search keywords such as "sports," "education," "college," and "athletics."

PHYSICAL EDUCATION TEACHER/SECONDARY SCHOOL

CAREER PROFILE

Duties: Developing activities for gym classes; teaching sports; following mandated physical education and fitness requirements; coaching.

Alternate Title(s): Phys. Ed. Teacher; Phys. Ed. Instructor; Gym Teacher; P.E. Teacher

Salary Range: $22,000 to $60,000+

Employment Prospects: Good

Best Geographical Location(s) for Position: Positions may be located throughout the country.

Prerequisites:

Education or Training—Minimum of four-year college degree in physical education; many schools may require master's degree.

Experience—Student teaching experience usually required.

Special Skills and Personality Traits—Enjoys sports; likes teaching; knowledge and understanding of sports games and rules; personable.

CAREER LADDER

```
┌─────────────────────────────┐
│      Department Head        │
│            or               │
│      Athletic Director      │
└─────────────────────────────┘

┌─────────────────────────────┐
│  Physical Education Teacher │
└─────────────────────────────┘

┌─────────────────────────────┐
│       College Student       │
└─────────────────────────────┘
```

Position Description

Physical Education Teachers working in secondary schools can work in junior high or high schools and in public, private, or parochial institutions. Their duties vary depending on the type of job they are hired for.

A secondary school Physical Education Teacher might teach boys, girls, or mixed gym classes. The individual usually must develop activities for each class and decide what sports should be taught to which students. Some states mandate minimum physical education and fitness requirements that the Physical Education Teacher must follow.

It is up to the Physical Education Teacher to help each student attain the best possible fitness. In some schools, he or she may be required to develop sports programs for handicapped and disabled students.

The Phys. Ed. Teacher or Gym Teacher, as he or she may be called, should be able to help students set realistic physical fitness goals and then help them reach them. Successful Teachers in this field will help all students, even those who don't seem to have any real interest in fitness or sports, attain a

fitness level and have fun participating in activities. Good Phys. Ed. Teachers make even nonjoiners want to be involved in sports.

The individual often has to handle paperwork and produce documentation. For example, the Physical Education Teacher is responsible for reporting both verbally and in writing any accidents that occur in the gym or during games. The individual usually is responsible for documenting students' progress in various sports and for reporting these on grade sheets, report cards, or during parent-teacher conferences.

Depending on the size and structure of the phys. ed. department, the individual may be required to plan budgets for the department, write up requests for equipment, and order supplies. This usually occurs in smaller schools where there is no head of the department or where the Teacher acts as the department head.

Physical Education Teachers may be responsible for putting together school sports teams. In some schools the individual is required to act as the coach for the various teams. In others he or she is responsible for finding coaches for the different sports teams.

The Instructor is responsible for keeping the gym, locker rooms, and other sports-oriented areas neat and safe. If equipment needs to be fixed or replaced, he or she usually is responsible for reporting the problem and following up on it.

In certain situations, the Physical Education Teacher may also be responsible for teaching other subjects, such as health, hygiene, and/or sex education classes.

Gym Teachers may be responsible to the head of the department, athletic director, assistant principal, principal, or headmaster, depending on the particular school system.

Individuals usually work normal school hours. Phys. Ed. Teachers have to put in extra time to plan classes, write up reports, attend meetings and other educational sessions, and attend school-sponsored sporting events. P.E. teachers who also coach work longer hours.

Many people enjoy the flexibility of teaching in a school system because schools are usually closed during holidays and the summer months.

Salaries

Salaries for Physical Education Teachers vary greatly depending on a number of variables. These include the type of school (private, parochial, public) and geographic location as well as the education, responsibilities, and seniority of the individual.

Salaries can range from $22,000 to $60,000 plus. Compensation is usually augmented by liberal fringe benefit packages. Physical Education Teachers can earn additional monies by coaching and teaching summer school.

Employment Prospects

Employment prospects are good for Physical Education Teachers who wish to work in secondary schools. While individuals may have to relocate to find specific jobs, employment may be found in almost every geographical area in the country.

Teachers also have the option of working in junior high schools or high schools, and public, private, or parochial institutions. Most secondary schools have at least two or more Physical Education Teachers on staff.

Advancement Prospects

Advancement prospects are good for Physical Education Teachers. Many individuals who stay at the same school for a number of years have the opportunity to be tenured. Usually tenured teachers cannot be fired or let go from their position. After teaching for a number of years, salaries usually rise. The individual might advance his or her career by locating another position at a larger school that pays more.

The Physical Education Teacher might also be promoted to head of the physical education department, assistant athletic director, or athletic director at either his or her school or at another institution.

Education and Training

A minimum of a four-year college degree is usually required in most teaching positions. It is common for individuals seeking positions such as this to have a degree in education with a major in physical education. Some schools might also require a graduate degree.

Experience/Skills/Personality Traits

Individuals who teach usually go through some type of student teaching experience while still in college. This helps prepare them for the job when they graduate.

Physical Education Teachers working in secondary schools should not only like sports but enjoy teaching and working with young adults. While all Phys. Ed. Teachers do not have to be terrific athletes, they should have a complete understanding of sports.

Successful teachers in all fields should be easygoing, understanding, and personable. Individuals should also have a knack for teaching.

Unions/Associations

Depending on the school, Physical Education Teachers may or may not belong to a bargaining union such as the National Educators Association (NEA) or the National Federation of Teachers (NFT). Organizations such as these work on behalf of teachers to help them obtain better benefits, working conditions, and salaries.

Teachers may also belong to any number of sports associations that offer seminars, conferences, booklets, and career guidance.

Tips for Entry

1. Certain employment agencies specialize in locating positions for teachers. Check these out. They are usually located in major cities.
2. Keep in touch with your college's placement office. These offices receive notices of schools that need to hire teachers.
3. Get letters of recommendation from several of your professors at school as well as your student teaching supervisor.
4. Apply for summer school positions. These are often easier to obtain and they help get your foot in the door of a school system.
5. Positions in education are often advertised in the classified or display section of the newspaper. The Sunday newspaper is one of the big days for advertising education jobs.
6. If you are interested in working in a specific area, write to the local newspaper and order a short-term subscription. In this way you will be able to keep track of all the job offerings.

PHYSICAL EDUCATION TEACHER/ELEMENTARY SCHOOL

CAREER PROFILE

Duties: Developing activities for gym classes; teaching physical education classes; instilling concepts of good sportsmanship.

Alternate Title(s): Phys. Ed. Teacher; Gym Teacher; P.E. Teacher.

Salary Range: $23,000 to $65,000+

Employment Prospects: Good

Best Geographical Location(s) For Position: Positions may be located throughout the country.

Prerequisites:

Education or Training—Minimum of a four-year college degree in physical education; many schools may require a master's degree

Experience—Student teaching experience usually required.

Special Skills and Personality Traits—Enjoys sports; likes teaching; flair for working with children; knowledge of sports and athletics; understanding.

CAREER LADDER

```
┌─────────────────────────────────┐
│     Head of Department          │
│             or                  │
│   Teacher at Larger School      │
└─────────────────────────────────┘

┌─────────────────────────────────┐
│  Physical Education Teacher/    │
│     Elementary School           │
└─────────────────────────────────┘

┌─────────────────────────────────┐
│       College Student           │
└─────────────────────────────────┘
```

Position Description

Physical Education Teachers working in elementary schools work with children. In some schools the Physical Education Teacher is responsible for all the school's gym classes. In others the individual might be responsible only for either the boys' or the girls' gym classes.

The Physical Education Teacher is also referred to as the P.E. or Gym Teacher. His or her duties vary depending on the specific job.

In some job situations, the P.E. Teacher is required to develop activities for each class. If the Teacher is working in a state where minimum physical education and fitness requirements are mandated, he or she must develop activities that follow the state guidelines. In other schools, the head of the department may develop specific activity rosters, and the individual Gym Teacher is required to put the activities into motion on a class level.

Physical Education Teachers must try to help each child attain the best fitness level possible. Elementary School Gym Teachers may have the added responsibility of assessing the needs of young students in their care and developing programs that help them gain coordination and confidence.

When teaching younger children, the individual must often deal with problems Phys. Ed. Teachers working with older students might not encounter. While all students must learn good sportsmanship, younger students often have a harder time dealing with such a concept. These problems could include a youngster losing a game, not being chosen for a team, and so on. The Gym Teacher must be able to deal with temper tantrums, crying, and other problems.

The P.E. Teacher must develop or teach sports programs for handicapped, emotionally disturbed, and disabled students.

Physical Education Teachers working with young children must have a great deal of patience. They must explain games, sports, and rules in a manner in which youngsters can understand. They must be able to help children set realistic physical fitness goals and then help them reach them.

Successful Teachers in the physical education field need to be able to draw all children into participating and having fun.

The Teacher is required to report both verbally and in writing any accidents that occur in the gym. The individual should know and be able to practice basic first aid techniques. He or she should also be able to know when a child has the wind knocked out of her and when a child is seriously hurt.

Depending on the grade level and school, the Phys. Ed. Teacher might be responsible for documenting students' progress in various sports and for reporting these on grade sheets, report cards, or during parent-teacher conferences.

In some schools, the individual may be required to plan budgets for the department, write up requests for equipment, and order supplies. In other situations, the Teacher passes requests on to the head of the department.

The Gym Teacher must make sure that the gym, locker rooms, and other sports-oriented areas are neat and safe. If any equipment needs to be fixed or replaced, he or she usually must report the problem to the head of the department or the proper authority and follow up on the repair order.

Elementary Physical Education Teachers may be responsible to the head of the department, assistant principal, principal, or headmaster, depending on the particular school system.

Individuals usually work normal school hours. In addition, they also have to put in extra hours writing reports, planning classes, and attending meetings. Most teachers have holidays and summers off.

Salaries

Salaries for Physical Education Teachers working in elementary schools can range from $23,000 to $65,000 or more. The variation in earning depends on whether the individual is working in a private, public, or parochial school, the size of the school system, and its geographic location. Salaries are also dependent on the education, responsibilities, and seniority of the individual. Earnings for most Elementary School Physical Education Teachers are augmented by liberal fringe benefit packages.

Employment Prospects

Employment prospects are good for Elementary School Physical Education Teachers. Almost every elementary school in the country has at least one Phys. Ed. Teacher on staff.

Teachers have the added benefit of being employable throughout the country.

Advancement Prospects

Advancement prospects are good for Elementary School Physical Education Teachers. Individuals who stay at the same school in the same position for a number of years have the opportunity to be tenured. Usually tenured teachers cannot be fired or let go from their position. This gives the individual a great amount of job stability.

Elementary School Phys. Ed. Teachers who wish to climb the career ladder may do so in a number of ways. Some individuals advance their career by locating a position in a larger school district that offers a higher salary. Other individuals seek promotion to the position of head of the physical education department.

Education and Training

A minimum of a four-year college degree is usually required in most teaching positions. It is common for individuals seeking positions such as this to have a degree in education with a major in physical education. Some positions might additionally require a graduate degree.

Seminars and classes in early childhood education as well as physical education are helpful.

Experience/Skills/Personality Traits

Elementary School Physical Education Teachers obtain experience by student teaching while in college. As a rule, the individual tries to do his or her student teaching in a situation simulating the general age group he or she wishes to work with after graduation.

Elementary School Physical Education Teachers must enjoy teaching and have a flair for working with children. They should have a good working knowledge of sports and athletics.

P.E. Teachers should be easygoing, understanding, compassionate, and personable.

Unions/Associations

The National Educators Association (NEA) and the National Federation of Teachers (NFT) are two of the bargaining unions that Elementary School Phys. Ed. Teachers may belong to. These organizations work on behalf of teachers to help them obtain better benefits, working conditions, and salaries. Teachers at some schools may not be members of any union.

Physical Education Teachers may also belong to any number of sports associations that offer educational and career guidance.

Tips for Entry

1. Volunteer time as a coach for a youngsters baseball, basketball, or football team. This will help you gain experience working with children.
2. Get letters of recommendation from several of your professors at school as well as your student teaching supervisor.
3. Certain employment agencies specialize in locating positions for teachers. Check these out. They are usually located in major cities. Check to find out who pays the employment agency fee. In some situations it is the school; in others it is the teacher.
4. Keep in touch with your college's placement office. These offices receive notices of schools that plan on hiring teachers.
5. Apply for summer school positions. These are often easier to obtain, and they help get your foot in the door of a school system.

6. Positions in education are often advertised in the display or classified section of the newspaper. The Sunday newspaper is one of the big days for advertising education jobs.

7. If you are interested in working in a specific area, write to the local newspaper and order a short-term subscription. In this way you will be able to keep track of all the job offerings.

8. Consider a summer position working in a town or city youth recreation department. This is another good way to gain valuable experience.

9. Search on-line for job openings. Type in keywords such as "teaching," "physical education," into job or career search sites.

CAREER OPPORTUNITIES
IN OFFICIATING
SPORTS TEAMS

UMPIRE/PRO BASEBALL

CAREER PROFILE

Duties: Officiating at professional baseball games; calling balls, strikes, and fouls; making out and safe calls; settling disputes on the field.

Alternate Title(s): Ump.; Official

Salary Range: $25,000 to $100,000+

Employment Prospects: Poor

Best Geographical Location(s) for Position: Cities hosting professional baseball teams.

Prerequisites:

Education or Training—Training at approved umpire school.

Experience—No experience necessary.

Special Skills and Personality Traits—Knowledge of rules, regulations, and policies of baseball; physically fit; good eyesight; ability to deal with stress and pressure; calm, cool, and collected; ability to travel.

CAREER LADDER

```
┌─────────────────────────────────┐
│  Umpire for Major League Games  │
└─────────────────────────────────┘

┌─────────────────────────────────┐
│  Umpire for Minor League Games  │
└─────────────────────────────────┘

┌─────────────────────────────────┐
│       Umpire Training           │
│       Camp Student              │
└─────────────────────────────────┘
```

Position Description

Umpires are the individuals who officiate at baseball games. Without them, a baseball game would not run smoothly. The individual's main function is to make sure that all rules and regulations of the game are followed and the game proceeds smoothly. Umpires participate in all professional baseball games, from those conducted in the minor leagues on up to the majors.

There are usually four Umpires in each professional baseball game. One stands behind home plate and the other three stand near each base. Depending on the situation, the Umpires take turns officiating in each position from game to game. Special games, such as World Series games, may use additional Umpires.

Umpires must know all the rules and regulations of the sport. They are responsible for calling fouls, balls, and strikes. Individuals in this position are also the ones who make the call on whether a player is safe or out on a play at a base. The Umpire standing behind home plate calls the fouls, balls, and strikes. The Umpire is also responsible for making sure the pitcher has a supply of balls when needed. Safe and out calls are made by the Umpire standing nearest the base where the action is occurring. These Umpires are also responsible for making calls regarding balls hit to the outfield.

Umpires must keep their eyes on the ball and the action on the field at all times. There is no time for daydreaming in this position. Looking away for even one second can mean missing important action.

A familiar scene in professional baseball is that of an athlete or a manager arguing with an Umpire over a decision. This arguing usually is in vain, as the Umpire's decision is final. If the Umpire's decision is not popular with the fans, he must also be able to deal with the booing that follows.

Umpires in professional baseball may have to travel a great deal in their jobs. They may be away from their home base for a third of the year during the baseball season. Individuals are assigned to officiate at a number of games in an area and then move on to another location. Umpires are usually treated well during their travels. Travel and lodging expenses are paid for as part of the job. Umpires are not allowed to fraternize with athletes, as this may lead to a conflict of interest during a game.

Individuals may work during afternoon games, evening games, and on weekends. Hours can be long. The Umpire is expected to be on the field for the entire game, which can take three hours or more. The individual also has to deal with the climate. Umpires may work on extremely hot or cold days, or in the rain.

Umpires in professional baseball are employed by the National League (NL) and the American League (AL). These leagues work under the auspices of the Baseball Commissioner's office.

Salaries

There is a large salary range for Umpires, depending on a number of variables. The most prominent variable is the level class the individual is officiating in. Those working in the minor leagues earn less than those in the majors. Umpires officiating at Class A games earn less than those doing the same job in AAA games. Individuals may earn annual salaries from $25,000 to $100,000 plus, depending on the level of game they are officiating at and their experience. Umpires may also earn more when officiating at major tournaments, such as the World Series.

Employment Prospects

Employment prospects are poor for those aspiring to be Umpires for professional baseball teams in the major leagues. Those who work in the minor leagues will have a better chance of getting their foot in the door.

Advancement Prospects

Advancement prospects are fair for Umpires officiating at professional baseball games if they have drive, determination, experience, and are skilled at what they do.

Individuals may climb the career ladder by being assigned to a position officiating for games between teams in a higher class. There are four classes in baseball, three in the minor leagues and one the major leagues. The lowest class is A, which is where the rookies usually start to play; the next is AA; AAA follows. The major leagues are the highest level. Most Umpires aspire to work in the majors. A great accomplishment for the individual is to officiate during the World Series.

Education and Training

There is no formal educational requirement for Umpires. Individuals must, however, be thoroughly training in the skills of officiating. This is usually accomplished at an Umpire training camp or school. After attending Umpire school, those who meet requirements go on to another training program. Individuals who complete this program are chosen to begin their careers as Umpires in the minor leagues.

Experience/Skills/Personality Traits

Umpires need to know all the rules, regulations, and policies of the sport. They must be able to make calls on balls, strikes, and fouls. Individuals should be in good physical condition. They must be able to stand for long periods of time while watching the game. Good eyesight is essential.

Umpires should be able to deal with stress and pressure. As a rule, whatever decision the Umpire makes, one side is unhappy and disagrees. Umpires must be able to make quick decisions and accurate, consistent, and fair judgments. Individuals must be able to work in a situation where others disagree with their decisions and judgments. Umpires must be calm, cool, and collected at all times.

Umpires must be able to travel away from the home base for a good portion of the year. It also helps to like traveling and living out of a suitcase.

Unions/Associations

Umpires work with the National League (NL) and American League (AL). Individuals also work with the Office for Baseball Umpire Development (OBUD). This organization holds development programs for Umpires and maintains standards within the industry.

Tips for Entry

1. If you are interested in being an Umpire, you must go to an Umpire training school. The names of these schools can be located in the Appendixes section. Contact them to find out application procedures.
2. Watch Umpires at professional games live or on television. This will give you some insight into how they make their calls.
3. Volunteer to act as Umpire for youth games or Little League. This will help you determine if you want to make a career commitment to the profession.
4. You might want to talk to an Umpire, either amateur or professional, to get insight into the career.

UMPIRE/AMATEUR—SCHOLASTIC BASEBALL

CAREER PROFILE

Duties: Officiating at baseball games; controlling the game; making calls; interpreting plays.

Alternate Title(s): Ump.; Baseball Official; Official.

Salary Range: 0 to $150 + per game

Employment Prospects: Good

Best Geographical Location(s) for Position: Positions located throughout the country.

Prerequisites:

Education or Training—No formal educational requirement; some schools and colleges may require official training or certification.

Experience—Experience playing or watching baseball needed.

Special Skills and Personality Traits—Thick skinned; ability to deal with stress and tension; knowledge of game of baseball; ability to deal with others; fair; consistent; even tempered.

CAREER LADDER

```
┌─────────────────────────────┐
│      Umpire for             │
│ College or University Games │
└─────────────────────────────┘

┌─────────────────────────────┐
│      Umpire for             │
│   Junior High School        │
│   or High School Games      │
└─────────────────────────────┘

┌─────────────────────────────┐
│   Little League Umpire      │
│           or                │
│       Entry Level           │
└─────────────────────────────┘
```

Position Description

Baseball Umpires working in amateur or scholastic situations are responsible for officiating at the games. Individuals may officiate at various levels, from Little League through junior high school, high school, and college.

The Umpire, Ump., or Game Official, as he or she may be called, is responsible for controlling the baseball game. Each game may have two or three Umpires. One is always positioned behind home plate. The others may be out in the field or at the bases. Together they try to make sure that each game is played fairly and consistent with the rules of the sport. In order to accomplish this, the Umpire must know the rules, regulations, and policies to the letter and be able to interpret them. One of the biggest mistakes an Umpire can make is not being consistent in his or her calls.

Many Umpires learn how to officiate by watching others do the same job. Others feel more comfortable performing their duties after attending clinics, workshops, and seminars on officiating and interpretation. Still others read and depend on rule books put out by associations and leagues.

Before each game the Umpire holds a pregame conference with the captains and/or coaches of both teams. During this conference or meeting, the individual goes over the rules, regulations, and policies that must be adhered to. Any questions by either side are discussed at this time. The Official also is given a line-up for each team.

The Umpire is the individual who calls out the familiar "play ball" at the beginning of each game. Once that call is made, he or she watches the game and each play carefully. He or she guides and controls the game from the beginning to the end.

One of the functions of the Umpire is to call balls, strikes, and fouls. The individual is responsible for making decisions and interpreting rules during the game. In the game of baseball, whatever the Umpire's decision, it stands. He or she is totally responsible for what happens on the field.

The Umpire's decision or call, however, is often controversial. Both sides may try to get him or her to change the call. Umpires, too, may disagree with each other. Individuals must remain calm, cool, and collected during these situations. They must also be able to handle unruly fans.

Baseball Umpires may work anytime a game is scheduled. They may officiate at an weekday afternoon game, an evening game, or on the weekends. Individuals must have the flexibility to fit into this type of schedule.

Salaries

As this is a part-time profession, individuals are paid on a per-game basis. In some amateur situations the Umpire does not get paid at all. In others, such as in Little League games, he or she may receive $10 to $20 for acting as Umpire. The individual might be paid a fee of $25 to $150 in a high school or college game. Umpires working at tournaments or games hosted by the National College Athletic Association (NCAA) may receive slightly more.

Employment Prospects

Employment prospects are good for individuals who are qualified and fully trained. It should be noted that the majority of amateur and scholastic Umpires and Officials perform in this field as an avocation, not a vocation. Those aspiring to officiate in the sport full time must usually move up to the professional level.

Positions may be located throughout the country.

Advancement Prospects

Advancement prospects are fair for the Baseball Umpire. As the individual gains experience officiating at games, he or she may move up the career ladder by officiating at more prestigious games. For example, the Umpire may begin his or her career officiating at Little League games and move up to working at junior high school games. After a while, the individual may climb the career ladder by officiating at high schools, colleges, and universities. The top level an Umpire can reach is officiating in the professionals at a major league game.

Education and Training

There is no formal educational requirement for Baseball Umpires in an amateur or scholastic setting. Usually, however, people perform this job in addition to having a full-time career in either a similar or a totally different field. Educational backgrounds of Umpires vary; some hold high school diplomas while others have doctorates.

Officials for some local games may just need a complete knowledge of the game, its rules, and regulations. Others officiating at many high schools and college games must have some sort of training from a baseball officiating camp, clinic, or seminar.

Experience/Skills/Personality Traits

Umpires working in baseball must be very thick skinned. No matter what decision the Umpire makes or how fair it seems, someone is usually not happy. Individuals who want to be friends with everyone should not be Umpires. There is a lot of stress and tension in this job. Individuals must understand that at the beginning and be able to deal with it without getting flustered. They should also be able to take criticism without letting it get to them personally.

The Umpire must have a total knowledge of baseball and all its rules, regulations, and policies. He or she must be diplomatic and firm. The individual must have the ability to make good, consistent, and quick judgments in game situations and stick to them. He or she should be confident in his or her decisions.

Communications skills are important. The Umpire must also have the ability to deal well with others, including officials who may have their own point of view about a call as well as players and fans.

The individual should be fair and consistent in his or her judgments. This is not the time to take sides. It is imperative that the Umpire be calm and even tempered and not lose his or her head during a call.

Most Umpires love the game. They may have been amateur ball players or may watch baseball every chance they get.

Unions/Associations

One of the major associations for amateur and scholastic Baseball Umpires is the National Association of Leagues, Umpires and Scorers (NALUS). Individuals may also be members of Little League Baseball (LLB) or Pony Baseball (PB).

Tips for Entry

1. Learn about the game of baseball as completely as possible. Know all the rules, regulations, and policies.
2. You can often get experience by volunteering your services as an Umpire to work with children's and other nonprofit organizations.
3. Take training courses, seminars, workshops, and clinics in umpiring. These courses will help keep you up on the newest rules as well as give you additional opportunities to make contacts.
4. Read rule books and training manuals on the subject. These will help you learn more about being a good Umpire.
5. Watch Umpires in action in both amateur and professional baseball. This will give you insight into the profession and teach you how other Umpires perform their job.

PRO FOOTBALL REFEREE

CAREER PROFILE

Duties: Officiating at professional football games; making sure rules and regulations are followed; calling fouls and imposing penalties.

Alternate Title(s): Official; Ref.

Salary Range: $600 to $2,500 per game

Employment Prospects: Poor

Best Geographical Location(s) for Position: Areas hosting professional football teams.

Prerequisites:

Education or Training—No formal educational requirements; training in refereeing and officiating game necessary.

Experience—Experience as a varsity college football referee necessary.

Special Skills and Personality Traits—Total knowledge of rules and regulations of pro football; fair; consistent; self-confident; ability to control emotions; calm, cool, and collected; thick skinned.

CAREER LADDER

```
┌─────────────────────────┐
│   Pro Football Referee  │
│      Assigned to        │
│   More Prestigious Games│
└─────────────────────────┘

┌─────────────────────────┐
│   Pro Football Referee  │
└─────────────────────────┘

┌─────────────────────────┐
│  College Football Referee│
└─────────────────────────┘
```

Position Description

Football Referees working in the pros are responsible for officiating at football games for professional teams. While high school games usually employ four Officials and colleges may use five or six, each professional game utilizes the services of seven Officials. Each individual is responsible for a specific officiating position on the field. For example, the person may officiate as a Referee, a headline judge, an umpire, line judge, backfield judge, or a side judge. An individual usually handles one position during a playing season. The Referee may stay in that position or request a change for the next season.

The main function of all Football Referees is to referee the game and make sure all the rules and regulations are followed. Individuals call fouls as they occur and impose penalties on players. The Referee is also expected to decide disputes within the game's framework according to the established regulations.

The main difference between officiating in professional and amateur or scholastic games is that if an individual makes a mistake in a call in a scholastic game, most people involved in football will never know about it. If the same mistake occurs in a pro game, the entire industry might learn about it. It could be televised, sportscasters might comment on it, and sports reporters would probably write about it in newspaper sports sections.

As pro football is usually played only once a week in an area, Pro Football Referees also work only once a week. Games may take place during the evenings or on weekends. The playing season is about four months.

Salaries

Earnings for Professional Football Referees can range from $600 to $2,500 a game. The major factor affecting the differences in salary levels is the individual's experience. As football games are not played every day of the week, most Professional Football Referees hold down full-time jobs in addition to refereeing. These other jobs may be in sports-related fields or may be in areas totally out of the sports industry.

Employment Prospects

Employment prospects are poor for Professional Football Referees. There are many more individuals who want to officiate at games than there are games. This is not to say that a Football Ref. cannot break into the pros. If the individual is good at the job, obtains a great deal of experience, and is willing to persevere, an opportunity may eventually open up.

Advancement Prospects

Once an individual makes it into officiating in the pros, advancement will mean that the Ref. is assigned to officiate at more prestigious games. Being assigned to work in the Super-bowl, for example, would be a step up the career ladder for most individuals. Advancement is attained mostly by being skilled at the job and by obtaining additional experience.

Education and Training

There is no formal educational requirement to become a Pro Football Referee. Some individuals on the job have a high school diploma; others have gone through law school. As noted, most individuals have another job in addition to working as a Referee. Educational requirements, therefore, depend on the individual's other occupation.

At the beginning of a Football Referee's career, the individual must go through a licensing procedure administered by the Professional Football Referees Association. Usually this involves reading rule, regulation, and policy books; attending training sessions; and taking an examination.

Experience/Skills/Personality Traits

In order to become a Pro Football Referee, an individual must move up the ranks. Most Refs. start working in the midget games, then go on to officiate at junior high and high school games. At that point, those aspiring to work in the pros begin officiating at college football games. An individual must have at least ten years experience refereeing varsity college football before applying to the National Football League (NFL) to move into the pros. By this time, the Referee knows all the rules and regulations of the game. It is also preferred that Pro Referees be over the age of 35. This gives them sufficient time to gain needed experience in the game.

After individuals apply to work pro games, they are asked to submit a schedule of college games where they will be officiating. Retired NFL officials, called observers, then scout the various college referees and observe the way they handle themselves, their job, and the game. It may take from two to four years from the time college Refs. fill in applications until the NFL decides they are ready. At that time psychological tests are given to the individual to make sure that they are mentally and emotionally prepared for refereeing important pro games.

Referees must be fair people. They need the ability to make quick, accurate judgments. Individuals should be self-confident and sure of their decisions.

Referees must be able to control their own emotions, especially when others have lost control. Individuals should be even tempered and able to deal with situations in a calm, cool, and collected manner.

Referees should be able to command respect for their judgment and work. Individuals must realize that they are not in these positions to be liked but to be respected and to keep the game fairly regulated. As in all officiating positions, it is important that Referees be thick skinned. Many of the calls and decisions they make will make someone unhappy.

Unions/Associations

There is no bargaining union for Professional Football Referees. Individuals belong to the Professional Football Referees Association. This organization works on behalf of the Referees to keep the standards of the profession high and provides professional and educational guidance and support.

Tips for Entry

1. Get as much experience refereeing games as you can. Start by volunteering to officiate at youth or community games. Go on to junior high school, high school, and so on. The more experience you have, the better you will be.
2. See if there is a chapter of your state's interscholastic athletic association near you and attend meetings. They can help you in many ways by offering information, training in officiating, guidance, and support.
3. Talk to a few football Referees working your school's games. Most will be happy to share their experience and knowledge.
4. Local school and college football coaches often will help you get into officiating.

AMATEUR/SCHOLASTIC FOOTBALL REFEREE

CAREER PROFILE

Duties: Officiating at amateur football games; making sure rules and regulations of game are followed; deciding disputes.

Alternate Title(s): Ref.; Active Referee; Associate Ref.; Cadet Football Referee; Football Official

Salary Range: $10 to $400 per game

Employment Prospects: Good

Best Geographical Location(s) for Position: Positions are located throughout the country in areas that host amateur and/or scholastic football.

Prerequisites:

Education or Training—Some positions may require amateur football officials' training; others require full knowledge of game rules and regulations.

Experience—Experience refereeing preferred for most positions.

Special Skills and Personality Traits—Knowledge of amateur football rules and regulations; decisive; confident; articulate; physically fit; even tempered.

CAREER LADDER

```
┌─────────────────────────────────────┐
│  Amateur/Scholastic Football Referee │
│                  at                  │
│       More Prestigious Games         │
└─────────────────────────────────────┘

┌─────────────────────────────────────┐
│  Amateur/Scholastic Football Referee │
└─────────────────────────────────────┘

┌─────────────────────────────────────┐
│           Football Player            │
└─────────────────────────────────────┘
```

Position Description

An Amateur/Scholastic Football Referee is responsible for officiating at amateur and/or scholastic football games. The individual's main function is to make sure that the rules and regulations of the game are followed. He or she is also required to decide disputes according to the established regulations of the game.

These rules are usually set up in a guide or regulation book. The individual must study these books and know every regulation and policy to the letter. Football Refs. must be aware when a player has committed a violation and how it affects the play. He or she must then decide whether or not to call a violation or let it go. It is important for the Ref. to be consistent in calling all violations. He or she can show no favoritism to either team. While a Referee is not the most popular person at a game, a fair individual earns the respect of most teams.

Amateur/Scholastic Football Referees may work in a variety of settings. They may referee junior or varsity high school football games, college games, or games in any other amateur situation.

Many Amateur Football Referees also serve various community youth football programs. Refs. who have a great deal of experience may officiate at championship games.

Depending on the specific situation, an individual may obtain a position as an Amateur Football Referee just by knowing the game and rules of football. Other positions may require that an individual is licensed, has passed examinations, and has received formal training from a football official's association.

While the Referee must have a thorough knowledge of the rules and regulations, he or she must also know how to interpret them. He or she must be able to do this quickly, consistently, and confidently. There is no room for indecision as an Amateur Football Official.

The Ref. should also keep abreast of rule and policy changes as they occur. Many Amateur Referees belong to local and state organizations that advise them of these changes. Individuals may be required to attend a number of meetings put on by these associations to help individuals improve their technique and offer a solid knowledge of the game.

Amateur/Scholastic Football Referees may work irregular hours. Games may take place during late afternoons, evenings, and on weekends. There can be a great deal of stress in this type of position. No matter what the call on a violation is, one side is usually upset. When a championship is on the line, there can be even more stress. The Ref. must have the ability to know he or she is right and stick with that decision even though people are yelling, screaming, and in some cases, calling names.

Salaries

Compensation for Amateur Football Referees varies depending on a number of things, including the geographic location, the individual's experience, and the type of game he or she is officiating at. Fees for Refs. working on a per-service basis will range from $10 to $25 per game for individuals officiating at midget or junior high games; $25 to $50 per game for those officiating at the high school level; and $50 to $400 for Referees officiating at college games.

Employment Prospects

Employment prospects are good for part-time Amateur and Scholastic Football Referees in the midget, junior high, and high school levels. Many areas are in desperate need of trained people. It may become more difficult for individuals to find employment officiating in varsity college settings.

Advancement Prospects

For an Amateur Football Referee to achieve career advancement, he or she has to move up to a higher level of the sport. For example, the Referee officiating at junior high school games moves up to officiating at high school games. The individual at the high school level may advance to the junior college level and then to varsity college football. Refs. who know the rules and regulations and are consistent and fair to both sides have a good chance at climbing the career ladder.

Education and Training

There is not usually any formal educational requirement to get a job as an Amateur Football Referee. Training requirements vary from position to position. In certain situations, the only requirement is that the individual understand amateur football and its rules and regulations.

Those hoping to advance, however, should try to obtain some type of amateur football officiating training. Many state and/or local amateur football associations hold training and interpretation meetings and seminars. At these seminars individuals can learn how to improve their officiating techniques as well as attain a greater knowledge of the rules and regulations of amateur football.

Certain associations also require that their officials take annual examinations in order to be certified as Amateur Football Referees.

Experience/Skills/Personality Traits

Many Amateur Football Referees have had personal experience playing the game themselves. Others have worked as coaches. The individual must have a total understanding and knowledge of the game and the rules. He or she will be making decisions based on these rules.

The Amateur Football Referee must be physically fit. He or she moves back and forth on the field in order to view the game. The Ref. must be decisive and confident. The individual must be able to make a decision quickly according to the rules and regulations of the game and have confidence in the decision.

Even in amateur games, tempers on both sides often flare. It is important that the individual be even tempered and able to speak calmly and articulately.

Unions/Associations

Amateur and Scholastic Football Referees may belong to a number of associations that provide training, and educational guidance and bring those interested in the sport on this level together. These might include the Football Officials Association, the National Association of Sports Officials, and the National Federation Interscholastic Officials Association. Individuals might also work with schools that are members of the National Association of Intercollegiate Athletics and/or the National Collegiate Athletic Association.

Tips for Entry

1. These positions are often advertised in the local newspaper classified sections. Look under heading classifications of "Sports Official," "Football," "Amateur Sports," "Scholastic Sports," or "Referee."
2. Many schools are in need of part-time officials. Call all the high schools and colleges that host football teams to check out their needs.
3. While it is not always necessary, try to obtain training from a state or local football officials association. This will put you a step above someone who doesn't have the proper training.
4. Join sports-oriented associations and organizations. This will help you build contacts.

AMATEUR/SCHOLASTIC BASKETBALL REFEREE

CAREER PROFILE

Duties: Officiating at amateur and scholastic basketball games; enforcing game rules and regulations; mediating court and other game disputes.

Alternate Title(s): Official; Ref.

Salary Range: $25 to $750+ per game

Employment Prospects: Good

Best Geographical Location(s) for Position: Positions may be located throughout the country.

Prerequisites:

Education or Training—Certification required for some positions; others require only total knowledge of game rules and regulations.

Experience—College conference games require officiating experience:

Special Skills and Personality Traits—Physically fit; self-confident; good judgment; knowledge of rules and regulations of amateur basketball; ability to deal with stress.

CAREER LADDER

```
┌─────────────────────────────┐
│    Amateur/Scholastic       │
│    Basketball Referee       │
│          for                │
│   More Prestigious Games    │
└─────────────────────────────┘

┌─────────────────────────────┐
│    Amateur/Scholastic       │
│    Basketball Referee       │
└─────────────────────────────┘

┌─────────────────────────────┐
│    Basketball Player, Fan,  │
│          or                 │
│       Entry Level           │
└─────────────────────────────┘
```

Position Description

Amateur or Scholastic Basketball Referees are responsible for officiating at amateur and scholastic basketball games. The function of the Ref. is to enforce rules and regulations of the game. Most basketball games have two Referees officiating. Together, the two make judgments about disputes that occur during the game.

Amateur Basketball Referees may work in a variety of settings. They may officiate at an area youth league game or at a small junior or varsity high school event. Individuals may also officiate at small college games as well as schools belonging to the National Collegiate Athletic Association. Despite the setting, Referee duties are usually very similar. He or she must make sure that the rules and regulations of the game are adhered to.

The individual usually has to study rule and regulation books provided by one of the amateur and scholastic basketball associations. It is extremely important that the Ref. know and understand the rules, policies, and regulations of the game. Without total knowledge of this information, he or she is not able to make correct calls. This can cause a great many difficulties.

Depending on the situation, the Amateur Basketball Referee must usually attend a good number of seminars and workshops to improve his or her officiating skills, keep up with rule changes, and continually learn more about the game. This is especially true of individuals who officiate at larger schools and colleges holding major tournaments and championships.

Most Amateur and Scholastic Basketball Referees do not consider officiating as their main source of income. They work games part time while holding other full-time jobs in related or unrelated areas.

Refereeing offers individuals the opportunity to work in the sport and make money too. Hours are usually irregular. Games may be played anytime, from early Saturday morning to a weekday evening. The individual needs to have flexibility in his or her main job to be able to referee at games.

This is not the type of job to have if you want everyone to like you. Making an unpopular call in a hometown crowd is not easy, but often necessary. Like most refereeing positions,

Amateur Basketball Refs. may also be put under a great deal of stress and tension. Individuals must have the ability to deal with these situations.

Salaries

Amateur and Scholastic Basketball Referees are usually paid on a per-game basis. Salaries vary depending on the type of game the individual is officiating at and his or her experience. Individual can earn from $25 to $75 for officiating at a high school basketball game. Compensation for officiating at college games can range from $40 to $750 plus, with the larger earnings going to individuals working important tournaments and championships.

Employment Prospects

Employment prospects for Amateur and Scholastic Basketball Referees are good. It must be kept in mind, however, that most people officiate at amateur games besides having another profession. This work might be in sports or in a totally different field.

Employment possibilities are located throughout the country in small schools and colleges that have basketball teams. As individuals gain training and experience, they may also find opportunities to officiate at larger colleges and those belonging to the National Collegiate Athletic Association. Jobs may also be found with area youth organizations.

Many colleges now have active men's and women's basketball teams. While a woman can officiate at a man's basketball game and vice versa, the addition of women's teams adds more work opportunities to the sport.

Advancement Prospects

Amateur and Scholastic Basketball Referees can advance their careers by officiating at more prestigious games, championships, and tournaments. Individuals who are good at what they do can make a name for themselves and climb the career ladder.

Education and Training

Educational and training requirements vary depending on the specific position. For example, while a high school Basketball Referee might just be required to know the game and its rules, an individual aspiring to become a Basketball Referee for a college game might need some sort of certification. Generally, this certification is mandatory to officiate in National Collegiate Athletic Association (NCCA) games.

This certification and training can be obtained by attending classes, seminars, camps, and workshops sponsored by various basketball organizations and associations. Officiating skills may also be taught in classes at colleges offering majors in sports administration and physical education.

Colleges that have intensive sports programs may also offer training programs.

Experience/Skills/Personality Traits

Basketball Referees, both professional and amateur, must be in extremely good physical condition. They generally run back and forth checking out plays during the entire game.

Individuals in officiating capacities must possess total self-confidence in themselves and their decisions. Basketball Refs. should be able to act quickly and calmly. Good judgment is a must. They need to be even tempered and articulate. Successful Basketball Referees do not yell and scream and are not easily shaken.

Amateur Basketball Referees must have a total understanding of the game and knowledge of all rules and regulations. While the Amateur Basketball Referee does not need to have played the game, he or she should certainly at least enjoy the sport.

Most college conference games are worked by individuals who have had a great deal of officiating experience.

Unions/Associations

Amateur Basketball Referees may belong to a number of local, state, and national associations that provide training, certification, and professional guidance. These include the National Federation of State High School Associations (NFSHSA), the International Association of Approved Basketball Officials (IAABO), the U.S.A. Basketball (USAB), the Eastern College Basketball Association (ECBA), and the Eastern Women's Amateur Basketball League of the AAU (EW-ABL/AAU).

Tips for Entry

1. Contact associations to find out when they are holding training sessions.
2. Apply for admission at a "summer camp" seminar for Basketball Referees. (Check the Appendix section for seminar information.) Seminars such as these will train you, give you confidence, and help you make contacts in the industry.
3. Amateur Basketball Referee positions are often advertised in the local newspaper display and classified sections. Look under such heading classifications as "Basketball," "Sports," "Officiating," "Referee," or "School Athletics."
4. Call schools and colleges that host basketball teams and inquire about their officiating needs.
5. Volunteer your services for area youth basketball games. This will give you experience and help make important contacts.

CAREER OPPORTUNITIES IN SPORTS JOURNALISM

SPORTS WRITER

CAREER PROFILE

Duties: Reporting news in the sports world; writing articles and feature stories on sporting events; attending games, tournaments, activities, and other sports-related events.

Alternate Title(s): Sports Reporter; Beat Writer

Salary Range: $15,000 to $1,000,000+

Employment Prospects: Fair

Best Geographical Location(s) for Position: Positions may be located throughout the country.

Prerequisites:

Education or Training—Minimum of two-year college degree required; many positions require four-year college degree.

Experience—Writing experience necessary.

Special Skills and Personality Traits—Excellent writing skills; good communication skills; basic knowledge of sports; enjoy attending sporting events; articulate; personable; dependable.

CAREER LADDER

```
┌─────────────────────────────┐
│      Sports Writer          │
│  for Larger, More Prestigious│
│        Publication          │
│            or               │
│     Sports Columnist        │
└─────────────────────────────┘

┌─────────────────────────────┐
│      Sports Writer          │
└─────────────────────────────┘

┌─────────────────────────────┐
│      College Student        │
│            or               │
│  Journalist in Other Field  │
└─────────────────────────────┘
```

Position Description

Sports Writers work for newspapers, magazines, or other periodicals. They are responsible for reporting news in the sports world, keeping the fans informed about scores, and writing both routine stories and feature articles on sports. Individuals may work for small local newspapers, larger metropolitan publications, or regional or national magazines.

Depending on the type of publication they work for, Sports Writers may write specifically about just one sport or may write stories on a variety of sports. A Sports Writer may cover a baseball game one day, a boxing match that night, and a golf tournament the next morning.

While good writers can often research almost any subject, it is helpful for a Sports Writer to both enjoy sports and know something about the field. Much of his or her time is spent attending games, tournaments, and matches, and talking to people in the sports industry.

When attending games and other sports events, the Sports Writer often sits in a special press section or press box with other Sports Writers, columnists, sportscasters, and photographers from other media.

Before the event, the team public relations person or publicist may pass out press releases, biographies, press kits, and other background information. The Sports Writer looks these over and decides what information to use in his or her story.

In addition to attending and watching events, the Sports Writer is responsible for talking to athletes, team players, coaches, and managers in order to gather material for articles. He or she may do this before an event, after it, or both. The Sports Writer also keeps track of scores, game highlights, and fan reactions.

The Sports Writer or Sports Reporter, as he or she may be called, is responsible for writing an article reporting the events in whichever game he or she is assigned. He or she might write a number of articles on events leading up to a specific game, the athletes, reactions after a game, and so on.

In certain situations, the Sports Writer writes the story or outlines it at the arena where the event is taking place and calls it in on the phone or faxes the article directly to the editor.

At times, the Sports Writer is responsible for developing sports-related feature stories for the publication. Subject matter could be anything from a hometown ball player making it in the big leagues, to a story on the winner of a local marathon, or an interview with a sports hero.

Sportswriters are expected to attend press conferences scheduled by sports teams and any other sports-related groups.

In areas that host professional sports teams, larger newspapers may assign an individual working in the sports department to cover the day-by-day activities of a specific team. These people are known as Beat Writers. The Sports Writers in these positions must report the news of every game played by that team.

Beat Writers are responsible for turning in a standard amount of copy about their assigned team even when there is little to write about. It is imperative that they build a good working relationship with the players, coaches, managers, etc., on the team they are covering. The Sports Writers can then turn to these people when they need extra copy or to obtain comments and/or quotes regarding the team or other related topics.

Sportswriters working for small local newspapers often are responsible for reporting news on school, college, and other amateur sports as well as professional sports. They may have additional writing and reporting responsibilities outside the sports field.

For an individual who loves being around sports, the job of a Sports Writer is ideal. He or she is paid to attend and watch ball games, boxing matches, wrestling tournaments, golf tournaments, horse races, and the like. The Sports Writer has the opportunity to meet athletes, team members, and coaches, and often socializes with them. In this way, he or she learns what is happening first in the sports world.

The individual in this position often works long, irregular hours. He or she may work at night and on weekends. The Sports Writer is usually responsible to the sports editor of the publication. In smaller newspapers, he or she may be responsible directly to the editor of paper.

Salaries

Salaries for Sports Writers vary greatly from job to job. Variables include the type of publication the individual is working for, its location, and his or her experience and responsibilities.

Sports Writers just starting out or those writing for local weeklies may earn salaries ranging from $15,000 to $18,000. Those who work for daily newspapers or monthly magazines may earn from $18,000 to $85,000 plus, depending on their experience and following. A very small number of Sports Writers with their own columns command salaries of $1,000,000 or more.

Employment Prospects

Employment prospects are good for Sports Writers. Almost every newspaper throughout the country has at least one Sports Writer. Many of the larger newspapers have an entire sports department on staff. There are also a number of local, regional, and national magazines and periodicals that need Sports Writers.

Individuals can often enter the field of sports writing by working at local and regional newspapers. Prospects get more difficult as the individual advances his or her career.

Advancement Prospects

Advancement prospects are fair for Sports Writers. The next step up the career ladder for individuals is to find a position writing in a larger, more prestigious newspaper or magazine. The higher the career level the individual reaches, the more difficult advancement becomes.

For example, after gaining some experience, those working for a weekly newspaper usually have no problem finding a job reporting sports in a daily paper. Individuals working in dailies have to locate positions in larger daily papers. Sports Writers working for newspapers in large cities often seek employment writing for national sports magazines.

Education and Training

While there are still a number of old-time Sports Writers hired years ago without a college background on staff at various papers throughout the country, most publications currently hiring expect some type of college background. Depending on the position, newspapers or magazines usually require a minimum of at least a two-year degree; most seek graduates of a four-year degree program.

Good choices for majors include journalism, English, public relations, and liberal arts. Any additional courses in writing are helpful as are those in sports studies, physical education, and the like.

Experience/Skills/Personality Traits

A Sports Writer needs to write well. He or she should have a good command of the English language, grammar, and be able to spell well. The individual should be able to write crisp, clean, informative copy. He or she should be able to spot an interesting story and to develop creative, unique angles for other articles.

The individual needs to be dependable and able to write quickly and meet deadlines. He or she may attend a game at night and have the story in for the early-morning edition. The Sports Writer should have a basic understanding of the sport he or she is writing about. An interest in sports is helpful.

The individual should be articulate with good verbal communication skills. He or she should be be friendly, personable, and easy to get along with and talk to.

Unions/Associations

Depending on the publication, Sports Writers may belong to local bargaining unions. Individuals might also belong to a trade association called the National Sportscasters and Sportswriters Association. This organization provides a forum for those in the industry and offers professional guidance and support.

Tips for Entry

1. Look for freelance assignments. Try to come up with an interesting story or a new angle on an old story. Then call, write, or visit the sports editor of your local newspaper and see if they might be interested. You may have to write on "spec," which means that you will have to come up with an idea, write the story, submit it, and see if the newspaper wants it. If they do use it, you will be paid. If they don't, you will at least have gained some experience.

2. Part-time positions are often available, especially in weekly newspapers and some of the smaller dailies.

3. Look in the display or classified section of newspapers under heading classifications of "Sportswriter," "Journalist," "Sports," "Reporter," or "Writer."

4. Get as much experience as you can writing. Become a member of your college's newspaper. If you can find a summer or part-time job working at a newspaper, take it, even if it isn't in the sports department. The experience will be worth it.

5. Offer to cover school sports for your local newspaper. You may not get paid very much (or not at all), but you will have a sportswriting job to put on your résumé.

6. Many newspapers and magazines offer internships or training programs. Ask for at least part of your training to be in the sports department.

7. Begin to put together a "portfolio" of your best work. When one of your stories or articles appears in a school or local newspaper, cut it out and have it photocopied, making sure the name of the publication and date are included. You can also include good writing pieces that you have done for college. These can help illustrate your talents when applying for a job.

8. Search for a position on the Internet. Go to a job or career site and type in keywords such as "sports reporter," "sports writer," or "reporter."

SPORTS COLUMNIST

CAREER PROFILE

Duties: Writing a sports column on a regular basis for a publication.

Alternate Title(s): Columnist

Salary Range: $12,000 to $1,000,000+

Employment Prospects: Fair

Best Geographical Location(s) for Position: Positions may be located throughout the country.

Prerequisites:

Education or Training—Most positions require a four-year college degree.
Experience—Writing experience necessary.
Special Skills and Personality Traits—Excellent writing skills; good communication skills; creative; enjoy sports; articulate; ability to work under pressure; personable.

CAREER LADDER

```
┌─────────────────────────────┐
│      Sports Columnist       │
│       for Larger,           │
│  More Prestigious Publication│
└─────────────────────────────┘

┌─────────────────────────────┐
│      Sports Columnist       │
└─────────────────────────────┘

┌─────────────────────────────┐
│        Sports Writer        │
└─────────────────────────────┘
```

Position Description

Sports Columnists may work for newspapers, magazines, or other periodicals. Their main responsibility is to write a column on a regular basis on some facet of the sports industry. The columns usually have a title. The Sports Columnist has a byline, and often, a head-and-shoulder photograph of the individual appears.

Individuals may write their column daily, once a week, biweekly, or monthly, depending on the publication. If they are very successful and popular, Sports Columnists may have their columns syndicated. This means that the column is bought and published by more than one publication. The writings of Sports Columnists may appear in small local newspapers, larger metropolitan publications, and regional or national magazines and papers.

While sports writers, as a rule, are responsible for reporting the sports news as it happens, the work of Sports Columnists usually reflects the writer's opinion in some way. Sports Columnists may write about one specific event and their feelings on the subject or may cover a number of newsworthy subjects on which they have varied opinions.

One of the main differences between a general sports writer and a Sports Columnist is that the former is usually assigned stories by editors while the latter must develop ideas for his or her column. Sports Columnists use their columns to write feature stories about athletes, sports events, specific sports, and the like. They constantly have to come up with and develop unique story ideas and feature articles about sports.

Depending on the type of publication they work for, Sports Columnists may write about just one sport or may create columns on sports in general. For example, Sports Columnist and newscaster Howard Cossell is remembered by many specifically for his stories about the boxing world.

Sports Columnists spend a lot of time on the phone talking to people who are in the sports industry. These might include athletes, team owners, fighters, other sportswriters, sportscasters, and public relations and publicity people. They also often attend and watch sports-related events, from games and tournaments to boxing matches. The emergence of cable television has greatly increased the number of sports events that can be watched. If an individual cannot be at an event or watch it on television, he or she can videotape it for later reference.

The Sports Columnist also spends a great deal of time talking to athletes, team players, coaches, and managers in person. Part of the job may include traveling to where these important sports figures and the sporting events are.

As a rule, Sports Columnists are totally sports oriented. They are the type of people who would watch sports, talk sports, and know about sports whether or not they worked in the industry.

When attending live events, Sports Columnists usually sit in a special press section or press box with other sports writers, sportscasters, and photographers. They also attend a great many press conferences, press parties, and dinners.

For those who love everything about sports, a Sports Columnist job is the ideal occupation. The individual is paid to talk and socialize with people he or she admires, attend sporting events and parties, and then give his or her opinion in a column.

Although the Sports Columnist may write only one column a week or one a day, he or she still works long, irregular hours gathering information for the piece. The individual in this position may be responsible to the sports editor or directly to the editor or publisher of the publication.

Salaries

Earnings of Sports Columnists can range greatly from person to person, depending on a number of variables. These include the size and type of publication the individual is working for and its location. Other variables include the experience and responsibilities of the individual as well as how popular and well known he or she is.

Sports Columnists just starting out or those writing for local weeklies may earn salaries ranging from $12,000 to $17,000. Those who work for daily newspapers or monthly magazines may earn from $15,000 to $1,000,000 plus. The syndication of a column by a major publication can also lead to earnings well above $1,000,000 for a popular Sports Columnist.

Employment Prospects

Employment prospects are fair for Sports Columnists. In many smaller papers, the publication's sports writer also is the Sports Columnist. Opportunities exist at almost every level from small, local newspapers to regional and national magazines and periodicals.

Individuals can often enter the field more easily by seeking a Sports Columnist position at a small local paper.

Some individuals may also write sports columns for sports oriented web sites on the Internet.

Advancement Prospects

Advancement prospects are fair for Sports Columnists. It is necessary to build a strong following in order to climb the career ladder. The next step for most Sports Columnists is to locate a position with a larger, more prestigious newspaper or magazine. The higher the career level the individual reaches, the more difficult advancement becomes.

Some Sports Columnists advance their careers by offering their column for syndication. This in turn leads to additional exposure in more publications and higher earnings.

Education and Training

Most publications today expect a sports writer or Sports Columnist to have a four-year college degree. While there are a number of Sports Columnists who may not have a degree, they are either very well known or have built up a following as a retired athlete, sportscaster, commentator, and so on.

Good choices for majors for this career might include journalism, English, public relations, and/or liberal arts. Any

additional courses in writing as well as those in sports studies and physical education would be helpful.

Experience/Skills/Personality Traits

A Sports Columnist should have a good command of the English language and grammar and be able to spell well. He or she should be able to write crisply, clearly, and concisely. The ability to develop creative angles is imperative.

The individual should have a keen interest in sports. Contacts with athletes and those involved in the sports industry are necessary to get scoops on information.

The individual needs good communication skills, verbally as well as on paper. While there are some Sports Columnists whom athletes don't particularly like, those seeking to enter the field should be friendly, personable, and easy to get along with and talk to.

Unions/Associations

Depending on the publication and other writing responsibilities, Sports Columnists may belong to local bargaining unions. Individuals might also belong to a trade association called the National Sportscasters and Sportswriters Association. This organization provides a forum for those in the industry and offers professional guidance and support.

Tips for Entry

1. Look in the display or classified section of newspapers under heading classifications of "Sports Columnist," "Sportswriter," "Journalist," "Sports," "Reporter," or "Writer."
2. Get as much experience as you can writing. Become a member of your college's newspaper. If you can find a summer or part-time job working at a newspaper, even if it isn't in the sports department, take it. The experience will be worth it.
3. Offer to cover school sports for your local newspaper. You may not get paid very much (or not at all), but you will have a sports-writing job to put on your résumé.
4. Many newspapers and magazines offer internships or training programs. Ask for at least part of your training to be in the sports department.
5. Begin to put together a "portfolio" of your best work. When one of your stories or articles appears in a school or local newspaper, cut it out and have it photocopied, making sure the name of the publication and date are included. You can also include good writing pieces that you have done for college. These examples can help illustrate your talents when applying for a job.
6. Write a sports column on "spec" for your local or school newspaper. Develop an interesting, unique angle to vent your opinion. Call, write, or visit the sports editor see if the paper might be interested. Even if they don't use it, you will have made an important contact.
7. Part-time positions are often available, especially in weekly newspapers and some of the smaller dailies.

SPORTSCASTER/TELEVISION

CAREER PROFILE

Duties: Reporting sports news to television audience; anchoring the sports desk on news programs; determining what information should go into a sportscast; providing color commentary during games.

Alternate Title(s): Sports Reporter; Announcer

Salary Range: $18,000 to $1,000,000+

Employment Prospects: Fair

Best Geographical Location(s) for Position: Positions may be located throughout the country.

Prerequisites:

Education or Training—Four-year college degree sometimes required.

Experience—Broadcast and writing experience necessary.

Special Skills and Personality Traits—Clear speaking voice; writing skills; communication skills; knowledge of sports; articulate dependable.

CAREER LADDER

```
┌─────────────────────────────────┐
│         Sportscaster            │
│ at Larger, More Prestigious Station │
│       or Sports Director        │
└─────────────────────────────────┘

┌─────────────────────────────────┐
│     Television Sportscaster     │
└─────────────────────────────────┘

┌─────────────────────────────────┐
│        College Student,         │
│        Desk Assistant,          │
│ Sportswriter, or Sports Journalist │
│      Professional Player        │
└─────────────────────────────────┘
```

Position Description

Television Sportscasters are responsible for reporting the sports news on television. They may work for local, regional, or national television stations. Individuals may also work for public or cable television stations.

The Television Sportscaster keeps fans informed about game scores as well as happenings in the sports world. A Television Sportscaster usually reports on all sports.

He or she usually is responsible for anchoring the sports desk on news programs. Depending on the job, the number of daily newscasts, and the size of the sports department, the individual may report sports news for all the station's newscasts, or may have specific spot. For example, the Sportscaster may anchor the sports desk on the nightly news or the midday report.

Television Sportscasters often go out into the field to cover the sports action. The individual may attend games, tournaments, matches, and bouts in a variety of sports. The Sportscaster may be required to interview athletes, managers, officials, or fans about specific events.

Most Sportscasters are avid sports fans who both enjoy sports and know a great deal about the industry. Sportscasters are fortunate to work in an environment they love. They attend sports events and interview people in the sports industry.

When attending games and other sports events, the Sportscaster may sit in a special press section or press box with other Sportscasters, writers, columnists, photographers, and press people. The Sportscaster may also be out on the field commenting on the game. Before or after games, he or she may do locker room interviews.

On occasion, the Sportscaster may be responsible for developing feature pieces on sports-related subjects or events. These features might cover a variety of areas. The Sportscaster may be required to develop the piece, research, interview, and also act as commentator.

The individual may write his or her own copy for the news report or may just read copy prepared by a writer. This usually depends on a number of variables, including the size of the sports department and the specific station and the writing talent of the Sportscaster.

Sportscasters may attend press conferences scheduled by sports teams and any other sports-related groups or may use video tape sections of the conference during his or her broadcast. The individual may also read and review wire service reports to determine what is relevant for news broadcasts.

Individuals may also be responsible for announcing the play-by-play action and doing color commentary. Many of the

Sportscasters who do this are former athletes with good communications skills.

Sportscasters working for small local stations often are responsible for reporting professional sports developments as well as news about school, college, and other amateur sports levels.

The work hours of a Sportscaster are difficult to determine. The individual may be required to attend luncheons, press parties, and conferences in the afternoon, attend sports events during the evening and on weekends, and still put together a sports spot for the television station. The Sportscaster is usually responsible to the sports director, news director, or the station manager.

Salaries

The salaries for Sportscasters vary greatly from job to job. Variables include the type of market the individual is working in, the specific station, and its location. Earnings also depend on the experience level, prestige, and duties of the individual.

Sportscasters who are working for local stations or those just beginning their career in television may have annual earnings from $18,000 to $20,000. Individuals with more experience and those working in larger markets may earn between $20,000 and $45,000. Sportscasters who have developed a large following and are working in a major market may have earnings of $150,000 plus. Some individuals who work nationwide earn over $1,000,000 a year. These positions, however, are extremely limited.

Employment Prospects

Employment prospects are fair for Sportscasters who are be willing to work on a local or regional level. As individuals aspire to work in larger markets, prospects become poorer.

Sportscaster hopefuls may find it easier to break in to the industry on a small, local level and work themselves up.

Advancement Prospects

Advancement prospects are fair for Sportscasters. Individuals who want to climb the career ladder find a position with a larger, more prestigious station. Unfortunately, it takes some time to achieve success in this industry. The higher the career level the individual reaches, the more difficult advancement becomes.

Another way for a Sportscaster to climb the career ladder is by becoming the sports director of a larger television station. However, many Sportscasters may not opt for this type of career advancement, as these positions may not always afford the individual an opportunity to be an on-air personality.

Education and Training

Competition is keen for positions as Sportscasters. Those with the best education will be better prepared for jobs. A four-year college degree with a major in communications is a good choice. A minor in sports administration or physical education might be helpful. Other possibilities for majors include journalism, English, or even liberal arts.

Courses, workshops, and seminars in writing, sports, and television are useful.

Experience/Skills/Personality Traits

Sportscasters come from a variety of backgrounds. Some individuals land a position with a local station right after graduation from college. Others worked in sports as radio announcers or newspaper sportswriters. Many come up the ranks from areas of the television broadcasting industry such as television sports writer, desk assistant, and others.

A Sportscaster needs a good, clear speaking voice. A command of the English language is necessary. The ability to write well is helpful. Individuals should be articulate and poised and be comfortable in front of a camera.

Dependability is necessary. No one will wait for a Sportscaster who doesn't appear for a live broadcast. The Sportscaster should have a basic understanding of the sport. An interest in sports is helpful but not always required.

The Sportscaster should have the ability to develop an on-air personality in order to build a viewer following.

Unions/Associations

Sportscasters may belong to a number of different bargaining unions depending on the specific position they hold and station they are working for. These might include the American Federation of Television and Radio Artists (AFTRA) or the Writers Guild of America (WGA). Individuals might also belong to trade association, such as the National Sportscasters and Sportswriters Association (NSSA), the American Sportscasters Association (ASA), and the Radio Television News Directors Association (RTNDA).

Tips for Entry

1. Work with your college television station even if you can't get into the sports department. Hands-on experience will be useful.
2. If your college does not have a television station, work on the radio station. Try to get as much experience working in broadcasting as you can.
3. Job availabilities may be located in the newspaper's display or classified section. Look under heading classifications of "Broadcasting," "Sportscaster," "Television," "Journalist," "Sports," "Reporter," or "Sports Writer."
4. Get experience writing. Most Sportscasters must write their own copy . . . at least at the beginning. Become a member of your college's newspaper. If you can, find a summer or part-time job working at a newspaper even if it isn't in the sports department. The experience will be worth it.
5. Look for a summer or part-time job at a local or cable radio station.
6. Many television stations and associations offer internships or training programs. Internships will give you on-the-job training and the opportunity to make important contacts.

SPORTSCASTER/RADIO

CAREER PROFILE

Duties: Reporting sports news, scores, and events on the air; giving color commentary during games, tournaments, and matches.

Alternate Title(s): Sports Announcer

Salary Range: $15,000 to $750,000+

Employment Prospects: Good

Best Geographical Location(s) for Position: Positions may be located throughout the country.

Prerequisites:

Education or Training—Four-year college degree required for most positions; others may accept broadcasting school certificate.

Experience—Experience in college radio helpful but not always required.

Special Skills and Personality Traits—Good speaking voice; comfortable in front of microphone; knowledge of sports; communications skills; ability to write well.

CAREER LADDER

```
┌─────────────────────────────────┐
│      Radio Sportscaster         │
│  for More Prestigious Station   │
└─────────────────────────────────┘

┌─────────────────────────────────┐
│      Radio Sportscaster         │
└─────────────────────────────────┘

┌─────────────────────────────────┐
│        Sports Writer,           │
│      Radio Announcer,           │
│             or                  │
│        Entry Level              │
└─────────────────────────────────┘
```

Position Description

Radio Sportscasters are responsible for reporting the sports news and events on the radio. They may work for local, regional, or network radio stations. Individuals may also work for public radio.

In addition to music and talk formats, there are a number of radio stations whose format is totally sports related. This type of station arrived on the scene when people began to prefer listening to music on FM stereo radio. Owners of AM stations had to try to maintain a listening audience and save their stations. Many owners opted for talk radio. As talk radio became more popular, so did entire formats dedicated to sports talk.

Radio Sportscasters working at sports talk stations may have different duties and responsibilities depending on their job description. They may serve as a sports reporter, host a sports-oriented talk show, perform as a color commentator for sporting events, and interview sports personalities.

While those working at sports radio stations will have more specific duties, Sportscasters on music, general talk format, or news stations may have more general responsibilities.

Music-oriented radio stations may have only a small sports department. Individuals working there may be expected to perform more varied functions. These Sportscasters usually are responsible for reporting current sports news, developments, and scores. Sportscasters may be responsible for national sports news as well as local developments. Those working in smaller local stations may also be required to report school, college, and amateur sports news.

Most Radio Sportscasters do not specialize in just one sport, but instead report on all sporting events. However, some individuals may specialize in reporting on one sport, such as baseball or boxing. This usually occurs as the Sportscaster gains a larger following and prestige. Other individuals comment on games, tournaments, and matches as they occur in order to help listeners follow the action.

The Radio Sportscaster may be expected to anchor the sports reports during all newscasts in his or her shift. He or she may get one- to six- minute spots to do this. The individual may also be responsible for longer sports spots during the nightly news or the midday or morning report.

Many Radio Sportscasters have scheduled shows one or more times a week during which they may discuss all aspects of sports, receive call-ins, or have special in-studio guests.

In some situations, the Radio Sportscaster may go into the field to cover the sports action. The individual may attend games, tournaments, matches, and bouts in a variety of sports. The Sportscaster may be expected to interview athletes, managers, officials, or fans about specific events.

Individuals may attend press conferences scheduled by sports teams and any other sports-related groups. They may also obtain audio sections of the conference from other reporters who were at the press conference to use during their broadcast.

Sportscasters can obtain their information firsthand or may get it from the wire services. Organizations such as United Press International (UPI) and Associated Press (AP) have large news and sports staffs as well as freelance individuals who report all the up-to-the-minute developments. These reports go over a wire or Teletype and are printed out in thousands of news rooms and television and radio stations throughout the world. Most newspapers, magazines, and television and radio stations pay for this service, which they use daily in reporting the news, weather, and sports.

Radio Sportscasters usually are fans who enjoy sports and know a great deal about them. Individuals may get to attend games and other sports events as part of their job. They can also be out on the field commenting on the game. Before or after games, Radio Sportscasters often do locker room interviews.

On occasion, the Sportscaster is responsible for developing feature pieces on sports-related subjects or events. These features might cover a variety of areas. The Sportscaster may be required to develop the piece, research, and interview, or just act as commentator.

A great number of Radio Sportscasters write their own copy for the sports report. Some individuals, however, just read copy prepared by another writer. This usually depends on the size of the sports department, the specific station, and the writing talent of the Radio Sportscaster.

Radio Sportscasters usually work shifts. Individuals can be assigned to the early-morning, late-morning, afternoon, drive, evening, or night shift. Hours vary. In some stations shifts are three hours long, while in others individuals may work eight. Most of the time they are preparing for a sportscast, not actually on the air. Sportscasters may attend a slew of events when not on the air, such as games, tournaments, sports-oriented luncheons, press parties, and conferences. The Radio Sportscaster is usually responsible to the sports director, news director, or station manager.

Salaries

Earnings for Radio Sportscasters vary greatly from job to job. Variables include the type of market the individual is working in, the specific station, and its location. Other factors determining income include the Sportscaster's experience level, prestige, following, and duties.

Sportscasters who are working for local stations or those just beginning their careers in radio may have annual earnings from $15,000 to $17,000. Individuals who have more experience and those working in larger markets may earn between $18,000 and $45,000. Radio Sportscasters who have developed a large following and are working in a major market may earn $100,000 plus. Some individuals working for radio networks earn $750,000 a year or more. These people, however, are in the minority.

Radio Sportscasters may also augment their income by writing sports columns for papers or magazines.

Employment Prospects

Employment prospects are good for Radio Sportscasters who are willing to work on a local or regional level. When individuals aspire to work in larger markets, prospects become dimmer. Openings may be located throughout the country.

It is easier to break in to the industry on a small, local level and work up from there. Many smaller stations hire individuals with little or no experience. While the salaries in these situations are usually very low, the experience is worth the opportunity.

Advancement Prospects

Advancement prospects are fair for Radio Sportscasters. After obtaining some experience, a Radio Sportscaster may advance his or her career by locating a position with a larger, more prestigious station. This, in turn, usually leads to higher earnings. The higher the career level the individual reaches, the more difficult advancement becomes. It is not easy to break into the major market radio stations, but it can be done.

A Radio Sportscaster may also climb the career ladder by becoming the sports director of the same or a larger station.

Education and Training

Most radio stations, even small local ones, require a minimum of a four-year college degree. While any major may be acceptable, good choices might be communications, journalism, liberal arts, broadcasting, or English.

Courses, workshops, and seminars in writing, sports, broadcasting, radio, and communications are useful.

Experience/Skills/Personality Traits

In some stations, the Radio Sportscaster can be an entry-level position. In others, he or she must have had experience working at another station. A great majority of Radio Sportscasters worked on college radio stations while in school. Many also were sports writers.

The Radio Sportscaster needs to have a clear speaking voice. A command of the English language is necessary. The ability to write well is most helpful. Individuals should be articulate and poised and be comfortable in front of a microphone.

Most but not all Radio Sportscasters are fans of at least one, if not more, sports. A basic basis understanding of the industry is helpful.

Unions/Associations

Sportscasters may belong to a number of different bargaining unions depending on the specific position they hold and the station they are working for. Some of the organizations offer individual membership, while others offer membership to the radio station. These groups often have seminars, conferences, and educational training for people working in radio. They also may provide trade journals, printed materials, and job guidance. Some of these organizations might include state Broadcasting Associations, the National Association of Broadcasting (NAB), the Radio and Advertising Bureau (RAB), or the National Association of Broadcast Employees and Technicians (NABET).

Other organizations Sportscasters might be members of include the American Federation of Television and Radio Artists (AFTRA) or the Writers' Guild of America (WGA), the National Sportscasters and Sportswriters Association (NSSA), the American Sportscasters Association (ASA), and the Radio Television News Directors Association (RTNDA).

Tips for Entry

1. Try to get as much experience working in broadcasting as you can. Work with your school radio station even if you can't get into the sports department. Hands-on experience will be useful.
2. Job openings are often advertised in the newspaper's display or classified section. Look under heading classifications of "Broadcasting," "Sportscaster," "Radio," "Announcer," "Sports," "Reporter," or "Sports Writer."
3. Many local stations advertise on their own station when there is an opening.
4. Make a demo tape and send it with your résumé and a cover letter to radio station owners, managers, or personnel directors. Look in the yellow pages of the phone book under "Radio" to find the stations available in an area.
5. Get experience writing copy. Become a member of your college newspaper. If you can, find a summer or part-time job working at a newspaper even if it isn't in the sports department. The experience will be worth it.
6. Many radio stations and associations offer internships or training programs. Internships will give you on-the-job training and the opportunity to make important contacts.

SPORTS PHOTOGRAPHER

CAREER PROFILE

Duties: Taking photographs of sport-related events and people.

Alternate Title(s): Photographer; Photojournalist

Salary Range: $15,000 to $100,000+

Employment Prospects: Fair

Best Geographical Location(s) for Position: Positions may be located throughout the country.

Prerequisites:

Education or Training—College background or degree may be required or preferred for some positions, others have no educational requirements.

Experience—Working on school or local paper helpful; taking photos of sports or action events.

Special Skills and Personality Traits—Photographic ability; enjoys sports; communications skills; creativity.

CAREER LADDER

```
┌─────────────────────────────┐
│     Sports Photographer     │
│             for             │
│  Larger, More Prestigous    │
│        Publication          │
└─────────────────────────────┘

┌─────────────────────────────┐
│     Sports Photographer     │
└─────────────────────────────┘

┌─────────────────────────────┐
│  College Student, Intern,   │
│          Reporter,          │
│             or              │
│    Amateur Photographer     │
└─────────────────────────────┘
```

Position Description

A Professional Sports Photographer has an interesting and varied job. He or she is responsible for taking photographs of sports-related events and people. The individual may work for a magazine or newspaper as a photojournalist. He or she might also work for an advertising agency, public relations firm, sports complex, sports team, specific individual, or as a freelance Sports Photographer.

Responsibilities depend on the individual's work situation and assignment. No matter what the responsibilities are, however, the individual's main function is taking active, creative sports photos.

Sports Photographers must be able to tell a complete story with their photos. This might be accomplished with one picture, or a photo-essay or montage might be required to describe a story.

Individuals working in small or weekly publications often are responsible for all photography. This could include sports-related as well as nonsports-related pictures. Individuals working in these types of publications might also have some writing responsibilities in addition to acting as the paper's Sports Photographer.

The Sports Photographer attends tournaments, games, matches, and events where athletes might show up, such as charity balls and nightclubs. Depending on the situation in which he or she works, the individual may be responsible for taking photographs of one sport or all sporting events in the area.

Individuals who work for major publications often travel to events, matches, and games. For example, a Sports Photographer working for a boxing magazine would be required to go to locations in which the major boxing matches were held.

The Sports Photographer working for a publication usually has intimate access to an event. He or she is right up there with the athletes taking pictures. For those who enjoy sports, this is an ideal situation.

The individual often works with a sports reporter on a project. Together the two develop stories for the sports page, section, or entire magazine.

Sometimes the Sports Photographer must be able to develop his or her own photographs. At other times the Photographer is just responsible for taking the photographs and turning in the exposed rolls of film.

The Sports Photographer may also be responsible for writing his or her own photo captions. Sometimes he or she is just required to obtain the information to match the photo. Someone else, such as a reporter, for example, is responsible for writing the caption.

Sports Photographers must go to a variety of sporting events. As many of these activities take place at night or weekends, these Photographers often work irregular hours. The Sports Photographer may be responsible to the sports editor or head editor, depending on the publication he or she is working for.

Salaries

Compensation for Sports Photographers varies widely. Salaries depend on the size, location, and prestige of the publication that the individual works for. Salaries are also dependent on the qualifications, skills, and experience of the Photographer.

Individuals working at smaller, local newspapers might have annual incomes ranging from $15,000 to $17,000. Those working at larger publications may have earnings ranging from $18,000 to $45,000. Successful Sports Photographers working for major publications may have annual salaries of $100,000 plus.

Freelance Sports Photographers sell single photographs of sport-related events to publications and wire services. Pictures can sell for from $10 to $500 and up.

Employment Prospects

Employment prospects are fair for those aspiring to be Sports Photographers. Depending on their skills, experience, and qualifications, individuals mights work for small weekly newspapers, larger daily newspapers, sports-oriented magazines, advertising agencies, public relations firms, sports complexes, specific athletes, sports teams, wire services, or they may be self-employed. Entry into the field is easier in the smaller, weekly publications.

Jobs are available throughout the country. Positions for major publications are often located in major cities where sports teams play and events take place.

Advancement Prospects

Advancement prospects are fair for Sports Photographers. A number of variables control the advancement process, including talent, contacts, and being in the right place at the right time.

Climbing the career ladder for most Sports Photographers can mean that they must locate positions with larger, more prestigious publications. This, in turn, leads to higher salaries.

Education and Training

Educational requirements vary from job to job. An impressive portfolio of photos may help an individual with a limited education land a job. However, many publications require or prefer their staff to hold college degrees.

As many Sports Photographers also function as journalists, courses in writing, journalism, and English are helpful. Courses or seminars in photography and darkroom techniques are useful.

Experience/Skills/Personality Traits

The most important skill of a Sports Photographer is the ability to take impressive, interesting, and unique photographs of sporting events and athletes.

Many Sports Photographers worked on their high school or college newspaper getting experience. Others enjoyed attending sporting events and found that they could capture a moment in time on film.

Individuals often have to write their own captions to photos. They should have good communications skills, written and verbal.

The Sports Photographer should be creative. Nobody wants to see the same picture that has been taken by others. He or she also needs that innate ability to feel when something special is going to occur or to know when something will turn into a unique, interesting picture. These are the types of photos everyone, including major editors and publishers, will remember.

Most successful Sports Photographers genuinely love sports and sports-related activities. While this isn't a job requirement, it certainly helps.

Unions/Associations

There is no specific bargaining union for Sports Photographers. However, individuals may be members of various unions depending on where they are employed.

Sports Photographers may belong to trade associations, such as the National Federation of Press Women (NFPW), the National Press Club (NPC), or the National Press Photographers Association (NPPA).

Tips for Entry

1. Work on your school newspaper. Try to write articles, reports, and captions besides taking photographs. This will help give you experience in all fields of journalism.
2. Put together a portfolio of your best work. Try to take photographs of a variety of sports in different types of situations. Make sure your portfolio is neat, clean, and creative.
3. Consider working during the summer or part time at your local hometown newspaper. Work in any department you can to gain experience.
4. Many newspapers and magazines offer internship programs for journalists and photojournalists
5. Positions as Sports Photographers are often advertised in the classified or display section of the newspaper. Look under heading classifications of "Photographer," "Sports Photographer," "Sports," or "Photojournalist."
6. Write to publications you are interested in working with and ask to set up an interview to see your portfolio. Always include a copy of your résumé.
7. You might also consider calling the personnel directors of larger publications or the editor in smaller publications to determine if an interview can be scheduled.
8. Take sports-oriented photographs and try to sell them on "spec" to local newspapers.

CAREER OPPORTUNITIES IN RECREATION AND FITNESS

SPORTS AND FITNESS PROGRAM COORDINATOR

CAREER PROFILE

Duties: Developing and implementing sports and fitness programs for a variety facilities; evaluating programs; supervising staff.

Alternate Title(s): Sports Program Coordinator; Recreation Specialist; Recreation Supervisor; Fitness Coordinator

Salary Range: $18,000 to $100,000+

Employment Prospects: Fair

Best Geographical Location(s) for Position: Positions may be located throughout the country.

Prerequisites:

Education or Training—Minimum of a four-year college degree required for most jobs.

Experience—Experience working as recreation staffer or physical education teacher may be preferred.

Special Skills and Personality Traits—Coordination skills; organized; detail oriented; knowledge of sports, fitness, and health; supervisory skills; communications skills; understanding of group dynamics; knowledge of exercise and/or dance.

CAREER LADDER

```
┌─────────────────────────────┐
│     Sports and Fitness       │
│     Program Coordinator      │
│   at More Prestigious Facility│
└─────────────────────────────┘

┌─────────────────────────────┐
│     Sports and Fitness       │
│     Program Coordinator      │
└─────────────────────────────┘

┌─────────────────────────────┐
│      College Student,        │
│      Recreation Staffer,     │
│            or                │
│   Physical Education Teacher │
└─────────────────────────────┘
```

Position Description

Sports and fitness programs are regularly sponsored by communities, nonprofit groups, recreational facilities, and schools. Recently business and industry management has begun to recognize that healthy, fit employees are of increased value in the workplace. Executives have begun implementing employee sports and fitness programs within the corporate structure. The person who develops and implements such activity programs is called a Sports and Fitness Program Coordinator.

Sports and Fitness Program Coordinators are also known as Recreation Specialists or Supervisors. The individual's main function is to assess the needs of the people who will be taking part in the program and develop its structure. Programs differ depending on individual group needs. Responsibilities, too, vary depending on the size and structure of the particular program.

Sports and Fitness Program Coordinators may work in a variety of settings, from community organizations and nonprofit groups, to town, county, city or state parks, schools, resorts, hotels, health clubs, and in major industries and business. Individuals may work with children, teenagers, adults, seniors, and those with special needs.

The first thing most Sports and Fitness Program Coordinators must do is to evaluate the program that is in use or to develop a new one. In performing this task, the individual must assess the needs of the people who will be participating. Sometimes the Program Coordinator must develop a budget. In others, he or she is given a budget to follow.

If the program is set up for company employees, it must accommodate their work schedule. The program must also take into account the various ages, fitness levels, and life-styles of participants. Program Coordinators must determine what types of activities and functions will be most useful. Sports and Fitness Program Coordinators in most business companies, for example, must develop programs that can fit into an active, busy life-style. The Coordinator may develop a program that includes group lectures on nutrition, dieting clubs, and exercise, dance, and aerobics classes. He or she may also set up a gym area and hire exercise, nutrition, and fitness instructors. The individual may be responsible for recommending equipment, pricing, obtaining bids, and purchasing. Another responsibility in this work situation may be to make employees aware of the program, get them involved, and monitor the success.

Individuals working in other types of situations can run small programs or large ones. These can run the gamut from exercise and fitness classes for community sports camps to city sports teams, tournaments, and the coordination of year-round recreational facilities.

Once the programs have been determined, the Coordinator may be expected to put in purchase orders for sporting equipment, make sure it arrives, and teach staff members how to use it. He or she may also be responsible for interviewing and hiring staff members to teach and instruct classes and supervise programs, sporting events, tournaments, and facilities.

The Coordinator is responsible for overseeing the work of each instructor, leader, and staff member. He or she is required to keep each staff member abreast of all programs. The individual may be expected to teach staff sporting, fitness, and recreational skills. In some situations, he or she may run regular workshops for these people. The Coordinator must explain goals and requirements of the program to all employees and see to it that they are met.

Sports and Fitness Coordinators need to keep up on the newest trends. They may be required to take classes, workshops, and seminars to accomplish this. Individuals must find ways to introduce the new trends to program participants.

Others functions of the Sports and Fitness Coordinator may include writing reports and handling paperwork on a variety of things, such as the success and/or failures of the program, proposals, budgets, and accidents or injuries.

The Coordinator must know how to motivate both staff members and people involved in the various programs. The individual is responsible for coordinating all the support personnel necessary to make programs work. He or she acts as the intermediary when other people need to be involved in a project.

The Coordinator is also expected to handle problems related to the program. These might include situations such as complaints by participants about a facet of the program, a staff member, or an activity. It is the Coordinator's job to look into all problems, respond to them accordingly, and report them to the appropriate people.

Salaries

Salaries for Sports Program Coordinators can range from $18,000 to $100,000 and up depending on the specific job and the individual's responsibilities and experience level.

Coordinators with little or no experience may earn between $18,000 and $20,000 yearly. Individuals with more experience

and responsibilities may have annual salaries between $23,000 and $40,000. Salaries are highest for Sports Program Coordinators running larger sports and fitness programs and those working in corporate and industry situations.

Employment Prospects

Employment prospects are fair and getting better. There are opportunities to work in this type of position in various setting throughout the country.

With the rise in health insurance and medical costs, it pays companies to keep their employees healthy and physically fit. Job opportunities will be especially plentiful in corporate industry settings as more companies try to keep up with this trend.

Advancement Prospects

Advancement prospects are good. Individuals can climb the career ladder by locating positions in more prestigious settings and by obtaining jobs with more responsibilities. Those who are good at their job and have the determination and drive to get better can easily accomplish this. Individuals should constantly try to improve their skills by attending workshops, seminars, training sessions, and classes.

Education and Training

Educational requirements for Sports Program Coordinators vary from job to job. Most positions require a minimum of a four-year college degree. Good choices for majors include physical education, recreation, or sports administration.

Classes, workshops, seminars, and training sessions in exercise, sports administration, fitness, business, and specialized sports will be useful to the individual in both obtaining a job and being successful at it.

Experience/Skills/Personality Traits

Sports Program Coordinators must be able to work well with people in all life-styles. Supervisory skills are mandatory for most positions.

Coordinators must be able to initiate and develop programs or work with those put together by others. They must be organized and detail oriented. The ability to work on many different projects at once without getting flustered is necessary.

Individuals should have good communications skills, both verbal and written. They are often expected to develop and draw up proposals for programs. At times, the Sports Program Coordinator may have to speak in public to groups to drum up support for a program or to get people interested.

The Coordinator should have a total knowledge of health, fitness, and sports. The more the Coordinator knows about individual sports and fitness programs, the more effective he or she can be.

The ability to instruct others in necessary. He or she should understand group dynamics. The individual must also be able to work with people who have special needs regarding fitness and sports. First aid skills are helpful to the Coordinator when injuries occur and in emergency situations.

Many individuals have obtained these positions right after graduation from college. Others worked as recreation staffers or physical education teachers prior to assuming their current Sports and Fitness Program Coordinator job.

Unions/Associations

Sports Program Coordinators may belong to a number of organizations relevant to the type of facility in which they work. They may also be members of the American Alliance for Health, Physical Education, Recreation and Dance (AAHPERD), the National Association for Sport and Physical Education (NASPE), the National Dance Association (NDA), and the National Employee Services and Recreation Association (NESRA).

Tips for Entry

1. Volunteer your services to the sports and fitness programs of a local community group for children or senior citizens.
2. Jobs are often advertised in the classified section of the newspaper. Look under heading classifications of "Recreation," "Fitness," "Sports," "Athletics," or "Sports Programs."
3. Get experience working in a local health club as a manager, exercise specialist, or exercise instructor.
4. Many community groups use part-time or free-lance people in this field. Call or write and inquire.
5. Send your résumé with a cover letter to nonprofit organizations hosting children's and seniors' programs as well as to industry and businesses. You may be able to create a position where there is none yet open.

PERSONAL TRAINER

CAREER PROFILE

Duties: Guiding clients on a one-to-one basis in an exercise and fitness regime; assisting individuals attain utmost level of fitness.

Alternate Title(s): Individual Trainer; Trainer

Salary Range: $25 to $500+ a session

Employment Prospects: Fair

Best Geographical Location(s) for Position: Positions may be located throughout the country.

Prerequisites:

Education or Training—No educational requirement; training in exercise, fitness, health, and nutrition helpful.
Experience—Experience working in gym, health club, spa, etc., preferred.
Special Skills and Personality Traits—Energetic; physically fit; health conscious; understanding of nutrition, fitness, and exercise; enthusiastic.

CAREER LADDER

```
┌─────────────────────────────────┐
│      Personal Trainer           │
│  with More Prestigious Clients  │
└─────────────────────────────────┘

┌─────────────────────────────────┐
│      Personal Trainer           │
└─────────────────────────────────┘

┌─────────────────────────────────┐
│      Exercise Instructor        │
└─────────────────────────────────┘
```

Position Description

Personal Trainers can lead very exciting lives depending on who their clients are. Personal Trainers may have clients who are well-known movie stars, executives in Fortune 500 companies or just ordinary people who are extremely interested in their fitness.

A Personal Trainer is responsible for helping a person, on a one-on-one basis, attain his or her utmost level of fitness. The Personal Trainer has varied duties and responsibilities, depending on the individual client.

This type of career is usually more like being self-employed than holding a full-time job. While a job in an exercise salon or gym may last from nine to five, Personal Trainers may have a much longer day. They not only work with people to get them or keep them in shape, but they must also find clients to work with. They may do this in a number of ways. One way is advertising for clients in newspapers, magazines, on radio, or television. Or Trainers might begin by working as exercise instructors in a gym and impress a number of patrons who in turn request private sessions. The best way for Personal Trainers to gain clients is by word of mouth. If people are happy with their Trainer, they will usually tell their friends. This method can build a highly successful business for the Personal Trainer.

One of the first responsibilities of the Personal Trainer is to assess the client to find what physical shape he or she is currently in. The Trainer must also determine what the client expects of training sessions. Does he or she want to lose weight, firm up, become more physically fit? The Trainer must make sure that the client is medically able to go through the particular program decided on.

The Personal Trainer meets with the client on a regular basis. The two go through an exercise routine that the Trainer has tailored specifically for the client.

The Personal Trainer begins by instructing the person on how to do each exercise correctly. He or she may then exercise with the individual or may just offer encouragement to help the client continue with the exercise routine. As the client is paying the Personal Trainer for individualized instruction, he or she is less likely to put off a workout.

In some instances the Personal Trainer also develops a diet regime for the client. This might be to lose weight or to help the individual improve his or her eating habits.

A Personal Trainer's hours are irregular. He or she may have one client or many. Training times may range from one hour per client to three or four hours for those training for a specific reason, such as an athletic event or a movie role.

Personal Trainers may schedule training sessions in a variety of locations. The sessions may take place in the client's home or place of business. The Personal Trainer might also train individuals in private or public gyms. Some Personal Trainers own mobile gyms, which they bring to the client's home or business.

Personal Trainers fortunate enough to be working with well-known athletes, movie stars, or other celebrities may travel with the individual around the world. While this seems like fun and may serve as a short holiday, the Personal Trainer who does this often loses out developing a clientele at home. He or she may schedule from three to five training sessions a day with other clients. Being on the road means that he or she can't take care of those commitments.

Personal Trainers are responsible to their clients. If a client is not happy with the training and workouts, he or she usually looks for another Trainer.

Salaries

It is extremely difficult to determine the earnings of Personal Trainers due to a number of variables. Compensation depends on the number and kind of clients the individual has. For example, if the Personal Trainer is working with major television or movie stars, he or she is usually able to charge more than an individual working with nonstars.

Earnings are also be dependent on the amount the Personal Trainer charges each client, his or her geographic location, experience, and responsibilities.

Personal Trainers can earn from $25 to $500 plus a session. Those earning the higher figure usually work for stars and celebrities. An average fee for a session in a large city could range from $50 to $100.

Employment Prospects

Employment prospects are fair for Personal Trainers. As noted previously, Personal Trainers must usually find their own clients. If the individual is aggressive, knowledgeable, and good at what he or she does, there should be no problem getting started as a Personal Trainer.

Advancement Prospects

Advancement prospects are fair for Personal Trainers. To climb the career ladder in this profession, an individual must get more clients, charge more for his or her services, or find additional prestigious clients who can pay more.

Keeping clients happy and satisfied with their workout regime will lead to to good word-of-mouth advertising. Personal Trainers may also advance their careers by opening up their own gyms or health clubs.

Education and Training

While there are no specific educational requirements for Personal Trainers, it is important that the individual know as much as possible about exercise and physical fitness. Some Personal Trainers have degrees in physical education, exercise physiology, exercise biochemistry, exercise science, and the like.

Some individuals have no formal training at all. Others received training in private gyms or health clubs by head instructors and by manufacturers of exercise equipment.

Personal Trainers should keep up on the newest trends in exercise, health, and nutrition. More and more classes and seminars on these subjects are being offered throughout the country.

Experience/Skills/Personality Traits

Personal Trainers should be energetic, physically fit people. They should like to exercise, be health conscious, and have an understanding about nutrition and fitness. They should also be personable, likable, and enthusiastic.

As Personal Trainers, they must not only obtain clients but also keep them. Individuals should have a basic knowledge of business. They should know how to advertise, charge people, do bookkeeping, and purchase equipment.

They should also be familiar with first aid procedures in case a client injures him or herself.

Unions/Associations

There are no unions or specific trade associations that Personal Trainers belong to. An individual in the business might belong to a local health, fitness, or nutritional organization.

Tips for Entry

1. Work in a local gym or health club. This will help you make important contacts as well as give you valuable training.
2. If you are considering college, try to find one with a program geared toward fitness, nutrition, or exercise.
3. If you are currently in college, volunteer to work with any of the sports teams to learn how they train for a season.
4. Volunteer to run exercise or fitness sessions for a local organization, such as a boys' club, girls' club, or senior citizen's center. It will be good experience.
5. Look in the newspaper display or classified section under heading classifications such as "Exercise," "Fitness," "Instructor," or "Personal Trainer."
6. Many exercise and fitness machine manufacturers look for representatives. They offer training and then either give you a job or ask you to be a company representative in a certain area. This is good for learning how to use various machines and equipment. It also opens up opportunities to make more contacts in the fitness world.
7. You might attempt to get clients by advertising your services in a local newspaper or circular.

AEROBICS INSTRUCTOR

CAREER PROFILE

Duties: Leading exercise, dance, and aerobics classes; developing dancing routines for exercise sessions.

Alternate Title(s):   Aerobics Leader

Salary Range: $12,000 to $35,000+

Employment Prospects: Excellent

Best Geographical Location(s) for Position: Positions located throughout the country.

Prerequisites:

Education or Training—No formal educational requirements; training in exercise, aerobics, and dance preferred.

Experience—No experience required.

Special Skills and Personality Traits—Physically fit; energetic; ability to lead classes; knowledge of exercise, aerobics, and dance.

CAREER LADDER

```
┌─────────────────────────────────┐
│       Aerobics Instructor       │
│     in More Prestigious Club    │
│               or                │
│        Exercise Director        │
└─────────────────────────────────┘

┌─────────────────────────────────┐
│       Aerobics Instructor       │
└─────────────────────────────────┘

┌─────────────────────────────────┐
│          Entry Level            │
│               or                │
│       Exercise Enthusiast       │
└─────────────────────────────────┘
```

Position Description

With the current trend toward physical fitness and health, gyms, fitness centers, spas, and health clubs are becoming a part of today's society. The Aerobics Instructor's function is to lead classes for individuals or groups in aerobics and other forms of exercise. Individuals may work in private health clubs, gyms, schools, and elsewhere.

The Aerobics Instructor is responsible for helping the patrons of a club or gym perform the exercises in a safe manner. It is important that he or she know the correct methods for doing the various exercise routines. The individual is responsible not only for teaching classes but for helping make the club a productive, fun place for the patrons. If people do not have a good time at the gym, they often do not return.

Many Aerobics Instructors utilize dancing routines as part of their exercise program. These individuals must develop routines, choose music, and put the entire production together.

Depending on the size of the club and the responsibilities of the Instructor, he or she may have additional duties. For example, the individual may teach club or gym members how to use the different types of equipment. He or she must, therefore, have a complete understanding not only of how each piece of equipment is used correctly, but what its benefits are.

In some health clubs, spas, or gyms, the Aerobics Instructor is responsible for putting together personal fitness programs for members. He or she might prescribe the number, type, and level of aerobics classes necessary to attain the best physical fitness with the least amount of strain for a new member.

The Aerobic Instructor must understand the fitness level of most people in the class. If not, class members may become so exhausted and strained that injuries may occur, or they may become so tired they lose interest in the class. The Aerobics Instructor may teach various levels of classes for people who are at different fitness levels.

In some health clubs and gyms, the Aerobics Instructor is the one who initially assesses the patrons to find what physical shape they are in. If the patron is not in good physical shape, or in specific age categories, the Aerobics Instructor may be required to determine if he or she is medically able to go through the selected programs. In other gyms, an exercise specialist, the receptionist, or the club manager may handle this. Some clubs require statements from physicians before allowing patrons to participate in programs.

The Aerobics Instructor begins by instructing the class on how to perform each exercise correctly. He or she may then stand in front of the class and exercise with them or may just offer encouragement.

Hours may be irregular for Aerobic Instructors. Individuals may work a variety of shifts, depending on the specific gym or spa. Usually, however, Aerobics Instructors work a set number of hours. Individuals are responsible to the gym or spa owner or general manager.

Salaries

Earnings for Aerobics Instructors depend on the specific spa or gym, its location and prestige, and the experience and duties of the individual.

Some Aerobics Instructors earn barely above the minimum wage. Others earn a great deal more. Annual compensation can range from $12,000 to $35,000 plus. Aerobics Instructors working in high-prestige spas in major cities usually earn even higher salaries.

Employment Prospects

Employment prospects are excellent for Aerobics Instructors. Job possibilities may be located in almost every part of the country. The better trained an individual is, the more opportunities there are for obtaining a good position.

Individuals can work in a variety of environments, from schools to gyms and franchise clubs to exclusive spas. They may work in male, female, or coed situations.

Advancement Prospects

Advancement prospects are fair for Aerobics Instructors. There are a number of ways of climbing the career ladder. The most common way for is for the Aerobics Instructor to locate a position in a larger or more prestigious club or spa. Another method of career advancement is for the individual to become an exercise director, specialist, or club manager.

Aerobics Instructors who provide stimulating, exciting workouts build a following. When Instructors are in demand, they can often command higher salaries.

Education and Training

While there are no specific educational requirements for Aerobics Instructors, it is important that the individual have as much exercise training as possible. Courses, seminars, or workshops in exercise physiology, exercise biochemistry, and exercise science will be useful. A number of colleges currently offer programs in exercise and fitness.

Other training may be obtained on the job at from spas and gyms. In some work situations an Aerobics Instructor must go through the gym's instructor training program before being hired. Manufacturers and representatives of exercise equipment companies are also good possibilities for training. These businesses often teach instructors about the correct use of their equipment.

Certain trade associations and organizations provide members with training in aerobics, dance, and exercise. Many of these organizations are now also beginning to offer certification.

Aerobics Instructors must keep up with the newest exercise trends. More and more classes and seminars on this subject are being offered nationwide. Basic first aid courses are also prove valuable to Instructors.

Experience/Skills/Personality Traits

Aerobics Instructors need to be in top physical shape. They should be energetic and enjoy exercising. Individuals should like being around and teaching people. Aerobics Instructors should be personable and have bubbly, enthusiastic personalities.

The individuals should also be familiar with first aid procedures in case a patron injures him- or herself.

Unions/Associations

Aerobics Instructors may belong to a number of trade associations providing educational guidance, training, and professional support. These might include the International Dance-Exercise Association (IDEA), or the Aerobics and Fitness Association of America (AFAA). Individuals might also belong to local fitness and health-oriented organizations.

Tips for Entry

1. If you are considering college, try to locate a school with a program geared toward fitness, exercise, and nutrition.
2. Volunteer your services running exercise sessions for local nonprofit organizations, such as boys' clubs, girls' clubs, and senior citizen's centers. This will provide good hands-on experience.
3. Positions for Aerobics Instructors are advertised in the the newspaper display or classified section under heading classifications such as "Aerobics," "Spa," "Health Club," "Gym," "Exercise," "Fitness," or "Instructor."
4. Many exercise and fitness machine manufacturers look for representatives. They provide training and may then either offer you a job or ask you to serve as a company representative in a certain territory. This is an excellent chance to learn how to use various machines and equipment. It also opens up opportunities to making contacts in the fitness world.
5. Send your résumé and a cover letter to spas, health clubs, and gyms. Ask that your résumé be kept on file if there are no current openings.
6. Write to the corporate headquarters of health industry and exercise franchise operations and chains. These spa and club organizations often offer training and job placement.

HEALTH CLUB MANAGER

CAREER PROFILE

Duties: Attending to the day-to-day activities of a health club; hiring qualified personnel; coordinating efforts of staff to run a safe, effective, and pleasant health club.

Alternate Title(s): Manager; Health Club Administrator

Salary Range: $17,000 to $50,000

Employment Prospects: Excellent

Best Geographical Location(s) for Position: Positions may be located throughout the country.

Prerequisites:

Education or Training—Minimum requirements vary from a high school diploma to a four-year college degree.

Experience—Experience working in health club facility or management of some type helpful but not always required.

Special Skills and Personality Traits—Management skills; ability to coordinate details; supervisory skills; self-confident; well groomed; good communication skills; physically fit.

CAREER LADDER

```
┌─────────────────────────────────────┐
│      Health Club Manager            │
│  at Larger, More Prestigious Club   │
│                or                   │
│       Owner of Health Club          │
└─────────────────────────────────────┘

┌─────────────────────────────────────┐
│         Health Club Manager         │
└─────────────────────────────────────┘

┌─────────────────────────────────────┐
│         Assistant Manager,          │
│           Entry Level,              │
│                or                   │
│        Health Club Worker           │
└─────────────────────────────────────┘
```

Position Description

More and more health and fitness clubs are springing up around the country. All of these clubs need managers. Health Club Managers are responsible for running the facilities in a safe, efficient manner. They also help make the club a productive, fun place for patrons to visit.

Health clubs usually offer a number of services for those who want to maintain a healthy, fit life-style. Most facilities have exercise machines, aerobic conditioning equipment, and classes. Some health clubs also have running tracks and tennis, handball, and racquetball courts. Depending on the club, it might also offer spa facilities, such as pools, steam rooms, and whirlpools.

The Health Club Manager is an administrative member of the club staff. Working with the rest of the personnel, he or she coordinates employee efforts to create a well-run facility.

Responsibilities of the Health Club Manager vary from job to job depending on the structure of the club. In smaller clubs, the Manager usually has more varied duties. In larger clubs, he or she can assign certain tasks to an assistant manager.

In some situations, the Health Club Manager is responsible for hiring and firing personnel, including the receptionist, assistant manager, exercise directors, and aerobics instructors. The individual is also responsible for hiring lifeguards, masseurs, masseuses, and attendants for the pool and locker room. To do this the Manager may call employment agencies, write and place advertisements, and make phone calls to qualified people to find staff members.

Once staff members are hired, the Manager is responsible for making sure that they are trained properly and are aware of club rules and regulations. He or she may be required to hold classes or seminars for new staff members. If the Manager finds that one of the staff is not performing the job correctly, he or she must either correct the situation or discharge the staff member.

The Manager must check all staff members who need to be licensed, such as lifeguards, have current licenses. If medical exams are required before hiring, he or she is responsible for making sure that examinations have been performed.

One of the major responsibilities of the Health Club Manager is to take care of the day-to-day problems that might occur in the club. If, for example, there is a disagreement between a patron and a staff member, the Health Club Manager must straighten it out and keep the patron happy.

If an accident occurs in the club, the Manager must call health care personnel, notify the owner of the club and the insurance company, and possibly write a report about the accident.

In some instances the Manager is responsible for doing payrolls, bookkeeping, and record keeping. In other clubs, this responsibility is handled by a bookkeeper or the club owner.

In some health clubs, the Manager greets new or prospective patrons and shows them around the club in hopes of signing them up. In other clubs, this duty is given to receptionists or sales people.

Another function of the Health Club Manager is to make sure that the physical club facility is kept safe, clean, and neat. He or she must make sure that all equipment is in proper working order. If something is broken, he or she arranges to have it repaired or replaced.

The Health Club Manager is often required to schedule exercise and aerobics classes. To do this, he or she must get to know the hours of the greatest patron influx. The Manager must keep up with everything that is happening in the club.

In some clubs, the Manager is responsible for advertising to bring in new members. He or she must get prices on the various media and decide on the type of ads, their frequency, and possible areas for placement. At times, the Manager may also be required to develop promotions to bring in new members. For example, he or she may try to bring in a new groups of members, such as pregnant women. In such cases, the Manager might schedule classes for pregnant women, run special programs, and offer special prices for those attending. In a similar vein, the Manager may decide that bringing singles together would be the method to attract additional members and schedule "singles" exercise parties. The more members a club can attract, the more successful the club will be.

The Health Club Manager must be accessible to members. Some Managers float around the club talking to patrons. In this way, they can see what problems exist and what services members are most satisfied with. In other clubs, the Manager might send out questionnaires.

The Health Club Manager may be required to fill in for staff members who call in sick or work at positions that have not yet been filled. If the individual is filling in for an exercise instructor, he or she must be aware of the newest exercise techniques.

The Health Club Manager is usually responsible directly to the owner of the club. The Health Club Manager may work varied hours depending on when the particular club is the busiest. He or she may have to work overtime when the club is extremely busy or when there is a problem, such as a staff member calling in sick.

Salaries

Salaries vary greatly for Health Club Managers. Variables include the size, type, geographic location, and prestige of the health club. Another important salary consideration is whether the facility is public, private, or part of a chain.

Compensation also is dependent on the education, experience, and responsibilities of the individual. Annual earnings may run from $17,000 to $50,000. Salaries on the lower end of the scale go to individuals with little experience who work in smaller local clubs. Many Health Club Managers also receive bonuses for bringing in and signing up new members.

An additional benefit for the Health Club Manager is that he or she is usually allowed to use club facilities at no cost.

Employment Prospects

Employment prospects are excellent for Health Club Managers. More and more clubs are opening every day all over the country. Positions may be found in almost every geographical location. There is also a need for Health Club Managers in clubs on cruise lines, resort hotels, and spas.

Advancement Prospects

Advancement prospects are fair for Health Club Managers. Individuals who wish to stay in this field usually climb the career ladder by seeking the same type of position in a larger, more prestigious club. This, in turn, generally leads to higher earnings. Other individuals try to advance their careers by starting up and owning their own health club.

Education and Training

Educational requirements vary depending on the specific job. Some health clubs demand that their staff be college graduates, while others just require high school diplomas. Other clubs require the individual to go through one of their own training programs.

Business or management classes are helpful in a career as a Health Club Manager. Classes in various facets of exercise and nutrition might also be useful.

Experience/Skills/Personality Traits

The Health Club Manager should be able to coordinate details, activities, and personnel. He or she needs to be able to supervise others in a strong yet friendly way. Self-confidence, composure, and good grooming are attributes in this type of job. The individual should also be articulate and have excellent communications skills, both in person and on the phone.

The Health Club Manager should be personable, friendly, and easy to get along with. He or she should be a people person.

The individual should be able to solve problems without losing his or her cool. The ability to deal with stress is necessary.

Most Health Club Managers are physically fit themselves and are equally interested in helping others attain a high fitness level. An understanding and knowledge of fitness and exercise is usually required.

Unions/Associations

There is no specific bargaining union for Health Club Managers. Individuals may, however, be working in a situation where all employees are unionized, such as a hotel or resort club or spa.

Health Club Managers may belong to the Association for Fitness In Business (AFFIB). This group provides educational support and career guidance to its members.

Tips for Entry

1. Positions for Health Club Managers are often advertised in newspaper display or classified sections. Look under heading classifications of "Health," "Health Club," "Management," "Fitness," "Spas," or "Sports."

2. If you don't have enough experience to manage a health club or can't find the position you want, try to get your foot in the door in some other way. For example, become the club's desk receptionist or a salesperson until a job opens up. In this way, you will be gaining experience and working in the health club atmosphere.

3. Look in the yellow pages of the phone book under "Health Club," "Spas," and the like. Send your résumé with a short cover letter to the owner inquiring about a job. Ask that your résumé be kept on file if a job is not currently available.

4. You might also consider calling the clubs listed in the yellow pages and ask to set up an interview.

5. If you are interested in working for a health club that is a part of a chain, write to their main office. Many companies offer training programs and then will place you in a job with the company.

6. Many hotels and resorts have health clubs that require Managers. Remember to check these when job hunting.

7. Remember to check out job possibilities on the Internet. Go to a career site and type in keywords such as "health club," "fitness," or "spas."

HEALTH CLUB ASSISTANT MANAGER

CAREER PROFILE

Duties: Helping manager run health club or spa; performing duties of manager when club manager is not on duty; handling day-to-day activities and problems in club; keeping club safe for patrons; handling paperwork.

Alternate Title(s):   Assistant; Health and Fitness Club Assistant Manager

Salary Range: $14,000 to $30,000+

Employment Prospects: Excellent

Best Geographical Location(s) for Position: Positions may be located throughout the country.

Prerequisites:

Education or Training—Minimum requirements vary from a high school diploma to a four-year college degree.
Experience—Experience working in health clubs preferred but not required.
Special Skills and Personality Traits—Administrative skills; business skills; detail oriented; self-confident; personable; communication skills; knowledge of health and fitness.

CAREER LADDER

```
┌─────────────────────────────────────┐
│        Health Club Manager          │
└─────────────────────────────────────┘

┌─────────────────────────────────────┐
│   Health Club Assistant Manager     │
└─────────────────────────────────────┘

┌─────────────────────────────────────┐
│      Exercise Class Instructor,     │
│        Club Receptionist,           │
│               or                    │
│           Entry Level               │
└─────────────────────────────────────┘
```

Position Description

Most health clubs in the country utilize the services of both a manager and an assistant. The time and work involved in running an operation usually makes this mandatory. The Assistant Health Club Manager is responsible for helping the manager run the facility. He or she assists in making sure the club is safe, productive, and enjoyable for patrons. The individual also is responsible for handling the duties of the club manager when he or she is not available.

Many clubs prefer to have the manager working one shift and an Assistant Manager working another so that the facility is always in the hands of a professional administrator. Some facilities also have more than one Assistant on staff.

The Assistant Manager has varied duties. He or she may be expected to offer input when other staff members are hired. The individual may also assist the manager in interviewing job applicants or reviewing applications. As new staff members join the club, the Assistant Manager may be responsible for helping the manager with training duties. The manager may also assign the Assistant to projects, such as checking that staff

members who require licensing are properly licensed and that paperwork is current and on file.

Individuals may be expected to handle a variety of paperwork. This can include anything from writing an accident report or recording staff hours for payroll to keeping track of money resulting from patron's fees. Assistant Managers may also be required to help the manager bill patrons who have not paid their membership fees. They may also be involved in sending out promotional material for the club.

The Assistant Manager is responsible for taking care of routine matters that occur when the manager is not on duty. These developments might include such areas as staff members calling in sick, broken equipment, or problems regarding patrons. Responsibilities regarding the handling of nonroutine difficulties may vary depending on the specific job. As a rule, if there is a major problem, the Assistant must contact the manager or club owner to get some direction on how it should be handled.

The individual assists the manager of the club in keeping the facility safe, clean, and neat. He or she is expected to routinely check all equipment to make sure it is in working order. The Assistant must also make sure that showers are working, towels are available, and everything is functioning correctly in the spa and sauna areas.

The Assistant Manager may be responsible for greeting prospective patrons on behalf of the manager. He or she may give patrons a tour of the club and may offer trial passes to use the facilities for the day. The individual is also expected to answer questions about club facilities, staff members' qualifications, and fee schedules. Depending on the facility, the Assistant Manager might also be responsible for demonstrating the correct use of various exercise machines. He or she might introduce new or potential members to other staff members and patrons to make them feel more comfortable at the club.

In many health clubs, especially smaller ones, the Assistant Manager may be required to teach exercise and aerobics classes. The individual must keep up with the latest techniques in exercise, dance, and aerobics. The Assistant may teach classes on a regular basis or just when other instructors are unavailable.

The Assistant Health Club Manager is directly responsible to the club manager. The individual may work various hours depending on the specific shift he or she is assigned. Assistant Managers are expected to work overtime when needed. This may occur when the manager cannot be at the club, when other staff members call in sick, or when the club is extremely busy and needs additional help.

Salaries

Assistant Health Club Managers may earn salaries that range from $14,000 to $30,000 plus. Factors affecting the range include the size, type, prestige, and geographical location of the facility. Other factors include the experience and responsibilities of the individual.

In some health clubs, staff members who bring in new patrons are awarded bonuses. Generally, individuals working in clubs in major cities earn more than those working in similar-size clubs in other areas.

Employment Prospects

There are excellent employment opportunities for Assistant Health Club Managers. Individuals may work in health and fitness clubs that are privately owned or that are part of a chain. Assistant Managers may also work in hotels, resorts, spas, or cruise ships. Job openings may be located throughout the country.

Advancement Prospects

Advancement prospects are good for Assistant Health Club Managers. The next step up the ladder is either to locate a similar position in a larger, more prestigious club or to become a full-fledged club manager. As a great many managers move to other positions, there are frequent opportunities for advancement.

Education and Training

Educational requirements vary for Assistant Managers depending on each job. Some clubs prefer that their staff be college graduates or at least have a college background, while others require only a high school diploma. Many clubs, such as those that are part of nationwide chains, have their own training programs for staff members.

Classes in business, management, exercise, nutrition, and fitness are helpful both in attaining a job and for career advancement.

Experience/Skills/Personality Traits

The Assistant Manager of a health club should have many of the skills that a full-fledged manager would have. Supervisory, business, and administrative skills are necessary. The individual should also be able to coordinate and handle many details and projects.

The Assistant Manager should be able to take control of a situation or problem and handle it. He or she should be self-confident and composed at all times.

Individuals in this position need good communications skills. They should be able to speak comfortably on a one-on-one basis as well as in front of groups and on the telephone. Assistant Health Club Managers should be personable and easy to get along with. They also should be service oriented.

Assistant Health Club Managers should look healthy and physically fit. Individuals should also be able to teach exercise, aerobics, and fitness classes.

Many Assistant Managers started their careers in health and fitness working as exercise or aerobics class instructors. Others held jobs as club receptionists. If individuals have a business or fitness background, this can also be an entry-level position.

Unions/Associations

Assistant Health Club Managers do not usually belong to any type of bargaining union. If, however, they are working in a club located in a resort or hotel that is unionized, they may be members.

Individuals may belong to health and fitness association, such as the Association for Fitness in Business (AFFIB). This organization offers educational support and career guidance to its members.

Tips for Entry

1. The easiest way to find a job in this area is to look in the newspaper. Openings are usually advertised in display or classified sections under heading classifications of "Health," "Health Club," "Exercise Salon," "Management," "Fitness," "Spas," or "Sports."
2. Many clubs post signs on their windows or inside advertising job openings.
3. You might also consider taking a day to visit the various clubs in your area to see if they have openings. Bring your résumé with you and ask the receptionist about job

possibilities. If there are openings, he or she will usually direct you to the club manager or ask you to fill out a job application.

4. If cold-call visiting to locate a job is not your style, you might want to send your résumé with a short cover letter to clubs in your area. You can find their names and addresses by looking in the yellow pages of the phone book under "Health Clubs," "Spas," and the like. Remember to request that your résumé be kept on file if a job is not currently available.

5. Job openings may be located on the Internet. Go to a job or career site and type in keywords such as "health clubs," "fitness," or "spas."

6. Be creative when looking for a job. Consider working for a health club or spa in a hotel, resort, or cruise ship.

7. Many health and fitness clubs and spas are chains or franchises. These businesses often offer training programs and then place you in a job at one of their facilities. If you are interested in this approach, write to the chain's or franchise's main office.

TENNIS DIRECTOR

CAREER PROFILE

Duties: Organizing tennis program for a facility; bringing in new members; giving lessons; operating a pro shop; maintaining courts; scheduling lessons, tournaments, and court time.

Alternate Title(s): Director of Tennis

Salary Range: $24,000 to $110,000+

Employment Prospects: Good

Best Geographical Location(s) for Position: Positions may be located throughout the country.

Prerequisites:

Education or Training—No formal educational requirement for some positions; others require or prefer a four-year college degree or background; training in tennis necessary.

Experience—Experience in business, management, and tennis needed.

Special Skills and Personality Traits—Skilled tennis player; business and marketing skills; communications skills; organizational skills; ability to teach all levels of tennis; detail oriented.

CAREER LADDER

```
┌─────────────────────────────────┐
│  Tennis Director at Larger, More│
│      Prestigious Facility       │
└─────────────────────────────────┘

┌─────────────────────────────────┐
│        Tennis Director          │
└─────────────────────────────────┘

┌─────────────────────────────────┐
│         Apprentice,             │
│         Assistant,              │
│            or                   │
│      Tennis Instructor          │
└─────────────────────────────────┘
```

Position Description

Tennis has always been a popular sport. With the current fitness trend hitting the country, it has become even more popular. Where once indoor courts were the exception, today thousands are located throughout the country. They can be found in various facilities, including country clubs, racquet clubs, resort hotels, and health and fitness clubs. There are even a couple of indoor tennis courts in the upper portion of Grand Central Station in New York City. The person who is in charge of the tennis program at these facilities is called the Tennis Director.

The individual in this position has varied duties depending on the specific job. His or her main function is to organize the tennis program for the facility. This responsibility is all-encompassing. The individual is responsible for everything from bookkeeping duties and staffing responsibilities to day-to-day facility operation.

The Tennis Director is expected to obtain members. To accomplish this, the individual may run various promotions or advertisements aimed at bringing new members into the facility. Once they are in, the Director must find ways to retain this membership. Many areas offer a number of tennis facilities. The Director, therefore, must develop ways to both obtain and retain patrons. A particular tennis club may, for example, have a well-known tennis pro teaching, or the club may be known for its posh surroundings or very helpful staff members.

The Director is also expected to develop tennis programs. These may include instructional workshops and seminars and tournaments for various levels of players. He or she may organize tournaments for juniors and seniors.

Most Tennis Directors are responsible for the operation of the pro shop. In some facilities, the Tennis Director owns the shop. In others, he or she just manages it. A pro shop is a small store within a tennis facility where people can purchase tennis equipment, supplies, and clothing. The individual receives a commission on sales made in the shop. He or she acts as the buyer, keeps stock in place, and recommends tennis equipment.

Court maintenance is another important function of the Tennis Director. He or she must see to it that courts are in perfect condition, clean, and safe. If they are not, the individual directs a maintenance person to fix the problem. The Tennis Director also is responsible for making sure all tennis racquets are in good shape. If not, he or she sees to it that they are repaired. The Tennis Director may do this him- or herself or may have an assistant or other staff member take care of repair. In addition to taking care of the club's racquets, the Director may also repair or have repaired patrons' racquets.

The individual must know how to schedule. The Director has a certain number of courts to fill, and he or she must know how to utilize them to the best advantage. For example, if the courts are always busy in the mornings and afternoons, but not the evenings, the Director may offer a discount for patrons willing to play at night.

The Tennis Director may be expected to do public relations work for the facility. He or she may write press releases on events held there and on special promotions, tournaments, and new professional tennis instructors. The individual may also invite the media to cover events or do feature stories.

Another major function of the Tennis Director is to provide instructions to patrons. The Director may give lessons him- or herself or may have a staff of tennis teachers and instructor professionals. The Director must schedule lessons for those who are interested. He or she may develop group lesson schedules and programs for those who have various levels of tennis playing skill.

The Tennis Director may work long hours. As he or she is ultimately responsible for every aspect of the organization of the tennis program, the individual may often have to work at night and on weekends as well as regular hours.

Salaries

Earnings can vary greatly for Tennis Directors depending on a great many factors. Some of these include the geographic location, prestige, and size of the facility. Other factors include the individual's experience and responsibilities. Another factor might be whether if the facility is open year-round or is seasonal. This might occur if the Director is working in a facility with outdoor courts in a geographical area with cold winters. Earnings are also dependent on the amount of sales generated in the pro shop and the number of lessons taught.

Salaries for Tennis Directors may range from $24,000 to $85,000 plus. Some individuals who run programs in very large or prestigious facilities earn $110,000 and over annually.

Employment Prospects

Employment prospects are good for Tennis Directors who are skilled in their profession. Individuals may work in any type of tennis and racquet club, tennis and swimming club, exercise facility, spa, resort, camp, country club, or hotel. They may work in indoor, outdoor, or dual facilities. Job openings may be located throughout the country.

Advancement Prospects

Advancement prospects are good for Tennis Directors. Individuals may advance their careers by locating similar positions in larger or more prestigious facilities. This will result in additional responsibilities and higher earnings.

Education and Training

Educational requirements vary for Tennis Directors. Some facilities require a college background or degree, while others do not. As a rule, most successful Tennis Directors do have a four-year college degree. As individuals are responsible for administering the tennis program, a degree or background in business or marketing is useful. A number of colleges currently offer degrees in tennis programming.

Individuals might also choose a college that places a heavy emphasis its school's tennis team. In this way they will obtain training, experience, and participate in competitive tennis situations.

Experience/Skills/Personality Traits

The Tennis Director should have a full range of business and marketing skills. He or she should have good communication skills, both verbal and written.

The Tennis Director needs supervisory skills as well. He or she administrates the entire tennis program. Therefore, the individual usually has a number of people working under him or her, including instructors, maintenance people, bookkeepers, and others.

The individual should be extremely organized. He or she must also know a great deal about scheduling. This comes in handy when scheduling lessons, court time, and tournaments.

The Tennis Director should know how to play tennis well. It is not necessary, however, for the Tennis Director to be a world-class player. It is more important that the individual is able to teach and communicate the methods and techniques of the sport. The individual must also be able to teach a variety of levels of players, from beginners through advanced.

Some positions may require or prefer certification.

Some individuals come out of college with a business or marketing degree and know a great deal about the sport. These people may locate a job as a Tennis Director right away. Other people obtain experience in the industry as assistants, interns, teachers, or tennis instructor professionals before becoming Tennis Directors.

Unions/Associations

The largest and oldest association in the professional tennis industry is the U.S. Pro Tennis Association (USPTA). This organization provides valuable help, professional guidance, and support as well as continuing education. It also licenses and certifies professionals working in the tennis industry.

Tips for Entry

1. If you aspire to be a successful Tennis Director, consider one of the colleges with a major in tennis programming. Ferris State in Big Rapids, Michigan, is one of these schools. Contact them for more information.

2. You might also consider attending a college with a strong tennis team.

3. Join the U.S. Pro Tennis Association. It is very helpful to those involved in the tennis industry. It offers classes, manuals, booklets, seminars, conferences, and other guidance and support. It is well worth getting involved with.

4. Get a part-time or summer job working in a local tennis club, tennis camp, or other tennis facility. This will provide you with good on-the-job experience.

5. Speak to a Tennis Director of a large facility to see if he or she might consider becoming your mentor.

TENNIS TEACHING PROFESSIONAL

CAREER PROFILE

Duties: Giving tennis lessons to all levels of players.

Alternate Title(s):   Tennis Teaching Pro; Pro; Tennis Pro; Instructor

Salary Range: $23,000 to $95,000+

Employment Prospects: Good

Best Geographical Location(s) for Position: Positions may be located throughout the country.

Prerequisites:

Education or Training—No formal educational requirement for some positions; others require certification.

Experience—Experience in playing or teaching tennis required.

Special Skills and Personality Traits—Skilled tennis player; organizational skills; ability to teach all levels of tennis; good communications skills.

CAREER LADDER

```
┌─────────────────────────────────────┐
│     Teaching Professional Level 1    │
│                  or                  │
│        Teaching Professional         │
│  at Larger, More Prestigious Facility│
└─────────────────────────────────────┘

┌─────────────────────────────────────┐
│        Teaching Professional         │
└─────────────────────────────────────┘

┌─────────────────────────────────────┐
│          Tennis Instructor           │
│                  or                  │
│            Tennis Player             │
└─────────────────────────────────────┘
```

Position Description

With tennis and racquet clubs becoming more popular throughout the country, a growing number of people want to learn how to play the sport or to refine their skills. The individual who can help accomplish this goal is called either a Tennis Instructor or a Teaching Professional. Teaching Professionals differ from Tennis Instructors in that they pass through a certification program, whereas Instructors may have no professional training.

As with the Tennis Instructor, the main function of the Teaching Professional is to give tennis lessons to those interested in the sport. He or she, however, is also trained in other facets of the tennis industry, which makes him or her a more valuable asset to a club, resort, or organization. In many instances, the Teaching Professional may assume many of the duties of a tennis director.

The Teaching Professional is certified by the U.S. Professional Tennis Association (USPTA). To be certified, the individual must pass an examination developed by the organization. The organization also holds courses and seminars to help prepare individuals for certification. For example, the individual is trained in merchandising and business. He or she may also be educated on court maintenance, racquet repair, and pro shop operation. The individual must know and demonstrate to those administering the exam the various techniques and shots used in the sport. He or she also has to demonstrate teaching abilities.

Teaching Professionals are expected to offer instruction in both private and group lessons. They also must be able to teach tennis techniques on all levels, from beginner to experienced. In many circumstances, individuals are responsible for a junior development program at the tennis facility.

The Teaching Professional might be expected to schedule lessons for his or her students as well as reserve court time. In some instances, the individual may also be responsible for racquet repair.

Depending on the specific job, the Teaching Professional often is expected to run tournaments for students and other players to participate in. He or she must know how to develop the tournaments, schedule court times for players, and divide the tournament for different skill or age levels. At the tennis director's request, the individual may also be responsible for obtaining players to participate as well as for handling public relations.

In some situations, the Teaching Professional also is expected to operate the pro shop. In these cases, he or she may recommend tennis equipment, clothing, shoes, and the like to patrons.

Many Teaching Professionals work at year-round indoor tennis courts. Others may work part of the year in one location and the rest in another section of the country. Individuals who love to play tennis and to teach and enjoy the sport can have a very fulfilling career.

Salaries

Earnings may vary greatly for Teaching Professionals in tennis depending on a number of variables. These may include the facility the individual is working at, its prestige, size, and location. Other factors determining earnings include the experience, skills, drive, determination, and responsibilities of the Teaching Professional. Individuals may earn between $23,000 and $95,000 plus annually.

Teaching Professionals may be paid a salary in addition to being entitled to all money they earn giving lessons. The average cost of a tennis lesson is between $25 and $50 per hour. The Teaching Professional may also earn a commission of proceeds from pro shop revenue.

Employment Prospects

Employment prospects are good for those trained in the sport and skilled in business. Individuals may work in a variety of settings, including resort hotels, tennis clubs, racquet clubs, exercise facilities, spas, tennis camps, country clubs, and hotels. Facilities may be indoors, outdoors, or dual. Jobs may be located throughout the country.

Advancement Prospects

Tennis Professionals who are certified may advance their career by obtaining continuing education in the field. There are three levels of professional, ranging from the highest level, Professional 1, through Professional 3. There is also a Master Professional certification. Those who advance their level of certification have an easier time locating similar positions in larger or more prestigious facilities. This results in increased responsibilities and higher earnings.

Education and Training

Some Tennis Instructors have no training whatsoever. They are self-taught, skilled in the sport, and like to teach. Teaching Professionals, however, go through a certification program offered by the U.S. Pro Tennis Association. The association gives a two-day examination that includes a written test as well as actual demonstrations. Prior to the test the USPTA offers training to assist individuals so that they will be able to pass the test. Once an individual is certified, he or she may take a variety of continuing education classes to help refine techniques in tennis, teaching, and business skills.

Experience/Skills/Personality Traits

The Tennis Teaching Professional must have good tennis skills. He or she need not, however, be a world-class tennis player. Individuals good enough to play on the tournament circuit usually do so for a while because they can make more money doing that. The Teaching Professional must be an excellent instructor. He or she must be able to show students techniques and communicate ways of performing them. The individual must be able to teach people in all levels of the sport. He or she must also be equally adept at teaching groups and individual students.

Teaching Professionals who attain success usually have good business and marketing skills. They are extremely organized and detail oriented. They know how to schedule classes, court time, and tournaments.

Individuals should enjoy working with people of all ages and at all levels of tennis. They should be pleasant, articulate, and well groomed. Communications skills are necessary.

Unions/Associations

The most prominent association in this field is the U.S. Pro Tennis Association. The USPTA certifies Teaching Professionals, provides continuing education, and offers job guidance and support for those in the field.

Tips for Entry

1. Join the U.S. Pro Tennis Association. The organization will be useful to you in getting your career started.
2. Attend tennis camps, seminars, workshops, and classes. The more techniques you learn from others, the more you will be able to teach to students.
3. Volunteer to teach tennis to a nonprofit or youth group in your area. It will be good on the job experience.
4. Positions are often advertised in the newspaper display or classified sections. Look under heading classifications of "Tennis," "Pro," or "Sports Instruction."
5. You might also consider sending your résumé and a cover letter to tennis clubs, health clubs, resorts, or hotels. Ask that your résumé be kept on file if there is no current opening.

GOLF PRO

Duties: Running a club, course, or resort's golf program; providing lessons; managing a pro shop; overseeing a golf course; recommending golf equipment.

Alternate Title(s): Pro

Salary Range: $25,000 to $150,000+

Employment Prospects: Good

Best Geographical Location(s) for Position: Positions located throughout the country; areas hosting a great many resort hotels may offer additional opportunities.

Prerequisites:

Education or Training—Completion of PGA training program is necessary in order to obtain PGA certification.
Experience—Experience as an assistant pro or apprentice may be required.
Special Skills and Personality Traits—Excellent golf skills; good teacher; personable; business and administrative skills; knowledge of first aid.

```
┌─────────────────────────────────┐
│   Golf Pro at More Prestigious  │
│     Club, Resort, or Facility   │
└─────────────────────────────────┘

┌─────────────────────────────────┐
│           Golf Pro              │
└─────────────────────────────────┘

┌─────────────────────────────────┐
│        Assistant Golf Pro       │
│               or                │
│           Apprentice            │
└─────────────────────────────────┘
```

Position Description

Golf is an extremely popular sport in this country and in other nations as well. Millions of people play regularly, and a great many business deals are developed and finalized on golf courses.

The Golf Pro is the individual responsible for running a golf course and a program for a facility. He or she may work at a driving range, a public golf course, a private golf club, a golf hotel, or a resort hotel. Individuals may have varied duties depending on the specific job. The Pro is expected to be an expert on everything from the skills of the sport and course maintenance to the type of equipment that golfers should use.

One of the main functions of the individual is to help people interested in playing the sport develop their skills. To do this, the Pro often offers private or group lessons to patrons of the golf facility. He or she is usually paid a fee by the golfers for this instruction. Individuals may take one or more lessons over a period of time in hopes of improving their golf game. As golfers begin to see their game improve, they generally seek additional instruction. The Pro must be able to give lessons to all levels of people, from beginners to advanced players. The Pro is expected to schedule his or her own lessons as well as those of any other instructors at the course. The individual

must also set fees for lessons. As a rule, the Pro is paid a higher fee for services than the other instructors.

In many golf clubs, the Pro may be responsible for hiring additional instructors, assistant pros, and the other personnel necessary to run the golf program successfully. He or she may be expected to advertise for openings, interview applicants, and talk with the press. Depending on the size and structure of a gold club, the Pro may also have to hire personnel for the food concessions, groundskeeping, maintenance, and pro shop, as well as caddies.

The Pro is responsible for the supervision and administration of staff members working under him or her. He or she is expected to schedule staff hours and make sure that enough personnel are on each shift to take care of the club patrons.

Another responsibility many Pros assume is running and managing of the pro shop. Here golfers can buy clubs, bags, balls, and other equipment for the game as well as golf clothes. In many cases, the Pro must do the buying for the shop, determining what brands of equipment and how much to purchase. He or she may be responsible for keeping track of inventory, invoices, pricing merchandise as it comes in, and displaying it in a pleasing manner, or assigning this duty to another staff member. People often patronize the shop to get the Pro's opinion and recommendation on the brand or type of clubs or other equipment to purchase.

The Pro is responsible for making sure that the course is in good shape. If there are dangerous or unsightly areas in need of repair, he or she is expected to have them taken care of in a timely manner.

If there is an emergency, accident, injury, or sick player in the club or on the course, the Pro is expected to call for an ambulance or medical personnel. He or she may administer first aid in emergencies. If there has been an accident, the Pro must fill out an accident report and notify the club or course owner or manager.

Other responsibilities of the Pro might include selling club memberships, obtaining greens fees, registrations, and renting equipment and golf carts.

Golf Pros are often asked to take part in charity events and golf tournaments to help raise money for worthwhile community causes. They may help put together players, find sponsors for prizes, and so on. Individuals may also find celebrity golfers to play in the tournament as well as play themselves.

Being a Golf Pro is the perfect job for those who enjoy the game. Pros have the opportunity to perfect their skills while helping others learn to perfect theirs. Pros working in the Midwest or eastern part of the country usually cannot work full time, because of the cold, snowy winters. Individuals who want to work full time must find a similar type of job in a warmer climate for the winter months. This is a drawback for some and a plus for others who like to travel.

Salaries

Earnings for Golf Pros vary greatly depending on a number of variables. These include the determination, drive, and personality of the individual as well as his or her skills, responsibilities, and experience level. Other factors include the location where the Pro is working and whether the individual has a recognized name in the golfing industry.

Pros often make a salary for running the golf program and managing the pro shop. They may earn commissions from sales of golf equipment, clothing, and shoes, and additional money by giving lessons.

Individuals may work part of the year in one section of the country and the balance of the time in another section. Earnings can range from $25,000 to $150,000 and up depending on the specific individual. Hourly rates for teaching golf skills to individuals may range between $30 and $250 plus.

Employment Prospects

Employment prospects are fair for individuals who are good at the sport. Golf Pros can work throughout the country. Pros in geographic areas that are cold and snowy in winter will have to move to warmer climates to continue working.

Individuals may work in a variety of settings, including driving ranges, community-owned golf courses, other public courses, private clubs, and luxurious resort hotels. Pros may also work for specific golf resorts.

While Pros can work throughout the country, more jobs may be located in areas in which many resort hotels are located.

Advancement Prospects

A Golf Pro can advance his or her career by locating a position at a more prestigious location. This usually results in higher earnings. For example, an individual working at a driving range might climb the career ladder by landing a job at a private golf club. Pros who run large pro shops and give lessons can increase their earnings.

Education and Training

There is no formal educational requirement to become a Golf Pro. Individuals, however, must usually go through a course of study offered by the Professional Golfer Association (PGA). The training offers courses in a number of areas of use to the Pro in his or her career.

Individuals must pass the training course in order to be approved and certified as a PGA Pro. PGA Pros also must serve as apprentices or assistants before becoming full-fledged Pros.

Experience/Skills/Personality Traits

The Golf Pro must be extremely talented and really enjoy the sport. He or she must know everything there is to know about golf. Many Pros began their career as professional golfers playing in tournaments. Some were top celebrities in their field. Others did not become household names but played in tournaments, enjoyed the sport, and want to work in it.

Pros need to be good teachers. They need the ability to instruct beginners through advanced golfers in the skills of the sport. Individuals should have a lot of patience and perseverance.

Pros must be personable and get along well with people. In order to be successful, the Pro must make people feel comfortable and confident. He or she must motivate them and help them enjoy the game.

As Golf Pros may be responsible for running the golf program, they must have both administrative and supervisory skills. A knowledge of business and management is needed.

Sales ability is required, especially if the Pro is paid a commission on golf equipment sold in the shop. It is also necessary for the Pro to sell his or her own skills in teaching.

Knowledge of first aid is helpful in cases of injury, sickness, or emergencies on the course.

Unions/Associations

The major trade association in the field of golf is the PGA. This organization provides training, support, certification, and professional guidance to those interested in golf.

Individuals might also belong to other organizations promoting the sport, such as the Ladies Professional Golf Association (LPGA).

Tips for Entry

1. Consider getting a part-time or summer job as a golf caddy. A caddy moves the golfer's equipment from hole to hole on the course. Being a caddy is an excellent way to work in the sport as you learn about the game.
2. If you are qualified, send your résumé and a cover letter to resort hotels, private golf clubs, or public courses. Ask that your résumé be kept on file if there are no current openings.
3. Play golf at various courses. Keep your ears open. You might hear of a job possibility. It will also help you make contacts that can in turn lead to a job offer.
4. Jobs openings may be located in trade magazines.
5. Positions may also be advertised in newspaper display or classified sections. Look under heading classifications of "Pro" or "Golf."

LIFEGUARD

CAREER PROFILE

Duties: Keeping water safe for swimmers; saving the lives of swimmers; overseeing activities at a pool or beach.

Alternate Title(s):   None

Salary Range: $10 to $28+ per hour; $20,000 to $39,000+ annually

Employment Prospects: Good

Best Geographical Location(s) for Position: Positions may be located throughout the country.

Prerequisites:

Education or Training—No formal educational requirement; individuals must be certified by the American Red Cross.

Experience—No experience necessary.

Special Skills and Personality Traits—Excellent swimmer; strong; physically fit; good eyesight; knowledge of lifesaving techniques; reliable; dependable; enjoy working with people.

CAREER LADDER

```
┌─────────────────────────┐
│   Chief Lifeguard       │
│        or               │
│  Lifeguard Supervisor   │
└─────────────────────────┘

┌─────────────────────────┐
│      Lifeguard          │
└─────────────────────────┘

┌─────────────────────────┐
│     Entry Level         │
└─────────────────────────┘
```

Position Description

Lifeguards have important jobs. Their presence in certain situations often means the difference between life and death. Lifeguards may work in a variety of settings, including public pools, private pools, lakes, or the ocean. They may work indoors or outdoors. Responsibilities of each individual vary depending on the specific job. The Lifeguard's main function, however, is to keep the water area safe for swimmers.

Individuals working at a pool have different duties from Lifeguards at the seashore. Those working in a pool setting are responsible for keeping the area around the pool hazard-free. The individual watches patrons using the facility. If they begin to play rough, in or out of the water, the Lifeguard instructs them to calm down.

When on duty, the Lifeguard must keep his or her eyes on the water at all times. The individual must be alert. Daydreaming, reading, or trying to handle any other activity might mean a potential drowning.

The Lifeguard at the pool may also be expected to check the pool temperature periodically and regulate it as necessary. He or she may also be required to check on the amount of chlorine and other chemicals used in the pool to keep the water clean and safe. When necessary, the Lifeguard is expected to disperse additional chemicals into the water.

In many job situations, the Lifeguard is required to teach swimming lessons. He or she may instruct on a one-on-one basis or offer group classes to various levels of swimmers.

Lifeguards working at lakes or at the seashore do not have to check water temperatures. Depending on where they are working, however, they may be required to check water for bacteria or chemical contamination, shark infestation, etc.

It is difficult to stare into the ocean or large lakes for hours on end. Therefore, individuals working in these types of settings usually do so in groups. One Lifeguard watches the water for an hour and then takes a break or attends to other duties. Another Lifeguard then takes his or her place.

Large stretches of beach are usually divided into sections. Each section has a Lifeguard station or tower. These look like very tall chairs that hover high above the beach. From those seats, Lifeguards can watch activities in the water.

The Lifeguard must make sure that swimmers stay in designated areas. Many beaches also have rules and regulations that patrons must follow. Some areas, for example, do not allow glass containers on the beach. The Lifeguard must enforce all the rules of the beach. If the individual sees an infraction, he or she usually tells the people and gives warnings.

When a swimmer has a problem, the Lifeguards jump into action. They are responsible for rapidly reaching the individual and trying to save him or her. They may do this by running to the water, swimming out to the person in trouble, and bringing him or her back to shore. In some instances, Lifeguards may also take a boat to save a swimmer. Lifesaving can be difficult if the drowning person becomes hysterical and disoriented. Rough surf and tides can also make swimming out to the individual difficult. Lifeguards may also assist boaters in need of assistance.

Lifeguards working on the beach often have lifesaving drills. One individual acts as the victim while others handle lifesaving duties.

Once a Lifeguard brings the distressed swimmer back to shore, he or she may have to perform cardiopulmonary resuscitation (CPR) or other first aid. All Lifeguards must know CPR. Often there is no time to wait for an ambulance.

Lifeguards may perform other functions, such as helping lost children find their parents, treating minor first aid problems, handling lost-and-found duties, and providing directions.

Salaries

Earnings vary for Lifeguards depending on the specific job. Variables include the individual's responsibilities and experience as well as place of employment.

Lifeguards may be compensated in a number of ways. Individuals may receive an hourly rate, a weekly salary, or may earn a set amount for a season.

Lifeguards may earn between $10 and $28 plus an hour. Individuals who are paid salaries can earn between $20,000 and $39,000 plus annually. This is common in areas such as California and Florida, where Lifeguards work year round on the beaches.

Lifeguards who teach swimming may also earn a fee for each lesson.

Employment Prospects

Employment prospects are good for Lifeguards. Individuals may work at indoor or outdoor pools. They may obtain positions in public or private settings. Many communities, cities, park services, and states hire Lifeguards.

Lifeguards may also work in camps, hotels, resorts, spas, clubs, or on cruise ships. Positions are also available at beaches on private or public lakes, or at the ocean.

Advancement Prospects

Lifeguards can advance their careers by becoming a supervising lifeguard or a chief lifeguard. Advancement is usually attained by seniority and by demonstrating supervisory abilities. Lifeguards can also advance their careers by obtaining positions at more prestigious or exciting locations.

Education and Training

There are usually no formal educational requirements needed to become a Lifeguard. Individuals must, however, be certified. The agency that ordinarily is responsible for setting certification requirements is the state's Department of Health. Requirements can vary from state to state.

The organization that provides certification is the American Red Cross. To obtain this certification, Lifeguards must take courses and pass tests in lifeguarding, first aid, and cardiopulmonary resuscitation and basic life support (CPRBLS). The American Red Cross sponsors these courses throughout the country.

Experience/Skills/Personality Traits

The most important skill a Lifeguard should possess is the ability to be an excellent swimmer. The individual should also be a fast swimmer and a quick runner. The Lifeguard probably will be required to take a swimming speed test. He or she should also be strong and physically fit. Good eyesight is necessary.

Lifeguards need to be skilled in lifesaving techniques. A working knowledge of CPR and first aid are imperative. Individuals should enjoy working near the water, and if working outside, enjoy the sun.

Lifeguards must be reliable and dependable. They need supervisory skills. The ability to take control of a situation is essential. Individuals must be able to work under intense, stressful conditions.

Unions/Associations

There is no specific trade association for Lifeguards. If, however, an individual is working as a city or state employee, he or she may be a member of a local municipal union. Most Lifeguards are members of their local chapter of the American Red Cross.

Tips for Entry

1. You need to be an excellent swimmer to be a Lifeguard. Take swimming lessons.
2. Contact your local chapter of the American Red Cross for information on certification classes and continuing education.
3. Positions are often advertised in the local newspaper's display or classified section. Look under heading classifications of "Lifeguard," "Pool," "Lake," "Summer Employment," "Seaside," or "Ocean."
4. Jobs may be located in state parks or recreation departments. Cities and local communities also frequently hire Lifeguards.
5. You might consider writing to camps, hotels, resorts, spas, or clubs with swimming pools. Send a copy of your résumé with a short cover letter. They may call you for an interview.
6. Jobs may be located on the World Wide Web. Search popular job sites, newspaper classifieds, or hotel and resort career opportunities.

CAREER OPPORTUNITIES
IN BOXING
AND WRESTLING

MATCHMAKER

CAREER PROFILE

Duties: Matching two opponents for professional fights; initiating entertaining, competitive bouts.

Alternate Title(s): None

Salary Range: $25,000 to $250,000+

Employment Prospects: Fair

Best Geographical Location(s) for Position: Atlantic City, Las Vegas, New York City, and other cities hosting boxing promoters and events.

Prerequisites:
Education or Training—No formal education or training.
Experience—Experience matchmaking.
Special Skills and Personality Traits—Complete knowledge of boxing and fighters; good memory; salesmanship.

CAREER LADDER

```
┌─────────────────────────────┐
│        Matchmaker           │
│     for More Prestigious     │
│    Promoters and Events      │
└─────────────────────────────┘

┌─────────────────────────────┐
│        Matchmaker           │
└─────────────────────────────┘

┌─────────────────────────────┐
│        Boxing Fan           │
│            or                │
│   Assistant to Matchmaker    │
└─────────────────────────────┘
```

Position Description

A Matchmaker works in the field of boxing. His or her main function is to place two opponents together in the ring for a professional fight. The Matchmaker's job is to initiate good, entertaining, and competitive bouts.

In most instances, Matchmakers are hired by the promoter of a fight. The promoter may instruct the individual about which specific fighters he or she wants on the card, or program. In other situations, the promoter leaves the choice of fighters to the Matchmaker.

The Matchmaker must first determine what the purse, or earnings, will be for the fighters and/or the fight. For example, if the purse is to be $800 for a fighter, the Matchmaker would not be able to have Mike Tyson on the card.

Sometimes fighters can earn multimillion-dollar purses. This usually occurs in major and championship fights. The Matchmaker must work within the budget the promoter sets for a fight and come up with the most exciting, competitive fighters available.

In addition to paying the fighters their purse, the Matchmaker may also be required to develop budgets for training, traveling expenses, food, and lodging for some of the fighters and their retinue. These expenses must be added into the event budget for the show.

In order for the Matchmaker to be successful "making" fights, he or she needs to have as much information as possible about as many fighters as possible. The Matchmaker must be familiar with managers, their fighters, fight records, amateur experience, fight styles, weights, statures, and so on. Matchmakers also must know how and where to locate this information. Just putting together two junior middleweights in a ring does not necessarily make a good fight. For example, one opponent might be making his professional debut, while the other might be a seasoned pro. It would probably be a better fight if the two opponents both had some experience fighting professionally.

In order to be completely aware of fight industry information, the Matchmaker must constantly ask questions. In making decisions, he or she must then weigh the answers and consider who was the information source.

After finding two fighters who are competitively matched and who will agree to a purse, the Matchmaker works with the promoter to have contracts drawn up and signed. These contracts usually specify the date and location of the fight, the agreed-upon purse, the number of rounds, and the weight the fighters are expected to be for the match.

Matchmakers are licensed in the states that have athletic governing bodies. In some states, in order to become licensed as a Matchmaker, the individual must first have a contract with a promoter to do the matchmaking. This can be a Catch-22 situation because one cannot be initiated without the other in place.

Matchmakers may work long hours doing the necessary research to put together good matches. Keep in mind that the individual usually is contracted to put together the entire fight card. This might run seven to ten different bouts.

The Matchmaker works under a great deal of stress. He or she is responsible directly to the fight promoter. The individual must both please the promoter and put together a good fight card. This might be difficult if the promoter also has promotional ties to fighters he or she wants on the card.

Salaries

Salaries vary depending on the Matchmaker and how successful or in demand he or she is. Earnings may be based on specific boxing promotions, a flat fee, an annual salary, or any combination of these systems.

Individuals working in a full-time situation where they are receiving weekly paychecks may earn from $25,000 to $250,000 plus.

Employment Prospects

Almost any individual who can find a promoter to hire him or her as a Matchmaker can find employment once. Some people think that anyone can promote and put together a successful boxing event. But Matchmakers who don't know what they are doing and put together an uncompetitive, unexciting show will not work in the profession again.

Employment prospects are fair for Matchmakers who are good at what they do. Most of the more established promoters in the country have had the same Matchmakers working with them for years. On the other hand, new promoters crop up all the time. An individual who is qualified as a Matchmaker might be able to build a relationship with a promoter who is just starting out.

While most of the major boxing shows are held in Atlantic City, Las Vegas, and New York, many other locations are beginning to host boxing events. This will give those starting out additional opportunities to break in to the profession.

Advancement Prospects

It is important to note that there is no logical job progression in boxing. Individuals can hit it lucky in any facet of this business and jump to the top of the industry.

Matchmakers climb the career ladder by working with more prestigious fight promoters. Advancement prospects could include matchmaking fights for television or cable or championships.

Those who are good at what they do can advance quickly.

Education and Training

There are no formal educational requirements for Matchmakers. Individuals must learn from watching others and personal experience. Some in the industry say that good Matchmakers learn how to make good fights by osmosis. If that is true, individuals pursuing a career in this field should watch and analyze as many fights as possible. Trying to find a skilled, expert Matchmaker to apprentice with might also be helpful.

Experience/Skills/Personality Traits

Successful Matchmakers have an extensive background in boxing as well as other sports. As a rule, individuals in this profession spend a lot of time watching and absorbing boxing events. A Matchmaker needs almost a sixth sense when it comes to fighters. He or she should either have or develop the ability to know when two boxers could put on a very exciting show.

It helps if the Matchmaker has a good memory. In this way, he or she will remember facts and data about fighters. The individual should be personable. Matchmakers want managers and fighters to talk to them honestly.

Being a good salesperson helps when the Matchmaker is trying to get opponents to fight each other.

Unions/Associations

There is no Matchmaker union in boxing. Individuals may belong to the various sanctioning organizations, such as the World Boxing Association (WBA), the World Boxing Council (WBC), the World Boxing Organization (WBO), and the International Boxing Federation (IBF). Matchmakers may also be affiliated with any of the state athletic commissions.

Tips for Entry

1. Find a gym where fighters train. Get to know the various fighters, managers, trainers, and promoters who visit. Make contacts. They might be able to guide you to helpful people in the industry.
2. Read boxing magazines and record books. This will help you to begin to know about fighters and their records.
3. Attend live fights and watch them on television. Get the feel for the way the fighters are matched up.
4. Try to obtain a job working as an assistant, secretary, or clerk for a promoter or Matchmaker. This will give you good hands-on experience.

BOXING REFEREE

CAREER PROFILE

Duties: Officiating during a boxing match; enforcing rules of the sport; giving eight counts; stopping fights; making sure that a fighter is not seriously injured.

Alternate Title(s):   Ref.; Official

Salary Range: $150 to $20,000+ per show

Employment Prospects: Fair

Best Geographical Location(s) for Position: Positions may be located throughout the country; major boxing capitals are Las Vegas, New York City, and Atlantic City.

Prerequisites:

Education or Training—No formal educational requirement; training in boxing officiating is necessary.

Experience—Experience officiating in amateur bouts is required.

Special Skills and Personality Traits—Enjoy sport of boxing; know rules and regulations of game; self-confident; ability to work under pressure; physically fit.

CAREER LADDER

```
┌─────────────────────────────────────┐
│         Boxing Referee              │
│          Assigned to                │
│   More Prestigious Boxing Show      │
└─────────────────────────────────────┘

┌─────────────────────────────────────┐
│         Boxing Referee              │
└─────────────────────────────────────┘

┌─────────────────────────────────────┐
│      Amateur Boxing Referee         │
└─────────────────────────────────────┘
```

Position Description

The Referee in professional boxing is the individual who stays in the ring with boxers during a bout. The individual in this position is responsible for enforcing the rules of the match. While doing this, the Referee tries to keep the bout running smoothly. One Referee is present in each boxing match. Individuals may officiate during one or more bouts during a boxing show.

One of the first duties of the Referee is to inspect both fighters' gloves. This is done to make sure that none of the gloves have been altered in any way. The individual must be sure that all glove padding is intact and that no substances have been put on the gloves.

Before a bout begins, the Referee explains the rules and regulations to the fighters and their "seconds." (Seconds are those people in the corner with the fighter between rounds. A second may be the fighter's manager or a trainer.) The Referee goes over the rules fully in the fighters' dressing rooms prior to the fight. Just before the bout starts, the individual calls both fighters and their seconds to the center of the ring and reviews the rules again briefly.

Once the fight has begun, the Referee follows the fighters around the ring making sure that they are adhering to the rules. The individual warns the fighters if they are delivering illegal punches, such as low blows, rabbit punches, punching on a break, or striking when a fighter is down on the canvas. If, after a couple of warnings, one of the fighters persists in the illegal punches, the Referee may call a time-out. The individual may then tell the judges to take points away from that fighter.

The Referee commands the fighters to break, or take a step apart, when they are in a clinch. The individual also keeps close watch on the actions of both fighters to see that they are fighting back.

When a fighter is getting hit, the Referee must watch the individual's eyes and the way he breathes to be sure he is trying to defend himself. One of the most important responsibilities of the Referee is to make sure that neither fighter is injured badly. This requires the Referee to have some basic medical knowledge and is often difficult to do. If it seems that a fighter is stunned or injured, the Referee may either end the fight or give the individual a standing eight count. The Referee might also call a time-out so that the ringside physician can inspect the fighter.

The Referee has the power to stop a fight at any time for a number of reasons. He or she may do this, if, as mentioned previously, one fighter is injured too badly to compete or will sustain permanent injuries if he continues. A Referee may also stop the bout if one fighter outclasses another so that the fight is one-sided. Another reason to end a bout is if one boxer is not fighting to the best of his ability or appears to be in there for the money. Under some circumstances, the Referee may also stop a fight if a boxer commits a major foul against another boxer while in the ring, such as an intentional low blow, head butt, or thumbing.

The major reasons Referees stop fights are KOs (knockouts) and TKOs (technical knockouts). Fights end when boxer cannot come out of his corner at the beginning of a round or when he is knocked down and cannot get up before the referee counts to ten. Some states specify the number of times a fighter can be knocked down during a round or during a fight before the Referee must stop the fight.

The Referee may be responsible for momentarily stopping the fight to have a fighter's gloves taped back up, grease wiped off his face or body, or to have a mouthpiece that was knocked out washed and replaced.

When one fighter is knocked down, the Referee must send the opponent to a neutral corner. At the same time, he or she counts to ten over the knocked-down fighter. So that no extra time is given to the downed boxer the Referee picks the count from the timekeeper, who begins counting as soon as the knockdown occurs. The downed fighter must take a count of eight even if he gets up before that.

At the end of the count, the Referee asks the fighter if he is okay and can continue fighting. If, in the Referee's opinion, the fighter cannot go on, he or she stops the fight (a technical knockout). This is a judgment call. Many times the fighter and his handlers do not agree. However, the decision of the Referee is final.

When the fight has ended, the Referee stands between the two contestants while the decision of the judges is read. When the winner is announced, the Referee holds up the winning fighter's hand and arm.

Salaries

Referees in professional boxing are paid by the promoter of the event. They are compensated on a per-event basis. Annual salaries depend on the number of shows they officiate at as well as the type of show and the sanctioning organization.

Individuals may earn from $150 to $20,000 plus per show for their refereeing duties. Higher fees usually go to well-known referees working high-profile fights.

Employment Prospects

Employment prospects are fair for individuals who are trained and licensed. Referees are usually assigned to bouts by the state's athletic commission. Individuals may officiate at fights in their state or may get authorization to work in other states or countries.

Advancement Prospects

Advancement prospects are fair for Referees who are consistent, concerned with the safety of fighters, fair, and skilled in their jobs. Referees advance their careers by being assigned to officiate at more prestigious and world-class fights. Most Referees aspire to officiate at a major world championship fight.

At the beginning of a Referee's professional career, the individual usually officiates at four-round matches. The Referee then officiates at matches that go six rounds. After being reviewed by other officials or members of a state commission, the Referee may go on to officiate at matches of eight or more rounds.

Education and Training

There is no formal educational requirement necessary to become a Referee. Some individuals in this profession have a high school diploma, while others hold master's and doctoral degrees.

In states hosting athletic commissions, Referees are usually required to be licensed. In order to become licensed, individuals may have to take written, oral, and medical examinations. Many states also require mandatory seminars and workshops and continuing education programs for Referees.

Experience/Skills/Personality Traits

Professional Boxing Referees must enjoy the sport of boxing and also know a great deal about it. They must know all the rules and regulations. Referees must not only know the illegal blows but be able to recognize them too.

Referees must be adept at watching the "looks" of fighters. They must know when a boxer is hurt and when he cannot fight any longer. Some basic medical knowledge may be necessary for this task. Individuals must be self-confident. They will often make judgment call decisions. Everyone will not agree. Referees must consider the safety of the fighters above all else.

The Referee may work under stressful conditions. When the champ is losing, it is not easy to stop a championship fight.

Referees usually officiate in amateur bouts to obtain experience before moving into the pros. Individuals must referee a certain number of rounds in amateur competitions before becoming a Referee in the pros.

Individuals move around the ring quickly and constantly following the fighters. In most states, Referees must undergo an annual medical examination to make sure that they are physically fit and in good shape.

Unions/Associations

Referees may be members of their state's athletic commission as well as any of the sanctioning organizations in boxing. They may also be members of various trade associations. Some of these include the International Boxing Federation (IBF), the International Veterans Boxers Association (IVBA), the National Veteran Boxers Associations (NVBA), the North American Boxing Federation (NABF), the World Boxing Association (WBA), and the World Boxing Organization (WBO).

Tips for Entry

1. Watch professional boxing either on television or live. Try to get a feel for the way the Referee works.

2. Read all about boxing. There are numerous books in the library on the subject as well as a great number of boxing magazines and periodicals.

3. If your state has an athletic commission, write to them inquiring about licensing.

4. Look for an amateur boxing club in your area and talk to the individuals administering the program about your aspirations. There usually will be someone who can help you with your career goals.

PROFESSIONAL BOXING JUDGE

CAREER PROFILE

Duties: Judging professional boxing matches; scoring rounds.

Alternate Title(s): Judge

Salary Range: $150 to $2,500+ per show

Employment Prospects: Fair

Best Geographical Location(s) for Position: Positions located throughout the country; most major shows are held in Atlantic City, New York, and Las Vegas.

Prerequisites:

Education or Training—No formal educational requirement; state license training sessions required in some states.

Experience—Experience judging in amateurs bouts.

Special Skills and Personality Traits—Good judgment; knowledge of boxing rules and regulations; confident; professional.

CAREER LADDER

```
┌─────────────────────────────────┐
│     Judge for Championships      │
│               and                │
│     More Prestigious Fights      │
└─────────────────────────────────┘

┌─────────────────────────────────┐
│     Professional Boxing Judge    │
└─────────────────────────────────┘

┌─────────────────────────────────┐
│       Amateur Boxing Judge       │
└─────────────────────────────────┘
```

Position Description

A Professional Boxing Judge is responsible for judging professional boxing matches. Bouts are judged by three official Judges. In some areas, a referee may also judge the fight from inside the ring. However, this is becoming less and less common.

Fights may be scored in a number of ways, including the point system or the round system. Fights in some states use a combination of the two.

Judges in states having an athletic commission must be licensed. Professional Judges may also be licensed by boxing sanctioning organizations. Individuals are required to apply for their license and take written and/or oral examinations, pass physical exams, and pay licensing fees. Officials may be required to attend workshops, seminars, and training sessions covering the rules and regulations of the specific state they are being licensed in. Judges in most states are prohibited from having any financial interest in fighters or promotional companies.

The Judges at a professional fight are chosen from a list of qualified individuals. Judges are usually selected by the athletic commissioner or his or her deputies in states having athletic commissions. They may also be chosen by the sanctioning organization in fights authorized by the major sanctioning groups.

The Judges are assigned a ringside seat to view the fight. Individuals are usually stationed at opposite sides of the ring so that each gets an unrestricted view of the action.

The Judge watches the fight and scores each round on an official scorecard. The fighters are given points or rounds for specific actions, such as clean hitting and ring generalship. Boxers also score points from the Judges by fighting aggressively and defensively. In most states, Judges are required to write down their scores in ink or indelible pencil so that there can be no question of anyone changing the scores. Sometimes the Judge is required to give a brief written explanation of why he or she scored each round in the way that he or she did.

The Judge must be aware of all moves a boxer makes. The individual must also know what major fouls can occur in the ring, including low blows, intentional head butting, and not paying attention to the referee's warnings and instructions. Other fouls might include a fighter hitting an opponent who is down on the mat or other unsportsmanlike conduct in the ring. The Judge must also listen and watch the referee. At times, the referee takes points away from fighters because of an infraction or foul in the ring. When the referee indicates to the Judge that a point is being taken away in a round, the individual must mark it on his or her scorecard against the appropriate fighter.

While watching the fight, the Judge must keep his or her attention on the fighters at all times. It only takes a split second for action to occur in boxing. To score each round accurately, a Judge cannot miss anything.

After the fight is over, the Judge must tally up his or her scorecard and turn it over to the ring announcer. The individual usually does this even in the event of a knockout (KO) or technical knockout (TKO).

A Judge may score one or more fights during a boxing show. He or she may be responsible to the state athletic commission, if there is one in the host state, or to the organization that sanctioned the fight.

Judges may have the opportunity to travel extensively both in the country and abroad to fulfill their duties.

Boxing shows are becoming more popular now than ever before. With coverage on network, local, and cable television, a growing number of shows are being promoted. Many individuals are also promoting small, local shows. This is good news for Professional Judges, as each show requires their services.

Salaries

Professional Boxing Judges are paid by the promoter of the event and compensated on a per-show basis. Individuals may judge one or more fights on the fight card. Earnings vary depending on whether the individual is judging a main event or a preliminary bout . Earnings in major championship fights may also depend on the total fight receipts and the organization sanctioning the fight.

Fees may range from $150 to $2,500 plus per show. Fees rise considerably for individuals judging major media events sanctioned by the boxing governing organizations.

Employment Prospects

Employment prospects are fair and are becoming better. There has been a rise in the number of fights promoted throughout the country in both live and televised events. National, regional, and cable TV are buying not just major championship fights but also run-of-the-mill events. On any given day, boxing can usually be viewed on at least one channel.

Individuals who have the best prospects are those who are fully trained, experienced, and licensed.

Advancement Prospects

Advancement prospects are fair for Professional Boxing Judges who exhibit skills, fairness, and professionalism in their work. Individuals may move up the career ladder by being selected to judge a larger number of fights.

The next step up for most individuals is to be assigned to judge a major fight. Each state's athletic commission may make different rulings about when an individual can be assigned to a championship bout. Depending on the state, individuals may have to judge professionally for over two years before they can be assigned as officials in an important heavyweight title fight.

Education and Training

While there is no formal educational requirement to become a Professional Boxing Judge, individuals may have to be licensed. Licensing is mandatory in states hosting athletic commissions and in fights sanctioned by the major sanctioning organizations, such as the World Boxing Association (WBA), the International Boxing Council (IBC), the World Boxing Council (WBC), and the International Boxing Federation (IBF).

Depending on the organization doing the licensing, the Professional Boxing Judge may have to take and pass a written and/or oral examination. Judges may also be required to attend seminars and workshops sponsored by boxing organizations.

Experience/Skills/Personality Traits

In addition to being aware of all the rules and regulations of the sport of boxing, individuals must display good judgment. It is often difficult to determine who is more aggressive or more defensive in a very close fight. This know-how comes with training and experience.

Most individuals work as amateur judges before becoming Professional Boxing Judges. Judges must have confidence in their abilities and their decisions. They must be fair and exhibit total professionalism.

It is important that Professional Judges enjoy boxing and can deal with injuries and accidents occurring in the ring. If a Judge is squeamish, he or she will not be able to concentrate on the fight.

Unions/Associations

Boxing Judges may belong to state athletic commissions, the International Boxing Federation (IBF), the North American Boxing Federation (NABF), the WBA, the WBC, the World Boxing Organization (WBO), or the Boxing Officials Association (BOA). These organizations offer training, educational guidance, and support, and bring together those interested in the sport.

Tips for Entry

1. Contact your state's athletic commission and request information about becoming a Professional Boxing Judge. Many commission hold training sessions. (If your state does not have an athletic commission, contact one of the states that do, such as New York, New Jersey, or Nevada.)
2. If your state has an athletic commission, get licensed.
3. Obtain as much training as possible. The better trained you are, the better your chances will be of being a good Judge.
4. Get experience. Most Professional Judges get their experience working with the amateurs. Contact an amateur boxing association such as the Golden Gloves to get information.

5. Attend live boxing shows and watch boxing on television. Try to score fights and see how your scorecard stacks up against the Judges'.
6. Learn as much as you can about the sport of boxing. Read books, periodicals, and so on.

7. Find the local gyms where boxers train in your area. Spend some time there and make contacts.
8. Join relevant associations. These groups often provide training as well as help individuals make contacts.

BOXING MANAGER

Duties: Developing a fighter's career; securing matches for a boxer; locating support personnel; providing financial backing for training when necessary.

Alternate Title(s): Fight Manager

Salary Range: Earns a percentage of fighter's income; impossible to determine earnings.

Employment Prospects: Good

Best Geographical Location(s) for Position: Positions may be located throughout the country.

Prerequisites:

Education or Training—No formal educational requirement; individual state athletic commissions may require completion of state training requirements.

Experience—No experience necessary; business background desirable but not required.

Special Skills and Personality Traits—Knowledge of boxing industry; business skills; negotiating skills; aggressive; persuasive.

```
┌─────────────────────────────────┐
│      Boxing Manager for         │
│   More Prestigious Fighters     │
└─────────────────────────────────┘

┌─────────────────────────────────┐
│        Boxing Manager           │
└─────────────────────────────────┘

┌─────────────────────────────────┐
│         Boxing Fan              │
│ with Business or Management Skills │
│              or                 │
│         Entry Level             │
└─────────────────────────────────┘
```

Position Description

A Boxing Manager is responsible for shaping and developing the career of professional fighters. Some Managers may start out with fighters who have been fighting in the amateurs and are planning on turning professional. Others, who were fighters themselves or involved in some phase of the profession, build a reputation for themselves as Boxing Managers. Experienced professional fighters then seek out their services.

In states that have an athletic commission governing boxing, Managers must be licensed. Boxing Managers usually have a contractual agreement with fighters they represent. These Managers are responsible for keeping the sport and the fighters clean of any improprieties.

The Boxing Manager, as a rule, only signs fighters he or she feels have potential. The Manager is a integral force in the life and success of a fighter. He or she helps put together the best possible team to work with the fighters.

A good Manager supervises and oversees the fighter's entire career. In return the fighter pays the Manager a percentage of monies earned. The money earned for fights is called the purse. The Boxing Manager often invests money in the fighter to help him or her keep financially stable until money begins to come in. For example, the Manager may pay for boxing equipment,

supplies, and clothing. He or she may pay gym and training expenses. Some Managers may even pay the fighter's room and board.

The Manager may be responsible for locating a trainer for the fighter. If a fighter already has a trainer, the Manager decides if he or she is suitable. The individual may also be required to find promoters, publicists, sparring partners, business managers, and the like.

Boxing or Fight Managers must carefully monitor the progress of their fighters. They must know when the fighter is ready for a fight and what type of challenger is suitable. For instance, a fighter who has had just two professional fights usually contracts for a three- or four-rounder. The boxer who has had ten or 15 pro fights might contract for a ten- or 12-rounder.

The Manager is responsible not only for finding good matches for his or her fighter but for negotiating deals and getting contracts signed. If the Manager is not an attorney, he or she may retain one to work with the team. In this way, it is hoped that the fighter will be protected legally.

The Manager has to make sure that the fighter is trained and ready for a fight at the contracted weight. He or she works with the boxer's trainer to do this.

As fighters begin to rise in the ranks, the Manager works with publicists, public relations people, and the media setting up interviews, television spots, and obtaining written press coverage.

Once the Manager has built up the fighter and his image, personal endorsements and advertisements for the fighter might develop. This will make the fighter an even bigger box office draw when there is a fight.

Many Boxing Managers represent more than one fighter. Some represent entire boxing camps. This situation is good for both the Manager and the fighters. The Manager can earn money from a number of fighters. He or she may also be able to use some of the fighters in the camp as sparring partners. One of the greatest benefits, however, is that when one boxer gets a shot at a big fight, some of the others in the training camp will have a better opportunity to get placed on the undercard (the bouts that precede the main event).

While a Boxing Manager may work very hard and possibly never represent a champion, most Managers feel their fighters are the best and will eventually have the opportunity for a championship bout. It can be very exciting for the Manager to know that he or she has helped someone make it to the top of the profession.

Salaries

Salaries for Boxing Managers are impossible to determine. Earnings depend on many things, including the number of fighters a Manager has under contract, the purse they receive for each bout, and the number of matches each boxer fights annually. Earnings may also be dependent on other factors, such as management contract inclusions. Some Managers receive a percentage of all the fighters' earnings, including television or public appearances, movies, publishing deals, and commercial endorsements.

Most but not all Boxing Managers receive $33\frac{1}{3}\%$ of the fighter's purse. As noted previously, some also receive a percentage of other income.

Most Managers handle more than one fighter. These individuals receive percentages of every fighter's purse. Managers representing champions who are fighting multimillion-dollar fights may earn many thousands of dollars each time their fighter gets in the ring. It must be noted that not all boxers make it to be world-class fighters. Some boxers get matches in local club shows and receive only minimal purses throughout their careers.

Employment Prospects

Employment prospects are good. Almost anyone can be a Boxing Manager. The only real requirements are that the Manager must find a boxer to represent and that he or she must be licensed in states that have athletic commissions. Boxing Managers may find potential fighters to represent in any part of the country or world.

Boxing Managers must remember that just because they have a contract with a fighter, the money will not automatically roll in. The Manager must work constantly to secure matches for his or her fighters and move them up the ranks.

Advancement Prospects

Advancement prospects are fair for Boxing Managers. The only way to advance in this position is to acquire more prestigious fighters who can command larger purses. Sometimes Managers sign contracts with fighters who have already made it. Generally, however, Managers work with fighters over a period of time. Eventually the fighter begins getting better fights, televised fights, or a chance at a championship.

Education and Training

There is no formal educational requirement for Boxing Managers. Some Managers who have been quite successful hold high school diplomas. Others have degrees in business or law. A background in either certainly cannot hurt.

Individuals who are representing boxers can benefit from taking courses or seminars in marketing, public relations, business, and boxing.

Managers who are licensed by state athletic commissions may have to complete individual state training requirements. These requirements may include an annual seminar, symposium, or workshop.

Experience/Skills/Personality Traits

Successful Boxing Managers should either have contacts in the boxing world or have the ability to make them. A great fighter may never have the opportunity of being seen by others if the Manager does not know how to obtain good fights.

The Manager should be articulate and have good communication skills, both verbal and written. The individual will be calling promoters to obtain fights for the boxers he or she represents. He or she may also be talking to the media.

The Manager needs to be persuasive and aggressive. These are many Managers in the fight world trying to push their fighters to the forefront of the industry. The individual must be persuasive enough to have promoters and media give his or her fighters a chance.

While it is not essential to personally know how to box, Managers should have a basic understanding of the industry. He or she will then be able to choose the best support team to help develop a fighter's career.

Negotiation skills are a good asset when negotiating the fighter's contracts and purses. Business skills are essential.

Unions/Associations

Boxing Managers may be members of any of the state athletic commissions, sanctioning organizations, or boxing trade associations. These might include the International Boxing Federation (IBF), the World Boxing Association (WBA), the World Boxing Organization (WBO), the World Boxing Federation (WBF), the International Boxing Hall of Fame (IBHF), the International Veteran Boxers Association (IVBA), and the National Veteran Boxers Association (NVBA).

Tips for Entry

1. Join state athletic associations and commissions. These organizations regulate the boxing world and offer training and support. (All states do not have athletic commissions. However, if your fighter is working in a state that does, you will usually have to be licensed by that state.)
2. Become a member of as many boxing trade associations as you can. These will help you make valuable contacts and provide support.
3. Read books and periodicals about boxing. Keep up on the latest news in the industry.
4. Watch live and televised boxing. This too will help keep you up with the news in the boxing business as well as with the progressive fighters.
5. Many Boxing Managers pick up new fighters while they are still amateurs and ready to turn pro. This is a good way to get into the business. However, it takes judgment, a background in the profession, and often funding to maintain the boxer until fights are obtained and purses earned.

BOXING TRAINER

CAREER PROFILE

Duties: Developing talents of fighters; teaching boxers skills, punches, blocks, and forms; building confidence of boxer.

Alternate Title(s): Trainer

Salary Range: Impossible to determine earnings.

Employment Prospects: Good

Best Geographical Location(s) for Position: Positions may be located throughout the country.

Prerequisites:

Education or Training—No formal educational requirement; complete knowledge about sport of boxing.

Experience—Experience in one or more facets of boxing.

Special Skills and Personality Traits—Ability to motivate and instill confidence in fighters; boxing knowledge and skills; energetic; first aid skills.

CAREER LADDER

```
┌─────────────────────────────────┐
│        Boxing Trainer           │
│  for a Greater Number of Fighters │
│               or                │
│    More Prestigious Fighters    │
└─────────────────────────────────┘

┌─────────────────────────────────┐
│        Boxing Trainer           │
└─────────────────────────────────┘

┌─────────────────────────────────┐
│            Boxer,               │
│       Assistant Trainer         │
│               or                │
│       Apprentice to Trainer     │
└─────────────────────────────────┘
```

Position Description

A Boxing Trainer develops the talents of fighters. The Trainer is responsible for teaching a fighter the skills of the sport. A good Trainer can take a fighter with drive and determination but only mediocre boxing skills and turn him or her* into a world-class fighter.

Many Trainers may start their careers as amateur boxers. After a few rounds in the ring, individuals may realize that they do not have what it takes to become a professional boxer, nor do they want to be one. However, they may still be fascinated with the sport. After spending time in the gym with other boxers, trainers, and managers, they realize that a career as a Boxing Trainer could keep them working in boxing and out of the range of an opponent's gloves. Other individuals get their start as Trainers through friends who are boxers, by participating in youth programs, or by going to the gym to work out, etc. All Trainers have a love of the sport and a respect for the two opponents who get in the ring to fight.

Boxing Trainers work in the gym. The gym may be located in a variety of settings, from a city building to a rustic training camp. A gym may even be set up for a championship fight in a luxurious hotel anyplace in the world.

Most boxing gyms have either a boxing ring or something suitably equivalent plus the equipment required to train the fighters, including a heavy bag, mirrors, punching bag, jump ropes, medicine balls, etc. The Trainer will often have additional equipment for fighters who do not have their own, such as boxing gloves, hand wraps, stop watches, pads, etc. The Trainer must know how to use and take care of each piece of equipment.

Trainers may work for one or more fighters. If the fighter is a professional, the Trainer may be retained by the fighter's manager. Some Trainers work for a specific gym and help anyone who does not have a personal Trainer. Other Trainers work for boxing camps or boxing management or promotional organizations. Each Trainer has a different job style.

Basically, the Trainer teaches a fighter how to use all the equipment in the gym. He or she shows the fighter how to wrap hands before putting on gloves and how to use a jump rope, heavy bag, punching bag, pads, etc. If the fighter is new to the game the Trainer explains the rules and regulations of the

---

*The field of boxing is opening up to women. While there are a small number of female Trainers working in the world of professional boxing, the prospects are still very limited. Gyms around the country are currently experiencing the phenomenon of women coming in to train. While some of the women are training for self-defense purposes as well as to get in shape, there are others training for the purpose of getting ready for a bout. If this continues, more women Trainers can be expected in the profession. There are a number of boxing associations already geared specifically for women boxers.

sport, such as round length, time between rounds, legal blows, illegal blows, mandatory counts.

The Trainer works to condition the fighter so that he or she is in top physical condition. This conditioning is accomplished by having the fighter jog, do aerobic exercises, jump rope, and perform other strengthening exercises. Fighters who are not in excellent physical shape usually do not perform well in the ring.

The Trainer is responsible for instructing the fighter on all the basic forms and styles used in boxing. He or she she also teaches the fighter the basic punches used in the sport. These blows include the left jab, straight right, left hook, combination, and uppercut. It is important that the fighter know how and when to use these punches. The fighter must also be familiar with the defenses he or she can use in the ring.

A successful Trainer can help the fighter know when to throw a left hook to the body or a right cross to the chin. He when to use a shoulder block and when to bob and weave.

Once a Trainer has taught the fighter the basic skills, punches, and blocks, he or she puts the fighter in the ring for a sparring session with an opponent. Boxers spar to practice and perfect their skills against opponents in the same weight category. During sparring sessions, the Trainer watches carefully to see what skills he or she must work on with the fighter. During an actual bout, the Trainer stays with his or her boxer ringside, making suggestions as the fight proceeds.

The Trainer may also use video equipment to illustrate to the boxer his or her strong and weak points. Videos of potential opponents' bouts are also used by the Trainer to study styles.

Many fighters use the same Trainer from the time they are amateurs up through the ranks of professional boxing. Others change Trainers when they lose a fight. Trainers have a difficult, stressful job. They must often be hard on fighters in order to have them attain success in the ring. As fighters become more successful it is often difficult to motivate them to train and stay in shape.

Trainers may be responsible to different people depending on the specific situation. Those working directly with fighters may be responsible to either the fighter or his or her manager. Individuals working for gyms or management organizations will be responsible to the owner or general manager.

Salaries

It is impossible to determine the annual salaries for Boxing Trainers. Earnings are based on a number of variables, including the amount the fighter is earning for a fight, the frequency of his or her bouts, and the number of other fighters the Trainer is working with.

Earnings for most individuals are usually based on the amount of money the boxer receives for a fight. The Trainer may earn a percentage of the money or purse, ranging from 5% to 20% with most receiving 10%.

For a championship fight, with a multimillion dollar purse, the Trainer can expect to do very well financially.

There are some Trainers who receive a set salary from a boxing management or promotional company to work full time with the company's fighters. A fighter may also pay a trainer a set amount to get him ready for an upcoming fight. There are also Trainers who work part time in boxing and hold full-time jobs in other professions.

Employment Prospects

Employment prospects are good for talented Trainers. Individuals may find employment throughout the country. Trainers may work with individual fighters or for management companies, promotional organizations, boxing gyms, and athletic organizations.

Advancement Prospects

Boxing Trainers may advance their career in a couple of ways. The next step up the ladder for a Boxing Trainer is the opportunity to either train a champion or someone fighting a current champion. Trainers may also develop a fighter over the years until they become championship material.

As Trainers usually receive a percentage of the fighter's purse, any individual who either trains a number of winning fighters or trains more prestigious fighters will advance both their career and their earnings.

Education and Training

There is no formal educational requirement for Boxing Trainers. Individuals usually pick up their training skills through either watching or apprenticing with other trainers. Some pick up skills working with amateur fighters. Many Trainers use what they learned as boxers themselves to teach other fighters.

Seminars and workshops offered by state athletic commissions, boxing organizations and associations, and sanctioning groups are very useful to Trainers.

In states with athletic commissions, Trainers must often be licensed. Depending on the state, the individual may have to fill out a form or may have to take a written or oral examination.

Experience/Skills/Personality Traits

Boxing Trainers need to know everything possible about boxing and fighters. Individuals must be totally familiar with basic blows, forms, defenses. They also should know all the rules of the sport.

Trainers should have the ability to instill confidence in their fighters. They should be good teachers and know how to get ideas across and motivate others.

Trainers should be energetic and physically fit themselves. They should be health conscious, and have a good understanding of nutrition and fitness. Individuals must also know basic first aid procedures in case a fighter is injured during a training session or a bout.

Unions/Associations

Boxing Trainers may belong to state athletic commissions, sanctioning organizations, and trade associations, including the International Boxing Federation (IBF), International Veterans Boxers Association (IVBA), National Veteran Boxers Associations (NVBA), North American Boxing Federation (NABF), World Boxing Association (WBA), and World Boxing Organization (WBO).

Tips for Entry

1. Find the local gyms in your area catering to training fighters. Spend time in them and try to make some contacts. Strike up a relationship with one or two of the Trainers and see if they can offer you some suggestions about getting into the field.

2. You might consider finding an amateur boxing club and offering to work with their fighters and staff. This should help you learn the business as you make contacts. When someone wants to turn pro, you can help.

3. Read all you can about all facets of boxing. There are a number of books on training and the sport of boxing that may help you.

4. Watch as much boxing as you can, both live and on television, to pick up boxing techniques.

5. Join local amateur boxing clubs, state athletic associations, sanctioning organizations, and any other relevant trade associations. These groups may provide training, professional guidance, and seminars, and they bring together people interested in the sport.

RING ANNOUNCER

CAREER PROFILE

Duties: Acting as M.C. of a boxing show; announcing all pertinent information about the fights to the public.

Alternate Title(s):   Master of Ceremonies; M.C.

Salary Range: $100 to $10,000+ per show

Employment Prospects: Fair

Best Geographical Location(s) for Position: Positions may be located throughout the country in cities hosting boxing shows.

Prerequisites:

Education or Training—No formal educational requirement; some states may require licensing.

Experience—Experience speaking in front of groups of people helpful.

Special Skills and Personality Traits—Pleasant speaking voice; comfortable speaking in front of groups of people; articulate; good verbal skills; knowledge of sport of boxing.

CAREER LADDER

> **Ring Announcer at More Prestigious or Televised Boxing Shows**

> **Ring Announcer**

> **Entry Level or Public Speaker in Other Field**

Position Description

A Ring Announcer in the field of boxing is the master of ceremonies for the entire boxing show. He or she is responsible for announcing all pertinent information to the public. During a fight, the only announcement the public may hear that is not made by the Ring Announcer is the referee's instructions to the fighters before each bout.

Ring Announcers are usually required to arrive at the boxing event a few hours before a fight to gather and prepare information on the various matches. The individual works closely with the promoter of the show gathering information before the event. To begin with, the Announcer must secure the names of all fighters who will be on the boxing card. He or she must find out their weights, hometowns, the color of the trunks they will be wearing, and which corner each will be fighting out of.

After gathering the information, the Ring Announcer writes down all information to be used when making the announcements in the ring. He or she always verifies everything to make sure the data are correct.

At the beginning of the event, the Ring Announcer may introduce celebrities in the audience or the promoter or copromoters of the fight. In championship fights, the individual may also be responsible for introducing an entertainer who sings the national anthem. In certain states, the Ring Announcer may not introduce any person who is not directly related to the sport of boxing without permission from the athletic commission.

The Ring Announcer announces the name, weight, hometown, and color of the trunks of the opponents. He or she may also give the audience other information about the fighters, such as their professional record, the championship belts held, who the champion is and who the challenger is, and so on.

Each round of a professional fight is three minutes long with a one-minute rest period. The Ring Announcer, or M.C., tells the audience how many rounds the fight is scheduled for. This varies from fight to fight. Championship fights are usually 12 rounds. A knockout (KO) or technical knockout (TKO) can end a fight in the first round.

The Ring Announcer also tells the audience what organization is sanctioning the fight. This might be a state athletic commission or an organization such as the World Boxing Association (WBA), the International Boxing Federation (IBF), the World Boxing Council (WBC), or others.

Some Ring Announcers may use their own unique sayings before a fight card begins. Others just give the information and announce the fights.

After a bout ends, the Ring Announcer gathers the scorecards from the judges. The individual must know the boxing terminology used. For example, he or she may be calling a split decision, a unanimous decision, or a draw. If one of the opponents is knocked out, the Ring Announcer must indicate the round and exact time into that round that the fight was stopped. In states hosting athletic commissions, the M.C. may be required to give the official scorecards to a member of the commission before making announcements of the decision.

The M.C. announces to the audience how each official judged the fight and then announces the winner. He or she continues on through the entire boxing card in the same manner. After all the bouts, the individual may thank everyone for coming and then end the event.

Announcing is usually done in the center of the boxing ring. The M.C. must be able to get in the ring before each bout and out of it after each announcement.

Ring Announcers may work for one promoter or many. Individuals are responsible directly to the promoter with whom they are working at the time.

Salaries

Ring Announcers are paid fees for each show they announce. These fees may have a wide range depending on the individual's experience, prestige, and personal demand.

Fees may range from $100 to $10,000 plus per show. The average fee for ring announcers working major shows is $1,000 per show. Announcers for club shows earn less. Annual earnings depend on the number of shows that the individual is contracted to announce each year.

Employment Prospects

Employment prospects are fair for individuals who are willing to work for smaller promoters. Prospects are fair for individuals aspiring to work as Ring Announcers for major promoters and televised events.

It should be noted that many Ring Announcers do this as a part-time profession.

Advancement Prospects

Advancement prospects are poor. Individuals may advance their career by obtaining additional jobs as Ring Announcers or by securing more prestigious assignments working for major promoters or televised events.

Some individuals climb the career ladder by becoming familiar with both athletes and their backgrounds in the boxing industry and then moving on to television reporting or boxing commentating.

Education and Training

There are no formal educational requirements for Ring Announcers. Individuals working in states with athletic commissions governing boxing may have to be licensed to be Ring Announcers. In some states this license is a written application; in others written or oral tests may be required.

Experience/Skills/Personality Traits

Ring Announcers should be comfortable speaking in front of large groups of people as well as into a microphone. Individuals should be articulate in their verbal communication skills and have a pleasant speaking voice. A good command of the English language is helpful. Announcers should be well-groomed individuals. They should be able to carry themselves with confidence.

Announcers need to gather information on the fighters quickly and accurately. They also have to be able to present the information clearly.

A knowledge and enjoyment of the sport is helpful, as the individual will be attending many boxing shows. Contacts in the boxing industry, or the ability to make them, are essential to the success of the Ring Announcer in obtaining jobs during his or her career.

Unions/Associations

There is no specific trade organization for Boxing Ring Announcers. Individuals may be members of state athletic commissions or sanctioning bodies, such as the WBA, the WBC or the IBF. Depending on the individual's other skills, he or she may also belong to the Boxing Writers' Association (BWA).

Tips for Entry

1. Obtain experience speaking in front of groups of people.
2. Volunteer to act as Master of Ceremonies for an amateur entertainment benefit.
3. Watch both live and televised boxing events to see the various Ring Announcers' work and styles.
4. Find the local boxing gyms in your area and visit them on a regular basis. Talk to the fighters, managers, and trainers. You will learn about boxing and make important contacts.
5. Make a demo tape of your voice and send it with your résumé and a cover letter to promoters. Try sending it to promoters holding smaller, local shows instead of the major promoters. Send it, wait a few days, and call up to make sure it was received. Ask for an interview. If they tell you there are no openings, wait a few months and try again. Persistence may pay off.

PROFESSIONAL WRESTLING REFEREE

CAREER PROFILE

Duties: Controlling a wrestling match; calling counts and breaks between opponents.

Alternate Title(s):   Ref.

Salary Range: $300 daily to $300,000+ annually

Employment Prospects: Poor

Best Geographical Location(s) for Position: Areas hosting professional wrestling leagues.

Prerequisites:

Education or Training—Training in officiating wrestling matches

Experience—Experience officiating matches.

Special Skills and Personality Traits—Ability to take punches, blows, and falls; good physical and medical shape; small stature; good showperson; knowledge of sport.

CAREER LADDER

```
┌─────────────────────────────────────┐
│         Referee for More            │
│ Prestigious Wrestling Organization  │
└─────────────────────────────────────┘

┌─────────────────────────────────────┐
│         Wrestling Referee           │
└─────────────────────────────────────┘

┌─────────────────────────────────────┐
│    Wrestling Referee Apprentice     │
│                or                   │
│          Wrestling Fan              │
└─────────────────────────────────────┘
```

Position Description

Within the past few years, professional wrestling has increased dramatically in popularity. Fans used to be able to attend live wrestling shows only on a limited basis. Today wrestling fans can attend live bouts in almost every corner of the country. Wrestling exhibitions are now shown on network television in prime time as well as on pay-for-view television, cable, local, and regional networks.

In professional wrestling, the official in the ring is called the Referee, or Ref. The function of this individual is to control the wrestling match from start to finish. Matches may last from 15 minutes to 1 hour in length.

The Referee is in charge of officiating during the entire match. It is the Ref.'s duty to tell the timekeeper when to start the match and when to end it. While the Referee does no judging, he gives counts to the wrestlers. Counts determine the number of seconds a wrestler has before he or she must release an illegal hold. Counts also determine the end of a match. The Referee must, therefore, be knowledgeable about the different counts that may be called. The Referee is also in charge of calling breaks between opponents during the match.

Due to the nature of professional wrestling, the Referee often gets bumped and banged around by the wrestlers during the match. He or she must be able to take these bumps without

getting seriously injured. The individual must also learn how to fall—falling frequently is all in a day's work in this sport.

The Referee is part of the action in professional wrestling. The better the showperson, the more excited the crowd will become.

Professional Wrestling Referees may travel extensively in the course of their work. Shows may be held anywhere in the country or abroad depending on the specific league the Ref. is involved with.

Referees may be called on to officiate at any type of match, for any sex or size wrestler. Individuals may officiate at world-class wrestling events, shows featuring women wrestlers, or others.

Individuals may work full or part time. Some Referees work 200 days a year. Others may work a couple days a month. It all depends on whether or not they have other jobs and how much in demand they are. The individuals are usually directly responsible to the promoter of the show or president of the league.

Salaries

There is a tremendous salary range for Professional Wrestling Referees. Differences in compensation depend on many things, including the type of bout in which the Referee officiates, the level of the league, and whether the show is being televised. Another variable might be the Referee's activity in the ring during the bout. The more action that occurs during a bout, the higher the individual's salary. Salaries are also dependent on the seniority of the official and whether he works full or part time.

Compensation for Professional Referees can be extremely lucrative. Earnings can run from $300 daily to $100,000 plus annually. Some officials earn salaries of $300,000 and more.

Traveling expenses, meals, and lodging for Professional Referees are covered when they work on the road.

Employment Prospects

Employment prospects are poor for Professional Wrestling Referees. Even with the increase of wrestling shows, individuals may have a difficult time finding employment in this area. The major reason for this is that professional wrestling appears to be a closed business. In order to become a Professional Wrestling Referee, an individual needs training and experience. As a rule, the only way to obtain this training and experience is to find a sponsor who will teach the individual the business. Many Referees are wary of giving out this information because it threatens their jobs.

Individuals who aspire to be Professional Wrestling Referees will have a better chance if they find a low-level wrestling league or one that is just starting out. These are be located throughout the country.

Advancement Prospects

Advancement prospects are determined by the Referee's drive and determination. To move to the top of this business, the individual must do two things: officiate at bouts put on by the top wrestling league in the world, the World Wrestling Federation (WWF), and officiate at bouts televised nationally and abroad.

Wrestling crowds enjoy action and like to see both the wrestlers and the Referee take chances in the ring. Individuals who take these chances will catch the eye of the fans and promoters and become more in demand.

It may take a Professional Wrestling Referee three to four years from the beginning of his career to reach this point. Some may never get there professionally.

Education and Training

While there is no formal educational requirement for this position, Professional Wrestling Referees must be fully trained before being appointed as officials. Unfortunately, as noted previously, most of this training is available only through other Professional Referees and wrestlers and not through classes or seminars. Those seeking training must locate a skilled professional who will teach them the ropes of the business.

Experience/Skills/Personality Traits

The most employable Professional Wrestling Referees are individuals of small stature. The smaller an individual appears in the ring, the larger the Wrestler will seem. Referees must be in good physical shape. Those who are not will have short careers.

Referees working televised bouts must be comfortable in front of a camera. They must also have a basic knowledge of the television industry. It is important that the Ref. officiating at a televised bout know where to stand and be familiar with TV cameras to know which camera is picking up the action. If not, the Ref. may block the wrestlers from camera view.

Successful Wrestling Referees must be good showpeople. Although professional wrestling is recognized as a sport, a good part of the action is its entertainment value. The Referee must be able and willing to take chances in the ring. Being thrown out of a ring by a wrestler, being chased and almost caught, and so on are actions that excite and entertain crowds.

Knowledge of the counts used in wrestling is essential. A love of the sport is necessary to work successfully in this area.

Unions/Associations

Professional Wrestling Referees have no bargaining union. Individuals may be members of the athletic commissions in states hosting them. They may also belong to the various wrestling leagues throughout the country and abroad.

Tips for Entry

1. This is one type of job where you have to be in the right place at the right time to get in. Keep plugging away. Don't let a few disappointments get you down.
2. If you have any contacts at all in the professional wrestling industry, use them. You will have to prove yourself once you make the initial contact. However, it is a way to get your foot in the door.
3. Look through wrestling magazines to locate small wrestling leagues. Contact them, one by one, to try to find someone willing to teach you the ropes.
4. Watch as much professional wrestling as possible. Try to see live shows as well as televised bouts. This will help give you a perspective on the industry.
5. Try to find gyms where professional wrestlers train. Consider a job doing anything in the gym, from maintenance to sweeping the floors or answering the phones. This will be your best way to make needed contacts.

CAREER OPPORTUNITIES
IN RACING

JOCKEY

Duties: Riding Thoroughbred horses in races and competitions; helping train and condition horses.

Alternate Title(s): None

Salary Range: $18,000 to $250,000+

Employment Prospects: Good

Best Geographical Location(s) for Position: Positions located in areas hosting Thoroughbred racetracks.

Prerequisites:

Education or Training—No formal educational requirement.

Experience—Experience as an apprentice required.

Special Skills and Personality Traits—Excellent riding skills; knowledgeable about horsemanship; lightweight body; small stature; love of horses; ability to work under stress and pressure.

```
┌─────────────────────────────────┐
│      Jockey Riding Horses in    │
│   More Prestigious Races with   │
│          Larger Purses          │
└─────────────────────────────────┘

┌─────────────────────────────────┐
│             Jockey              │
└─────────────────────────────────┘

┌─────────────────────────────────┐
│            Apprentice           │
└─────────────────────────────────┘
```

Position Description

There are two different varieties of horse racing. One is called harness horse racing. This is where the horse pulls a two-wheeled cart called a sulky with a driver seated in the cart and guiding it. The other is called Thoroughbred or flat horse racing. This is the type of race where a man or woman called a Jockey rides astride the horse during a competition.

Jockeys' responsibilities may vary depending on the situation. Their main function, however, is to ride horses in competitions at racetracks. These individuals are often crucial to the success of a horse in a race.

As Jockeys sit on the horse's back when racing, it is important they keep their body weight down. The lighter they are the better. Their average weight is around 100 pounds.

Most Jockeys begin their careers working in the stables taking care of horses. Individuals must learn how to care for the animals, how to feed them, clean them, and get them ready for exercising. Aspiring Jockeys help trainers exercise and train the horses on a daily basis. When they are 18 years old, they can apply for an apprentice license.

Jockeys often travel extensively in the course of their job. Many tracks are seasonal. Individuals may work at one track for a couple of months and then move on. They may also travel between tracks when a horse is being raced in a number of tracks during a season.

When racing a horse, the Jockey must be strong enough to control the animal. He or she must also know how to guide and motivate the horse into a winning position. The Jockey must know the specific horse well enough to know what its strengths, weaknesses, and abilities are. In this way he or she can develop a strategy to race the horse. To accomplish this, individuals must know if a horse is a slow starter, quick starter, quick finisher, and so on.

A lot of this knowledge and understanding comes from the Jockey working with the horse. He or she may help with the daily training of the animals as well as with their general conditioning.

Jockeys are responsible to either the horse owner or trainer, depending on who hired the individual. This may be a stressful job. If the horse does not win, the Jockey is often the one blamed. To stay successful in the industry, he or she must constantly have winners. Jockeys must also be concerned with injuries. Working with animals is unpredictable. Jockeys may be bitten, kicked, or thrown off horses and injured. For those who love horses and the exciting life of racing, however, none of these drawbacks is overwhelming.

Salaries

Earnings for Jockeys vary greatly depending on a number of factors. These include the experience and skills of the individual and the type of race he or she is riding in. Other variables include how often the Jockey rides and the number of winners he or she has. Salaries also depend on the type of financial arrangement the Jockey has made. He or she may be under contract with a trainer or owner and/or may also earn various percentages of winning purses.

Individuals may earn from $40 to $100 or more every time they ride in a race. Jockeys may also earn a percentage of the winning purse. Although percentages vary, an average may be 10% of the purse if the horse a Jockey rides comes in first. If it comes in second or third, their Jockey's share may be only 5%.

For Jockeys riding in races with major purses, earnings can be quite high. Some individuals in this field earn only $18,000 a year, while others earn $250,000 plus.

Employment Prospects

Employment prospects are good for Jockeys who are skilled in their trade. Individuals usually are hired by horse owners. They may be under contract with the owners or may ride on a free-lance basis. Jockeys who have proven themselves in a number of races have no problem finding work. Thoroughbred racetracks are located around the country. However, many tracks located in colder climates are seasonal.

Advancement Prospects

Advancement prospects are good for Jockeys who are willing to learn their craft and really want to make it in the horse racing industry. Climbing the career ladder for a Jockey might mean that he or she obtains a position riding a champion in a major race. Other paths the Jockey may take to career advancement include riding more prestigious horses or in more prestigious races, or obtaining a greater number of horses to ride.

As Jockeys often receive a percentage of winning purses, riding winners in races with big purses can mean large earnings.

Education and Training

There are no formal educational requirements for Jockeys. Individuals must, however, have a complete knowledge of horses and experience working with them. Individuals must be licensed in order to be Jockeys. To obtain a license, the Jockey must first go through an apprenticeship program. Programs may be administered by the state or by organizations, depending on the specific state.

Individuals must be at least 18 years old to apply for an apprentice license. They may obtain a free-lance apprentice certificate or a contract apprentice license. The former means that the individual can ride for any trainer at any stable, while the latter means that he or she can ride only for one specific stable. While an apprentice, the individual rides in races, getting experience. After riding a number of winners in races, an individual can become a full-fledged Jockey and receive his or her journeyman's license. Licensing may be done by individual organizations or the state, depending on the location the individual is in.

Experience/Skills/Personality Traits

Most successful Jockeys are people who are small and lightweight. Individuals must know how to to ride horses expertly and be skilled in every facet of horsemanship. In order for Jockeys to be successful, they must also love horses. Like many other domestic animals, horses are sensitive to people who deal with them. They can instinctively tell if a Jockey is comfortable doing his or her job.

Jockeys must be dependable, honest, and trustworthy. They must not use any type of stimulants or illegal drugs on the animals. Not only could this endanger the horse's health, but the Jockey could lose his or her license for life.

Individuals must be able to deal with the pressure of people wanting them to win constantly. They also must recognize that when a horse does not win, they may be made to feel it is their fault.

Unions/Associations

Jockeys may belong to a number of local, state, and national organizations and associations that bring members of the profession together. One of the most prominent in the field is the Jockey's Guild, Inc. (JGI).

Tips for Entry

1. Get a job working at a racetrack or in a local stable. This will give you on-the-job experience and help you make important contacts in the field.
2. Locate trainers and jockeys to talk with about your aspirations. They are usually glad to offer advice and help.
3. Go to a racetrack and watch the races. Get a feel for what Jockeys do and how they handle the horses.
4. Go to the library and get some books on horse racing. The more you know about the industry, the better chance you will have to be successful in it.

HARNESS DRIVER

CAREER PROFILE

Duties: Racing horses; training horses.

Alternate Title(s): Driver; Harness Race Driver

Salary Range: $15,000 to $1,000,000+

Employment Prospects: Fair

Best Geographical Location(s) for Position: Areas hosting harness racetracks.

Prerequisites:

Education or Training—No formal educational requirement; licensing necessary.

Experience—Experience as a groom or trainer's assistant required.

Special Skills and Personality Traits—Knowledge of horse care and training; ability to drive sulkies; enjoy working with horses; self-confident; quick reflexes.

CAREER LADDER

```
Harness Driver
for Horses in
More Prestigious Races
and with Larger Purses
```

```
Harness Driver
```

```
Harness Driver Apprentice
or
Harness Driver/Trainer Apprentice
```

Position Description

In harness horse racing, horses pull carts competitively around a track. These carts, called sulkies, are guided by skilled individuals known as Harness Horse Race Drivers. Individuals may be Harness Drivers or Harness Driver/Trainers. The latter train the horses and race them. In order to drive professionally, individuals must be licensed.

There are two varieties of harness races, one for trotters and the other for pacers. Drivers may work in either type of race.

The road to becoming a Harness Driver is much like that of becoming a jockey. Individuals usually begin working at jobs in racetrack stables. They become grooms and help trainers work with the horses, feeding them, brushing them, and cleaning and exercising them.

After gaining some experience working with horses as a groom or a trainer's assistant, aspiring Harness Drivers may apply for a license. The first license many Drivers obtain is the matinee license. This license is valid only for matinee meets that do not involve wagering or purses.

The next license individuals may apply for is a qualifying license for extended paramutual meets. In order to obtain this license, Drivers are required to take a written exam as well as a practical test demonstrating their ability to drive. They have to demonstrate to those giving the test that they are safe,

talented drivers. Individuals must also provide references before they are issued such a license.

Drivers hold their qualifying license for six months and must participate in at least 12 satisfactory drives with a licensed paramutual judge watching. They must then obtain the approval of both the judge and the local district track committee in their area.

After these requirements are met, they obtain their provisional license. Now they are similar to apprentices. Drivers who hold a provisional license for a year must then drive either 25 satisfactory drives and obtain the same approvals as noted above or hold the license for less than a year and drive 50 satisfactory extended paramutual drives. They must also then obtain judge and committee approvals. Individuals who complete these requirements are then granted a full or A license. Once this license is obtained, they can drive in any track in the country.

Harness Drivers may travel from track to track to race horses. Some are under contract with a stable or trainer, driving only for those people. Others, called Catch Drivers, are not under contract. These individuals drive for hire, for any stable or trainer.

Individuals who have made a name for themselves often are asked to drive a number of horses in the same race. As Drivers often are paid on a percentage of the money earned by the horse (or purse), they will likely choose to drive the horse that appears to have the best chance to win. Harness Drivers may travel extensively to race horses in tracks across the country.

Harness Drivers may prefer just to drive in races or may also train the horses. Those who act as trainers must also have a trainer's license. Trainers spend a great many hours training and driving horses that are destined to become winners. Crossing the finish line a winner makes all of the work that has been put into the animal worth it.

Salaries

Salaries vary greatly for Harness Drivers depending on a number of factors. These include the driver's experience level and the number of races he or she drives in. Other determining factors include the tracks the individual is racing at and the amount of the purse for each horse the individual drives.

Drivers earn a percentage of the purse when the horse comes in first through fifth. If the individual is a Driver-Trainer, he or she earns 10% of the purse. If, however, the Driver is not helping with the training, the percentage is split. The Driver receives 5% and the trainer receives 5%.

In a major competition with a large purse, Drivers can win a great deal of money.

Annual earnings for Drivers who are racing full time may range from $15,000 to $500,000+. Those who drive and train can double that amount.

Employment Prospects

Employment prospects are fair for Harness Drivers. There is a great deal of competition in this industry, but there is always room for skilled drivers. Individuals must be dedicated and committed to the sport to make it in harness racing. One of the best ways to obtain work is to find owners who are interested in having their horses trained and raced. If owners are impressed with the skills of a Driver, they often purchase other horses for the Driver/Trainer to work with.

Advancement Prospects

Drivers who do their job well will have no trouble advancing their careers. Individuals can climb the career ladder by driving horses in more prestigious races that have larger purses. As Drivers begin to win races and show that they can drive well, owners and others will seek out their services.

Education and Training

There are no formal educational requirements necessary to become a Harness Race Driver. Individuals must, however, be trained in working with horses and driving a sulky in races.

This skill usually comes from experience working as an apprentice to a trainer and/or driver. Harness Drivers must be licensed in order to work. Licensing is handled through the United States Trotting Association (USTA). Drivers may have a variety of licenses from matinee to qualifying to provisional. Most states also require state licensing as well.

Experience/Skills/Personality Traits

In order to become a Harness Driver or Driver/Trainer, individuals usually obtain experience by becoming an apprentice to an established driver or driver/trainer. They should have experience training and jogging horses.

Harness Drivers and Driver/Trainers must like to work around horses. They must have a feel for the the way the animals think, act, and behave. Individuals must have a complete knowledge of maintaining horses as well as of training and racing them.

Drivers should be confident in their abilities. They must have quick reflexes. Driving a sulky is not as easy as it looks. Individuals must have a feel for driving.

Drivers usually are required to wear helmets and to observe safety measures. However, as in other sports, accidents in horse racing do occur. While driving, the individual cannot express any fear. If he or she does, the horse can often sense this fear and will not perform well.

Unions/Associations

The major association for those involved in this industry is the USTA. This organization licenses Drivers and offers guidance and support to those in the industry.

Tips for Entry

1. Go to a harness race track and watch Drivers in action.
2. Consider a part-time or summer job in a stable or at a racetrack to give you the feel for harness racing. It will also give you a good opportunity to get your foot in the door of the industry and make important contacts. You have to make a major commitment to be involved in horse racing. This experience will help you decide if it is the career for you.
3. Contact the U.S. Trotting Association for more information on getting into harness driving and licensing requirements.
4. When you are ready to begin your career, try to find an established Trainer or Driver whom you like and respect. You will be spending a great deal of time with this individual. Learn as much as you can from your mentor.

HARNESS RACING JUDGE

CAREER PROFILE

Duties: Supervising all racing activity at racetrack; presiding over the running of races; making sure all rules and regulations are followed; handling complaints and infractions; suspending or fining participants for infractions.

Alternate Title(s):   Judge; Steward; State Steward; Paddock Judge; Patrol Judge; Presiding Judge; Associate Judge

Salary Range: $75 to $400 per day

Employment Prospects: Fair

Best Geographical Location(s) for Position: Areas hosting harness racetracks.

Prerequisites:

Education or Training—No formal educational requirement; licensing required.

Experience—Prior experience required within industry.

Special Skills and Personality Traits—Common sense; good judgment; fair; consistent; horse racing background; ability to work under pressure; communication skills.

CAREER LADDER

```
┌─────────────────────────────────┐
│            Judge                │
│ at Larger, More Prestigious Track│
│              or                 │
│         State Steward           │
└─────────────────────────────────┘

┌─────────────────────────────────┐
│      Harness Racing Judge       │
└─────────────────────────────────┘

┌─────────────────────────────────┐
│        Clerk for Judge          │
│              or                 │
│          Fair Judge             │
└─────────────────────────────────┘
```

Position Description

In horse racing, as in all sports, officials preside over each race. The officials in horse racing are known as either Judges or Stewards.

For each race there are Patrol Judges, Associate Judges, Presiding Judges, and State Stewards. While they are all judges, they may perform different duties. The main function of these Judges is to supervise all racing activity at the particular track to which they are assigned. The Judges also preside over the actual running of races. They must make sure that all track rules and regulations are followed. They oversee the actual racetrack as well as the areas where the horses are kept, where the drivers stay, and where patrons bet.

Judges' duties vary depending on the type of Judge they are and what work they are assigned to do. Judges inspect horses to make sure that they are in compliance with all commission rules. They may also confer with veterinarians about the fitness of horses on the race card.

Stewards are the highest level of Judges at the track. They and the other Judges serve on judiciary boards that make decisions about occurrences at the racetrack. Judges may receive written or verbal complaints on any number of issues, from a driver not

agreeing with the order of horses finishing a race to a trainer accused of injecting a horse with an illegal substance. The Judges must determine the validity of the complaints and then decide how to deal with them. The Steward is responsible for writing reports on all complaints, actions taken, and penalties imposed and then filing them with the state's racing commission.

Some Judges are responsible for inspecting the equipment of horses and their drivers in the paddock before a race. This is done to make sure that equipment meets regulations. Other individuals observe the races to determine if there are any infractions or fouls committed. In order to get a good view, Judges watch the race from elevated stands. They may also view videos and use photographs of the race to determine infractions.

If, during a race, a driver feels that another driver or trainer has done something against the rules, he or she can bring the matter to the attention of the Judges. The Judges then must determine if the complaint is valid.

Judges preside over the entire racing community. When a rule is broken or there is a regulation infraction, the Judge or Steward has the power to take action. Individuals may suspend or fine participants for violations of the rules. Their powers, however, are limited by state regulations. Some states have more lenient fines and suspension policies than others. For example, one state may have a limit of a 15-day suspension for an infraction while in another state the limit might be as high as 90 days.

Racing is a highly regulated industry. A major function of Judges is the approval of licenses for all individuals involved at the track, from the drivers and trainers to the grooms and mutual clerks.

Judges are also responsible for determining the order of the winning horses at the finish line. Before the racetrack announcer tells patrons the order of the winners in a race, often he or she must wait for the Judges to determine which horse came in first. To do this, the Judges may look at photographs and videos taken at the finish line. A photo finish occurs when two horses appear to reach the finish line at the same moment. The video or photograph allows the Judges to make an accurate decision.

It is the Judge's duty to protect the interest of the state, the betting public, the track owners, and the actual participants. To accomplish this, Judges are responsible for many of the day-to-day activities at the track.

Judges and Stewards often work split shifts. That means that they will perform some of their duties in the morning and the rest in the evening hours.

Salaries

Earnings for Judges and Stewards vary depending on a number of factors. These include the individual's experience and education as well as the size and location of the track. Individuals are usually paid on a per-day basis.

A Patrol Judge can earn from $75 to $110 a day. Associate Judges may earn from $150 to $350 per day. Presiding Judges or State Stewards may earn $150 to $400 or more per day.

Employment Prospects

While there is a great deal of competition for these positions, talented, skilled Judges are always in demand. Individuals who are educated and experienced in the racing industry and who are willing to relocate to areas requiring Judges will have an easier time finding work.

In some situations, Judges are state employees. Others are appointed by the specific track they are working at.

Advancement Prospects

Individuals advance their careers in judging by obtaining experience and education in the field. Individuals can move up from the position of a Paddock Judge to become a Patrol Judge. They can then climb the career ladder to the next step, which is Associate Judge and then Presiding Judge. The top level of officials are called State Stewards.

Education and Training

A college degree is not required to become a Judge in the racing industry, but it does help. As there is so much competition for these jobs, individuals who are the most qualified will get the positions.

All Judges must be licensed. The organization licensing individuals is the the United States Trotting Association (USTA). Individuals must pass a written examination in order to be licensed. The USTA offers an intensive weeklong course covering information needed to pass the test. This organization also offers a great deal of other education and school opportunities for those interested in becoming Judges or advancing their careers.

Experience/Skills/Personality Traits

Two of the most important traits officials should have are good judgment and common sense. They should also be fair and consistent.

Individuals should have a high self-esteem and be confident in their decisions. Judges often work under a great deal of pressure. They should be able to function in stressful situations.

A racing background is necessary to perform this job well. Some individuals grew up in the racing industry. Others had family or friends who were involved with it. Still other individuals worked at tracks or in the racing profession in other capacities.

Communications skills, both written and verbal, are necessary for this job.

Unions/Associations

Judges and Stewards in the racing industry can be members of the North American Judges and Stewards Association (NAJSA). Individuals may also be members of the USTA. These organizations provide educational and professional guidance and support.

Tips for Entry

1. Contact the USTA to learn more about licensing requirements.
2. It is also a good idea to inquire about the classes, seminars, and other educational programs available.
3. Remember that you are going to have to start at the lowest level and advance your career from there.
4. A background in the racing industry is necessary. Consider a part-time or summer job at a racetrack in some capacity to help you learn more about racing.
5. Look in your library for books on the subject. Read as much as you can about the racing industry.

RACING SECRETARY

CAREER PROFILE

Duties: Arranging the daily race card; making sure horses in each race are competitive; scrutinizing stall applications; determining purses.

Alternate Title(s): Director of Racing

Salary Range: $30,000 to $150,000+

Employment Prospects: Poor

Best Geographical Location(s) for Position: Positions may be located in areas hosting horse racing tracks.

Prerequisites:

Education or Training—No specific educational requirement.

Experience—Experience in horsemanship needed.

Special Skills and Personality Traits—Understanding of horses and horsemanship; ability to deal with stress; good memory; communications skills.

CAREER LADDER

```
┌─────────────────────────────────────┐
│         Racing Secretary            │
│   at Larger, More Prestigious Track │
└─────────────────────────────────────┘

┌─────────────────────────────────────┐
│         Racing Secretary            │
└─────────────────────────────────────┘

┌─────────────────────────────────────┐
│          Horse Race Fan             │
│                or                   │
│          Track Worker               │
│                or                   │
│          College Student            │
└─────────────────────────────────────┘
```

Position Description

A Racing Secretary works at a horse racing track. His or her function is to make sure that the horses in each race are competitive with each other. The individual in this position is responsible for arranging the daily race card for the racetrack. Depending on the particular track, this schedule may be from seven to 11 races.

There are a certain number of stalls available for horses at each racetrack. Owners and trainers apply for these stalls so that their horses can train and compete at the track. The Racing Secretary prepares for races by scrutinizing stall applications. He or she decides which horses will be given stall space by determining the individual animal's qualifications and potential.

The Racing Secretary reviews data from the animal's past workout and performance records. He or she prepares a condition sheet based on an evaluation of the horses already on the grounds. The individual strives to put together a race card of horses that are competitively matched with each other.

In some situations, the Racing Secretary may handicap horses for races using criteria such as the animal's age and sex. Other data that may be used include the horse's past money winnings and the distance of the races won.

The individual then must classify horses for the proper type of race; these include claiming, condition, and stake races. Races may be classified by money earnings or by the type of horse racing, such as mares, fillies, horses, or geldings.

In order to do his or her job properly, the Racing Secretary must know as much as possible about each horse's background. After the preliminary work is completed, the individual plans the races that will be run. The Racing Secretary may also be responsible for determining the purse, or amount of money to be won, for each of those races. The Secretary uses his or her research and data on the horses scheduled to participate in the race to determine the purse. Patrons and fans use the race card to place bets on the races.

Functions of the Racing Secretary may also include registering and keeping track of the names of people who have a financial interest in each horse and changes in ownership. He or she may also be required to obtain the entrance and application fees for races from owners.

The individual is ultimately responsible for racing information that is supplied to newspapers, racing forms, and daily racing programs. Depending on the specific position, the Racing Secretary may supervise the individuals who compile the racing information. He or she is also required to keep records of the results of each horse in every race.

While most of the work of the Racing Secretary is accomplished prior to the actual races, he or she is usually on hand during the races too. At this time, the individual might verify the specific selection of entries in the race as well as the shape, form, and ability of the animals taking part in the competition.

The Racing Secretary is usually responsible to the track's owner or general manager. Hours can be long in this job. The individual might put in a full day preparing for the races and then, as noted, be required to be at the track for the entire card. It must also be noted that many racetracks are seasonal. Race Secretaries may work at one track during the spring and summer and another during the fall and winter.

Salaries

Salaries for Racing Secretaries vary widely depending on a number of variables, including the size and prestige of the track and the length of its season. Earnings will also be dependent on the experience level of the individual.

Some Racing Secretaries are paid by the draw or race day for which they have drawn up the race card. Others are paid by the week. Salaries for Racing Secretaries can range from $30,000 for individuals working at smaller tracks around the country to $150,000 plus for those working at larger, more prestigious tracks.

Employment Prospects

Employment prospects are poor for Racing Secretaries. As a rule, each track needs the services of only one individual for this position. As there is only a limited number of racetracks in the country and their number is dwindling, it is extremely difficult to find jobs.

Those who aspire to be Racing Secretaries might find it easier to break into the field by trying to locate positions with smaller tracks. Then as the individual gains experience, he or she will be able to move up in the ranks to larger tracks.

Advancement Prospects

In order for the Racing Secretary to climb the career ladder, he or she must usually find a similar position at a larger, more prestigious racetrack. This will lead to higher earnings.

Other Racing Secretaries advance their careers by becoming officials at the tracks.

Education and Training

There usually is no formal educational requirement for this position. However, a college degree might be helpful in attaining a position.

There are Racing Secretaries with degrees in everything from communications to animal science. Training and any type of background in horsemanship is extremely useful. Seminars and workshops are often offered through racing associations.

Experience/Skills/Personality Traits

Racing Secretaries must be able to deal with constant stress and tension. With each race that they classify, there can be only one winner. Owners and trainers of horses that did not win often try to place blame on the person who did the classifying.

Individuals in this position should have good memories. The Race Secretary must read about horses constantly and must be able to remember the data. In this way, he or she is able to put horses that belong together in the same races.

The Racing Secretary should have good communications skills, both written and verbal. He or she needs to be able to deal well with a variety of people. Experience dealing with horses and in horsemanship is essential to the success of the Racing Secretary.

Unions/Associations

There is no union for Racing Secretaries working at horse racing tracks. Individuals may belong to a number of trade associations, including the Racing Secretaries Association (RSA) and the United States Trotting Association (USTA). These organizations offer meetings, symposiums, conventions, and workshops that bring together those interested in working in the sport. The associations also often training, professional guidance, and support.

Tips for Entry

1. Consider a summer or part-time job at a local racetrack. While working as a clerk or an assistant to a Racing Secretary would be ideal, experience in any facet of racing will prove helpful.
2. Try to obtain an intern position with the Racing Secretary of a racetrack. This too will provide valuable experience and on-the-job training.
3. Contact relevant trade associations for help in training and professional guidance.
4. Attend workshops, seminars, and symposiums on horsemanship. You will make a lot of contacts and gain valuable information.
5. Send your résumé and a cover letter to racetracks where you might want to work. Ask that you résumé be kept on file if there is no current opening.

RACETRACK ANNOUNCER

CAREER PROFILE

Duties: Announcing and calling races at horse or dog racetracks.

Alternate Title(s): Race Announcer; Race Broadcaster; Race Caller

Salary Range: $100 to $300+ a day; $15,000 to $45,000 annually

Employment Prospects: Poor

Best Geographical Location(s) for Position: Positions may be located throughout the country.

Prerequisites:

Education or Training—No educational requirement for most positions.

Experience—Public speaking or radio announcing helpful but not always necessary.

Special Skills and Personality Traits—Pleasant speaking voice; good memory; articulate; good eyesight; familiarity with the sport of horse or dog racing; enjoy horse or dog racing.

CAREER LADDER

```
┌─────────────────────────────────┐
│   Racetrack Announcer at Larger,│
│   More Prestigious Racetrack    │
└─────────────────────────────────┘

┌─────────────────────────────────┐
│      Racetrack Announcer        │
└─────────────────────────────────┘

┌─────────────────────────────────┐
│      Backup Announcer or        │
│         Entry Level             │
└─────────────────────────────────┘
```

Position Description

A Racetrack Announcer works at either a horse or a dog racetrack. He or she is responsible for announcing the races as they occur. The Racetrack Announcer's main function is to let the track patrons know what is going on before, during, and after each race.

The individual is required to announce races as they occur, beginning with the number of each race. He or she then usually gives the name and number of the horse or dog in each race and often the odds as the animals parade around the track. On occasion, the Announcer gives the track fans other information, such as the name of the jockey, driver, or trainer. He or she might also tell patrons in what position the animal finished the last time it raced.

The Racetrack Announcer tells patrons how many minutes there are until post time (the time the race starts). He or she may give updates during this prerace period on the various odds that are on the specific horses or dogs.

The individual announces the beginning of each race. He or she then monitors the race and tells fans about the progress of each horse or dog. He or she is expected to do this quickly and accurately. Before the race, the Announcer must memorize the color each horse, dog, driver, and/or jockey is wearing and the

number accompanying each color. In this way he or she can tell what is happening as the race progresses.

As the race get close to the finish line, the Announcer tells the fans who is in first, second, and third positions and who is moving up. Successful track announcers can make a race even more exciting.

The Racetrack Announcer is the track representative who tells patrons which horse or dog has won a race. He or she also announces the numbers and names of the winning, place, and show animals. The individual then tells patrons the official race results or, in the case of a photo finish, instructs fans to hold their tickets until the track judges make a final decision.

Once race results are official, the individual may announce the cash winnings in each category. The racing process then begins again until all races on the card are run.

Sometimes the Racetrack Announcer may also be required to make other types of announcements. These might include broadcasting the names of people or businesses visiting the track, indicating the celebrities who are attending, and previewing special events that will be taking place at the track.

Racetrack Announcers may work in the morning, afternoon, or evenings, depending on the specific track's racing schedule. Most Announcers work a full card, which may run anywhere from seven to 11 races. They do a lot of talking. For people who enjoy the sport of racing and like to comment on its activities, this can be a very interesting career.

Racetrack Announcers may be responsible to the track general manager, assistant manager, or owner, depending on the specific situation.

Salaries

Salaries for Racetrack Announcers vary from job to job. Some tracks pay their Announcers weekly, while others compensate Announcers on a per-day basis. Earnings can range from $100 to $300 plus a day. Those paid on a weekly basis may earn from $15,000 to $45,000 or more a year.

Most tracks are seasonal and do not operate all year. In some situations, where the Announcer has built a reputation over the years, he or she is compensated throughout the year, even when not working. In other situations, the individual has to work part of the year in one part of the country and another part of the year in a different part.

Employment Prospects

Employment prospects are poor for those who seek positions as Racetrack Announcers. There are only a limited number of racetracks in the country. Once an individual gets a job as a track Announcer, he or she often stays in that position for years.

Individuals who aspire to be Racetrack Announcers may be more successful obtaining jobs at smaller tracks. Once they gain some experience, Racetrack Announcers can often become substitute or backup Announcers at larger tracks.

Advancement Prospects

Advancement prospects can be poor to fair depending on a number of variables. These include the speaking personality of the individual and his or her experience level. Advancement also depends on a certain amount of luck and contacts, and the individual being at the right place at the right time.

Those who climb the career ladder in this profession do so by obtaining jobs at larger, more prestigious tracks or by becoming the track's main Announcer.

Education and Training

There is usually not any educational requirement for the job of Racetrack Announcer. Knowledge about using the track's P.A. (public address) system is useful but can usually be learned in a short time.

Seminars about the sport of horse racing or dog racing may help the individual understand more about the sport and the industry.

Experience/Skills/Personality Traits

Some racetracks do not require Racetrack Announcers to have any experience. Others require that applicants have had prior announcing experience at tracks. The amount of experience required is dependent on the specific position and racetrack.

It is important that the Racetrack Announcer have a pleasant speaking voice, free of speech impediments. He or she should be both articulate and understandable. The Announcer should either have or be able to develop an announcing personality or voice that distinguishes him or her from other announcers. This approach is the equivalent of Ed McMahon announcing Johnny Carson in his unique style.

The Racetrack Announcer must have a good memory. He or she must memorize the colors that the jockeys, horses, and/or dogs are wearing before the race in order to accurately announce the race's progress. While Announcers often use binoculars and/or cameras to see the horses and/or dogs clearly, it helps to remember the relationship of color to number on each animal.

Unions/Associations

While there are no specific associations for Racetrack Announcers, individuals may belong to a number of organizations and associations related to the racing industry. These might include the International Trotting and Pacing Association (ITPA) and the Racing Fans Club of America.

Tips for Entry

1. Send your résumé and a demo tape of your voice calling a race to the personnel director of racetracks that you are interested in working with.
2. Call up racetracks and ask if they have any openings for backup announcers.
3. Get experience speaking into a microphone. You might consider working at your school radio station.
4. If you are in school, see if you can get a summer or part-time job working at a racetrack in some capacity. This will help you make important contacts and give you an understanding of the way a track works.
5. On occasion, openings are advertised in local newspaper display and classified sections. Look under heading classifications of "Announcer," "Racetrack Announcer," "Horse Racing," "Dog Racing," or "Broadcaster."

CAREER OPPORTUNITIES IN WHOLESALING AND RETAILING

MANUFACTURER'S REPRESENTATIVE/ SPORTING GOODS OR EQUIPMENT COMPANY

CAREER PROFILE

Duties: Representing manufacturers by selling their sporting goods and equipment to shops, sporting departments, schools, teams, etc.

Alternate Title(s):   Sales Representative; Rep.; Sporting Goods Representative; Salesperson; Salesman; Saleswoman

Salary Range: $22,000 to $125,000+

Employment Prospects: Excellent

Best Geographical Location(s) for Position: Positions located throughout the country.

Prerequisites:

Education or Training—Minimum educational requirement is high school diploma; some positions may require or prefer college degree.

Experience—Sales experience in either wholesale or retail helpful but not always required.

Special Skills and Personality Traits—Sales ability; detail oriented; communications skills; aggressive; motivated.

CAREER LADDER

```
┌─────────────────────────────┐
│   Manufacturer's Representative │
│        at Larger, More         │
│      Prestigious Company       │
│             or                 │
│        Sales Manager           │
└─────────────────────────────┘
```

```
┌─────────────────────────────┐
│   Manufacturer's Representative │
└─────────────────────────────┘
```

```
┌─────────────────────────────┐
│         Entry Level            │
│             or                 │
│  Salesperson in Retail Trade   │
│             or                 │
│      Manufacturer's Rep.       │
│       in Other Industry        │
└─────────────────────────────┘
```

Position Description

A Manufacturer's Representative working for a sporting equipment company is responsible for selling the company's line of products at a wholesale level. The individual may handle a single line of goods and products or may represent diversified or several lines. The Manufacturer's Representative may also be called a Rep. or Sales Representative.

The Manufacturer's Representative may sell products to sporting goods stores or departments, professional teams, amateur, college and high school teams, and others. The Manufacturer's Rep. may work for the manufacturer of any type of sporting equipment, supplies, accessories, machines, and/or sports clothing.

Individuals are usually assigned a territory. The territory is an area, region, or district consisting of a few cities, counties, states, or an entire section of the country. When assigned a territory, Reps. try to sell their product line in the specific area

and that area only. If a store outside that territory wants to purchase company goods, a different Rep. is responsible for the sale. Sizes and locations of sales zones may vary depending on the size of the company, company policy, product sold, and salesperson.

While it is not imperative to know everything about sports and athletics in this line of work, the Manufacturer's Rep. must have a complete knowledge of the product or equipment sold. He or she should also know as much as possible about both competitors' products and those of his or her own company. Knowing the similarities and differences will help the Manufacturer's Rep. speak to store buyers knowledgeably and honestly concerning comparisons. For the same reason, it is important that the Manufacturer's Rep, be aware of both the strengths and weaknesses of all competitive products. Being knowledgeable about the line will help the indiviudal develop a good, strong sales pitch to use when trying to sell products.

Manufacturer's Reps. use a number of methods to sell goods. They may work from the office making sales calls on the phone and mailings to distribute literature. Individuals might also make "cold" sales calls in person, actually visiting shop owners or store buyers. Most successful Manufacturer's Reps. use a combination of the two systems.

The Rep. might visit established accounts to see what goods and equipment have moved since the last sales call and what sales support is needed. The individual also discusses any problems that might have developed regarding the product, such as defective pieces, returns, or warranties.

The Rep. discusses with the store buyer or owner new trends and developments in the sporting goods industry and the way they relate to new equipment or products the company manufactures. In this manner, the Rep. develops a good client rapport and obtains orders for products.

The Manufacturer's or Sales Rep. generally seeks out new customers or accounts. To do this he or she may call to set up appointments, send correspondence, product brochures, and other mailings, or just drop in at a potential new customer's place of business. While he or she may not get an order on that first call, persistence usually pays off.

The Manufacturer's Representative is responsible for demonstrating the use of products, pointing out salable features, and answering relevant questions regarding the product.

Representatives must build good, honest working relationships with their customers. Buyers must feel comfortable with both the the salesperson and the manufacturing company or they will not continue placing orders.

Depending on the Rep.'s territory, he or she may visit schools, colleges, or professional teams to try to sell his or her products. The Rep. constantly strives to create and develop new markets for the product.

The Rep. must handle a great deal of paperwork. He or she is expected regularly to send mailings, letters, spec sheets, and brochures about products to both new and established accounts. The Rep. must also keep accurate records regarding orders, call-backs, and customers. Not following this procedure could mean a forgotten order, an invoice unbilled, or a dissatisfied customer.

The Manufacturer's Representative is usually responsible to either the district or sales manager of the company. If the Rep. has a large territory, he or she may be required to travel extensively. The individual must set up appointments at the convenience of the buyer. He or she must also put in a number of office hours making calls and keeping records.

Salaries

Manufacturer's Representatives may be paid straight salaries, commissions, or a combination of the two. Reps. are also often rewarded with bonuses for outstanding sales.

Salaries vary extensively depending on the company the individual is working for, the product or products sold, territories,

experience, and sales ability. Earnings for Manufacturer's Representatives of sporting goods and products may range from $22,000 to $125,000 and up.

One of the most exciting things about being paid on any type of commission basis is that the sky is the limit in relation to earnings.

Employment Prospects

Employment prospects are excellent for those aspiring to Manufacturer's Representatives positions. Individuals must be good salespeople who are highly motivated with a lot of drive and determination. Companies are constantly on the lookout for people who fit this mold.

Prospective manufacturers may be located throughout the country.

Advancement Prospects

Advancement prospects are usually determined by sales ability. The individual advances by meeting and exceeding sales quotas, developing good relationships with customers, and opening up new accounts.

Manufacturer's Reps. may advance their careers by locating similar positions in larger, more prestigious companies, obtaining better sales territories, or by becoming sales managers.

Education and Training

Educational requirements differ with each position. Many companies just require their Manufacturer's Reps. to have high school diplomas. Others prefer or require college graduates.

Seminars and workshops in all aspects of selling and salesmanship will be useful in both obtaining a position and being successful with it.

Experience/Skills/Personality Traits

Manufacturer's Representatives must have sales ability. They must be able to develop good sales pitches and deliver them to potential customers. It is essential that individuals be motivated, driven, and aggressive without being pushy.

Reps. should be organized and detail oriented. The ability to keep clear, concise records is necessary. Writing skills may be necessary for some positions.

Some Reps. working for manufacturers of sporting goods and equipment have had experience in either retail or wholesaling positions. For others the Rep. position is entry level.

The Rep. should have good verbal communications skills and be comfortable talking to a variety of people. The individual should be as articulate communicating on the phone as he or she is in person. The Rep. should have a neat and well-groomed appearance.

Unions/Associations

Manufacturer's Representatives may belong to any number of professional trade organizations specifically relevant to the type of product or products represented. Individuals might also be members of the Manufacturer's Agents National Association (MANA) or the Sporting Goods Agents Association (SGAA). Both these organizations provide training and professional guidance to their members.

Tips for Entry

1. Consider getting some experience working with sporting goods and equipment prior to seeking a Manufacturer's Representative position. Find a job in a retail sporting goods shop or department. An added bonus might be meeting and talking with Reps. who come in the store.
2. When you do apply for a job, try to learn as much as possible about the company and its products. It is also helpful to know about competing products. In this manner, you can discuss the company knowledgeably with your interviewer.
3. Manufacturer's Representative positions are often advertised in the newspaper display or classified sections. Look under heading classifications of "Sales," "Salesperson," "Manufacturer's Reps.," "Sporting Goods," "Wholesale," "Athletics," or "Sports Equipment."
4. If there are specific companies you would like to work with, obtain their addresses by checking their product packaging, asking for the information in a sporting goods store, or looking up the data in *Standard and Poors*, a directory found in most libraries.
5. Look in the yellow pages of the phone book to locate sporting goods and equipment manufacturers. Send your résumé with a cover letter requesting an interview or information on job openings.
6. Positions may be located on the Internet. Search various career and job sites as well as sporting goods and equipment manufacturers' sites.

SPORTS STORE MANAGER

CAREER PROFILE

Duties: Managing sporting goods, athletic equipment, or general sports store; overseeing operation of store; supervising employees; handling customers' problems.

Alternate Title(s): Sporting Goods Store Manager; Athletic Equipment Store Manager.

Salary Range: $20,000 to $75,000+

Employment Prospects: Excellent

Best Geographical Location(s) for Position: Positions located throughout the country.

Prerequisites:

Education or Training—Minimum educational requirement is high school diploma; some positions may require or prefer college background or degree.

Experience—Experience working in retail sales necessary.

Special Skills and Personality Traits—Supervisory skills; administrative skills; detail oriented; honest; dependable; communications skills; knowledgeable about sporting goods and athletic equipment.

CAREER LADDER

```
┌─────────────────────────────────┐
│      Sports Store Manager of      │
│   Larger or More Prestigious Store │
└─────────────────────────────────┘

┌─────────────────────────────────┐
│       Sports Store Manager        │
└─────────────────────────────────┘

┌─────────────────────────────────┐
│        Retail Salesperson         │
└─────────────────────────────────┘
```

Position Description

Every city and many small towns throughout the country have at least one if not more sporting goods and athletic equipment shops. These stores sell everything from inexpensive fishing lines to costly exercise equipment. For individuals who have an interest in the sport and athletic industries as well as some retail or business experience, becoming a Sports Store Manager is a good way to get involved in an interesting and lucrative career.

Sports Store Managers may work in various settings. These include the all-purpose sporting goods shop or the specialized sporting goods store. Managers also may work in sports store chains that are located throughout the country. Shops may sell equipment, machines, accessories, and clothing for exercise, camping, recreation, and other sporting goods. Store Managers have varied duties depending on the specific job and store they are working for.

The Store Manager is responsible for the operation of the entire store. An important function of the Manager is hiring of personnel. The individual may be responsible for placing advertisements in the paper, notifying employment agencies,

or putting up signs in the store window in order to find staff. He or she is also expected to interview potential employees. The Store Manager must be sure that the staff he or she hires is competent, trustworthy, and dependable.

In this position, the Store Manager needs supervisory skills. Depending on the size of the store, he or she may be in charge of a large number of employees. These staff people may include salespeople, clerks, cashiers, stock people, maintenance people, and bookkeepers.

He or she must make sure that they are trained in all phases of the operation, from running the cash register to helping a customer choose an expensive piece of sports equipment. In some situations, the Store Manager must run training sessions for new employees. In others, the Manager may train each new employee personally as he or she comes on the job or assign another staff member to the task.

The Store Manager is responsible for scheduling staff members in an effective manner. This is often a difficult job, because the store must always be fully staffed. The Manager must also make contingency plans in case someone calls in sick or there is an emergency.

The Manager must be totally knowledgeable about all the store's stock. He or she must become an expert on everything in the store. The Store Manager must know about different types of exercise equipment, recreational equipment, and sporting supplies that the store stocks. He or she also must know how the various machines and equipment work in order to demonstrate it to both staff and buyers. It also helps if the Manager has a knowledge of competitors' products.

The Store Manager oversees everything and everybody. At times, the individual may assume the duties of a salesperson, clerk, or cashier. The Manager may be responsible for approving checks and making sure large bills are not counterfeit. He or she may also be responsible for arranging for layaways and putting through credit card purchases.

An important role of the Store Manager is to handle customer service problems. When a customer has a problem, the Store Manager is expected to find a solution. For example, a customer may return an expensive rowing machine after the warranty has expired because it fell apart. To keep goodwill between the customer and the store, the Manager may authorize an exchange or may fix the piece of equipment at no charge. The Store Manager is also expected to handle any problems arising between employees and patrons. The successful Store Manager's motto is usually "The customer is always right."

Another major function of the Store Manager may be acting as the buyer of the store. The individual may talk with various representatives of sporting goods and equipment companies about their products. When ordering merchandise, he or she also listens to the needs of customers who come into the store. The Manager gets price quotes and writes orders.

In some situations, such as a large sporting good chain store, he or she may not do the purchasing. Instead, the individual reports stock deficiencies to the main office. Headquarters, in turn, sends needed equipment from the main warehouse.

The Manager is expected to check inventory on a regular basis. In this way, he or she knows what items are low in stock or have sold out completely. The Manager may assign this duty to an assistant or to a salesperson.

When stock arrives at the store, the Manager is responsible for making sure every piece is accounted for. He or she may count and sort merchandise and verify the receipt of items on invoices personally or assign this duty to an assistant or salesperson. The individual must also make sure that all items are priced for sale.

In some situations, the Manager is responsible for advertising store specials. In others, he or she receives advertising circulars from a main office. The Manager must be sure that all items advertised are available in the store and sale priced.

Another duty of the Manager is to keep stock arranged attractively and samples of the product line assembled for customers to see and try out. If a customer was purchasing an exercise bicycle or treadmill, he or she would not only want to look at the product when it was assembled but would probably want to try it out too.

In most situations the Store Manager is responsible for obtaining time sheets and work hours of employees for payroll purposes. He or she may then be expected to personally draw up payroll checks or may give the information to the store owner or district manager.

The Sports Store Manager may be responsible to the owner of the store or, in chain stores, to the regional manager. The individual may often work overtime if an employee calls in sick, there is an emergency, a shipment of stock comes in, or there is work to be completed.

Salaries

Earnings for Sports Store Managers vary depending on the experience of the individual, his or her responsibilities, the size of the store, and the geographical location. Salaries can range from $20,000 to $75,000 plus per year.

Individuals with little experience working in smaller stores may earn from $20,000 to $25,000. Those with a modest amount of experience in a larger store setting may have annual salaries from $24,000 to $35,000. Earnings for Store Managers with a great deal of experience and responsibilities working in a large sports store in a major city may range between $24,000 and $75,000 plus.

Employment Prospects

Employment prospects are currently excellent for Sports Store Managers. Positions are located throughout the country in sporting goods and athletic equipment stores. Individuals may work in large or small stores.

Advancement Prospects

Advancement prospects are good for Sports Store Managers. The next rung on the career ladder for the Sports Store Manager is to locate a similar position in a larger, more prestigious sports store. This usually results in increased responsibilities and higher earnings. As there is quite a bit of mobility in all aspects of the retail market, jobs open up frequently.

Education and Training

Educational requirements vary depending on the specific position. Almost all sports stores require their Managers to hold at least a high school diploma. Many either require or prefer Managers to have either a college background or a four-year college degree.

A college degree in almost any major will be useful. Good choices for those interested in this field might include sports administration, business, marketing, communications, retailing, or liberal arts.

Experience/Skills/Personality Traits

Sports Store Managers need to be informed about the stock level in the store. Any experience working with sporting equipment, athletic equipment, athletic shoes, or clothing is useful. The more sports and athletic oriented the individual is, the more successful he or she will be in this position.

The Store Manager should have supervisory and administrative skills. He or she is responsible for the organization, administration, and running of the store. The ability to organize and handle many details at one time is necessary.

Honesty and dependability are important traits. Communication skills are imperative. The Store Manager should not only like working with people but be good with them as well.

Store Managers need experience in retail sales. While it helps to have experience in retail sales in a sports store, it is not always necessary. Some Store Managers landed their position after a stint as an assistant manager, while others moved up from a sales position.

Unions/Associations

There are no associations geared specifically toward Managers of Sports Stores.

Tips for Entry

1. Positions as Sports Store Managers may often be located in the display or classified section of the newspaper. Look under heading classifications of "Retail Sales," "Sales Manager," "Sports Store," or "Athletic Equipment."

2. Malls and shopping centers also advertise management positions in their store windows. Visit these areas and browse looking for signs.

3. You might consider sending your résumé and a cover letter to some of the sporting goods, athletic equipment, or sports stores in your area. Ask that your résumé be kept on file if there are no current openings. As noted previously, there is a great deal of mobility in retail jobs. If your résumé is on file, you may get a call. Get names and addresses of stores by looking in the yellow pages of the phone book.

4. Carry copies of your résumé with you when job hunting. Make sure that they are neat, clean, and well put together. If you do not type yourself, have someone else type your résumé for you. Bring it to a quick print shop to have copies made.

5. Job opportunities may be located on the World Wide Web. Search popular job and career sites as well as the sites of major chain sporting goods stores.

SPORTING GOODS SALESPERSON

CAREER PROFILE

Duties: Selling sporting equipment, machines, accessories, supplies, and clothing; acting as cashier; taking inventory; arranging merchandise.

Alternate Title(s): Sporting Equipment Salesperson; Sales Associate

Salary Range: $12,000 to $40,000+

Employment Prospects: Excellent

Best Geographical Location(s) for Position: Positions located throughout the country.

Prerequisites:

Education or Training—Minimum of a high school diploma required for full-time position.

Experience—Experience working with public helpful but not necessary in many positions.

Special Skills and Personality Traits—Sales skills; dependable; ability to work well with people; personable; articulate; good communications skills.

CAREER LADDER

```
┌─────────────────────────────────────┐
│     Sporting Goods Salesperson       │
│   at Larger, More Prestigious Store  │
│                 or                    │
│       Sporting Goods Store            │
│                 or                    │
│       Department Manager              │
└─────────────────────────────────────┘

┌─────────────────────────────────────┐
│     Sporting Goods Salesperson       │
└─────────────────────────────────────┘

┌─────────────────────────────────────┐
│            Entry Level               │
│                 or                    │
│    Salesperson in Other Industry     │
└─────────────────────────────────────┘
```

Position Description

The trend toward attaining health and fitness is increasing today. With the importance placed on health and fitness, sports equipment shops and departments are becoming more common.

As more shops open up throughout the country and additional department stores begin carrying fuller lines of sports equipment, informed, knowledgeable Salespeople have become increasingly necessary. Sporting Goods Salespeople are responsible for selling sports-oriented equipment, supplies, accessories, machines, and clothing.

The Salesperson must know how the various machines and equipment work so that he or she can demonstrate their functions to buyers. The individual must also be able to explain the differences between brands of the same types of equipment. The Salesperson may specialize in one type of equipment or may be required to be fully informed about all of the store's merchandise. For example, one Salesperson may specialize in exercise machines, while another may be knowledgeable about recreational equipment.

Other functions of the Salesperson may include serving as a cashier, closing sales, totaling up customers' purchases, arranging for layaways, putting through credit card purchases, taking payments for products, and giving change to customers.

Good Salespeople try to find out exactly what the customers' needs are. When a customer comes in to a store asking about purchasing an exercise bicycle, rowing machine, cross-country ski machine, or treadmill, the Salesperson must try to determine certain things. He or she accomplishes this by talking and questioning: What is the price range? What brands would the buyer consider? What types of options are desired? How long has the customer been exercising? How many people will be using the machine? Approaching the sale in this way, the Salesperson can assist the customer in making a wise purchase.

In some shops, the Salesperson may repair or assemble equipment. The individual might also explain directions concerning assembly or instructions for repair to customers. The Salesperson in some stores must also help carry and load equipment into customers' cars after purchase.

Others duties of the Salesperson might include counting and sorting merchandise and verifying the receipt of items on invoices. The individual checks that stock arriving is the merchandise that was ordered. He or she may stamp, mark, or attach price tags to equipment and other products in the stores.

The Salesperson may be required to stock shelves, set up advertising displays, and arrange merchandise under the supervision of the store manager.

Depending on the situation, the Salesperson may be responsible for checking inventory and reporting to store management items that have sold out or are low in stock. The individual may order special items for customers if the store does not have specific items in stock.

Salespeople may work in various settings. These include all-purpose sporting goods shop, specialized sporting goods shop, or sports department in a department store. Individuals may sell equipment, machines, accessories, and clothing for exercise, camping, recreation, and any other sporting goods carried by the store.

The Salesperson is directly responsible to the manager of the sporting equipment shop or department. Hours vary depending on the shift the individual works. He or she may or may not work overtime, depending on the specific job.

Salaries

Earnings for Salespeople working in sporting goods and equipment stores or departments vary, depending on the experience of the person, the size of the store, the geographical location, and method of payment. Salaries can range from $12,000 to $40,000 plus per year.

Salespeople may be compensated in a number of different ways. The individual may receive a straight salary, a commission on equipment sold, or a combination of the two.

Employment Prospects

Employment prospects are currently excellent in every facet of retail sales, and sporting equipment sales is no exception. Individuals aspiring to work in sporting equipment shops or departments may find positions throughout the country.

Virtually anyone can enter the sports industry as a Sporting Goods Salesperson. With hard work, an individual can also advance quickly.

Advancement Prospects

Advancement prospects are excellent for Sporting Goods Salespersons. There are two methods of career advancement. The individual might find a similar position in a larger, more prestigious sporting goods store. This could result in added responsibilities and higher earnings. The other option for climbing the career ladder is for the Salesperson to become a sporting goods store or department manager.

Both paths are wide open at this time. There is a growing need for personnel in all areas of retail sales. An individual with drive and determination will have no problem moving up in this type of job.

Education and Training

Salespeople working full time in sporting goods stores or department must usually hold at least a high school diploma. Part-timers may still be attending school. Some stores now require a college background or degree. A college background may be necessary for advancement.

Experience using any sporting goods or equipment is helpful in both attaining a job and achieving success in it.

Experience/Skills/Personality Traits

While sales skills are necessary for this type of position, the most important trait an individual can have is to be a personable, likable individual who works well with the public. The Salesperson needs to make customers feel comfortable when purchasing equipment and other items from the store. He or she should be able to make customers feel they are important. The individual should know how to talk to customers without being pushy and pressuring them into a purchase.

The more informed a Salesperson is about the products being sold, the more successful he or she will be. The individual needs to be able to give concise, honest information about equipment and other products.

The Salesperson should be dependable, articulate, and have good communications skills. He or she should be neat, clean, and well groomed.

Any experience in retail sales or dealing with the public will be helpful.

Unions/Associations

Many stores are represented by bargaining unions that negotiate minimum salaries and working conditions. Employees including the Sports Equipment Salesperson may be members of these organizations.

If the Salesperson is working in a store specializing in selling equipment or uniforms to schools or colleges, he or she may be a member of the Athletic Goods Team Distributors (AGTD).

Tips for Entry

1. One of the easiest ways to find a sales position is to look in the newspaper. Look in the display or classified section under heading classifications of "Sales," "Selling," "Salesperson," "Sales Associate," "Retail," "Athletics," "Fitness," "Sports," or "Exercise."

2. Another method of locating a sales job in a sports equipment shop is to visit malls and shopping centers in your area and look in store windows. There will often be signs stating "Help Wanted," "Salesperson Wanted," or "Sales Associate Wanted." All you have to do is go into the store, ask to speak to the manager, fill out an application, and wait to be called for an interview.

3. It is always a good idea to carry copies of your résumé with you when job hunting. Make sure that they are neat, clean, and well put together. If you do not type yourself, have someone else type your résumé for you. Bring it to a quick print shop to have copies made.

4. Once you have a résumé put together, think about sending it out to sports shops in your area with a cover

letter inquiring about openings. You can obtain names and addresses by looking in the yellow pages of the phone book. You can also get leads by looking through the local newspaper. Sports shops often advertise sales and specials. Their addresses are usually somewhere in the advertisement.

5. If you cannot find a job right away working in a sport equipment shop, consider getting a sales job in another field until a suitable position opens up. This will give you good hands-on experience working with people.
6. Positions may be located on the Internet. Search popular job and career sites.

CAREER OPPORTUNITIES IN SPORTS MEDICINE

ATHLETIC TRAINER

CAREER PROFILE

Duties: Working with athletes to prevent injuries; evaluating injuries; making sure athletes are physically capable and ready to play.

Alternate Title(s):   None

Salary Range: $23,000 to $115,000+

Employment Prospects: Excellent

Best Geographical Location(s) for Position: Positions may be located throughout the country.

Prerequisites:

Education or Training—Minimum of four-year college degree.

Experience—Experience as student athletic trainer or apprentice helpful but not always required.

Special Skills and Personality Traits—First aid skills; ability to evaluate injuries; communications skills; understanding of sports; knowledge of psychology and physiology.

CAREER LADDER

```
┌─────────────────────────────────────┐
│       Athletic Trainer in           │
│  Larger, More Prestigious School    │
│               or                     │
│   for Professional Sports Team      │
└─────────────────────────────────────┘

┌─────────────────────────────────────┐
│         Athletic Trainer            │
└─────────────────────────────────────┘

┌─────────────────────────────────────┐
│     Student Athletic Trainer        │
│               or                     │
│   Apprentice to Athletic Trainer    │
└─────────────────────────────────────┘
```

Position Description

Athletic Trainers may work in amateur or professional sports. Individuals in this position have a number of duties. Their main responsibility is to work with athletes in an effort to prevent injuries. Once injuries do occur, the Athletic Trainer is required to evaluate the problem and get the athlete the proper medical treatment. He or she also makes sure that athletes are physically ready and able to play after an injury.

Athletic Trainers often work with team coaches in the development and implementation of programs that can be used to help athletes get in the best possible physical condition. This is important because athletes who are in good condition will have fewer injuries. Athletes are also interested in conditioning; they know their performance will peak with proper training and good conditioning.

Athletic Trainers also work with the equipment manager to make sure that playing and training areas are in working order. Depending on the situation, the Athletic Trainer requests from the equipment manager or head coach supplies he or she needs to do the job. These items might include braces, bandages, cold packs, and the like. The Athletic Trainer is responsible for recommending the types of supplies he or she needs and making sure that they are available as required.

One of the major functions of the Athletic Trainer occurs during games and practice sessions. He or she is on the sidelines watching the athletes. As soon as someone looks injured or does not look quite right after a move, the Athletic Trainer rushes out on the field to evaluate the injury. Sometimes injuries are slight and just need a simple treatment, such as an ice application. The Trainer must determine if the athlete needs medical attention and, if so, must get it for him or her immediately.

Another of the Athletic Trainer's duties is to work with the physician in a rehabilitation program for injured players. The Trainer discusses prognoses with the physician and with the athletes. The Trainer is then responsible for developing and implementing a program that will help the athletes regain use of the injured body part. This program may include prescribed exercises, heat treatments, whirlpools, or massages.

The Trainer must keep records of each athlete's progress throughout his or her injury and rehabilitation. Good record keeping of all injuries is necessary. Often an injury does not seem serious at first but can cause problems later. Records must indicate when an athlete was injured, where, what the injury was, the prognosis, prescribed rehabilitation, and progress.

The Athletic Trainer is responsible for deciding when an athlete's injuries have healed sufficiently for the individual to get back to the game. This may be difficult because athletes usually do not like to miss games. They have been known to tell Trainers they are no longer in pain, when in reality they still are. The Trainer may also have to deal with coaches who want players back in games before they are ready.

Individuals working in a school setting may have additional responsibilities. Athletic Trainers in these situations may be responsible for teaching classes, working in health centers, or coaching sports teams, or some combination of these jobs.

Individuals work long hours preparing playing and practice areas, keeping records, attending games and practice sessions, evaluating and taking care of injuries, supervising rehabilitation, and soothing players who are frightened that an injury might end their careers. Their job is extremely important. Most Athletic Trainers and athletes are aware that their expertise can mean the difference between a permanent injury and one that can be rehabilitated.

Salaries

Salaries vary greatly depending on the specific setting in which the Athletic Trainer works. Athletic Trainers working in schools or colleges may earn salaries ranging from $23,000 to $60,000 plus. The range depends on the type and size of the school, the importance the administration puts on sports programs and teams, prestige, and location. Earnings are also be based on the duties and responsibilities of the individual and his or her experience.

Athletic Trainers working for professional teams earn from $25,000 to $115,000 plus. These salaries too depend on the type of team, its prestige, and the responsibilities and experience of the individual Trainer.

Employment Prospects

Employment prospects are excellent for Athletic Trainers. Individuals may find employment throughout the country in a variety of different settings. Athletic Trainers are hired in public and private high schools, junior colleges, four-year colleges and universities, and professional sports teams. One or more Athletic Trainer may be required.

Advancement Prospects

Advancement prospects are excellent for Athletic Trainers. An individual might begin his or her career working in a high school situation and advance to the college level. The Athletic Trainer might then climb the career ladder by locating a position in a larger college or university that puts more emphasis on its sports and athletic teams.

The next level of advancement, with professional teams, becomes more difficult to reach. This is not to say that advancement is impossible. Athletic Trainers who have proven themselves in the field may advance to pro levels.

Education and Training

Most positions for Athletic Trainers require the individual to have a four-year college degree. While many jobs do not require an individual be certified as an Athletic Trainer, it might be useful. Individuals who wish to be certified should consider a college accredited by the National Athletic Trainer's Association. Others may obtain a degree with a major in physical education. Certain positions may also require graduate degree.

Good course choices might include those in anatomy, exercise physiology, kinesiology, nutrition, physics, chemistry, first aid, coaching, and psychology.

Athletic Trainers who want to be certified but who have not attended one of NATA's accredited colleges, may take part in an apprenticeship program.

Workshops, seminars, and courses in athletic training, coaching, and health education are also useful to the individual in this profession. Continuing education may be required for some positions.

Experience/Skills/Personality Traits

Athletic Trainers need the ability to get along well with people. Individuals will be interacting with all the athletes on the team as well as coaches and physicians. Those who are not people oriented and personable are usually not successful in this type of job.

Athletic Trainers need to feel comfortable working with injured people. This is not the job for individuals who feel faint at the sight of blood. Athletic Trainers should be able to deal well in crisis situations. Individuals need to know basic first aid procedures. They should also be able to do preliminary evaluations of injured athletes.

Athletic Trainers must understand the psychology of both team athletes and coaches. Some athletes who want to get back to a game say that their injuries are not serious or have healed when they really have not. The Trainer must have a sixth sense in such matters. Sending an individual back to a game before he or she is ready might cause permanent injury.

Trainers must have good communications skills. They deal with a variety of people. Individuals are also responsible for written reports dealing with team injuries.

It is helpful for the Athletic Trainer to have an understanding and enjoyment of sports. He or she must attend a great many games. Trainers who are not sports fans may not be able to enjoy their work fully, while those who are fans will be very happy.

Unions/Associations

Athletic Trainers may belong to the National Athletic Trainers Association (NATA). The NATA offers education, training, certification programs, and career guidance. It also brings people in this profession together to maintain high standards. This group also sponsors student memberships.

Tips for Entry

1. Become a student member of NATA. This will give you constant, up-to-date information about the profession and help you make important contacts in the field.
2. Volunteer to work with your school team. If your school has an Athletic Trainer, ask if you can assist him or her. If not, talk to the head coach or athletic director.

3. Learn the proper first aid procedures. You will need to know them when you get a job.
4. Look for and attend seminars in athletic training, advanced first aid, sports injuries, sports medicine, and the like. These will give you additional training and help you make more contacts.
5. Read books and periodicals on the subject of athletic training.
6. Subscribe to trade journals. These will suggest other relevant reading material and may advertise job opportunities.
7. There are a number of workshops, clinics, and camps around the country for student Athletic Trainers. Attending one of these will be very valuable to an individual for training purposes and to instill added confidence. It will also look good on your résumé.

PHYSICAL THERAPIST

CAREER PROFILE

Duties: Assessing physical therapy needs; performing initial evaluations for patients; performing physical therapy procedures on patients.

Alternate Title(s): None

Salary Range: $21,000 to $60,000+

Employment Prospects: Excellent

Best Geographical Location(s) for Position: Positions may be located throughout the country.

Prerequisites:

Education or Training—Four-year college degree in physical therapy or graduate of a certificate program; some positions may require master's degree

Experience—Experience in physical therapy setting helpful for most positions.

Special Skills and Personality Traits—Patience; compassion; empathy; enthusiasm; personability articulateness; physical and mechanical ability to use equipment related to job.

CAREER LADDER

```
┌─────────────────────────────────────────┐
│       Physical Therapist Supervisor      │
│        or Physical Therapist at          │
│    Larger, More Prestigious Facility      │
└─────────────────────────────────────────┘

┌─────────────────────────────────────────┐
│           Physical Therapist             │
└─────────────────────────────────────────┘

┌─────────────────────────────────────────┐
│            College Student               │
│                   or                     │
│       Physical Therapy Assistant         │
└─────────────────────────────────────────┘
```

Position Description

A Physical Therapist is a registered professional. In many states the Physical Therapist must be licensed by the state. He or she is responsible for a variety of functions, including assessing physical therapy needs, performing initial patient evaluations, performing physical therapy procedures, and revising patient's therapeutic plan of care. The individual in this position may also assist in directing physical therapy ancillary personnel.

The Physical Therapist may work with athletes or nonathletes. Physical therapy is an adjunct to the growing field of sports medicine. At one time or another during their careers, many professional sportsmen and women use the services of a Physical Therapist.

Physical Therapists develop therapies and exercise treatments for their patients. These therapies can help patients ease pain, recover from injuries or illness, or regain use of body parts.

Individuals become patients as a result of accidents or, in the case of athletes, sports-related injuries. People may also be born with physical disabilities or may become disabled through an illness, such as a stroke, heart attack, polio, or other diseases.

Physical therapy is very important to athletes who have been injured whether or not they are professionals. Almost any type of athlete, from an amateur runner to a professional ball player, may become a physical therapy patient. Physical therapy may also be used by handicapped individuals who would like to excel or just participate in some type of physical activity.

The Physical Therapist works with a variety of rehabilitative personnel, including physiatrists and physical therapy assistants. Specific duties depend on the situation and the specific job.

One of the first things a Physical Therapist does with a new patient is evaluate the individual and develop a rehabilitation plan. The Therapist may put the individual through a battery of tests to determine the extent of his or her injuries.

The individual must know which type of procedures and treatments will help ease a patient's pain and be therapeutic. He or she must set realistic rehabilitation goals for all patients.

The Physical Therapist may instruct and supervise physical therapy assistants in all phases of their work. He or she is required to instruct the assistant on how to run tests and how to keep proper documentation on each patient.

The Physical Therapist is responsible for reevaluating patients after a series of treatments have been completed. After the reevaluation, the individual revises the patient's therapy accordingly.

Records and documentation are extremely important in this field. In some situations, the Physical Therapist may be responsible for all paperwork and documentation of patient's progress, therapy, reactions, and so on. In other situations, the individual passes this responsibility on to an assistant.

Depending on the situation, the Physical Therapist may be required to participate in patient care conferences with individuals in the nursing or social services department, or even with families of the patient.

Often the individual must know about all aspects of the patient's medical care. The Therapist is also responsible for instructing family members, coaches, and trainers in the patient's physical therapy program.

Depending on the requirements of the job, the Physical Therapist may be required to perform additional duties, including ordering equipment, scheduling daily workloads, assessing departmental needs, and assisting in the maintenance of the physical environment of the therapy department.

The Physical Therapist may be responsible to any number of people, depending on the institution in which he or she works. The individual may report directly to the head physical therapist, physical therapist supervisor, physiatrist, or director of rehabilitative services.

He or she usually works normal or fairly normal hours. While most hospitals and health care facilities usually schedule physical therapy sessions during the day, some facilities keep Physical Therapists on staff during all hours. During an emergency, Physical Therapists may be called in and asked to work beyond normal working hours.

Salaries

Salaries for Physical Therapists vary greatly depending on a number of variables, including geographical location of the facility and its size and prestige.

Earnings also depend on the individual's education, experience, and responsibilities. The Physical Therapist can earn from $21,000 to $60,000 plus annually. In addition, compensation is also usually augmented by liberal fringe benefit packages.

Employment Prospects

A nationwide shortage of qualified individuals makes employment prospects excellent for Physical Therapists. Positions may be located throughout the country in sports medicine clinics, independent physical therapy centers, hospitals, rehabilitation centers, nursing homes, and other health care facilities.

Advancement Prospects

Advancement prospects are good for Physical Therapists. Individuals can advance their career by becoming supervisors or by locating positions in larger, more prestigious facilities.

Education and Training

A Physical Therapist must be a graduate of an approved school of physical therapy. The individual may be required to hold a Bachelor of Science degree, a certificate, or a master's degree in physical therapy.

Some states also require that Physical Therapist be licensed by their state.

Experience/Skills/Personality Traits

The Physical Therapist should genuinely like to help others. Compassion and empathy are also traits that will help the individual to excel in his or her career.

The Physical Therapist should be articulate. He or she may be required to explain procedures and therapies to both patients and their families, coaches, and trainers. He or she should be able to give directions to others in a way they understand. Physical Therapists must be able to supervise others, including assistants and aides.

The individual should be positive, personable, and enthusiastic so that he or she can motivate patients to help themselves.

The Physical Therapist must also have both the physical and the mechanical ability to use equipment relevant to the job, such as wheelchairs, stretchers, lifts, geriatric chairs, whirlpools, and traction equipment.

Unions/Associations

Physical Therapists working in health care facilities may or may not belong to a variety of unions that represent workers in hospitals or health care facilities.

Individuals may also belong to trade associations, including the American Physical Therapy Association (APTA). This organization provides educational guidance and support for those working in the physical therapy field.

Tips for Entry

1. Locate sports medicine clinics and private physical therapy centers in the area by looking in the yellow pages of the phone book.
2. Positions are often advertised in the display or classified section of the newspaper. Look under heading classifications of "Health Care," "Hospitals," "Physical Therapy," "Sports Medicine," or "Therapists."
3. Consider sending your résumé to hospitals or health care facilities with a cover letter. Ask that your résumé be kept on file if a position is not currently available.
4. Call the personnel director of hospitals and health care facilities in the areas where you want to work to try to set up an appointment for an interview.
5. If you are still in school or taking part in an accredited training program, contact the job placement office for job possibilities.
6. Employment agencies located throughout the country specialize in jobs in the health care industry. Check to see who pays the fee if you do get a job (you or the employer) before getting involved.

PHYSICAL THERAPY ASSISTANT

CAREER PROFILE

Duties: Assisting physical therapist in treating patients; administering physical therapy treatments such as hydrotherapy, massage, heat treatments, etc.; doing paperwork.

Alternate Title(s): Assistant Physical Therapist; Physical Therapist Assistant

Salary Range: $15,000 to $28,000

Employment Prospects: Excellent

Best Geographical Location(s) for Position: Positions may be located throughout the country.

Prerequisites:

Education or Training—Two-year associate's degree from college offering physical therapy or physical therapy assistant program.

Experience—No experience required; work in health care facility may be preferred.

Special Skills and Personality Traits—Patience; compassion; empathy; enthusiasm; personality; articulateness; strong; ability to follow instructions.

CAREER LADDER

```
┌─────────────────────────────────────┐
│        Physical Therapist           │
└─────────────────────────────────────┘

┌─────────────────────────────────────┐
│     Physical Therapy Assistant      │
└─────────────────────────────────────┘

┌─────────────────────────────────────┐
│          College Student            │
└─────────────────────────────────────┘
```

Position Description

A Physical Therapy Assistant is a paraprofessional who is responsible for providing direct patient care under immediate direction and supervision. He or she is also required to assist the physical therapist, physiatrist, and/or other rehabilitation specialist in any procedure or function, including those not related to direct patient care when directed to do so.

The individual may work with athletes or nonathletes depending on the situation. Physical therapy is an adjunct to the growing field of sports medicine.

Physical Therapy Assistants or Physical Therapist Assistants, as they may be called, provide patients with various therapies and exercise modalities developed by the physical therapist. These therapies help the patient ease pain, recover from an injury or illness, or regain use of a body part.

Individuals become patients as a result of accidents or, in the case of athletes, game-related injuries. People may also be born with physical disabilities or may become disabled through an illness, such as a stroke, heart attack, polio, or other diseases.

Physical therapy is very important to athletes who have been injured whether or not they are professionals. Almost any type of athlete, from a amateur runner to a professional ball player, may become a physical therapy patient. Physical therapy may also be used by handicapped individuals who would like to excel or just participate in some type of physical activity.

The Physical Therapy Assistant takes orders from the head physical therapist, physiatrist, or other rehabilitation specialist. Duties depend on the situation and the specific job.

The Physical Therapy Assistant may work with the physical therapist or physiatrist in evaluating a new patient and implementing a care or rehabilitation plan. For example, if an athlete comes in after a sports-related injury, the Assistant may be instructed on which particular tests to put him or her through. In physical therapy treatment it is important to know the extent of injuries.

The Assistant may be asked to do tests, such as checking the amount of weight an athlete can put on his or her leg or how far the individual can bend. The Assistant may help the patient walk, climb stairs or inclines, or perform other exercises to regain mobility. If the Assistant does not do his or her job correctly, a patient may have a treatment that is too strenuous or not strenuous enough to help.

In many cases, the Physical Therapy Assistant helps a patient not only ease the pain but also learn how to deal with pain. He or she may, for example, assist the patient by providing heat therapy, hydrotherapy, such as whirlpool baths or wet packs, massages, and so on.

In some cases, the Assistant helps the physical therapist reevaluate patients after a series of treatments have been completed. The Physical Therapy Assistant often must do a great deal of the paperwork documentation, from making original records of a patient's problems, capabilities, and so on to evaluating his or her current capabilities and progress.

The Physical Therapy Assistant often builds a close bond with his or her patients. It is exciting to watch someone who couldn't walk take his or her first step after a major injury.

Physical Therapy Assistants are responsible directly to the head physical therapist, physiatrist, or rehabilitation specialist, depending on the institution they are working in. They usually work normal or fairly normal hours. While most hospitals and health care facilities usually schedule physical therapy sessions during the day, some facilities keep both physical therapists and Assistants on staff at all hours.

Salaries

Salaries for Physical Therapy Assistants vary greatly depending on a number of variables, including the geographical location of the facility and its size and prestige.

Earnings also depend on the individuals' education, experience, and responsibilities. The Physical Therapy Assistant's annual earnings can range from $15,000 to $28,000. In addition, compensation is also usually augmented by liberal fringe benefit packages.

Employment Prospects

Employment prospects are excellent for Physical Therapy Assistants as there is currently a nationwide shortage of qualified individuals. There are many opportunities in hospitals, rehabilitation centers, nursing homes, and other health care facilities. Physical Therapy Assistants may also work in sports medicine clinics, which are springing up throughout the country, or in independent physical therapy centers. One of the good things about this position is that jobs may be found in almost any geographical location.

While some institutions only have one or two people in this position, many hire a number of Physical Therapy Assistants. Part-time work as a Physical Therapy Assistant in a variety of different health care facilities is also available.

Advancement Prospects

Advancement prospects are excellent for Physical Therapy Assistants. Individuals can advance their career by becoming full-fledged physical therapists. In order to climb the career ladder, however, the Physical Therapy Assistant must take additional training. This usually includes at least another two years of schooling in an institution that has an accredited program in physical therapy.

Education and Training

Physical Therapy Assistants are usually required to hold an associate's degree from a two-year college that offers a physical therapy or physical therapy assistants' program.

Experience/Skills/Personality Traits

The Physical Therapy Assistant should have a great deal of patience. This is important because the individual often works with patients who can't do very much. A small step by a patient may be a major accomplishment, and it may take a long time to achieve.

The Assistant should be a giving person who genuinely likes to help others. Compassion and empathy are also traits that will help the individual excel in his or her career.

The Physical Therapy Assistant should be articulate. He or she should be able to follow directions and explain them to others in a way they understand. The Assistant should also be positive, personable, and enthusiastic so that he or she can motivate patients to help themselves. Many patients who work with the Assistant are under severe emotional and physical strain. A smiling face at a therapy session can sometimes make the difference between success and failure.

If the individual is working in a health care facility, he or she must be able to handle the situation both physically and emotionally.

Unions/Associations

Many Physical Therapy Assistants working in health care facilities do not belong to unions. Others may belong to a variety of unions that represent workers in hospitals or health care facilities.

The individual may belong to trade associations, including the American Physical Therapy Association (APTA). This organization provides educational guidance and support for those working in the physical therapy field.

Tips for Entry

1. Positions can often be located in display or classified advertisements in the newspaper. Look under heading classifications of "Health Care," "Hospitals," "Physical Therapy," "Sports Medicine," or "Therapists."
2. You might want to send your résumé to hospitals or health care facilities with a cover letter. Ask that your résumé be kept on file if a position is not currently available.
3. You might also consider calling the personnel director of hospitals and health care facilities in the areas where you want to work to try to set up an appointment for an interview.
4. If you are still in school or taking part in an accredited training program, contact the job placement office for job possibilities.

SPORTS AND FITNESS NUTRITIONIST

CAREER PROFILE

Duties: Analyzing nutritional needs of individuals; planning nutritious, healthful meals for athletes; counseling athletes on nutritional problems.

Alternate Title(s): Nutritionist; Sports Nutritionist; Sports Nutrition Counselor

Salary Range: $20,000 to $100,000+

Employment Prospects: Good

Best Geographical Location(s) for Position: Positions may be located throughout the country.

Prerequisites:

Education or Training—Educational requirements vary from one-year program through master's degree in nutritional science.

Experience—Experience in nutrition and fitness helpful.

Special Skills and Personality Traits—Complete knowledge of nutrition; understanding of exercise, athletics, and fitness; personable; communication skills; understanding; compassionate.

CAREER LADDER

```
┌─────────────────────────────────┐
│   Director of Sports Nutrition   │
│               or                 │
│  Sports and Fitness Nutritionist │
│            for More              │
│  Prestigious Team or Facility    │
└─────────────────────────────────┘

┌─────────────────────────────────┐
│  Sports and Fitness Nutritionist │
└─────────────────────────────────┘

┌─────────────────────────────────┐
│         College Student          │
└─────────────────────────────────┘
```

Position Description

It is important to both professional and amateur athletes to be physically fit and healthy. This is accomplished by exercising, sleeping a sufficient number of hours, living an appropriate and healthy life-style, and eating correctly. The field of sports nutrition is becoming more popular as people realize the importance of good nutrition to athletes. Studies have shown that an athlete's performance can often increase if he or she eats balanced and nutritious meals. The Sports Nutritionist is the individual called on to develop nutritional programs for individual athletes or athletic teams and organizations.

The Sports Nutritionist can work in a variety of settings. He or she may work with professional sports teams, collegiate or amateur teams, individual athletes, sports training camps, hospitals, health clubs, or sports clinics. The individual's responsibilities vary depending on the specific job. Many of the responsibilities of the Sports and Fitness Nutritionist also depend on the level of education the individual has secured.

The main function of the Sports and Fitness Nutritionist is to plan nutritious, healthful meals and menus for athletes. To do this, the Nutritionist may talk to the athlete to determine what type of diet he or she has been following, foods currently

on his or her menus, and so on. The Nutritionist determines the physical activities that the athlete does routinely and his or her height, weight, and other factors.

The individual then analyzes the nutritional requirements of the athlete and plans meals around this information. The Nutritionist must understand the athlete's food likes and dislikes as well as eating routines and schedules. Planning a nutritious food program is useless unless someone can and will follow it. The Sports and Fitness Nutritionist may be expected to explain the correlation between eating correctly and potential athletic performance to many of his or her clients.

The individual may work on a one-on-one basis with athletes helping them learn what foods will be most beneficial to their performance level. He or she may also develop a nutritional analysis for a team or group of people and use this analysis to plan meals and menus. The Nutritionist may be required to develop food budgets and keep within set dollar limits when putting together menus.

The Sports and Fitness Nutritionist may, for example, work for a professional sports team at a training camp. The individual is expected to plan meals to be prepared and served to the athletes during the training camp.

The individual may also be expected to counsel athletes about what they should eat after leaving training camp. He or she is expected to keep records of client needs, prescribed programs, and progress. In some cases, athletes may have to either take off or put on weight. The Sports and Fitness Nutritionist works with these individuals prescribing diets to help them attain their goals.

At times, the Sports and Fitness Nutritionist may be required to lecture groups of athletes on nutrition and healthy eating patterns. He or she may also explain how various foods can affect their athletic performance. The individual may also offer cooking lessons to either athletes or chefs. This is done to help explain how to prepare nutritious food when away from camp or out of the Nutritionist's jurisdiction.

The individual may work long hours analyzing dietary needs. However, watching an athlete excel because of a suggested change in his or her diet can be exciting and fulfilling for the Nutritionist.

Salaries

Earnings for Sports Nutritionists may range from $20,000 to $100,000 plus per year. Variables affecting salaries include the experience, education, responsibilities, and duties of the individual as well as the specific job.

Individuals with a master's degree or higher earn considerably more than a person with less education.

Employment Prospects

Employment prospects for Sports and Fitness Nutritionists are good and steadily increasing. As more and more people begin to realize the importance of nutrition in relation to athletic performance, there is a greater need for individuals working in the field. Jobs may be located throughout the country.

Sports and Fitness Nutritionists may be on staff with professional sports teams as well as scholastic and/or amateur teams. They may also work on a consulting basis for teams or individual athletes.

Sports medicine clinics are also beginning to utilize the services of Sports and Fitness Nutritionists. Many health and fitness clubs have individuals in this capacity on staff.

Advancement Prospects

Advancement prospects are fair for Sports and Fitness Nutritionists. Individuals may climb the career ladder by locating a position with a more prestigious, well-known team or athlete. Sports and Fitness Nutritionists might also advance their careers by becoming directors of sports nutrition for a team or a clinic.

For many individuals, career advancement may be attained by obtaining additional education.

Education and Training

Educational requirements vary for Sports and Fitness Nutritionists. While some jobs require a minimum of a one-year program in nutrition or a two-year associate's degree in food and nutrition, most require at least a four-year college degree with a major in foods and nutrition. Many professional sports teams and sports medicine clinics may prefer individuals with advanced degrees, such as a master's in nutrition.

Continuing education in the form of classes, seminars, and symposiums on athletics, fitness, exercise, nutrition, and food will be helpful.

Many jobs also require an individual to be a registered member of the American Dietary Association (ADA).

Experience/Skills/Personality Traits

Sports and Fitness Nutritionists should enjoy working with people. They should be able to relate to individuals on a variety of levels. The Nutritionist should be understanding, compassionate, and nonjudgmental. It is often difficult for people to change their dietary patterns even if their professional career depends on it.

Nutritionists should have a complete knowledge of nutrition and food and its effect on the body. They should be healthy, fit people themselves with an understanding of exercise and fitness.

Individuals should be easy to talk to and personable. They should have good communications skills, both verbal and written.

Unions/Associations

There are no specific trade associations for Sports and Fitness Nutritionists. Individuals may, however, be members of the ADA.

Tips for Entry

1. Get as much education as you can in this field. The better your educational background, the better chance you will have of obtaining a job and advancing your career.

2. Contact health and fitness clubs about openings. If the clubs do not have a staff Nutritionist, try to create a position for yourself. You may have to work part time at a couple of clubs in order to get your career started.

3. If you can't find a job in sports and fitness and you have the educational requirements, consider a job in a hospital dietary department. This will give you hands-on experience working with nutrition. You can then move on to the sports and fitness fields.

4. Jobs may be advertised in the newspaper's classified or display section. Look under heading classifications of "Nutritionist," "Sports Nutritionist," "Fitness," or "Dietary."

5. You may also search for job openings on the Internet. Go to any of the popular job sites and look for keywords such as "nutritionist" or "nutrition counselor."

APPENDIXES

APPENDIX I
DEGREE PROGRAMS

A. COLLEGES AND UNIVERSITIES THAT OFFER MAJORS IN SPORTS ADMINISTRATION

The following is a list of four-year schools that grant degrees with majors in sports administration and management. They are grouped by state. More colleges are beginning to grant degrees in this area every year. Check the newest copy of *Lovejoy's* (found in the reference section of libraries or in guidance counseling centers) for additional schools offering degrees in this field.

ALABAMA

Faulkner University
5345 Atlanta Highway
Montgomery, AL 36193

Huntingdon College
1500 East Fairview Avenue
Montgomery, AL 36194

ARKANSAS

Arkansas State University
P.O. Box 1630
State University, AR 72467

Harding University
Station A, Box 2255
Searcy, AR 72149

CALIFORNIA

Concordia University
1530 Concordia West
Irvine, CA 92612-3299

Fresno Pacific University
1717 South Chestnut Avenue
Fresno, CA 93702

University of San Francisco
Ignatian Heights
San Francisco, CA 94177

University of the Pacific
3601 Pacific Avenue
Stockton, CA 95211

CONNECTICUT

Eastern Connecticut State University
Willimantic, CT 06226

Sacred Heart University
5151 Park Avenue
Fairfield, CT 06432

Teikyo Post University
800 Country Club Road
P.O. Box 2540
Waterbury, CT 06723

University of New Haven
300 Orange Avenue
New Haven, CT 06516

DELAWARE

Wilmington College
320 DuPont Highway
New Castle, DE 19720

FLORIDA

Flagler College
King Street
St. Augustine, FL 32084

Florida Southern College
111 Lake Hollingworth Drive
Lakeland, FL 33801

Florida State University
Tallahassee, FL 32306

Lynn University
3601 North Military Trail
Boca Raton, FL 33431

Nova Southeastern University
3301 College Avenue
Fort Lauderdale, FL 33314

Saint Leo College
P.O. Box 2008
Saint Leo, FL 33574

Saint Thomas University
16400 Northwest 32nd Avenue
Miami, FL 33054

Webber College
1201 Alternate 27 South
P.O. Box 96
Babson Park, FL 33827

GEORGIA

Berry College
Mount Berry, GA 30149

Georgia Southern University
Box 8024
Statesboro, GA 31709

Kennesaw State University
P.O. Box 444
Marietta, GA 30061

IDAHO

Albertson College of Idaho
2112 Cleveland Boulevard
Caldwell, ID 83605

ILLINOIS

Elmhurst College
190 Prospect Avenue
Elmhurst, IL 60126

Judson College
1151 North State Street
Elgin, IL 60120

MacMurray College
447 East College Street
Jacksonville, IL 62650

Principia College
Elsah, Illinois
62028-9799

Quincy University
1800 College Avenue
Quincy, IL 62301

INDIANA

Ball State University
Muncie, IN 47306

Indiana State University
217 North Sixth Street
Terre Haute, IN 47809

Indiana University–Bloomington
814 Third Street
Bloomington, IN 47405

IOWA

Graceland College
700 College Avenue
Lamoni, IA 50140

Iowa Wesleyan College
601 North Main Street
Mount Pleasant IA 52641

Lorus College
1450 Alta Vista
Dubuque, IA 52001

Luther College
Decorah, IA 52101

Simpson College
Indianola, IA 50125

University of Iowa
108 Calvin Hall
Iowa City, IA 52242

William Penn College
201 Trueblood Avenue
Okaloosa, IA 52577

KANSAS

Benedictine College
North Campus
Atchison, Kansas 66002

KENTUCKY

Union College
College Street
Barbourville, KY 40906

University of Louisville
Louisville, KY 40292

LOUISIANA

**Northwestern State University
of Louisiana**
College Avenue
Natchitoches, LA 70402

Tulane University
6823 St. Charles Avenue
New Orleans, LA 70118

MAINE

Husson College
One College Circle
Bangor, ME 04401

University of New England
University Campus
Hills Beach Road
Biddeford, ME 04005

MARYLAND

Morgan State University
Cold Spring Lane and Hillen Road
Baltimore, MD 21239

MASSACHUSETTS

Becker College–Leicester Campus
3 Paxton Street
Leicester, MA 01524-1197

Becker College–Worcester Campus
61 Sever St.
Worcester, MA 01615-0071

Endicott College
376 Hale Street
Beverly, MA 01915

Salem State College
352 Lafayette Street
Salem, MA 01970

Springfield College
Box M
Springfield, MA 01109

**University of Massachusetts–
Amherst**
255 Whitmore Administration Building
Amherst, MA 01003

MICHIGAN

Concordia College
4090 Geddes Road
Ann Arbor, MI 48105

Cornerstone College
1001 E. Beltline Avenue NE
Grand Rapids, MI 49525

University of Michigan–Ann Arbor
1220 Student Activities Building
Ann Arbor, MI 48109

MINNESOTA

Bemidji State University
Bemidji, MN 56601

Winona State University
Winona, MN 55987

College of St. Scholastica
1200 Kenwood Avenue
Duluth, MN 55811

Crown College
6425 County Road 30
St. Bonifacius, MN 55375

Mankato State University
Box 55
Mankato, MN 56001

MISSISSIPPI

Mississippi University For Women
Columbus, MS 39701

University of Southern Mississippi
Box 5011–Southern Station
Hattiesburg, MS 39401

MISSOURI

Northwest Missouri State University
Maryville, MO 64468

Southwest Baptist University
623 South Pike
Bolivar, MO 65613

MONTANA

Carroll College
1601 North Benton Avenue
Helena, MT 59625-0002

NEBRASKA

Nebraska Wesleyan University
5000 St. Paul Avenue
Lincoln, NE 68504

Wayne State College
200 East Tenth
Wayne, NE 68787

NEW HAMPSHIRE

Colby-Sawyer College
100 Main Street
New London, NH 03257

Daniel Webster College
Twenty University Drive
Nashua, NH 03063

Franklin Pierce College
College Road
Rindge, NH 03461

Keene State College
Main Street
Keene, NH 03431

New Hampshire College
2500 North River Road
Manchester, NH 03106

University of New Hampshire
Garrison Avenue-Grant House
Durham, NH 03824

NEW JERSEY

Jersey City State College
2039 Kennedy Boulevard
Jersey City, NJ 07305

Rutgers, The State University of New Jersey
Cook College
P.O. Box 2101
New Brunswick, NJ 08903

Rutgers, The State University of New Jersey
Douglass College
P.O. Box 2101
New Brunswick, NJ 08903

Rutgers, The State University of New Jersey
Livingston College
P.O. Box 2101
New Brunswick, NJ 08903

Rutgers, The State University of New Jersey
Rutgers College
P.O. Box 2101
New Brunswick, NJ 08903

Seton Hall University
400 South Orange Avenue
South Orange, NJ 07079

NEW YORK

Daemen College
4380 Main Street
Amherst, NY 14226

Ithaca College
Ithaca, NY 14850

Medaille College
18 Agassiz Circle
Buffalo, NY 14214

St. John's University
8000 Utopia Parkway
Jamaica, NY 11439

State University of New York
College at Brockport
Kenyon Street
Brockport, NY 14420

NORTH CAROLINA

Barton College
Box 5000
Wilson, NC 27893

Belmont Abbey College
Belmont, NC 28012

Campbell University
P.O. Box 546
Buies Creek, NC 27506

Chowan College
Murfreesboro, NC 27855

Elon College
2700 Campus Box
Elon College, NC 27244

Gillford College
5800 West Friendly Avenue
Greensboro, NC 27410

High Point University
University Station, Montlieu Avenue
High Point, NC 27262

Livingstone College
701 West Monroe Street
Salisbury, NC 28144

Mars Hill College
Mars Hill, NC 28754

Methodist College
5400 Ramsey Street
Fayetteville, NC 28311

Pfeiffer University
Misenheimer, NC 28109

Western Carolina University
520 H.F. Robinson Administration
  Building
Cullowhee, NC 28723

Wingate University
Wingate, NC 28174

Winston-Salem State University
Wallace Street
Winston-Salem, NC 27110

OHIO

Baldwin-Wallace College
275 Eastland Road
Burea, OH 44017

Bluffton College
280 West College Avenue
Bluffton, OH 45817-1196

Bowling Green State University
110 McFall Center
Bowling Green, OH 43403

Defiance College
701 North Clinton Street
Defiance, OH 43512

Miami University
Oxford, OH 45056

Mount Union College
1972 Clark Street
Alliance, OH 44601

Mount Vernon Nazerene College
800 Martinsburg Road
Mount Vernon, OH 43050

Ohio Northern University
Main Street
Ada, OH 45810

Ohio University
120 Chubb Hall
Athens, OH 45701

Shawnee State University
940 Second Street
Portsmouth, OH 45662

Tiffin University
155 Miami Street
Tiffin, OH 44883

University of Dayton
300 College Park Avenue
Dayton, OH 45469

Xavier University
3800 Victory Parkway
Cincinnati, OH 45207

OKLAHOMA

Phillips University
P.O. Box 2000 University Station
Enid, OK 73702

University of Tulsa
600 South College Avenue
Tulsa, OK 74104

PENNSYLVANIA

Allentown College of St. Francis de Sales
2755 Station Avenue
Center Valley, PA 18034

Loch Haven University of Pennsylvania
Loch Haven, PA 17745

Mercyhurst College
Glenwood Hills
Erie, PA 16546

Robert Morris College
881 Narrows Run Road
Moon Township, PA 15108

Slippery Rock University of Pennsylvania
Slippery Rock, PA 16057

Temple University
Philadelphia, PA 19122

University of Pittsburgh at Bradford
300 Campus Drive
Bradford, PA 16701

SOUTH CAROLINA

Anderson College
316 Boulevard
Anderson, SC 29621

Erskine College
Due West, SC 29639

University of South Carolina at Columbia
Columbia, SC 29208

TENNESSEE

Lincoln Memorial University
Harrogate, TN 37752

Tennessee Wesleyan College
P.O. Box 40–College Street
Athens, TN 37303

Tusculum College
P.O. Box 5097
Greeneville, TN 37743

University of Tennessee–Knoxville
320 Student Services Building
Knoxville, TN 37996

TEXAS

LeTourneau University
2100 S. Mobberly Avenue
Longview, TX 75602

Texas Weslyan College
P.O. Box 50010–3101 East Rosedale
Fort Worth, TX 76105

University of the Incarnate Word
4301 Broadway
San Antonio, TX 78209

UTAH

Brigham Young University
Brigham Young University Campus
Provo, UT 84602

VERMONT

Lyndon State College
Lyndonville, VT 05851

VIRGINIA

Averett College
West Main Street
Danville, VA 24541

Christopher Newport University
50 Shoe Lane
Newport News, VA 23606

Liberty University
3765 Candlers Mountain Road
Lynchburg, VA 24506

Longwood College
Farmville, VA 23901

Old Dominion University
Hampton Boulevard
Norfolk, VA 24142

Virginia Intermont College
1013 Moore Street
Bristol, VA 24201

**Virginia Polytechnic Institute and
    State University**
104 Burruss Hall
Blacksburg, VA 24016

WASHINGTON

Pacific Lutheran University
Tacoma, WA 98447

WEST VIRGINIA

Bethany College
Bethany, WV 26032

Davis & Elkins College
100 Campus Drive
Elkins, WV 26241

Glenville State College
Glenville, WV 26351

Marian College of Fond du Lac
45 South National Avenue
Fond Du Lac, WI 54935

Marshall University
4th Avenue and Hal Greer Boulevard
Huntington, WV 25705

Salem-Teikyo University
Salem, WV 26426

Shepherd College
Shepherdstown, WV 25443

West Virginia University
P.O. Box 6009
Morgantown, WV 26506

WISCONSIN

University of Wisconsin-La Crosse
1725 State Street
La Crosse, WI 54601

CANADA

Laurentian University
935 Ramsey Lake Road
Sudbury, Ontario, Canada
P3E 2C6

University College of Cape Breton
P.O. Box 5300
Sydney, Nova Scotia, Canada
B1P 6L2

University of Alberta
120 Administration Building
Edmonton, Alberta, Canada
T6G 2M7

University of Victoria
Box 1700
Victoria, British Columbia, Canada
V8W 2Y2

York University
4700 Keele Street
Toronto, Ontario, Canada
M3J 1P3

B. COLLEGES AND UNIVERSITIES THAT OFFER MAJORS IN PHYSICAL EDUCATION

The following is a list of four-year schools that grant degrees with majors in physical education. They are grouped by state. More colleges are beginning to grant degrees in this area every year.

Check the newest copy of *Lovejoy's* (found in the reference sections of libraries or in guidance counseling centers) for additional schools offering degrees in this field.

ALABAMA

Alabama A & M University
P.O. Box 284
Normal, AL 35762

Alabama State University
P.O. Box 271
915 South Jackson Street
Montgomery, AL 36101

Athens State College
P.O. Box 2216
Beaty Street
Athens, AL 35611

Auburn University
Mary E. Martin Hall
Auburn University, AL 36849

Auburn University-Montgomery
Montgomery, AL 36193

Huntingdon College
1500 East Fairview Avenue
Montgomery, AL 36194

Jacksonville State University
North Pelham Road
Jacksonville, AL 36265

The University of West Alabama
Livingston, AL 35470

Mobile College
Box 13220
Mobile, AL 36613

Oakland College
Huntsville, AL 35896

Samford University
800 Lakeshore Drive
Birmingham, AL 35229

Southeastern Bible College
3001 Highway 280 East
Birmingham, AL 35243

Stillman College
P.O. Box 1430
Tuscaloosa, AL 35403

Troy State University
University Avenue
Troy, AL 36082

Tuskegee University
Carnegie Hall
Tuskegee, AL 36088

University of Alabama
Box 870132
Tuscaloosa, AL 35487

University of Alabama–Birmingham
University Station–University Center
Birmingham, AL 35294

University of Montevallo
Montevallo, AL 35115

University of North Alabama
Wesleyan Avenue
Florence, AL 35632

University of South Alabama
307 University Boulevard
Mobile, AL 36688

ALASKA

University of Alaska–Anchorage
3211 Providence Drive
Anchorage, AK 99508

University of Alaska–Fairbanks
320 Signers Hall
Fairbanks, AK 99701

ARIZONA

Grand Canyon College
3300 West Camelback Road
Phoenix, AZ 85017

Northern Arizona University
Box 4084
Flagstaff, AZ 86011

University of Arizona
Tuczon, AZ 85721

ARKANSAS

Arkansas College
Batesville, AR 72501

Arkansas State University
P.O. Box 1630
State University, AR 72467

Arkansas Tech University
Caraway Hall
Russellville, AR 72801

Harding University
Box 762–Station A
Searcy, AR 72143

Henderson State University
Arkadelphia, AR 71923

Hendrix College
Conway, AR 72023

John Brown University
Siloam Springs, AR 72761

Philander Smith College
812 West 13th Street
Little Rock, AR 72202

Quachita Baptist University
410 Quachita Street
Arkadelphia, AR 71998

Southern Arkansas University
SAU Box 1382
Magnolia, AR 71753

University of Arkansas
Administration 222
Fayetteville, AR 72701

University of Arkansas–Monticello
Monticello, AR 71655

University of Arkansas–Pine Bluff
1200 University Drive
Pine Bluff, AR 71601

University of Central Arkansas
Conway, AR 72032

University of the Ozarks
415 College Avenue
Clarksville, AR 72830

CALIFORNIA

Azusa Pacific University
P.O. Box 7000
901 East Alosta
Azusa, CA 91702

California Baptist College
8432 Magnolia Avenue
Riverside, CA 92504

California Lutheran University
60 Olsen Road
Thousand Oaks, CA 91360

California State University–Bakersfield
9001 Stockdale Highway
Bakersfield, CA 93311

California State University–San Bernadino
5500 University Parkway
San Bernadino, CA 92407

California State University–Stanislaus
801 West Monte Vista Avenue
Turlock, CA 95380

California Polytechnic State University
San Luis Obispo, CA 93407

California State Polytechnic University–Pomona
3801 West Temple Avenue
Pomona, CA 91768

California State University–Chico
Chico, CA 95929

California State University–Dominquez Hills
Carson, CA 90747

California State University–Fresno
Shaw and Cedar Avenues
Fresno, CA 93740

California State University–Fullerton
Fullerton, CA 92634

California State University–Hayward
Hayward, CA 94542

California State University–Long Beach
1250 Bellflower Boulevard
Long Beach, CA 90840

California State University–Los Angeles
5151 State University Drive
Los Angeles, CA 90032

California State University–Northridge
18111 Nordoff Street
Northridge, CA 91330

California State University–Sacramento
6000 J Street
Sacramento, CA 95819

Chapman College
333 North Glassell Street
Orange, CA 92666

Concordia College
1530 Concordia
Irvine, CA 92715

Christian Heritage College
2100 Greenfield Drive
El Cajon, CA 92019

Fresno Pacific College
1717 South Chestnut Avenue
Fresno, CA 93702

Humboldt State University
Arcata, CA 95521

La Sierra University
4700 Pierce Street
Riverside, CA 92515

The Master's College
P.O. Box 878
Newhall, CA 91322

Pacific Union College
Angwin, CA 94508

Pepperdine University–Seaver College
24255 Pacific Coast Highway
Malibu, CA 90265

Point Loma Nazarene College
3900 Lomaland Drive
San Diego, CA 92106

San Diego State University
5300 Campanile Drive
San Diego, CA 92182

San Francisco State University
1600 Holloway Avenue
San Francisco, CA 94132

San Jose State University
One Washington Square
San Jose, CA 95192

Southern California College
55 Fair Drive
Costa Mesa, CA 92626

St. Mary's College of California
Moraga, CA 94575

University of California–Davis
Davis, CA 95616

University of La Verne
1950 Third Street
La Verne, CA 91750

University of San Francisco
Ignatian Heights
San Francisco, CA 94177

University of the Pacific
3601 Pacific Avenue
Stockton, CA 95211

Westmont College
955 La Paz Road
Santa Barbara, CA 93108

Whittier College
13406 East Philadelphia
Whittier, CA 90608

COLORADO

Adams State College
Alamosa, CO 81102

Colorado State University
Administration Annex
Fort Collins, CO 80523

Fort Lewis College
College Heights
Durango, CO 81301

Mesa State College
P.O. Box 2647
Grand Junction, CO 81502

University of Northern Colorado
Greeley, CO 80639

Western State College of Colorado
College Heights
Gunnison, CO 81230

CONNECTICUT

Central Connecticut State University
1615 Stanley Street
New Britain, CT 06050

Eastern Connecticut State University
Hurley Hall
Willimantic, CT 06226

Southern Connecticut State University
501 Crescent Street
New Haven, CT 06515

University of Connecticut
Storrs, CT 06269

DELAWARE

University of Delaware
116 Hullihen Hall
Newark, DE 19716

Wesley College
Dover, DE 19901

WASHINGTON, DC

American University
4400 Massachusetts Avenue NW
Washington, DC 20016

Howard University
2400 Sixth Street NW
Washington, DC 20059

FLORIDA

Barry University
11300 Northeast Second Avenue
Miami Shores, FL 33161

Bethune-Cookman College
640 Second Avenue
Daytona Beach, FL 32015

Clearwater Christian College
3400 Gulf-To-Bay Boulevard
Clearwater, FL 33519

Edward Waters College
1658 Kings Road
Jacksonville, FL 32209

Flagler College
P.O. Box 1027
St. Augustine, FL 32085

Florida Agriculture and Mechanical University
Tallahassee, FL 32307

Florida International University
Tamiami Trail
Miami, FL 33199

Florida Memorial College
15800 Northwest 42nd Avenue
Miami, FL 33054

Florida Southern College
111 Lake Hollingsworth Drive
Lakeland, FL 33801

Florida State University
Tallahassee, FL 32306

Jacksonville University
2800 University Boulevard
Jacksonville, FL 32211

Palm Beach Atlantic College
1101 South Olive Avenue
West Palm Beach, FL 33401

Stetson University
DeLand, FL 32720

University of Central Florida
P.O. Box 160111
Orlando, FL 32816

University of Florida
303 Little Hall
P.O. Box 118140
Gainesville, FL 32611

University of North Florida
4567 St. John Bluff Road, South
Jacksonville, FL 32224

University of South Florida
4202 Fowler Avenue
Tampa, FL 33620

University of Tampa
401 West Kennedy Boulevard
Tampa, FL 33606

University of West Florida
11000 University Parkway
Pensacola, FL 32514

Warner Southern College
U.S. Highway 27 South
Lake Wales, FL 33853

GEORGIA

Albany State College
504 College Drive
Albany, GA 31705

Armstrong State College
11935 Abercorn Street
Savannah, GA 31419

Augusta College
2500 Walton Way
Augusta, GA 30910

Berry College
P.O. Box 159
Mount Berry Station
Mount Berry, GA 30149

Clark Atlanta University
240 James P. Brawley Drive
Atlanta, GA 30314

Columbus College
422 University Avenue
Richards Building
Columbus, GA 31907

Fort Valley State College
805 State College Drive
Fort Valley, GA 31030

Georgia College
Campus Box 499
Milledgeville, GA 31061

Georgia Southern College
Box 8024
Statesboro, GA 30458

Georgia Southwestern University
Wheatey Street
Americus, GA 31709

Georgia State University
University Plaza
Atlanta, GA 30303

Kennesaw College
P.O. Box 444
Marietta, GA 30061

Morehouse College
830 Westview Drive Southwest
Atlanta, GA 30314

Morris Brown College
643 Martin Luther King Jr. Drive NW
Atlanta, GA 30314

North Georgia College
Dahlonega, GA 30597

University of Georgia
212 Terrell Hall
Athens, GA 30602

Valdosta State College
1500 North Patterson Street
Valdosta, GA 30698

West Georgia College
Carrollton, GA 30118

HAWAII

Brigham Young University–Hawaii
55–220 Kulanui Street
Laie, Oahu, HI 96762

IDAHO

Boise State University
1910 University Drive
Boise, ID 83725

Albertson College
2112 Cleveland Boulevard
Caldwell, ID 83605

Idaho State University
P.O. Box 8270
Pocatello, ID 83209

Lewis Clark State College
8th Avenue and 6th Street
Lewiston, ID 83501

Northwest Nazerene College
623 Holly Street
Nampa, ID 83651

University of Idaho
141 Administration Building
Moscow, ID 83843

ILLINOIS

Augustana College
639 38th Street
Rock Island, IL 61201

Aurora University
347 South Gladston
Aurora, IL 60506

Blackburn College
700 College Avenue
Carlinville, IL 62626

Chicago State University
95th Street at King Drive
Chicago, IL 60628

Concordia College
7400 Augusta Street
River Forest, IL 60305

DePaul University
25 East Jackson Boulevard
Chicago, IL 60604

Eastern Illinois University
Old Main
Charleston, IL 61920

Elmhurst College
190 Prospect Avenue
Elmhurst, IL 60216

Eureka College
College Avenue
Eureka, IL 61530

Greenville College
315 East College Avenue
Greenville, IL 62246

Illinois Benedictine College
5700 College Road
Lisle, IL 60532

Illinois College
West College Avenue
Jacksonville, IL 62650

Illinois State University
Campus Box 2200
Normal, IL 61761

Judson College
1151 North State Street
Elgin, IL 60120

MacMurray College
447 East College Street
Jacksonville, IL 62650

McKendree College
701 Chicago Road
Lebanon, IL 62258

Millikin University
1184 West Main Street
Decatur, IL 62522

Monmouth College
700 East Broadway
Monmouth, IL 61462

North Central College
30 North Brainard
Naperville, IL 60566

North Park College
3225 West Forester Avenue
Chicago, IL 60625

Northeastern Illinois University
5500 North St. Louis Avenue
Chicago, IL 60625

Northern Illinois University
De Kalb, IL 60115

Olivet Nazerene University
P.O. Box 592
Kankakee, IL 60901

Quincy University
1800 College Avenue
Quincy, IL 62301

Rockford College
5050 East State Street
Rockford, IL 61108

**Southern Illinois University–
Carbondale**
Woody Hall
Carbondale, IL 62901

Southern Illinois University–Edwardsville
Box 1047
Edwardsville, IL 62026

St. Xavier College
3700 West 103rd Street
Chicago, IL 60655

Trinity Christian College
6601 West College Drive
Palos Heights, IL 60463

Trinity International University
2077 Half Day Road
Deerfield, IL 60015

University of Illinois at Chicago
Box 5220
Chicago, IL 60680

University of Illinois at Urbana–Champaign
506 South Wright Street
Urbana, IL 61801

Western Illinois University
900 West Adams Street
Macomb, IL 61455

Wheaton College
501 East College
Wheaton, IL 60187

INDIANA

Anderson University
Anderson, IN 46012

Ball State University
2000 University Avenue
Muncie, IN 47306

Bethel College
1001 West McKinley Avenue
Mishawaka, IN 46545

Butler University
46th and Sunset Avenue
Indianapolis, IN 46208

DePauw University
313 South Locust Street
Greencastle, IN 46135

Franklin College
Monroe Street
Franklin, IN 46131

Goshen College
1700 South Main Street
Goshen, IN 46526

Grace College
200 Seminary Drive
Winona Lake, IN 46590

Hanover College
Hanover, IN 47243

Huntington College
2303 College Avenue
Huntington, IN 46750

Indiana State University
217 North Sixth Street
Terre Haute, IN 47809

Indiana University–Bloomington
Bloomington, IN 47405

Indiana University–Purdue University at Indianapolis
425 North University Boulevard
Indianapolis, IN 46202

Indiana Wesleyan University
4201 South Washington Street
Marion, IN 46953

Manchester College
North Manchester, IN 46962

Marian College
3200 Cold Spring Road
Indianapolis, IN 46222

Oakland City College
Lucretia Street
Oakland City, IN 47660

Purdue University
Schleman Hall
West Lafayette, IN 47907

Taylor University
Reade Avenue
Upland, IN 46989

Tri-State University
Angola, IN 46703

University of Evansville
1800 Lincoln Avenue
Evansville, IN 47722

University of Indianapolis
1400 East Hanna Avenue
Indianapolis, IN 46227

University of Southern Indiana
8600 University Boulevard
Evansville, IN 47712

Valparaiso University
Valparaiso, IN 46383

IOWA

Briar Cliff College
3303 Rebecca Street
Sioux City, IA 51104

Buena Vista College
4th and College Streets
Storm Lake, IA 50588

Central College
812 University Street
Pella, IA 50219

Coe College
1220 First Avenue
Cedar Rapids, IA 52402

Cornell College
600 First Street West
Mount Vernon, IA 52314

Dordt College
Sioux Center, IA 51250

Graceland College
Lamoni, IA 50140

Iowa State University
Alumni Hall
Ames, IA 50011

Iowa Wesleyan College
601 North Main Street
Mount Pleasant, IA 52641

Loras College
1450 Alta Vista
Dubuque, IA 52001

Luther College
Decorah, IA 52101

Morningside College
1501 Morningside Avenue
Sioux City, IA 51106

Northwestern College
101 College Lane
Orange City, IA 51041

Simpson College
Indianola, IA 50125

St. Ambrose University
518 West Locust Street
Davenport, IA 52803

University of Dubuque
University Avenue
Dubuque, IA 52001

University of Iowa
107 Calvin Hall
Iowa City, IA 52242

University of Northern Iowa
West 27th Street
Cedar Falls, IA 50614

Upper Iowa University
Fayette, IA 52142

Wartburg College
P.O. Box 1003–222 9th Street NW
Waverly, IA 50677

Teikyo Westmar University
1002 3rd Avenue Southeast
Le Mars, IA 51031

William Penn College
201 Trueblood Avenue
Okaloosa, IA 52577

KANSAS

Baker University
Baldwin City, KS 66006

Benedictine College
North Campus
Atchison, KS 66002

Bethany College
421 North First
Lindsborg, KS 67456

Bethel College
300 East 27th Street
North Newton, KS 67117

Emporia State University
12th and Commercial Streets
Emporia, KS 66801

Fort Hays State University
600 Park Street
Hays, KS 67601

Friends University
2100 University Avenue
Wichita, KS 67213

Kansas Newman College
3100 McCormick
Wichita, KS 67213

Kansas Wesleyan University
200 East Claflin
Salina, KS 67401

McPherson College
1600 East Euclid
McPherson, KS 67460

Mid America Nazarene College
P.O. Box 1776–2030 College Way
Olathe, KS 66061

Ottawa University
1001 South Cedar Street
Ottawa, KS 66067

Pittsburgh State University
1701 South Broadway
Pittsburgh, KS 66762

Southwestern College
100 College Street
Winfield, KS 67156

Sterling College
North Broadway
Sterling, KS 67579

Tabor College
Hillsboro, KS 67063

University of Kansas
126 Strong Hall
Lawrence, KS 66045

Washburn University
1700 College Street
Topeka, KS 66621

Witchita State University
1845 Fairmount Street
Wichita, KS 67208

KENTUCKY

Alice Lloyd College
Purpose Road
Pippa Passes, KY 41844

Ashbury College
North Lexington Avenue
Wilmore, KY 40390

Berea College
CPO 2344
Berea, KY 40404

Campbellsville College
200 College Street West
Campbellsville, KY 42718

Cumberland College
6178 College Station Drive
Williamsburg, KY 40769

Eastern Kentucky University
Lancaster Avenue
Richmond, KY 40475

Georgetown College
400 East College Street
Georgetown, KY 40324

Kentucky State University
East Main Street
Frankfort, KY 40601

Kentucky Wesleyan College
3000 Frederica Street
Owensboro, KY 42301

Morehead State University
Morehead, KY 40351

Murray State University
Murray, KY 42071

Northern Kentucky University
Nunn Drive
Highland Heights, KY 41076

Pikeville College
Sycamore Street
Pikeville, KY 41501

Transylvania University
300 North Broadway
Lexington, KY 40508

Union College
College Street
Barbourville, KY 40906

University of Kentucky
100 Funkhouser Building
Lexington, KY 40506

University of Louisville
Louisville, KY 40292

Western Kentucky University
Potter Hall
1 Big Red Way
Bowling Green, KY 42101

LOUISIANA

Centenary College of Louisiana
2911 Centenary Boulevard
Shreveport, LA 71104

Dillard University
2601 Gentilly Boulevard
New Orleans, LA 70122

Grambling State University
Grambling, LA 71245

Louisiana College
LC Box 560
Pineville, LA 71359

**Louisiana State University and
    Agricultural and Mechanical
    College**
110 Thomas Boyd Hall
Baton Rouge, LA 70803

Louisiana State University–Shreveport
One University Place
Shreveport, LA 71115

Louisiana Tech University
P.O. Box 3168–Tech Station
Ruston, LA 71272

McNeese State University
Lake Charles, LA 70609

Nicholls State University
P.O. Box 2004–University Station
Thibodaux, LA 70310

Northeast Louisiana University
700 University Avenue
Monroe, LA 71209

**Northwestern State University
    of Louisiana**
College Avenue
Natchitoches, LA 71497

Southeastern Louisiana University
Box 752–University Station
Hammond, LA 70402

Southern University–Baton Rouge
P.O. Box 9901 Southern Branch
Bato Rouge, LA 70813

Southern University at New Orleans
6400 Press Drive
New Orleans, LA 70126

Tulane University
6823 St. Charles Avenue
New Orleans, LA 70118

University of New Orleans
Lakefront
New Orleans, LA 70148

University of Southwestern Louisiana
P.O. Box 41770
Lafeyette, LA 70504

Xavier University of Louisiana
7325 Palmetto Street
New Orleans, LA 70125

MAINE

Saint Joseph's College
Windham, ME 04062

University of Maine at Orono
Chadbourne Hall
Orono, ME 04469

University of Maine at Presque Isle
181 Main Street
Presque Isle, ME 04769

MARYLAND

Bowie State College
Jericho Park Road
Bowie, MD 20715

Coppin State College
2500 West North Avenue
Baltimore, MD 21216

Frostburg State University
Frostburg, MD 21532

Morgan State University
Cold Spring Lane and Hillen Road
Baltimore, MD 21239

Salisbury State University
Camden Avenue
Salisbury, MD 21801

Towson State University
Towson, MD 21204

University of Maryland–College Park
College Park, MD 20742

University of Maryland–Eastern Shore
Princess Anne, MD 21853

MASSACHUSETTS

Atlantic Union College
Main Street
South Lancaster, MA 01561

Boston University
121 Bay State Road
Boston, MA 02215

Bridgewater State College
Bridgewater, MA 02325

Eastern Nazarene College
23 East Elm Avenue
Quincy, MA 02170

Endicott College
376 Hale Street
Beverly, MA 01915

Salem State College
352 Lafayette Street
Salem, MA 01970

Springfield College
263 Alden Street
Springfield, MA 01109

University of Massachusetts–Boston
10 Morrissey Boulevard
Boston, MA 02125

Westfield State College
Western Avenue
Westfield, MA 01085

MICHIGAN

Adrian College
110 South Madison Street
Adrian, MI 49221

Albion College
Albion, MI 49224

Andrews University
Berrien Springs, MI 49104

Aquinas College
1607 Robinson Road SE
Grand Rapids, MI 49506

Calvin College
Grand Rapids, MI 49506

Central Michigan University
100 Warriner Hall
Mouth Pleasant, MI 48859

Concordia College
4090 Geddes Road
Ann Arbor, MI 48105

Eastern Michigan University
214 Pierce Hall
Ypsilanti, MI 48197

Grand Rapids Baptist College
1001 East Beltline
Grand Rapids, MI 49505

Grand Valley State University
1 Seidman House
Allendale, MI 49401

Hillsdale College
33 East College Street
Hillsdale, MI 49242

Hope College
Holland, MI 49423

Michigan State University
Administration Building
East Lansing, MI 48824

Northern Michigan University
Cohodas Administration Center
Marquette, MI 49855

Olivet College
Main Street
Olivet, MI 49076

Saginaw Valley State University
2250 Pierce Road
University Center, MI 48710

Spring Arbor College
106 Main Street
Spring Arbor, MI 49283

University of Detroit Mercy
4001 West McNicholls Road
Detroit, MI 48221

University of Michigan–Ann Arbor
515 East Jefferson
Ann Arbor, MI 48109

Wayne State University
Detroit, MI 48202

Western Michigan University
Administration Building
Kalamanzoo, MI 49008

MINNESOTA

Augsburg College
2211 Riverside Avenue
Minneapolis, MN 55454

Bemidji State University
Bemidji, MN 56601

Bethel College
3900 Bethel Drive
St. Paul, MN 55112

College of St. Catherine
2004 Randolph Avenue
St. Paul, MN 55105

University of St. Thomas
2115 Summit Avenue
St. Paul, MN 55105

Concordia College
Moorhead, MN 56560

Concordia College
Hamline and Marshall Avenue
St. Paul, MN 55104

Crown College
6425 County Road 30
St. Bonifacius, MN 55375

Gustavus Adolphus College
St. Peter, MN 56082

Hamline University
St. Paul, MN 55104

Mankato State University
Box 55
Mankato, MN 56001

Moorhead State University
1104 7th Avenue South
Moorhead, MN 56560

Northwestern College
3003 Snelling Avenue North
St. Paul, MN 55113

Southwest State University
Marshall, MN 56258

St. Cloud State University
7th Street and 4th Avenue South
St. Cloud, MN 56303

St. Olaf College
Northfield, MN 55057

University of Minnesota–Duluth
184 Darland Administration Building
Duluth, MN 55812

University of Minnesota–Twin Cities
231 Pillsbury Drive SE
Minneapolis, MN 55455

Winona State University
Winona, MN 55987

MISSISSIPPI

Alcorn State University
P.O. Box 300
Lorman, MS 39096

Blue Mountain College
Blue Mountain, MS 38610

Delta State University
P.O. Box 3151
Cleveland, MS 38732

Jackson State University
1325 J.R. Lynch Street
Jackson, MS 39217

Mississippi College
P.O. Box 4203
Clinton, MS 39058

Mississippi State University
Box 5268
Mississippi State, MS 39762

Mississippi University for Women
Columbus, MS 39701

Mississippi Valley State University
1400 Highway 92 West
Itta Bena, MS 38941

Rust College
1 Rust Avenue
Holly Springs, MS 38635

Tougaloo College
Tougaloo, MS 39174

University of Southern Mississippi
Box 5011–Southern Station
Hattiesburg, MS 39401

William Carey College
Tuscan Avenue
Hattiesburg, MS 39401

MISSOURI

Central Methodist College
411 Central Methodist Square
Fayette, MO 65248

Central Missouri State University
Warrensburg, MO 64093

College of the Ozarks
Point Lookout, MO 65726

Culver-Stockton College
Canton, MO 63435

Drury College
900 North Benton Avenue
Springfield, MO 65802

Evangel College
1111 North Glenstone
Springfield, MO 65101

Lindwood College
St. Charles, MO 63301

Missouri Baptist College
12542 Conway Road
St. Louis, MO 63141

Missouri Southern State College
Newman and Duquesne Roads
Joplin, MO 64801

Missouri Valley College
500 East College
Marshall, MO 65340

Northwest Missouri State University
Maryville, MO 64468

Rockhurst College
5225 Troost Avenue
Kansas City, MO 64110

Southeast Missouri State University
One University Place
Cape Girardeau, MO 63701

Southwest Baptist University
623 South Pike
Bolivar, MO 65613

Southwest Missouri State University
901 South National
Springfield, MO 65854

University of Missouri–Kansas City
5100 Rockhill Road
Kansas City, MO 64110

University of Missouri–St. Louis
8001 Natural Bridge Road
St. Louis, MO 63121

Westminster College
501 Westminster Avenue
Fulton, MO 65251

William Jewell College
Liberty, MO 64068

William Wood College
Fulton, MO 65251

MONTANA

College of Great Falls
1301 20th Street South
Great Falls, MT 59405

Montana State University–Billings
1500 North 30th Street
Billings, MT 59101

Montana State University
Montana Hall
Bozeman, MT 59717

Northern Montana College
Havre, MT 59501

Rocky Mountain College
1511 Poly Drive
Billings, MT 59102

University of Montana
Lodge 101
Missoula, MT 59812

Western Montana College
Dillon, MT 59725

NEBRASKA

Bellevue College
Galvin Road South
Bellevue, NE 68005

Chadron State College
10th and Main Streets
Chadron, NE 69337

Concordia College
800 North Columbia Avenue
Seward, NE 68434

Dana College
Blair, NE 68008

Donane College
Crete, NE 68333

Hastings College
7th and Turner Avenues
Hastings, NE 68901

University of Nebraska at Kearney
905 West 25th Street
Kearney, NE 68849

Midland Lutheran College
720 East 9th Street
Fremont, NE 68025

Nebraska Wesleyan University
5000 St. Paul Avenue
Lincoln, NE 68504

Peru State College
Peru, NE 68421

Union College
3800 South 48th Street
Lincoln, NE 68506

University of Nebraska–Lincoln
14th and R Streets
Lincoln, NE 68588

University of Nebraska–Omaha
60th and Dodge Streets
Omaha, NE 68182

Wayne State College
200 East Tenth
Wayne, NE 68787

NEVADA

University of Nevada–Las Vegas
4505 Maryland Parkway
Las Vegas, NV 89154

University of Nevada–Reno
Reno, NV 89557

NEW HAMPSHIRE

Keene State College
Main Street
Keene, NH 03431

New England College
Henniker, NH 03242

Plymouth State College
Plymouth, NH 03264

University of New Hampshire
Garrison Avenue–Grant House
Durham, NH 03824

NEW JERSEY

Glassboro State College
Glassboro, NJ 08028

Kean College of New Jersey
Morris Avenue
Union, NJ 07083

Montclair State College
Valley Road and Normal Avenue
Upper Montclair, NJ 07043

Rowan College of New Jersey
201 Mullica Hill Road
Glassboro, NJ 08028

**Rutgers, The State University of
New Jersey Livingston College**
P.O. Box 2101
New Brunswick, NJ 08903

Seton Hall University
400 South Orange Avenue
South Orange, NJ 07079

Trenton State College
CN 4700 Hillwood Lakes
Trenton, NJ 08650

William Paterson College
300 Pompton Road
Wayne, NJ 07470

NEW MEXICO

Eastern New Mexico University
Highway 70, Portales, NM 88130

New Mexico Highlands University
P.O. Box 13
Las Vegas, NM 87701

New Mexico State University
Box 30001–Department 3A
Las Cruces, NM 88003

University of New Mexico
Albuquerque, NM 87131

Western New Mexico University
Box 680
Silver City, NM 88061

NEW YORK

Adelphi University
South Avenue
Garden City, NY 11530

CUNY–Brooklyn College
Bedford Avenue and Avenue H
Brooklyn, NY 11210

CUNY–City College
Convent Avenue at 138th Street
New York, NY 10031

CUNY–Hunter College
695 Park Avenue
New York, NY 10021

CUNY–York College
94–20 Guy R. Brewer Boulevard
Jamaica, NY 11451

Canisium College
2001 Main Street
Buffalo, NY 14208

Hofstra University
Hempstead, NY 11550

Houghton College
Houghton, NY 14744

Ithaca College
Ithaca, NY 14850

**Long Island University–Brooklyn
Campus**
University Plaza
Brooklyn, NY 11201

**Long Island University–C.W. Post
Campus**
Northern Boulevard–College Hall
Greenvale, NY 11548

Manhattan College
Manhattan College Parkway
Riverdale, NY 10471

Russell Sage College
51 First Street
Troy, NY 12180

St. Bonaventure University
Route 417
St. Bonaventure, NY 14778

St. Francis College
180 Remsen Street
Brooklyn Heights, NY 11201

St. Lawrence University
Canton, NY 13617

Skidmore College
Saratoga Springs, NY 12866

SUNY–College at Brockport
Kenyon Street
Brockport, NY 14420

SUNY–College at Cortland
Box 2000–Graham Avenue
Cortland, NY 13045

Syracuse University
201 Administration Building
Syracuse, NY 13244

NORTH CAROLINA

Appalachian State University
Boone, NC 28608

Barber–Scotia College
145 Cabarrus Avenue
Concord, NC 28025

Bennett College
900 East Washington Street
Greensboro, NC 27401

Campbell University
P.O. Box 546
Buies Creek, NC 27506

Catawba College
2300 West Innes Street
Salisbury, NC 28144

East Carolina University
Greenville, NC 27834

Elizabeth City State University
Parkview Drive
Elizabeth City, NC 27909

Elon College
Elon College, NC 27244

Fayetteville State University
Murchison Road
Fayetteville, NC 28301

Gardner-Webb College
P.O. Box 817
Boiling Springs, NC 28017

Greensboro College
815 West Market Street
Greensboro, NC 27401

Guilford College
5800 West Friendly Avenue
Greensboro, NC 27410

High Point College
University Station
High Point, NC 27261

Johnson C. Smith University
100 Beatties Ford Road
Charlotte, NC 28216

Lenoir-Rhyne College
Box 7227
Hickory, NC 28603

Livingstone College
701 West Monroe Street
Salisbury, NC 28144

Mars Hill College
Mars Hill, NC 28754

Methodist College
5400 Ramsey Street
Fayetteville, NC 28311

**North Carolina Agricultural and
    Technical State University**
1601 East Market Street
Greensboro, NC 27411

North Carolina Central University
P.O. Box 19719
1902 Fayetteville Street
Durham, NC 27707

North Carolina Wesleyan College
College Station
Rocky Mount, NC 27801

Pembroke State University
Pembroke, NC 28372

Pfeiffer College
Misenheimer, NC 28109

Piedmont Bible College
716 Franklin Street
Winston-Salem, NC 27101

Shaw University
118 East South Street
Raleigh, NC 27611

St. Andrews Presbyterian College
Laurinburg, NC 28352

St. Augustine's College
1315 Oak Avenue
Raleigh, NC 27611

**University of North Carolina–
    Chapel Hill**
Campus Box 2200
Chapel Hill, NC 27514

**University of North
    Carolina–Greensboro**
1000 Spring Garden Street
Greensboro, NC 27412

**University of North
    Carolina–Wilmington**
601 South College Road
Wilmington, NC 28403

Western Carolina University
520 H.F. Robinson Administration
    Building
Cullowhee, NC 28723

Wingate College
Wingate, NC 28174

Winston-Salem State University
601 Martin Luther King Jr. Drive
Winston-Salem, NC 27110

NORTH DAKOTA

Dickinson State University
Dickinson, ND 58601

Jamestown College
Jamestown, ND 58401

Mayville State University
330 3rd Street NE
Mayville, ND 58257

Minot State University
Minot, ND 58701

North Dakota State University
124 Ceres Hall
Fargo, ND 58105

University of Mary
7500 University Drive
Bismarck, ND 58504

University of North Dakota
Grand Forks, ND 58202

Valley City State University
Valley City, ND 58072

OHIO

Ashland College
College Avenue
Ashland, OH 44805

Baldwin-Wallace College
275 Eastland Road
Berea, OH 44017

Bluffton College
Box 638–Marbeck Center
Bluffton, OH 45817

Bowling Green State University
110 McFall Center
Bowling Green, OH 43403

Capital University
2199 East Main Street
Columbus, OH 43209

Cedarville College
Box 601
Cedarville, OH 45314

Central State University
Brush Row Road
Wilberforce, OH 45384

Cleveland State University
East 24th and Euclid Avenue
Cleveland, OH 44115

College of Mount St. Joseph
5701 Delhi Road
Cincinnati, OH 45233

The Defiance College
701 North Clinton Street
Defiance, OH 43512

Denison University
P.O. Box H
Granville, OH 43023

Heidelberg College
310 East Market Street
Tiffin, OH 44883

Hiram College
P.O. Box 96
Hiram, OH 44234

John Carroll University
20700 North Park Boulevard
University Heights, OH 44118

Kent State University
P.O. Box 5190
Kent, OH 44242

Malone College
515 25th Street NW
Canton, OH 44709

Marietta College
Fifth Street
Marietta, OH 45750

Miami University
Oxford, OH 45056

Mount Union College
1972 Clark Street
Alliance, OH 44601

Mount Vernon Nazarene College
800 Martinsburg Road
Mount Vernon, OH 43050

Muskingum College
New Concord, OH 43762

Ohio Dominican College
1216 Sunbury Road
Columbus, OH 43219

Ohio Northern University
Main Street
Ada, OH 45810

Ohio State University–Columbus
1800 Cannon Drive–Lincoln Tower
Columbus, OH 43210

Ohio University
120 Chubb Hall
Athens, OH 45701

Ohio Wesleyan University
Delaware, OH 43015

Otterbein College
Westerville, OH 43081

University of Rio Grande
P.O. Box 909
Rio Grande, OH 45674

University of Akron
381 East Buchtel Commons
Akron, OH 44325

University of Dayton
300 College Park Avenue
Dayton, OH 45469

University of Toledo
2801 West Bancroft Street
Toledo, OH 43606

Urbana University
579 College Way
Urbana, OH 43078

Walsh College
2020 Easton Street NW
Canton, OH 44720

Wilmington College of Ohio
Box 1325–Pyle Center
Wilmington, OH 45177

Wright State University
Colonel Glenn Highway
Dayton, OH 45435

Xavier University
3800 Victory Parkway
Cincinnati, OH 45207

Youngstown State University
Youngstown, OH 44555

OKLAHOMA

Bartlesville Wesleyan College
2201 Silver Lake Road
Bartlesville, OK 74003

Cameron University
2800 Gore Boulevard
Lawton, OK 73505

University of Central Oklahoma
100 North University
Edmond, OK 73034

East Central University
Ada, OK 74820

Langston University
P.O. Box 838
Langston, OK 73050

Northeastern State University
Tahglequah, OK 74464

**Northwestern Oklahoma State
University**
Alva, OK 73717

Oklahoma Baptist University
500 West University
Shawnee, OK 74801

Oklahoma Christian College
P.O. Box 11000
Oklahoma City, OK 73136

Oklahoma City University
2501 North Blackwelder
Oklahoma City, OK 73106

**Oklahoma Panhandle State
University**
Goodwell, OK 73939

Oklahoma State University
103 Whitehurst Hall
Stillwater, OK 74078

Oral Roberts University
7777 South Lewis
Tulsa, OK 74171

Phillips University
P.O. Box 2000 University Stations
Enid, OK 73702

**Southeastern Oklahoma State
University**
Box 4118–Station A
Durant, OK 74701

**Southwestern Oklahoma State
University**
Weatherford, OK 73096

University of Oklahoma–Norman
1000 Asp Avenue
Norman, OK 73019

**University of Science and Arts
of Oklahoma**
17th Street and Grand Avenue
Chickasha, OK 73018

University of Tulsa
600 South College Avenue
Tulsa, OK 74104

OREGON

Columbia Christian College
9101 East Burnside Street
Portland, OR 97216

Concordia College
2811 Northeast Holman
Portland, OR 97211

Eastern Oregon State College
8th and K Avenues
La Grande, OR 97850

George Fox College
Newberg, OR 97132

Linfield College
McMinnville, OR 97128

Oregon State University
Corvallis, OR 97331

Pacific University
2043 College Way
Forest Grove, OR 97116

Warner Pacific College
2219 Southeast 68th Avenue
Portland, OR 97215

Western Oregon State College
Monmouth, OR 97361

Willamette University
900 State Street
Salem, OR 97301

PENNSYLVANIA

**East Stroudsburg University
of Pennsylvania**
East Stroudsburg, PA 18301

Eastern College
10 Fairview Drive
St. Davids, PA 19087

Edinboro University of Pennsylvania
Edinboro, PA 16444

Gannon University
University Square
Erie, PA 16541

Gettysburg College
300 Carlisle Street
Gettysburg, PA 17325

Indiana University of Pennsylvania
Indiana, PA 15705

Kutztown University
College Hill
Kutztown, PA 19530

Lincoln University
Lincoln Hall
Lincoln University, PA 19352

**Loch Haven University of
    Pennsylvania**
Loch Haven, PA 17745

Marywood College
2300 Adams Avenue
Scranton, PA 18509

Messiah College
College Avenue
Grantham, PA 17027

**Slippery Rock University
    of Pennsylvania**
Slippery Rock, PA 16057

Temple University
Philadelphia, PA 19122

University of Pittsburgh
4200 Fifth Avenue
Pittsburg, PA 15260

Ursinus College
Main Street–Box 1000
Collegeville, PA 19426

**West Chester University
    of Pennsylvania**
West Chester, PA 19383

RHODE ISLAND

Rhode Island College
Providence, RI 02908

University of Rhode Island
Green Hall
Kingston, RI 02881

SOUTH CAROLINA

Charleston Southern University
P.O. Box 10087
Charleston, SC 29411

Benedict College
Harden and Blanding Streets
Columbia, SC 29204

Bob Jones University
Wade Hampton Boulevard
Greenville, SC 29614

Central Wesleyan College
Central, SC 29630

**Citadel–The Military College of
    South Carolina**
Citadel Station
Charleston, SC 29409

Claflin College
700 College Avenue N.E.
Orangeburg, SC 29115

Coastal Carolina University
P.O. Box 1954
Myrtle Beach, SC 29578

Coker College
College Avenue
Hartsville, SC 29550

College of Charleston
66 George Street
Charleston, SC 29424

Erskine College
Due West, SC 29639

Furman University
Poinsett Highway
Greenville, SC 29613

Lander University
Stanley Avenue
Greenwood, SC 29646

Limestone College
1115 College Drive
Gaffney, SC 29340

Newberry College
Newberry, SC 29108

South Carolina State University
Orangeburg, SC 29117

University of South Carolina
Columbia, SC 29208

**University of South Carolina–
    Spartanburg**
800 University Way
Spartanburg, SC 29303

Winthrop University
Oakland Avenue
Rock Hill, SC 29733

SOUTH DAKOTA

Augusta College
29th and Summit Avenue
Sioux Falls, SD 59197

Black Hills State College
1200 University Street
Spearfish, SD 57783

Dakota State College
Hetson Hall
Madison, SD 57301

Dakota Wesleyan University
1200 West University Avenue
Mitchell, SD 57301

Huron College
Huron, SD 57350

Mount Marty College
1105 West Eighth
Yankton, SD 57078

Northern State College
Aberdeen, SD 57401

Sioux Falls College
1501 South Prairie Street
Sioux Falls, SD 57105

South Dakota State University
Box 2201–Administration Building
Brookings, SD 57007

University of South Dakota
414 East Clark
Vermillion, SD 57069

TENNESSEE

Austin Peay State University
601 College Street
Clarksville, TN 37040

Belmont University
1900 Belmont Boulevard
Nashville, TN 37203

Bethel College
McKenzie, TN 38201

Carson-Newman College
Russell Avenue
Jefferson City, TN 37760

Cumberland University of Tennessee
Lebanon, TN 37087

David Lipscomb College
Nashville, TN 37203

East Tennessee State University
Campus Box 24430-A
Johnson City, TN 37614

Free Will Baptist Bible College
3606 West End Avenue
Nashville, TN 37205

Freed–Hardeman College
158 East Main Street
Henderson, TN 38340

Knoxville College
901 College Street
Knoxville, TN 37921

Lambuth College
Lambuth Boulevard
Jackson, TN 38301

Lane College
Lane Avenue
Jackson, TN 38301

Le Moyne–Owen College
807 Walker Avenue
Memphis, TN 38126

Lee College
Cleveland, TN 37311

Lincoln Memorial University
Harrogate, TN 37752

Memphis State University
Memphis, TN 38152

Middle Tennessee State University
Murfreesboro, TN 37132

Milligan College
Milligan College, TN 37682

**Southern College of Seventh-
Day Adventists**
Box 370
Collegedale, TN 37315

Tennessee State University
John Merritt Boulevard
Nashville, TN 37203

Tennessee Technological University
Dixie Avenue
Cookeville, TN 38505

Tennessee Wesleyan College
P.O. Box 40–College Street
Athens, TN 37303

Trevecca Nazarene College
333 Murfreesboro Road
Nashville, TN 37210

Tusculum College
Greenville, TN 37743

Union University
2447 Highway 45 By-Pass
Jackson, TN 38305

University of Tennessee–Chattanooga
McCallie Avenue-129 Hooper Hall
Chattanooga, TN 37402

University of Tennessee–Knoxville
320 Student Services Building
Knoxville, TN 37996

University of Tennessee–Martin
Martin, TN 38238

Vanderbilt University
401 24th Avenue South
Nashville, TN 37212

TEXAS

Abilene Christian University
Box 6000–ACU Station
Abilene, TX 79699

Angelo State University
P.O. Box 11009–ASU Station
San Angelo, TX 76909

Baylor University
P.O. Box 97008
Waco, TX 76706

Concordia Lutheran College
3400 Interstate 35 North
Austin, TX 78705

**Texas A & M University–
Corpus Christi**
6300 Ocean Drive
Corpus Christi, TX 78412

Dallas Baptist University
3000 Mountain Creek Parkway
Dallas, TX 75211

East Texas Baptist University
1209 North Grove
Marshall, TX 75670

East Texas State University
East Texas Station
Commerce, TX 75428

Hardin-Simmons University
Abilene, TX 79698

Houston Baptist University
7502 Fondren Road
Houston, TX 77074

Howard Payne University
Howard Payne Station Box 174
Brownwood, TX 76801

Jarvis Christian College
P.O. Drawer G
Hawkins, TX 75765

Lamar University
P.O. Box 10009
Beaumont, TX 77710

Lubbock Christian University
5601 West 19th Street
Lubbock, TX 79407

McMurry College
Box 85–McMurry Station
Abilene, TX 79697

University of North Texas
Box 13797
Denton, TX 76203

Prairie View A & M University
P.O. Box 2610
Prairie View, TX 77446

Rice University
P.O. Box 1892
Houston, TX 77251

Sam Houston State University
Huntsville, TX 77341

Schreiner College
Kerrville, TX 78028

Southwest Texas State University
429 North Guadalupe
San Marcos, TX 78666

Stephen F. Austin State University
Nacogdoches, TX 75962

Sul Ross State University
P.O. Box C-1
Alpine, TX 79832

Texas College
2404 North Grand Avenue
Tyler, TX 75702

Texas Lutheran College
1000 West Court
Seguin, TX 78155

Texas Southern University
3100 Cleburne
Houston, TX 77004

Texas Tech University
P.O. Box 45005
Lubbock, TX 79409

Texas Wesleyan College
P.O. Box 50010–3101 East Rosedale
Fort Worth, TX 76105

Texas Woman's University
P.O. Box 22909–TWU Station
Denton, TX 76204

University of Houston
4800 Calhoun
Houston, TX 77004

University of Mary Hardin–Baylor
P.O. Box 403
Belton, TX 76513

University of Texas–Austin
Austin, TX 78712

University of Texas–Permian Basin
Box 8422–UTPB
Odessa, TX 79762

University of Texas–San Antonio
San Antonio, TX 78285

Wayland Baptist University
1700 West 7th Street
Plainview, TX 79072

West Texas State University
Canyon, TX 79016

Wiley College
711 Rosborough Springs Road
Marshall, TX 75670

UTAH

Brigham Young University
A-153 ASB
Provo, UT 84602

Southern Utah State College
351 West Center
Cedar City, UT 84720

University of Utah
250 Student Services Building
Salt Lake City, UT 84112

Utah State University
Logan, UT 84322

Weber State College
3750 Harrison Boulevard
Ogden, UT 84408

VERMONT

Castleton State College
Castleton, VT 05735

Johnson State College
Stowe Road
Johnson, VT 05656

University of Vermont
194 South Prospect Street
Burlington, VT 05401

VIRGINIA

Avarett College
West Main Street
Danville, VA 24541

Bluefield College
Bluefield, VA 24605

Bridgewater College
East College Street
Bridgewater, VA 22812

Christopher Newport University
50 Shoe Lane
Newport News, VA 23606

College of William and Mary
Williamsburg, VA 23185

Eastern Mennonite College
Harrisonburg, VA 22801

Ferrum College
Ferrum, VA 24088

George Mason University
4400 University Drive
Fairfax, VA 22030

Hampton University
Hampton, VA 23688

James Madison University
Harrisonburg, VA 22807

Liberty University
3765 Candlers Mountain Road
Lynchburg, VA 24506

Longwood College
Farmville, VA 23901

Norfolk State University
2401 Corprew Avenue
Norfolk, VA 23504

Old Dominion University
Hampton Boulevard
Norfolk, VA 23508

Radford University
Radford, VA 24142

Roanoke College
226 High Street
Salem, VA 24153

Shenandoah College and Conservatory
1460 College Drive
Winchester, VA 22601

University of Richmond
Sarah Brunet Hall
Richmond, VA 23173

University of Virginia
Box 9017–University Station
Charlottesville, VA 22906

Virginia Commonwealth University
P.O. Box 2526
821 West Franklin Street
Richmond, VA 23284

Virginia Intermont College
1013 Moore Street
Bristol, VA 24201

**Virginia Polytechnic Institute and
  State University**
104 Burruss Hall
Blacksburg, VA 24016

Virginia State University
Box 468
Petersburg, VA 23803

WASHINGTON

Central Washington University
Mitchell Hall
Ellensburg, WA 98926

Eastern Washington University
Showalter Hall
Cheney, WA 99004

Gonzaga, University
Spokane, WA 99258

Pacific Lutheran University
Tacoma, WA 98447

Seattle Pacific University
337 Third Avenue West
Seattle, WA 98119

University of Puget South
1500 North Warner
Tacoma, WA 98416

Walla Walla College
College Place, WA 99324

Washington State University
342 French Administration
Pullman, WA 99164

Western Washington University
Old Main–Room 200
Bellingham, WA 98225

Whitworth College
Spokane, WA 99251

WEST VIRGINIA

Alderson–Broaddus College
Philippi, WV 26416

Bethany College
Bethany, WV 26032

Bluefield State College
Bluefield, WV 24701

Concord College
Athens, WV 24712

Davis and Elkins College
Elkins, WV 26241

Fairmont State College
Locust Avenue Extension
Fairmont State College
Fairmont, WV 26554

Glenville State College
Glenville, WV 26351

Marshall University
4th Avenue and Hal Greer Boulevard
Huntington, WV 25705

Shepherd College
Shepherdstown, WV 25443

University of Charleston
2300 McCorkle Avenue SE
Charleston, WV 25304

West Liberty State College
West Liberty, WV 26074

West Virginia State College
Institute, WV 25112

West Virginia University
P.O. Box 6009
Morgantown, WV 26506

West Virginia Wesleyan College
59 College Avenue
Buckhannon, WV 26201

WISCONSIN

Carroll College
100 North East Avenue
Waukesha, WI 53186

Carthage College
2001 Alford Drive
Kenosha, WI 53140

University of Wisconsin–Eau Claire
Eau Claire, WI 54701

University of Wisconsin–La Crosse
1725 State Street
La Crosse, WI 54601

University of Wisconsin–Madison
750 University Avenue
Madison, WI 53706

University of Wisconsin–Oshkosh
135 Depsey Hall
Oshkosh, WI 54901

University of Wisconsin–Platteville
1 University Plaza
Platteville, WI 53818

University of Wisconsin–River Falls
112 South Hall
River Falls, WI 54022

University of Wisconsin–Stevens Point
Stevens Point, WI 54481

University of Wisconsin–Superior
1800 Grand Avenue
Superior, WI 54880

University of Wisconsin–Whitewater
800 West Main Street
Whitewater, WI 53190

WYOMING

University of Wyoming
Box 3435–University Station
Laramie, WY 82071

APPENDIX II
PROGRAMS IN SPORTS OFFICIATING

The following is a list of schools, training camps, and other programs developed or sponsored by organizations that train officials for various sports. Write or call to obtain information. This is not a complete list by any means. Use these names to get you started. To locate additional programs, contact associations and organizations relevant to the sport you want to officiate.

Academy of Professional Umpiring
P.O. Box 164165
Austin, TX 78716
512-328-1923
(baseball)

Affiliated Boards of Officials (ABO)
1900 Association Drive
Reston, VA 22091
703-476-3452
(girls' and women's sports)

Amateur Softball Association of America (ASA)
2801 N.E. 50th Street
Oklahoma City, OK 73111
405-424-5266
(softball)

Brinkman Froemming Umpire School
1021 Indian River Drive
Cocoa, FL 32922
407-639-1515
(baseball)

Eastern College Soccer Association (ECSA)
P.O. Box 3
Centerville, MA 02632
508-771-5060
(soccer)

International Association of Approved Basketball Officials (IAABO)
P.O. Box 270661
West Hartford, CT 06127
203-232-7530
(basketball)

National Association of Sports Officials (NASO)
2017 Lathrop Avenue
Racine, WI 53405
414-632-5448
(various)

National Gymnastics Judges Associations (NGJA)
c/o Harry W. Bjerke
44 Lawrence Lane
Bay Shore, NY 11705
516-665-2103
(gymnastics)

National Intercollegiate Soccer Officials Association (NISOA)
541 Woodview Drive
Longwood, FL 32770
407-862-3305
(soccer)

Harry Wendelstedt Umpire School
88 South Street & Andrews Drive
Ormond Beach, FL 32074
904-672-4879
(baseball)

APPENDIX III
WORKSHOPS, SEMINARS, AND SYMPOSIUMS

The following is a listing of workshops, seminars, courses, and symposiums and the general subject matter covered. This is by no means a complete listing. Many associations, schools, companies, and organizations offer other workshops. As subject matter changes frequently, a number of people running these workshops and seminars did not wish to have their programs listed. You may want to contact associations related to the area of employment you are interested in to obtain more information on programs not listed here.

**Academy of Professional
Umpiring (APU)**
P.O. Box 164165
Austin, TX 78716
512-328-1923
The Academy of Professional Umpiring offers accredited programs needed to become a major league umpire.

**Amateur Softball Association of
America (ASA)**
2801 N.E. 50th Street
Oklahoma City, OK 73111
405-424-5266
The ASA holds clinics and workshops for umpires in amateur softball.

**American Athletic Trainers
Association and Certifications
Board (AATACB)**
660 West Duarte Road
Arcadia, CA 91006
818-445-1978
This organization conducts continuing education for the field of athletic trainers.

**American Baseball Coaches
Association (ABCA)**
108 South University Avenue Suite 3
Mount Pleasant, MI 48858
517-775-3300
Coaching clinics are offered by the ABCA to coaches working in schools, colleges and universities.

American Fitness Association (AFA)
6285 East Spring Street
No. 404
Long Beach, CA 90808
310-402-3952
This organization holds seminars and clinics individuals interested in education for health and fitness.

**American Sportscasters
Association (ASA)**
5 Beekman Street
Suite 814
New York, NY 10038
212-227-8080
The ASA offers seminars, clinics, and workshops for individuals aspiring to enter the sportscasting field.

**American Youth Soccer Organization
(AYSO)**
5403 West 138th Street
Hawthorne, CA 90250
310-643-6455
The American Youth Soccer Organization offers regional training conferences for those involved in the sport.

**Association for Fitness in Business
(AFB)**
310 North Alabama
Indianapolis, IN 46204
317-636-6621
The Association for Fitness in Business sponsors seminars, training programs and workshops, in fitness, health, and nutrition.

**Athletic Equipment Managers
Association (AEMA)**
6224 Hester Road
Oxford, OH 45056
419-352-2027
The AEMA offers a number of workshops and clinics throughout the year to equipment managers and purchasers working in amateur or professional sports.

Brinkman Froemming Umpire School
1021 Indian River Drive
Cocoa, FL 32922
305-639-1515
The Joe Brinkman Umpire School offers training programs for individuals aspiring to be professional baseball umpires.

Center for Sports Sponsorship (CSS)
P.O. Box 280
Plainsboro, NJ 08536
609-799-4722
The Center for Sports Sponsorship offers seminars during the year to businesses and individuals interested in the area of sports sponsorship.

**Eastern College Soccer Association
(ECSA)**
P.O. Box 3
Centerville, MA 026732
617-771-5060
The Eastern College Soccer Association sponsors annual clinics and workshops for soccer officials.

**International Association of Approved
Basketball Officials (IAABO)**
P.O. Box 270661
West Hartford, CT 06127
203-232-7530
IAABO offers annual workshops for basketball officials.

**International Association of Dive
Rescue Specialists (IADRS)**
P.O. Box 5259
San Clemente, CA 92674
714-489-2004
The IADR holds conferences and seminars in a variety of aspects of water rescue and recovery.

**National Athletic Trainers Association
(NATA)**
2952 Stemmons Freeway
Suite 200
Dallas, TX 75247
214-637-6282
The National Athletic Trainers Association conducts clinics and continuing education seminars on a variety of subjects of interest to athletic trainers.

National Association of Sports Officials (NASO)

2017 Lathrop Avenue
Racine, WI 53405
414-632-5448

NASO organizes seminars, clinics, and camps for sports officials.

National Dance-Exercise Instructors Training Association (NDEITA)

1503 South Washington Avenue
Minneapolis, MN 55454
612-340-1306

The National Dance-Exercise Instructors Training Association offers workshops regarding aerobic teaching certification.

National Health Club Association (NHCA)

12596 West Bayaud Avenue
Denver, CO 80228
303-753-6422

This organization offers certification courses for fitness instructors and sponsors programs on fitness, sports medicine, and nutrition.

National Gymnastics Judges Association (NGJA)

44 Lawrence Lane
Bay Shore, NY 11706
516-665-2103

The National Gymnastics Judges Association provides training, certification, and refresher courses for individuals in this field.

National Soccer Coaches Association of America (NSCA)

4220 Shawnee Mission Parkway
Suite 105 B
Fairway, KS 66205
913-362-1747

The NSCA sponsors a number of clinics for soccer coaches throughout the year.

National Strength and Conditioning Association (NSCA)

530 Communications Circle
Suite 204
Colorado Springs, CO 80905
719-632-6722

NSCA develops clinics and workshops throughout the country for coaches, athletic trainers, and others in the field of sports medicine.

Professional Basketball Athletic Trainers Society (PBATS)

400 Colony Square
Suite 1220

Atlanta, GA 30361
404-875-4000

PBATS holds annual seminars for minor league trainers.

Professional Football Athletic Trainers Society (PFATS)

P.O. Box 386
Atlanta, GA 30361
404-875-4000

PFATS holds seminars, workshops, and continuing education courses for members on various aspects of the profession.

Professional Ski Instructors of America (PSIA)

133 South Van Gordon Street
Lakewood, CO 80228
303-447-0842

The Professional Ski Instructors of America (PSIA) sponsors clinics and management seminars in the field of ski instruction.

Public Relations Society of America (PRSA)

33 Irving Place
New York, NY 10003
212-995-2230

The PRSA offers seminars and educational courses throughout the year in a variety of public relations subjects.

Sporting Good Agents Association (SGAA)

P.O. Box 998
Morton Grove, IL 60053
312-296-3670

The Sporting Goods Agent Association offers training seminars to manufacturer's agents.

United States Association of Independent Gymnastic Clubs (USAIGC)

235 Pinehurst Road
Wilmington, DE 19803
302-656-3706

The USAIGC offers a number of national and regional gymnastic clinics in a variety of subject matters from business management to coaching techniques.

United States Competitive Aerobic Federation (USCAF)

9000 Sunset Boulevard
No. 1408

Los Angeles, CA 90069
213-658-7223

The United States Competitive Aerobic Federation offers educational programs for aerobic dance competition.

United States Youth Soccer Association (USYSA)

2050 North Plano Road
Suite 100
Richardson, TX 75082
214-235-4497

This organization sponsors clinics on the officiating and administration of soccer.

United States Sports Academy (USSA)

One Academy Drive
Daphne, AL 36526
205-626-3303

The USSA offers master's degrees in sport science in sport coaching, fitness management, sports medicine and sports research. They also sponsor workshops, seminars, and clinics in a variety of subjects.

U.S.A. Coaches Clinics, Inc.

8420 Delmar
Suite 200
St. Louis, MO 63124
314-991-8600
800-COACH-13

U.S.A. Coaches Clinics, Inc. conducts seminars for coaches in all sports.

U.S.A. Wrestling

6155 Leham Drive
Colorado Springs, CO 80918
719-598-8181

This organization holds clinics for officials, coaches, and amateur wrestlers on a various subjects of interest to those working in amateur wrestling.

U.S. Ski Coaches Association (USSCA)

P.O. Box 100
Park City, UT 84060
801-649-9090

The U.S. Ski Coaches Association holds courses and clinics for ski instructors and coaches.

Harry Wendelstadt Umpire School

88 South Street & Andrews Drive
Ormond Beach, FL 32074
904-872-4879

The Harry Wendelstadt Umpire School offers programs and training for those who want to become professional baseball umpires.

APPENDIX IV
TRADE ASSOCIATIONS AND UNIONS

The following is a list of associations and unions discussed in this book. There are also numerous other associations listed that might be useful to you.

The names, addresses, and phone numbers are included so that you can get contact any of the associations or unions for further information regarding membership, career guidance, scholarships, or internships.

Many of the organizations have branch offices located throughout the country. Organization headquarters can provide you with the phone number and address of the branch closest to you.

AAU/U.S.A. Junior Olympics (AAU/USA JO)
3400 West 86th Street
Indianapolis, IN 46268
317-872-2900

Academy of Television Arts and Sciences (ATAS)
5220 Lankershim Boulevard
North Hollywood, CA 91601
818-754-2800

Advertising Council (AC)
261 Madison Avenue
New York, NY 10016
212-922-1500

Aerobics and Fitness Association of America (AFAA)
1520 Ventura Boulevard
Sherman Oaks, CA 91403
818-905-0040

Affiliated Boards of Officials (ABO)
c/o National Association For Girls and Women In Sport
1900 Association Drive
Reston, VA 22091
703-476-3452

All American Amateur Baseball Association (AAABA)
c/o Tom J. Checkush
340 Walker Drive
Zanesville, OH 43701
614-453-7349

Amateur Athletic Union of the United States (AAU)
3400 West 86th Street
P.O. Box 68207
Indianapolis, IN 46268
317-872-2900

Amateur Softball Association of America (ASA)
2801 N.E. 50th Street
Oklahoma City, OK 73111
405-424-5266

American Advertising Federation (AAF)
1101 Vermon Avenue NW
Suite 500
Washington, DC 20005
202-898-0089

American Alliance for Health, Physical Education, Recreation and Dance (AAHPERD)
900 Association Drive
Reston, VA 22091
703-476-3400

American Amateur Baseball Congress (AABC)
118-19 Redfield Plaza
Marshall, MI 49068
616-781-2002

American Athletic Trainers Association and Certification Board (AATACB)
660 West Duarte Road
Arcadia, CA 91007
818-445-1978

American Auto Racing Writers and Broadcasters Associatioin (AARWBA)
922 North Pass Avenue
Burbank, CA 91505
818-842-7005

American Baseball Coaches Association (ABCA)
108 South University Avenue
Suite 3
Mount Pleasant, MI 48858
517-775-3300

American Federation of Teachers (AFT)
555 New Jersey Avenue NW
Washington, DC 20001
202-879-4400

American Federation of Television and Radio Artists (AFTRA)
260 Madison Avenue
New York, NY 10016
212-532-0800

American Fitness Association (AFA)
6285 East Spring Street
No. 404
Long Beach, CA 90208
310-402-3592

American Football Coaches Association (AFCA)
5900 Old McGregor Road
Waco, TX 76712
817-776-5900

American Guild of Variety Artists (AGVA)
184 Fifth Avenue
New York, NY 10010
212-675-1003

American Hockey Coaches Association (AHCA)
c/o Bruce Delventhal
Achilles Rink
Union College
Schenectady, NY 12308
518-388-6134

American Hockey League (AHL)
425 Union Street
No. D-3
West Springfield, MA 01809
413-781-2030

American Judges Association (AJA)
300 Newport Avenue
Williamsburg, VA 23187
804-259-1841

American Legion Baseball (ALB)
P.O. Box 1055
Indianapolis, IN 46206
317-630-1213

American Marketing Association (AMA)
250 South Wacker Drive
Chicago, IL 60606
312-648-0536

American Medical Athletic Association (AMAA)
P.O. Box 4704
North Hollywood, CA 91607
818-706-2049

American Physical Therapy Association (APTA)
1111 North Fairfax Street
Alexandria, VA 22314
703-684-2782

American Running and Fitness Association (ARFA)
4405 East-West Highway
Suite 405
Bethesda, MD 20814
301-913-9517

American Society of T.V. Cameramen (ASTVC)
4314 Hillary Street
Las Vegas, NV 89117
702-228-6704

American Sportscasters Association (ASA)
5 Beekman Street
Suite 814
New York, NY 10038
212-227-8080

American Swimming Coaches Association (ASCA)
301 SE 20th Street
Ft. Lauderdale, FL 33316
305-462-6267

American Turners (AT)
1127 East Kentucky Street
P.O. Box 4216
Louisville, KY 40204
502-636-2395

American Tennis Association (ATA)
P.O. Box 3277
Silver Springs, MD 20918
202-291-8993

American Women in Radio and Television (AWRT)
1650 Tysons Boulevard
McLean, VA 22102
703-506-3290

American Youth Soccer Organization (AYSO)
5403 West 138th Street
Hawthorne, CA 90251
310-643-6455

Associated Press Broadcasters (APB)
1825 K. Street NW
Suite 710
Washington, DC 20006
202-736-1100

Association for Fitness in Business (AFB)
310 North Alabama
Indianapolis, IN 46204
317-636-6621

Association of National Advertisers, Inc. (ANA)
155 East 44th Street
New York, NY 10017
212-697-5950

Association of Professional Ball Players of America (APBPA)
12062 Valley View Street
Suite 211
Garden Grove, CA 92645
714-892-9900

Association of Representatives of Professional Athletes (ARPA)
1000 Santa Monica Blvd.
Suite 312
Century City, CA 90067
213-553-5607

Athletic Equipment Managers Association (AEMA)
6224 Hester Road
Oxford, OH 44056
419-352-2027

Athletic Goods Team Distributors (AGTD)
1699 Wall Street
Mount Prospect, IL 60056
708-439-4000

Athletic Institute (AI)
200 Castlewood Drive
North Palm Beach, FL 33408
407-842-3600

Babe Ruth Baseball (BRB)
P.O. Box 5000
1770 Brunswick Pike
Trenton, NJ 08638
609-695-1434

Baseball Hall of Fame Committee on Baseball Veterans (IBHFCBV)
P.O. Box 590
Cooperstown, NY 13326
607-547-9988

Baseball Writers Association of America (BBWAA)
78 Olive Street
Lake Grove, NY 11755
516-981-7938

Boating Writer's International (BWI)
P.O. Box 10
Greentown, PA 18426
717-857-1557

Bowling Writers Association of America (BWAA)
6357 Siena Street
Centerville, OH 45459
513-433-8363

Boxing Writers Association (BWA)
50 Mary Street
Tappan, NY 10983
914-359-6334

Business/Professional Advertising Association (B/PAA)
21 Kilmer Road
Edison, NJ 08899

Center for Sports Sponsorship (CSS)
P.O. Box 280
Plainsboro, NJ 08536
609-799-4722

Central Intercollegiate Athletic Association (CIAA)
P.O. Box 7349
Hampton, VA 23666
804-865-0071

Central Collegiate Hockey Association
1000 South State Street
Ann Arbor, MI 48109
313-764-2590

Club Managers Association of America (CMAA)
1733 King Street
Alexandria, VA 22314
703-739-9500

College Athletic Business Managers Association (CABMA)
19009-398 Laurel Park Road
Rancho Dominguez, CA 90220
310-637-0560

College Football Association (CFA)
6688 Gunpark Drive
Suite 201
Boulder, CO 80301
303-530-5566

College Sports Information Directors of America (CSIDA)
c/o Fred Nuesch
Campus Box 114 S
Texas A & M University
Kingsville, TX 78363
512-595-3908

College Swimming Coaches Association of America (CSCA)
c/o Don Megerly
Tufts University
College and Sports Avenue
Medford, MA 02155
617-628-5000

Collegiate Commissioners Association (CCA)
800 South Broadway
Walnut Creek, CA 94056
510-932-4411

Consolidated Athletic Commission (CAC)
851 N. Leavitt Street
Chicago, IL 60622
312-276-3762

Continental Basketball Association (CBA)
425 S. Cherry Street
Denver, CO 80222
303-331-0404

Cosmopolitan Soccer League (CSL)
7800 River Road
North Bergen, NJ 07047
201-861-6606

Council of Sales Promotion Agencies
750 Summer Street
Stamford, CT 06901
203-325-3911

Eastern College Basketball Association (ECBA)
P.O. Box 3
1311 Craigville Beach Road
Centerville, MA 02632
508-771-5060

Eastern College Hockey Association (ECHA)
P.O. Box 3
1311 Craigville Beach Road
Centerville, MA 02632
617-771-5060

Eastern College Soccer Association (ECSA)
P.O. Box 3
1311 Craigville Beach Road
Centerville, MA 02632
508-771-5060

Eastern Intercollegiate Gymnastic League (EIGL)
P.O. Box 3
1311 Craigville Beach Road
Centerville, MA 02632
617-771-5060

Federation of Professional Athletes (FPA)
2021 L Street NW
Washington, DC 20036
202-463-2200

Football Writers Association of America (FWAA)
Box 1022
Edmond, OK 73083
405-341-4731

George Khoury Association of Baseball Leagues (GKABL)
5400 Meramec Bottom Road
St. Louise, MO 63128
314-282-1125

Golden Gloves Association of America (GGAA)
3535 Kenilworth Lane
Knoxville, TN 37914
615-522-5885

Golf Writers Association of America (GWAA)
6-7 25822 Orchard Lake Road
Farmington Hills, MI 48336
810-442-1481

Harness Horse Youth Foundation (HHYF)
14950 Greyhount Court
Suite 210
Carmel, IN 46032
317-848-5132

Harness Horsemen International (HHI)
14 Main Street
Robinsonville, NJ 08691
609-259-3717

Harness Tracks of America (HTA)
4640 East Sunrise
Tucson, AZ 85718
602-259-2525

Intercollegiate Association of Amateur Athletes of America (ICAAA)
c/o Eastern College Athletic Conference
P.O. Box 3
Centerville, MA 02632
508-771-5060

Intercollegiate Soccer Association of America (ISAA)
1821 Sunny Drive
St. Louis, MO 63122
314-822-2814

Intercollegiate Tennis Coaches Association (ITCA)
c/o David A. Benjamin
P.O. Box 71
Princeton, NJ 08544
609-452-6332

International Association of Dive Rescue Specialists (IADRS)
P.O. Box 5259
San Clemente, CA 92674
714-489-2044

International Association of Approved Basketball Officials (IAABO)
P.O. Box 27–661
West Hartford, CT 62127
203-232-7530

International Boxing Federation (IBF)
134 Evergreen Point
East Orange, NJ 07018
201-414-0300

International Boxing Hall of Fame (IBHF)
Hall of Fame Drive
P.O. Box 425
Canastota, NY 13032
315-697-7095

International Boxing Writers Association (IBWA)
50 Mary Street
Tappan, NY 10983
914-359-6334

International Cheerleading Foundation (ICF)
10660 Barkley
Overland Park, KS 66212
913-649-3666

International Collegiate Sports Foundation (ICSF)
P.O. Box 866
Plano, TX 75074
214-424-8227

International Council-National Academy of Television Arts and Sciences (IC/NATAS)
142 West 57th Street
New York, NY 10019
212-489-6969

International Dance Alliance (IDA)
c/o Renee Renouf
1120 Broderick Street
San Francisco, CA 94115
415-922-0560

International Dance-Exercise Association (IDEA)
6190 Cornerstone Street E.
San Diego, CA 92121
619-535-8979

International Hockey League (NHL)
3850 Priority Way
Suite 100
Indianapolis, IN 46240
317-573-3888

International League of Professional Baseball Clubs (ILPBC)
55 South High Street
Suite 202
Dublin, OH 43017
614-791-9300

International Physical Fitness Association (IPFA)
415 W. Court Street
Flint, MI 48503
810-239-2166

International Public Relations Association (IPRA)
18 Loveton Circle
P.O. Box 6000
Sparks, MD 21152

International Society of Sports Psychology (ISSP)
c/o Professor Glyn C. Roberts
Department of Kinesiology
906 South Goodwin Avenue
University of Illinois at
Urbana-Champaign
Urbana, IL 61801
217-333-6563

International Trotting and Pacing Association (ITPA)
575 Broadway
Hanover, PA 17331
717-637-5777

International Veteran Boxing Association (IVBA)
35 Brady Avenue
New Rochelle, NY 10805
914-235-6820

Jockey's Guild, Inc. (JGI)
250 West Main Street
Suite 1820
Lexington, KY 40507
606-259-3211

Knights Boxing Team International
2350 Vetura Boulevard
Smyra, GA 30080
404-432-3632

Ladies Professional Golf Association of America (LPGA)
2570 West International Speedway
Building
Suite B
Daytona Beach, FL 32114
914-254-8800

Little League Baseball (LLB)
P.O. Box 3485
Williamsport, PA 17701
717-326-1921

Major Indoor Soccer League Players Association (MISLPA)
2021 L Street NW
6th Floor
Washington, DC 20036
202-463-2200

Major League Baseball Players Association (MLBPA)
12 East 49th Street
24th Floor
New York, NY 10017
212-826-0808

Major League Baseball Umpire Development Program (MLBUDP)
Box A
St. Petersburg, FL 33731
813-823-1286

Major League Umpires Association (MLUA)
Mellon Bank Center
Suite 3420
1735 Market Street
Philadelphia, PA 19103
215-959-3200

Manufacturer's Agents National Association (MANA)
P.O. Box 3467
23016 Mill Creek Road
Laguna Hills, CA 92654
717-859-4040

National Academy of Sports (NAS)
220 East 63rd Street
New York, NY 10021
212-838-2980

National Academy of Television Arts and Sciences (NATAS)
111 West 57th Street
New York, NY 10019
212-586-8424

National Amateur Baseball Federation (NABF)
P.O. Box 705
Bowie, MD 20718
301-262-5005

National Association of Collegiate Womens Athletic Administrators (NACWAA)
Northern Illinois University
Dekalb, IL 60115
815-753-3700

National Association for Sport and Physical Education (NASPE)
1900 Association Drive
Reston, VA 22091
703-476-3410

National Association for Stock Car Auto Racing (NASCAR)
P.O. Box 2875
1801 Volosia Avenue
Daytona Beach, FL 32015
904-253-0611

National Association of Athletic Development Directors (NAAD)
P.O. Box 16428
Cleveland, OH 44116
216-892-4000

National Association of Basketball Coaches of the United States (NABC)
9300 West 110th Street
Overland Park, KS 66210
913-469-1001

National Association of Broadcast Employees and Technicians (NABET)
501 3rd Street NW
8th Floor
Washington, DC 20001
202-434-1254

National Association of Broadcasters (NAB)
1771 N Street NW
Washington, DC 20036
202-429-5300

National Association of Collegiate Directors of Athletics (NACDA)
P.O. Box 16428
Cleveland, OH 4116
216-892-4000

National Association of Collegiate Gymnastics Coaches (NACGC)
c/o A.B. Grossfeld
Southern Connecticut State University
Department of Physical Education
501 Crescent Street
New Haven, CT 06515
203-397-4245

National Association of Intercollegiate Athletics (NAIA)
6120 South Yale
Suite 1450
Tulsa, OK 74136
918-498-8828

National Association of Leagues, Umpires and Scorers (NALUS)
Box 1420
Wichita, KS 67201
316-267-7333

National Association of Professional Baseball Leagues (NAPBL)
P.O. Box A
St. Petersburg, FL 33731
813-822-6937

National Association of Sporting Goods Wholesales (NASGW)
P.O. Box 11344
Chicago, IL 60611
312-565-0233

National Association of Sports Officials (NASO)
2017 Lathrop Avenue
Racine, WI 53405
414-632-5448

National Athletic Trainers Association (NATA)
2952 Stemmons Freeway
Suite 200
Dallas, TX 75247
214-637-6282

National Baseball Congress (NBC)
Box 1420
Wichita, KS 67201
316-267-3372

National Basketball Association (NBA)
645 Fifth Avenue
New York, NY 10022
212-826-7000

National Basketball Players Association (NBPA)
1775 Broadway
Suite 2401
New York, NY 10019
212-333-7510

National Basketball Referees Association (NBRA)
P.O. Box 6093
Huntington Beach, CA 92615
714-894-9564

National Club Sports Association (NCSA)
c/o Stan Gural
15 Tulipwood Drive
Commack, NY 11725
516-543-0730

National Collegiate Athletic Association (NCAA)
6201 College Boulevard
Overland Park, KS 66211
913-339-1906

National Collegiate Baseball Writers Association (NCBWA)
University of Florida
P.O. Box 14485
Gainsville, FL 36204
904-375-4683

National Collegiate Football Association (NCFA)
c/o Stan Gural
15 Tulipwood Drive
Commack, NY 11725
516-543-0730

National Dance Association (NDA)
1900 Association Drive
Reston, VA 22091
703-476-3436

National Dance-Exercise Instructor's Training Association (NDEITA)
1503 South Washington Avenue
Minneapolis, MN 55454
612-340-1306

National Employee Services and Recreation Association (NESRA)
2211 York Road
Suite 207
Oak Brook, IL 60521
708-368-1280

National Federation Interscholastic Coaches Association (NFICA)
P.O. Box 20626
11724 Plaza Circle
Kansas City, MO 64195
816-464-5400

National Federation Interscholastic Officials Association (NFIOA)
P.O. Box 20626
11724 Plaza Circle
Kansas City, MO 64195
816-464-5400

National Federation of Press Women (NFPW)
Box 99
Blue Springs, MO 64015
816-229-1666

National Federation of State High School Associations (NFSHSA)
P.O. Box 20626
11724 NW Plaza Circle
Kansas City, MO 64195
816-464-5400

National Football League (NFL)
410 Park Avenue
New York, NY 10022
212-758-1500

National Football League Players Association (NFPLA)
2021 L Street, NW
Washington, DC 20036
202-463-2200

National Gymnastics Judges Association (NGJA)
c/o Harry Bjerke
44 Lawrence Lane
Bay Shore, NY 11706
516-665-2103

National Health Club Association (NHCA)
12596 West Bayaud Avenue
Denver, CO 80228
303-753-6422

National High School Athletic Coaches Association (NHSACA)
2265 Lee Road
3321 B
Winter Park, FL 32789
407-628-8555

National Hockey League (NHL)
1800 McGill College Avenue
Suite 2600
Montreal, Quebec, Canada
H3A 3J6
514-268-9220

National Hockey League Player's Association (NHLPA)
1 Dundes Street West
Suite 2300
Toronto, Ontario, Canada
M5G 1Z3
416-408-4040

National Intercollegiate Soccer Officials Association (NISOA)
541 Woodview Drive
Longwood, FL 32779
407-862-3305

National Intramural-Recreational Sports Association (NIRSA)
850 SW 15th Street
Corvallis, OR 97333
503-737-2088

National Interscholastic Swimming Coaches Association of America (NISCA)
c/o Donald R. Allen
Glenbrook South High School
4000 West Lake Avenue
Glenview, IL 60025
708-729-2000

National Junior College Athletic Association (NJCAA)
P.O. Box 7305
Colorado Springs, CO 80933
719-590-9788

National Football League Officials Association (NFLOA)
609 Brainerd Place
Exton, PA 19341
215-363-1733

National League of Professional Baseball Clubs (NL)
350 Park Avenue
New York, NY 10022
212-339-7300

National Press Club (NPC)
National Press Building
529 14th Street NW
Room 1386
Washington, DC 20045
202-662-7500

National Press Photographers Association (NPPA)
3200 Croasdaile Drive
Suite 306
Durham, NC 27705
919-383-7246

National Semi-Professional Baseball Association (NSPBA)
P.O. Box 29965
Atlanta, GA 30359
402-908-3339

National Small College Athletic Association (NSCAA)
c/o Gary Dallman
1844 College Heights
New Ulm, MN 56073
507-359-9791

National Soccer Coaches Association of America (NSCA)
4220 Shawnee Mission Parkway
Suite 105 B
Fairway, KS 66205
913-362-1747

National Professional Soccer League (NPSL)
229 Third Street NW
Canton, OH 44702
216-455-4625

National Soccer League (NSL)
4534 North Lincoln Avenue
Chicago, IL 60625
312-275-2850

National Sporting Goods Association (NSGA)
Lake Center Plaza Building
1699 Wall Street
Mt. Prospect, IL 60056
708-439-4000

National Sportscasters and Sportswriters Association (NSSA)
Box 559
Salisbury, NC 28144
704-633-4275

National Strength and Conditioning Association (NSCA)
530 Communication Circle
Suite 204
Colorado Springs, CO 80905
719-632-6722

National Veterans Boxers Association (NVBA)
1110 McKinley Street
Philadelphia, PA 19111
215-289-0850

National Women Bowling Writers Association (NWBW)
5161 West 136th Street
Hawthorn, CA 90250
410-284-6884

National Wrestling Coaches Association (NWCA)
c/o Les Anderson
Iowa State University
10 Sate Gym
Ames, IA 50011
515-294-4642

National Youth Sports Coaches Association (NYSCA)
2611 Old Okeechobee Road
West Palm Beach, FL 33409
407-684-1141

NCCA Division 1 Track Coaches Association
1705 Evanston
Kalamazoo, MI 49008
616-349-1008

North American Boxing Federation (NABF)
14340 Sundance Drive
Reno, NV 89511
702-853-1236

North American Ski Journalists Association (NASJA)
P.O. Box 5334
Takoma Park, MD 20913
301-864-6428

North American Youth Sport Institute (NAYSI)
4985 Oak Garden Drive
Kernersville, NC 27284
919-784-4926

Office for Baseball Umpire Development
201 Bayshore Drive SE
St. Petersburg, FL 33731

Pony Baseball (PB)
P.O. Box 225
Washington, PA 15301
412-225-1060

Pop Warners Football (PWF)
920 Town Center Drive
Suite I-25
Langhorne, PA 19047
215-752-2691

Professional Basketball Writer's Association of America (PBWAA)
30 Oakland Park Boulevard
Pleasant Ridge, MI 48069
313-222-2260

Professional Football Athletic Trainers Society (PFATS)
P.O. Box 386
Atlanta, GA 30361
404-875-4000

Professional Football Referees Association (PFTA)
1175 Hilltop Lane
Coatesville, PA 19320
215-363-1622

Professional Football Researchers Association (PFRA)
12870 Rt. 30
North Huntingdon, PA 15642
412-863-6345

Professional Football Writers of America (PFWA)
3235 East Flamingo
No. 204
Las Vegas, NV 89121
702-434-0319

Professional Golfers Association of America (PGA)
100 Avenue of Champions
Palm Beach Garden, FL 33418
407-624-8400

Professional Hockey Writers' Association (PHWA)
1480 Pleasant Valley Way
No. 44
West Orange, NJ 07052
201-669-8607

Professional Photographers of America
57 Forsyth Avenue NW
Suite 1000
Atlanta, GA 30303
404-522-8600

Professional Ski Instructors of America (PSIA)
133 South Van Gordon Street
Suite 101
Lakewood, CO 80228
303-987-9390

Public Relations Society of America (PRSA)
33 Irving Place
New York, NY 10003
212-995-2230

Public Relations Student Society of America (PRSSA)
33 Irving Place
New York, NY 10003
212-460-1474

Racing Fans Club of America (RFCA)
P.O. Box 6518
Philadelphia, PA 19115
215-342-2821

Radio Advertising Bureau (RAB)
304 Park Avenue South
New York, NY 10010
212-387-2100

Radio Television News Directors
Association (RTNDA)
1000 Connecticut Avenue NW
Suite 615
Washington, DC 20036
202-659-6510

Society for American Baseball
Research (SABR)
P.O. Box 93183
Cleveland, OH 44101
216-575-0500

Sporting Goods Agents Association
(SGAA)
P.O. Box 998
Morton, Grove, IL 60053
312-0296-3670

Sporting Goods Manufacturers
Association (SGMA)
200 Castlewood Drive
North Palm Beach, FL 33048
407-842-4100

Sports Foundation (SF)
Lake Center Plaza Building
1699 Wall Street
Mt. Prospect, IL 60506
708-439-4000

Sports Therapy Division
1600 James Naismith Drive
Gloucester, Ontario, Canada
K1B 5N4
613-748-5671

The Athletics Congress of the U.S.A.
(TAC/USA)
P.O. Box 120
Indianapolis, IN 46206
317-638-9155

Thoroughbred Club of America (TCA)
P.O. Box 8098
Lexington, KY 40533
606-254-4282

Trotting Horse Museum (THM)
P.O. Box 590
240 Main Street
Goshen, NY 10924
914-294-6330

United Soccer League (USL)
c/o Dr. William Burfeind
R.D. 2, Box 112
Merztown, PA 19539
215-682-6386

United States Amateur Wrestling
Foundation (USAMF)
Wrestling Division
Amateur Athletic Union
3400 West 86th Street
Indianapolis, IN 46269
317-872-2900

United States Association of
Independent Gymnastic Clubs
(USAIGC)
235 Pinehurst Road
Wilmington, DE 19803
302-656-3706

United States Athletes Association
(USAA)
3735 Lakeland Avenue, N.
Suite 230
Minneapolis, MN 55422
612-522-5844

United States Basketball Writers
Association (USBWA)
c/o Joseph F. Mitch
Missouri Valley Conference
100 North Broadway
Suite 1135
St. Louise, MO 63102
314-421-0339

United States Cross Country Coaches
Association (USCCCA)
c/o Bill Bergan
207 State Gym
Iowa State University
Ames, IA 50011
515-294-3723

United States Gymnastics Federation
(USGF)
201 South Capitol
Suite 300
Indianapolis, IN 46225
317-237-5050

United States Harness Writers'
Association (USHWA)
P.O. Box 10
Batavia, NY 14020
716-343-5900

United States Lifesaving Association
(USLA)
P.O. Box 366
Huntington Beach, CA 92648
714-536-5283

United States Ski Association (USSA)
P.O. Box 100
Park City, UT 84060
801-649-9090

United States Soccer Federation
(USSF)
1801-1811 S Prairie Avenue
Chicago, IL 60616
312-808-1300

United States Sports Academy (USSA)
One Academy Drive
Daphne, AL 36526
205-626-3303

United States Swimming, Inc. (USS)
1 Olympic Plaza
Colorado Springs, CO 80909
719-578-4578

United States Swimming Foundation
(USSF)
3318 Park Sorrento
Calabassas Park, CA 91302
818-951-1379

United States Trotting Association
(USTA)
750 Michigan Avenue
Columbus, OH 43215
614-224-2291

United States Women's Track
Coaches Association (USWTCA)
c/o Karen Dennis
Michigan State University
Women's Athletic Department
East Lansing, MI 48824
517-353-9299

United States Youth Soccer
Association (USYSA)
2050 North Plano Road
Suite 100
Richardson, TX 75082
214-235-4499

U.S.A. Boxing (USAB)
1 Olympic Plaza
Colorado Springs, CO 80909
719-578-4506

USA Basketball (USAB)
5465 Mark Dabling Boulevard
Colorado Springs, CO 80918
719-590-4800

U.S.A. Field Hockey Association
(USAFHA)
225 South Academy Boulevard
Colorado Springs, CO 80910
719-597-8333

USA Hockey (USAH)
4965 N 30th Street
Colorado Springs, CO 80919
719-599-5500

U.S.A. Wrestling
405 West Hall of Fame Avenue
Stilwater, OK 74075
405-377-5242

U.S. Ski Coaches Association (USSCA)
P.O. Box 100
Park City, UT 84060
801-649-9090

U.S. Tennis Writers Association (USTWA)
c/o Thomas Bonk
Los Angeles Times
Times Mirror Square
Los Angeles, CA 90053
213-237-7145

Western Winter Sports Representatives Association (WWSRA)
2621 Thorndyke Avenue, W.
Seattle, WA 98199
206-284-0751

Women In Communications, Inc. (WIC)
3717 Columbia Pike
No. 310
Arlington, VA 22204
703-528-4200

Women In Soccer (WIS)
242 East 75th Street
New York, NY 10021
212-744-1565

Women's Basketball Association (WBA)
2 Penn Plaza
Suite 1500
New York, NY 10001
212-643-6677

Women's Basketball Coaches Association (WBCA)
4646 B Lawrenceville Highway
Liburn, GA 30247
404-279-8027

Women's Sports Foundation (WSF)
Eisenhower Park
East Meadow, NY 11554
516-542-4700

World Boxing Association (WBA)
c/o Nick P. Kerasiotis
412 Colorado Avenue
Aurora, IL 60506
312-897-4765

World Boxing Council (WBC)
Genova 33–Desp 503
06600 Mexico, D.F.
Mexico
905-525-3787

World Boxing Federation (WBF)
P.O. Box 3966
Bristol, TN 53762
615-764-1161

World Boxing Organization (WBO)
412 Colorado Avenue
Aurora, IL 60506
708-897-4765

APPENDIX V
MAJOR LEAGUE BASEBALL CLUBS

The following is a listing of the clubs in Major League baseball as well as related organizations. Names, addresses, and phone numbers are included for each. Use them to obtain general information, locate internships, and/or to send your résumés for job possibilities.

Office of the Commissioner
350 Park Avenue
New York, NY 10022
212-339-7800

Major League Baseball (MLB)
Players Association
12 East 49th Street
New York, NY 10017
212-826-0808

AMERICAN LEAGUE OF
PROFESSIONAL BASEBALL
CLUBS (AL)

American League Office
350 Park Avenue
New York, NY 10022
212-339-7600

Anaheim Angels
P.O. Box 2000
Anaheim, CA 92803
714-940-2000

Baltimore Orioles
333 West Camdem Street
Baltimore, MD 21201
410-685-9800

Boston Red Sox
Fenway Park
Boston, MA 02215
617-267-9440

Chicago White Sox
333 West 35th Street
Chicago, IL 60616
312-674-1000

Cleveland Indians
2401 Ontario Street
Cleveland, OH 44115
216-420-4200

Detroit Tigers
2121 Trumbell Avenue
Detroit, MI 48216
313-962-4000

Kansas City Royals
P.O. Box 419969
Kansas City, MO 64141
816-921-2200

Milwaukee Brewers
P.O. Box 3099
Milwaukee, WI 53201
414-933-4114

Minnesota Twins
34 Kirby Puckett Place
Minneapolis, MN 55415
612-375-1366

New York Yankees
Yankee Stadium
Bronx, NY 10451
212-293-4300

Oakland Athletics
Oakland Coliseum
Oakland, CA 94621
510-638-4900

Seattle Mariners
P.O. Box 4100
Seattle, WA 98104
206-628-3555

Tampa Bay Devil Rays
One Tropicana Drive
St. Petersburg, FL 33705
813-825-3137

Texas Rangers
P.O. Box 90111
Arlington, TX 76004
817-273-5222

Toronto Blue Jays
1 Blue Jays Way # 3200
Toronto, Ontario, Canada
M5V 1J1
416-341-1000

NATIONAL LEAGUE OF
PROFESSIONAL BASEBALL
CLUBS (NL)

National League Office
350 Park Avenue
New York, NY 10022
212-339-7700

Arizona Diamondbacks
P.O. Box 2095
Phoenix, AZ 85001
602-514-8500

Atlanta Braves
P.O. Box 4064
Atlanta, GA 30303
404-522-7630

Chicago Cubs
1060 West Adison Street
Chicago, IL 60613
773-404-2827

Cincinnati Reds
100 Cinergy Field
Cincinnati, OH 45202
513-421-4510

Colorado Rockies
2001 Blake Street
Denver, CO 80205
303-292-0200

Florida Marlins
2267 NW 199th Street
Miami, FL 33056
305-626-7400

Houston Astros
P.O. Box 288
Houston, TX 77001
713-799-9500

Los Angeles Dodgers
1000 Elysian Park Avenue
Los Angeles, CA 90012
213-224-1500

Montreal Expos
P.O. Box 500
Station M
Montreal, Quebec, Canada
H1V 3P2
514-253-3434

New York Mets
Shea Stadium
Flushing, NY 11368
718-507-6387

Philadelphia Phillies
P.O. Box 7575
Philadelphia, PA 19101
215-463-6000

Pittsburgh Pirates
P.O. Box 7000
Pittsburgh, PA 15212
412-323-5000

St. Louis Cardinals
250 Stadium Plaza
St. Louis, MO 63102
314-421-3060

San Diego Padres
P.O. Box 2000
San Diego, CA 92112
619-881-6500

San Francisco Giants
3Com Park at Candlestick Point
San Francisco, CA 92124
415-468-3700

APPENDIX VI
NATIONAL ASSOCIATION
OF PROFESSIONAL
BASEBALL LEAGUES MEMBERS

The following is a listing of the members of the National Association of Professional Baseball Leagues, Inc. provided by that organization. This will help you find the various clubs in the minor leagues. Names, addresses and phone numbers are included for each as well as league association, club affiliation and class designation. Use them to obtain general information, locate interships and/or to send your resumes for job possibilities.

NATIONAL ASSOCIATION OF PROFESSIONAL BASEBALL LEAGUES, INC. (NAPBL)
P.O. Box A
St. Petersburg, FL 33703
813-822-6937

AMERICAN ASSOCIATION (AAA)
6801 Miami Avenue # 3
Cincinnati, OH 45243
513-271-4800

Buffalo Bisons P.O. Box 450 Buffalo, NY 14205 716-846-2000	American Association	Cleveland Indians	(AAA)
Indianapolis Indians 501 West Maryland Street Indianapolis, IN 46225 317-267-3545	American Association	Cincinnati Reds	(AAA)
Iowa Cubs 350 SW First Street Des Moines, IA 50309 515-243-6111	American Association	Chicago Cubs	(AAA)
Louisville Redbirds P.O. Box 36407 Louisville, KY 40233 502-367-9121	American Association	St. Louis Cardinals	(AAA)
Nashville Sounds P.O. Box 23290 Nashville, TN 37202 615-242-4371	American Association	Chicago White Sox	(AAA)
New Orleans Zephyrs 6000 Airline Highway Metairie, LA 70003 504-734-5155	American Association	Houston Astros	(AAA)
Oklahoma RedHawks P.O. Box 75089 Oklahoma City, OK 73147 405-218-1000	American Association	Texas Rangers	(AAA)

Omaha Royals P.O. Box 3665 Omaha, NE 68103 402-734-2550	American Association	Kansas City Royals	(AAA)

INTERNATIONAL LEAGUE (AAA)
55 South High Street # 202
Dublin, OH 43017
614-791-9300

Charlotte Knights P.O. Box 1207 Fort Mills, SC 29716 803-548-8050	International League	Florida Marlins	(AAA)
Columbus Clippers 1155 West Mound Street Columbus, OH 43223 614-462-5250	International League	New York Yankees	(AAA)
Norfolk Tides Harbor Park 150 Park Avenue Norfolk, VA 23510 757-622-2222	International League	New York Mets	(AAA)
Ottawa Lynx 300 Coventry Road Ottawa, Ontario, Canada K1K 4P5 613-747-5969	International League	Montreal Expos	(AAA)
Pawtucket Red Sox P.O. Box 2365 Pawtucket, RI 02861 401-724-7300	International League	Boston Red Sox	(AAA)
Richmond Braves P.O. Box 6667 Richmond, VA 23230 804-359-4444	International League	Atlanta Braves	(AAA)
Rochester Red Wings One Morris Silver Way Rochester, NY 14608 716-454-1001	International League	Baltimore Orioles	(AAA)
Scranton/Wilkes-Barre Barons P.O. Box 3449 Scranton, PA 18505 717-969-2255	International League	Philadelphia Phillies	(AAA)
Syracuse SkyChiefs P & C Stadium Syracuse, NY 13208 315-474-7833	International League	Toronto Blue Jays	(AAA)
Toledo Mud Hens P.O. Box 6212 Toledo, OH 43614 419-893-9483	International League	Detroit Tigers	(AAA)

PACIFIC COAST LEAGUE (AAA)
2345 South Alma School Road
10
Mesa, AZ 85210
602-838-2171

Albuquerque Dukes 1601 Avenida Cesar Chavez SE Albuquerque, NM 87106 505-243-1791	Pacific Coast League	Los Angeles Dodgers	(AAA)
Calgary Cannons 2255 Crowchild Trail NW Calgary, Alberta, Canada T2M 4S7 403-284-1111	Pacific Coast League	Pittsburgh Pirates	(AAA)
Colorado Springs Sky Sox 4385 Tutt Boulevard Colorado Springs, CO 80922 719-597-1449	Pacific Coast League	Colorado Rockies	(AAA)
Edmonton Trappers 10233 96th Avenue Edmonton, Alberta, Canada T5K OA5 403-429-2934	Pacific Coast League	Oakland A's	(AAA)
Las Vegas Stars 850 Las Vegas Boulevard, North Las Vegas, NV 89010 702-386-7200	Pacific Coast League	San Diego Padres	(AAA)
Phoenix Firebirds P.O. Box 8528 Phoenix, AZ 85252 602-275-0500	Pacific Coast League	San Francisco Giants	(AAA)
Salt Lake Buzz P.O. Box 4108 Salt Lake City, UT 84110 801-485-3800	Pacific Coast League	Minnesota Twins	(AAA)
Tacoma Rainers P.O. Box 11087 Tacoma, WA 98411 206-752-7707	Pacific Coast League	Seattle Mariners	(AAA)
Tucson Toros P.O. Box 27045 Tucson, AZ 85726 520-325-2621	Pacific Coast League	Milwaukee Brewers	(AAA)
Vancouver Canadians 4601 Ontario Street Vancouver, BC V5V 3H4 604-872-5232	Pacific Coast League	California Angels	(AAA)

EASTERN LEAGUE (AA)
P.O. Box 9711
Portland, ME 04104
207-761-2700

Akron Aeros 300 South Main Street Akron, OH 44308 330-253-5151	Eastern League	Cleveland Indians	(AA)
Binghamton Mets P.O. Box 598 Binghamton, NY 13902 607-723-6387	Eastern League	New York Mets	(AA)

Bowie Baysox P.O. Box 1661 Bowie, MD 20717 301-805-6000	Eastern League	Baltimore Orioles	(AA)
Harrisburg Senators P.O. Box 15757 Harrisburg, PA 17105 717-231-4444	Eastern League	Montreal Expos	(AA)
New Britain Rock Cats P.O. Box 1718 New Britain, CT 06050 860-224-8383	Eastern League	Minnesota Twins	(AA)
New Haven Ravens 252 Derby Avenue West Haven, CT 06516 203-782-3140	Eastern League	Colorado Rockies	(AA)
Norwich Navigators P.O. Box 6003 Yantic, CT 06839 860-887-7962	Eastern League	New York Yankees	(AA)
Portland Sea Dogs P.O. Box 636 Portland, ME 04104 207-874-9300	Eastern League	Florida Marlins	(AA)
Reading Phillies P.O. Box 15050 Reading, PA 19612 610-375-8469	Eastern League	Philadelphia Phillies	(AA)
Trenton Thunder One Thunder Road Trenton, NJ 08611 609-394-3300	Eastern League	Boston Red Sox	(AA)

SOUTHERN LEAGUE (AA)
1 Depot Street
Suite 300
Marietta, GA 30060
770-428-4749

Birmingham Barons P.O. Box 360007 Birmingham, AL 35236 205-988-3200	Southern League	Chicago White Sox	(AA)
Carolina Mudcats P.O. Box 1218 Zebulon, NC 27597 919-269-2287	Southern League	Pittsburgh Pirates	(AA)
Chattanooga Lookouts P.O. Box 11002 Chattanooga, TN 37401 423-267-2208	Southern League	Cincinnati Reds	(AA)
Greenville Braves P.O. Box 16683 Greenville, SC 29606 864-299-3456	Southern League	Atlanta Braves	(AA)

Huntsville Stars P.O. Box 2769 Huntsville, AL 358045 205-882-2562	Southern League	Oakland A's	(AA)
Jacksonville Suns P.O. Box 4756 Jacksonville, FL 32201 904-358-2846	Southern League	Detroit Tigers	(AA)
Knoxville Smokies 633 Jessamine Street Knoxville, TN 37917 423-637-9494	Southern League	Toronto Blue Jays	(AA)
Memphis Chicks 800 Home Run Lane Memphis, TN 38104 901-272-1687	Southern League	Seattle Mariners	(AA)
Mobile BayBears P.O. Box 161663 Mobile, AL 36616 334-476-2287	Southern League	San Diego Padres	(AA)
Orlando Rays 287 South Tampa Avenue South Orlando, FL 32805 407-649-7297	Southern League	Tampa Bay Devil Rays	(AA)

TEXAS LEAGUE
2442 Facet Oak
San Antonio, TX 78232
210-545-5297

Arkansas Travelers P.O. Box 55066 Little Rock, AR 72215 510-664-1555	Texas League	St. Louis Cardinals	(AA)
El Paso Diablos P.O. Drawer 4797 El Paso, TX 79914 915-755-2000	Texas League	Milwaukee Brewers	(AA)
Jackson Generals P.O. Box 4209 Jackson, MS 39296 601-981-4664	Texas League	Houston Astros	(AA)
Midland Angels P.O. Box 51187 Midland, TX 79710 915-683-4251	Texas League	Anaheim Angeles	(AA)
San Antonio Missions 5757 West US Highway 90 San Antonio, TX 78227 210-675-7275	Texas League	Los Angeles Dodgers	(AA)
Shreveport Captains P.O. Box 3448 Shreveport, LA 71133 318-636-5555	Texas League	San Francisco Giants	(AA)

Tulsa Drillers P.O. Box 4448 Tulsa, OK 74159 918-744-5901	Texas League	Texas Rangers	(AA)
Wichita Wranglers P.O. Box 1420 Wichita, KS 67201 316-267-3372	Texas League	Kansas City Roytals	(AA)

CALIFORNIA LEAGUE (A)
2380 South Bascom Avenue
#200
Campbell, CA 95008
408-369-8038

Bakersfield Blaze P.O. Box 10031 Bakersfield, CA 93389 805-322-1363	California League	San Francisco Giants	(A)
High Desert Mavericks 12000 Stadium Way Adelanto, CA 92301 909-245-4487	California League	Arizona Diamondbacks	(A)
Lake Elsinore Storm P.O. Box 535 Lake Elisnore, CA 92531 909-245-4487	California League	California Angels	(A)
Lancaster JetHawks 45116 Valley Central Way Lancaster, CA 93536 805-726-5400	California League	Seattle Mariners	(A)
Modestos A's P.O. Box 883 Modesto, CA 95353 209-572-4487	California League	Oakland A's	(A)
Rancho Cucamonga Quakes P.O. Box 4139 Rancho Cucamonga, CA 91729 909-481-5000	California League	San Diego Padres	(A)
San Bernardino Stampede 280 South E Street San Bernardino, CA 92401 909-888-9922	California League	Los Angeles Dodgers	(A)
San Jose Giants P.O. Box 21727 San Jose, CA 95151 408-297-1435	California League	San Francisco Giants	(A)
Stockton Ports P.O. Box 8550 Stockton, CA 95208 209-944-5943	California League	Milwaukee Brewers	(A)
Visalia Oaks P.O. Box 48 Visalia, CA 93279 209-625-0480	California League	Oakland A's	(A)

CAROLINA LEAGUE (A)
P.O. Box 9503
Greensboro, NC 27429
910-691-9030

Durham Bulls P.O. Box 507 Durham, NC 27702 919-687-6500	Carolina League	Atlanta Braves	(A)
Frederick Keys P.O. Box 3169 Frederick, MD 21701 301-662-0013	Carolina League	Baltimore Orioles	(A)
Kinston Indians P.O. Box 3542 Kinston, NC 28501 919-527-9111	Carolina League	Cleveland Indians	(A)
Lynchburg Hillcats P.O. Box 10213 Lynchburg, VA 24506 804-528-1144	Carolina League	Pittsburgh Pirates	(A)
Prince William Cannons P.O. Box 2148 Woodbridge, VA 22193 703-590-2311	Carolina League	St. Louis Cardinals	(A)
Salem Avalanche P.O. Box 842 Salem, VA 24153 540-389-3333	Carolina League	Colorado Rockies	(A)
Wilmington Blue Rocks 801 South Madison Street Wilmington, DE 19801 302-888-2015	Carolina League	Kansas City Royals	(A)
Winston-Salem Warthogs P.O. Box 4488 Winston-Salem, NC 27115 910-759-2233	Carolina League	Chicago White Sox	(A)

FLORIDA STATE LEAGUE (A)
P.O. Box 349
Daytona Beach, FL 32115
904-252-7479

Brevard County Mantees 5800 Stadium Parkway Melbourne, FL 32940 407-633-9200	Florida State League	Florida Marlins	(A)
Charlotte Rangers 2300 El Jobean Road Port Charlotte, FL 33948 941-625-9500	Florida State League	Texas Rangers	(A)
Clearwater Phillies P.O. Box 10336 Clearwater, FL 34617 813-441-8638	Florida State League	Philadelphia Phillies	(A)

Daytona Cubs P.O. Box 15080 Daytona Beach, FL 32115 904-257-3172	Florida State League	Chicago Cubs	(A)
Dunedin Blue Jays P.O. Box 957 Dunedin, FL 34697 813-733-9302	Florida State League	Toronto Blue Jays	(A)
Ft. Myers Miracle 14400 Six Mile Cypress Parkway Ft. Myers, FL 33912 941-768-4210	Florida State League	Minnesota Twins	(A)
Kissimmee Cobras P.O. Box 422229 Kissimmee, FL 34742 407-933-5500	Florida State League	Houston Astros	(A)
Lakeland Tigers P.O. Box 90187 Lakeland, FL 33804 941-688-7911	Florida State League	Detroit Tigers	(A)
St. Lucie Mets 525 NW Peacock Boulevard Port St. Lucie, FL 34986 561-871-2100	Florida State League	New York Mets	(A)
St. Petersburg Devil Rays P.O. Box 12557 St. Petersburg, FL 33733 813-822-3384	Florida State League	Tampa Bay Devil Rays	(A)
Sarasota Red Sox P.O. Box 2816 Sarasota, FL 34230 941-365-4460	Florida State League	Boston Red Sox	(A)
Tampa Yankees 3802 West Dr. Martin Luther King Boulevard Tampa, FL 33614 813-875-7753	Florida State League	New York Yankees	(A)
Vero Beach Dodgers P.O. Box 2887 Vero Beach, FL 32961 561-569-4900	Florida State League	Los Angeles Dodgers	(A)
West Palm Beach Expos P.O. Box 3566 West Palm Beach, FL 33402 561-684-6801	Florida State League	Montreal Expos	(A)

MIDWEST LEAGUE (A)
P.O. Box 936
Beloit, WI 53511
608-364-1188

Beloit Snappers P.O. Box 855 Beloit, WI 53511 608-362-2272	Midwest League	Milwaukee Brewers	(A)

Burlington Bees P.O. Box 824 Burlington, IA 52601 319-754-5705	Midwest League	Cincinnati Reds	(A)
Cedar Rapids Kernels P.O. Box 2001 Cedar Rapids, IA 52406 319-363-3887	Midwest League	California Angels	(A)
Clinton LumberKings P.O. Box 1295 Clinton, IA 52733 319-242-0727	Midwest League	San Diego Padres	(A)
Fort Wayne Wizards 4000 Parnell Avenue Fort Wayne, IN 46805 219-482-6400	Midwest League	Minnesota Twins	(A)
Kane County Cougars 34W002 Cherry Lane Geneva, IL 60134 630-232-8811	Midwest League	Florida Marlins	(A)
Lansing Lugnuts 505 East Michigan Avenue Lansing, MI 58912 517-485-4500	Midwest League	Kansas City Royals	(A)
Michigan Battle Cats 1392 Capital Avenue NE Battle Creek, MI 49017 616-660-2287	Midwest League	Boston Red Sox	(A)
Peoria Chiefs 1524 West Nebraska Avenue Peoria, IL 61604 309-688-1622	Midwest League	St. Louis Cardinals	(A)
Quad-City River Bandits P.O. Box 3496 Davenport, IA 52808 319-324-2032	Midwest League	Houston Astros	(A)
Rockford Cubbies P.O. Box 6748 Rockford, IL 61125 815-962-2827	Midwest League	Chicago Cubs	(A)
South Bend Silver Hawks P.O. Box 4218 South Bend, IN 46634 219-235-9988	Midwest League	Arizona Diamondbacks	(A)
West Michigan Whitecaps P.O. Box 428 Comstock Park, MI 49321 616-784-4131	Midwest League	Detroit Tigers	(A)
Wisconsin Timber Rattlers P.O. Box 464 Appleton, WI 54912 414-733-4152	Midwest League	Seattle Mariners	(A)

SOUTH ATLANTIC LEAGUE (A)
P.O. Box 38
Kings Mountain, NC 28086
704-739-3466

Asheville Tourists P.O. Box 1556 Asheville, NC 28802 704-258-0428	South Atlantic League	Colorado Rockies	(A)
Augusta GreenJackets P.O. Box 3746 Hill Station Augusta, GA 30914 706-736-7889	South Atlantic League	Pittsburgh Pirates	(A)
Cape Fear Crocs P.O. Box 64939 Fayettville, NC 28306 910-424-6500	South Atlantic League	Montreal Expos	(A)
Capital City Bombers P.O. Box 7845 Columbia, SC 29201 803-256-4110	South Atlantic League	New York Mets	(A)
Charleston Alley Cats P.O. Box 4669 Charleston, WV 25304 304-344-2287	South Atlantic League	Cincinnati Reds	(A)
Charleston River Dogs P.O. Box 20849 Charleston, SC 29413 803-723-7241	South Atlantic League	Tampa Bay Devil Rays	(A)
Columbus Redsticks P.O. Box 1886 Columbus, GA 31902 706-571-8866	South Atlantic League	Cleveland Indians	(A)
Delmar Shorebirds P.O. Box 1557 Salisbury, MD 21802 410-219-3112	South Atlantic League	Baltimore Orioles	(A)
Greensboro Bats 510 Yanceyville Street Greensboro, NC 27405 910-333-2287	South Atlantic League	New York Yankees	(A)
Hagerstown Suns P.O. Box 230 Hagerstown, MD 21741 301-791-6266	South Atlantic League	Toronto Blue Jays	(A)
Hickory Crawdads P.O. Box 1268 Hickory, NC 28063 704-322-3000	South Atlantic League	Chicago White Sox	(A)
Macon Braves P.O. Box 4525 Macon, GA 31208 912-745-8943	South Atlantic League	Atlanta Braves	(A)
Piedmont Boll Weevils P.O. Box 64 Kannapolis, NC 28082 704-932-3267	South Atlantic League	Philadelphia Phillies	(A)

Savannah Sand Gnats   South Atlantic League   Los Angeles Dodgers   (A)
P.O. Box 3783
Savannah, GA 31404
912-351-9150

NEW YORK-PENN LEAGUE (S-A)
1629 Oneida Street
Utica, NY 13501
315-733-8036

Auburn Doubledays   New York-Penn League   Houston Astros   (S-A)
108 North Division Street
Auburn, NY 13021
315-255-2489

Batavia Clippers   New York-Penn League   Philadelphia Phillies   (S-A)
Dwyer Stadium
299 Bank Street
Batavia, NY 14020
716-343-5454

Hudson Valley Renegades   New York-Penn League   Tampa Bay Devil Rays   (S-A)
P.O. Box 661
Fishkill, NY 12524
914-838-0094

Jamestown Jammers   New York-Penn League   Detroit Tigers   (S-A)
P.O. Box 338
Jamestown, NY 14702
716-664-0915

Lowell Spinners   New York-Penn League   Boston Red Sox   (S-A)
P.O. Box 778
Lowell, MA 01853
508-459-1702

New Jersey Cardinals   New York-Penn League   St. Louis Cardinals   (S-A)
94 Championship Place
Suite 2
Augusta, NJ 07822
201-579-7500

Oneonta Yankees   New York-Penn League   New York Yankees   (S-A)
95 River Street
Oneonta, NY 13820
607-432-3151

Pittsfield Mets   New York-Penn League   New York Mets   (S-A)
P.O. Box 328
Pittsfield, MA 01202
413-499-6387

St. Catharines Stompers   New York-Penn League   Toronto Blue Jays   (S-A)
426 Merritt Street
St. Catharines, Ontario, Canada
L2P 1P3
905-641-5297

Utica Blue Sox   New York-Penn League   Florida Marlins   (S-A)
P.O. Box 751
Utica, NY 13503
315-738-0999

Vermont Expos   New York-Penn League   Montreal Expos   (S-A)
1 Main Street
Box 4
Winoski, VT 05404
802-655-4200

Watertown Indians P.O. Box 802 Watertown, NY 13601 315-788-8747	New York-Penn League	Cleveland Indians	(S-A)
Williamsport Cubs P.O. Box 3173 Williamsport, PA 17701 717-3389	New York-Penn League	Chicago Cubs	(S-A)

NORTHWEST LEAGUE (S-A)
P.O. Box 848 (from June through October)
Eugene, OR 97440
541-686-5412

P.O. Box 4941 (from October through June)
Scottsdale, AZ 85261
602-483-8224

Boise Hawks 5600 North Glenwood Street Boise, ID 83714 208-322-5000	Northwest League	California Angels	(S-A)
Eugene Emeralds P.O. Box 5566 Eugene, OR 97405 541-342-5367	Northwest League	Atlanta Braves	(S-A)
Everett AquaSox 3802 Broadway Everett, WA 98201 425-258-3673	Northwest League	Seattle Mariners	(S-A)
Portland Rockies P.O. Box 998 Portland, OR 97207 503-223-2837	Northwest League	Colorado Rockies	(S-A)
Salem-Keizer Volcanos P.O. Box 20936 Keizer, OR 97303 503-390-2225	Northwest League	San Francisco Giants	(S-A)
Southern Oregon Timberjacks P.O. Box 1457 Medford, OR 97501 541-770-5364	Northwest League	Oakland A's	(S-A)
Spokane Indians P.O. Box 4758 Spokane, WA 99202 509-535-2922	Northwest League	Kansas City Royals	(S-A)
Yakima Bears P.O. Box 483 Yakima, WA 98907 509-457-5151	Northwest League	Los Angeles Dodgers	(S-A)

APPALACHIAN LEAGUE (R)
283 Deerchase Circle
Statesville, NC 28677
704-873-5300

Bluefield Orioles P.O. Box 356 Bluefield, WV 24701 540-326-1326	Appalachian League	Baltimore Orioles	(R)
Bristol Sox P.O. Box 1434 Bristol, VA 24203 540-645-7275	Appalachian League	Chicago White Sox	(R)
Burlington Indians P.O. Box 1143 Burlington, NC 27216 910-791-3346	Appalachian League	Cleveland Indians	(R)
Danville Braves P.O. Box 3637 Danville, VA 24543 804-791-3346	Appalachian League	Atlanta Braves	(R)
Elizabethton Twins 136 South Sycamore Elizabethton, TN 37643 423-543-4395	Appalachian League	Minnesota Twins	(R)
Johnson City Cardinals P.O. Box 568 Johnson City, TN 37601 423-461-4850	Appalachian League	St. Louis Cardinals	(R)
Kingsport Mets P.O. Box 1128 Kingsport, TN 37662 423-392-8533	Appalachian League	New York Mets	(R)
Martinsville Phillies P.O. Box 3614 Martinsville, VA 24115 540-666-2000	Appalachian League	Philadelphia Phillies	(R)
Princeton Devil Rays P.O. Box 5646 Princeton, WV 24740 304-487-2000	Appalachian League	Tampa Bay Devil Rays	(R)
Pulaski Rangers 630 Lafayette Avenue Pulaski, VA 24301 540-980-8878	Appalachian League	Texas Rangers	(R)

PIONEER LEAGUE (R)
P.O. Box 2564
Spokane, WA 99220
509-456-7615

Billings Mustangs P.O. Box 1553 Billings, MT 59103 406-252-1241	Pioneer League	Cincinnati Reds	(R)
Butte Copper Kings P.O. Box 186 Butte, MT 59703 406-723-8206	Pioneer League	California Angels	(R)

Great Falls Dodgers P.O. Box 1621 Great Falls, MT 59403 406-452-5311	Pioneer League	Los Angeles Dodges	(R)
Helena Brewers P.O. Box 4606 Helena, MT 59604 406-449-7616	Pioneer League	Milwaukee Brewers	(R)
Idaho Falls Braves P.O. Box 2183 Idaho Falls, ID 83403 208-522-8363	Pioneer League	San Diego Padres	(R)
Lethbridge Black Diamonds P.O. Box 1986 Lethbridge, Alberta, Canada T1J 4K5 403-327-7975	Pioneer League	Arizona Diamondbacks	(R)
Medicine Hat Blue Jays P.O. Box 465 Medicine Hat, Alberta, Canada T1A 7G2 403-526-0404	Pioneer League	Toronto Blue Jays	(R)
Ogden Raptors 2330 Lincoln Avenue Ogden, UT 844011 801-393-2400	Pioneer League	Milwaukee Brewers	(R)

ARIZONA STATE LEAGUE (R)

P.O. Box 4941
Scottsdale, AZ 85261
602-483-8224

GULF COAST LEAGUE (R)

1503 Clower Creek Drive, # H-262
Sarasota, FL 34231
941-966-6407

MEXICAN LEAGUE (AAA)

Angel Pola #16
Col. de Periodis
11220 Mexico, D.F.
Mexico
011-525-557-1007

DOMINICAN SUMMER LEAGUE

Av. John F. Kennedy, No. 3
Santo Domingo, Dominican Republic
809-563-3223

APPENDIX VII
NATIONAL BASKETBALL ASSOCIATION

The following is a listing of the teams in the National Basketball Association (NBA) provided by that organization. Names, addresses, and phone numbers are included for each in case you would like to contact them. The main address for the National Basketball Association's office is also included, as well as that for the NBA Players Association. Use them to obtain general information, locate internships, and/or to send your résumé for possible jobs.

National Basketball Association
Olympic Tower
555 Fifth Avenue
New York, NY 10022
212-826-7000

NBA Players Association
1775 Broadway
Suite 2401
New York, NY 10019
212-333-7510

Atlanta Hawks
One CNN Center
South Tower
Suite 405
Atlanta, GA 30303
404-827-3800

Boston Celtics
151 Merrimac Street
Boston, MA 02114
617-523-6050

Charlotte Hornets
100 Hive Drive
Charlotte, NC 28717
704-357-0252

Chicago Bulls
United Center
1901 West Madison
Chicago, IL 60612
312-455-4000

Cleveland Cavaliers
Gund Arena
100 Gateway Plaza
Cleveland, OH 44115
216-420-2000

Dallas Mavericks
Reunion Arena
777 Sports Street
Dallas, TX 75205
214-748-1808

Denver Nuggets
1635 Clay Street
P.O. Box 4658
Denver, CO 80204
303-893-6700

Detroit Pistons
The Palace of Auburn Hills
Two Championship Drive
Auburn Hills, MI 48326
810-377-0100

Golden State Warriors
Oakland Coliseum Arena
1221 Broadway
20th Floor
Oakland, CA 94612
510-986-2200

Houston Rockets
2 Greenway Plaza
Suite 400
Houston, TX 77046
713-627-3865

Indiana Pacers
300 East Market Street
Indianapolis, IN 46204
317-263-2100

Los Angeles Clippers
Los Angeles Sports Arena
3939 South Figueroa Street
Los Angeles, CA 90037
213-745-0400

Los Angeles Lakers
Great Western Forum
3600 West Manchester Boulevard
Ingelwood, CA 90305
310-419-3100

Miami Heat
SunTrust International Center
One Southeast Third Avenue
Miami, FL 33131
305-577-4328

Milwaukee Bucks
The Bradley Center
1001 North Fourth Street
Milwaukee, WI 53203
414-227-0500

Minnesota Timberwolves
Target Center
600 First Avenue North
Minneapolis, MN 55403
612-673-1600

New Jersey Nets
405 Murray Hill Parkway
East Rutherford, NJ 07073
201-935-8888

New York Knicks
Madison Square Garden
Two Pennsylvania Plaza
New York, NY 10121
212-465-6499

Orlando Magic
Orlando Arena
One Magic Place
Orlando, FL 32801
407-649-3200

Philadelphia 76ers
Veterans Stadium
P.O. Box 25040
Broad Street & Pattison Avenue
Philadelphia, PA 19147
215-339-7600

Phoenix Suns
Phoenix Sun Plaza
201 East Jefferson
Phoenix, AZ 85004
602-379-7900

Portland Trail Blazers
One Center Court
Suite 200
Portland, OR 97227
503-234-9291

Sacramento Kings
One Sports Parkway
Sacramento, CA 95834
916-928-0000

San Antonio Spurs
100 Montana Street
San Antonio, TX 78203
210-554-7700

Seattle Supersonics
190 5th Avenue North
Seattle, WA 98109
206-281-5800

Toronto Raptors
20 Bay Street
Suite 1702
Toronto, Ontario, Canada
M5J 2N8
416-214-2255

Utah Jazz
Delta Center
301 West South Temple
Salt Lake City, UT 84101
801-325-2500

Vancouver Grizzliers
General Motors Place
800 Griffiths Way
Vancouver, British Columbia, Canada
V6B 6G1
604-899-7400

Washington Bullets
US Air Arena
One Harry S. Truman Drive
Landover, MD 20785
301-773-2255

APPENDIX VIII
WOMEN'S NATIONAL BASKETBALL ASSOCIATION

The following is a listing of the teams in the Women's National Basketball Association (WNBA). Names, addresses, and phone numbers are included for each, in case you would like to contact them. Use these resources to obtain general information, locate internships, and/or to send your résumé for possible jobs.

Women's National Basketball Association
645 Fifth Avenue
New York, NY 10022
212-688-9622

EASTERN CONFERENCE

Charlotte Sting
27069 Water Ridge Parkway
Suite 400
Charlotte, NC 28717
704-329-4960

Cleveland Rockers
Gund Arena
1 Center Court
Cleveland, OH 44145
216-420-2000

Houston Comets
Two Greenway Plaza
Suite 400
Houston, TX 77046
713-627-9622

New York Liberty
Two Penn Plaza
New York, NY 10121
212-564-9622

WESTERN CONFERENCE

Los Angeles Sparks
Great Western Forum
3900 W. Manchester Boulevard
Ingewood, CA 90306
310-330-2434

Phoenix Mercury
America West Arena
201 East Jefferson
Phoenix, AZ 85004
602-514-8333

Sacramento Monarchs
Arco Arena
One Sports Parkway
Sacramento, CA 95834
916-928-3650

Utah Starzz
Delta Center
301 West South Temple
Salt Lake City, UT 08104
801-325-2000

APPENDIX IX
NATIONAL FOOTBALL LEAGUE

The following is a listing of the teams and organizations in the National Football League. Those in the American Football Conference (AFL) are listed first; those in the National Football Conference follow.

Names, addresses, and phone numbers are included for each. Use them to obtain general information, locate internships, and/or to send your résumé for possible jobs.

National Football League (NFL)
280 Park Avenue
New York, NY 10017
212-450-2000

NFL (National Football League) Players Association
2021 L Street NW
Washington, DC 20036
202-463-2200

AMERICAN FOOTBALL CONFERENCE (AFC)

Baltimore Ravens
1101 Owings Mills Road
Owings Mills, MD 2117
410-654-6200

Buffalo Bills
One Bills Drive
Orchard Park, NY 14127
716-648-1800

Cincinnati Bengals
One Bengals Drive
Cincinnati, OH 45204
513-621-3550

Cleveland Browns Trust*
80 First Avenue
Berea, OH 44017

Denver Broncos
13655 E. Dove Valley Parkway
Engelwood, CO 80112
303-649-9000

Indianapolis Colts
7001 West 56th Street
Indianapolis, IN 46254
317-297-2658

Jacksonville Jaguars
One ALLTEL Stadium Place
Jacksonville, FL 32202
904-633-6000

Kansas City Chiefs
One Arrowhead Drive
Kansas City, MO 64129
816-924-9300

Miami Dolphins
7500 SW 30th Street
Davie, FL 33329
954-452-7000

New England Patriots
Foxboro Stadium/Route 1
Foxboro, MA 02035
508-543-8200

New York Jets
1000 Fulton Avenue
Hempstead, NY 11550
516-538-6600

Oakland Raiders
1220 Harbor Bay Parkway
Alameda, CA 94502
510-864-5000

Pittsburgh Steelers
300 Stadium Circle
Pittsburgh, PA 15212
412-323-1200

San Diego Chargers
Qualcomm Stadium
San Diego, CA 92160
619-280-2111

Seattle Seahawks
11220 N.E. 53rd Street
Kirkland, WA 98033
206-827-9777

Tennessee Oilers
Baptist Sports Park
7640 Highway 70 South
Nashville, TN 37221

NATIONAL FOOTBALL CONFERENCE (NFC)

Arizona Cardinals
8701 South Hardy Drive
Phoenix, AZ 85284
602-379-0101

Atlanta Falcons
One Falcon Place
Suwanee, GA 30174
770-945-1111

Carolina Panthers
800 South Mint Street
Charlotte, NC 28202
704-358-7000

Chicago Bears
1000 Football Drive
Lake Forest, IL 60045
847-295-6600

Dallas Cowboys
One Cowboys Parkway
Irving, TX 75063
214-556-9900

Detroit Lions
1200 Featherstone Road
Pontiac, MI 48342
313-335-4131

Green Bay Packers
1265 Lombardi Avenue
Green Bay, WI 54307
414-496-5700

Minnesota Vikings
9520 Viking Drive
Eden Prairie, MN 55344
612-828-6500

New Orleans Saints
5800 Airline Highway
New Orleans, LA 70003
504-733-0255

* The name is owned by the city of Cleveland. They have the opportunity to obtain the next franchise available.

New York Giants
Giants Stadium
East Rutherford, NJ 07073
201-935-8111

Philadelphia Eagles
3501 Broad Street
Philadelphia, PA 19148
215-463-2500

St. Louis Rams
One Rams Way
St. Louis, MO 63045
314-982-7267

San Francisco 49ers
4949 Centennial Boulevard
Santa Clara, CA 95054
408-562-4949

Tampa Bay Buccaneers
One Buccaneer Place
Tampa, FL 33607
813-870-2700

Washington Redskins
21300 Redskin Park Drive
Ashburn, VA 20147
703-478-8900

APPENDIX X
CANADIAN FOOTBALL LEAGUE

The following is a listing of the teams in the Canadian Football League (CFL). Names, addresses, and phone numbers are included for each. Use them to obtain general information, to locate internships, and/or to send your résumé for possible jobs. When sending mail from the United States to Canada, remember to check postage rates.

**CANADIAN FOOTBALL
    LEAGUE (CFL)**
1200 Bay Street
Toronto, Ontario, Canada
M5R 2A5
416-322-9650

EAST DIVISION

Hamilton Tiger-Cats
Lloyd D. Jackson Square
2 King Street West
Hamilton, Ontario, Canada
L8P 1A2
905-521-5666

Montreal Alouettes
Olympic Stadium
4545 Avenue Pierre-de Coubertin
P.O. Box 65, Station M
Montreal, Quebec, Canada
H1V 3L6
514-252-4666

Toronto Argonauts
Skydome Gate 9
P.O. Box 2005
Station B
Toronto, Ontario, Canada
M5T 3H8
416-341-5151

Winnipeg Blue Bombers
1465 Maroons Road
Winnipeg, Manitoba, Canada
R3G 0L6
204-784-2583

WEST DIVISION

B.C. Lions
10605 135th Street
Surrey, British Columbia, Canada
V3T 4C8
604-930-5466

Calgary Stampeders
McMahon Stadium
1817 Crowchild Trail N.W.
Calgary, Alberta, Canada
T2M 4R6
403-289-0205

Edmonton Eskimos
9023 - 111 Avenue
Edmonton, Alberta, Canada
T5B 0C3
403-448-1525

Saskatchewan Roughriders
2940 - 10th Avenue
P.O. Box 1277
Regina, Saskatchewan, Canada
S4P 3B8
308-569-2323

APPENDIX XI
NATIONAL HOCKEY LEAGUE TEAMS

The following is a listing of the teams and related organizations in the National Hockey League (NHL). Names, addresses, and phone numbers are included for each. Use them to obtain general information, locate internships, and/or to send your résumé for possible jobs.

Remember when sending mail from the United States to Canada to check postage rates.

National Hockey League (NHL)
800 McGill College Avenue
Suite 2600
Montreal, Quebec, Canada
H3A 3J6
514-288-9220

1251 Avenue of the Americas
New York, NY 10020
212-789-2000

(NHL) National Hockey League
 Players Association
1 Dundas Street West
Suite 2300
Toronto, Ontario, Canada
M56 1Z3
416-408-4040

Mighty Ducks of Anaheim
Arrowhead Pond of Anaheim
695 Katelia Avenue
Anaheim, CA 92803

Boston Bruins
Fleet Center
Boston, MA 02114
617-624-1050

Buffalo Sabres
Marine Midland Arena
One Seymour H. Knox III Plaza
Buffalo, NY 14203
716-855-4100

Calgary Flames
Canadian Airlines Saddledome
Box 1540-Station M
Calgary, Alberta, Canada
T2P 3B9
403-777-2177

Carolina Hurricanes
5000 Aerial Center
Suite 100
Morrisville, NC 27560
919-467-7825

Chicago Blackhawks
1901 West Madison Street
Chicago, IL 60612
312-455-7000

Colorado Avalanche
McNichols Sports Arena
1635 Clay Street
Denver, CO 80204
303-893-6700

Dallas Stars
211 Cowboy Parkway
Irving, TX 75063
972-868-2890

Detroit Red Wings
Joe Louis Sports Arena
600 Civic Drive
Detroit, MI 48226
313-396-7544

Edmonton Oilers
11230-110 Street
Edmonton, Alberta T5G 3G8
403-474-8561

Florida Panthers
100 N.E. Third Avenue
Fort Lauderdale, FL 33301
954-768-1900

Los Angeles Kings
The Great Western Forum
3900 West Manchester Boulevard
Inglewood, CA 90306
310-419-3160

Montreal Canadians
1260 Rue de la Gauchetiere Ouest
Montreal, Quebec, Canada
H3B 5E8
514-932-2582

New Jersey Devils
Continental Airlines Arena
500 Route 120 North
East Rutherford, NJ 07073
201-935-6050

New York Islanders
Nassau Coliseum
Uniondale, NY 11553
516-794-4100

New York Rangers
Madison Square Garden
2 Pennsylvania Plaza
10th Floor
New York, NY 10121
212-465-6000

Ottawa Senators
Corel Centre
1000 Palladium Drive
Kenasta, Ontario, Canada
K2V 1A5
613-599-0250

Philadelphia Flyers
CoreStates Center
1 CoreStates Complex
Philadelphia, PA 19148
215-465-4500

Phoenix Coyotes
One Renaissance Square
2 North Central, Suite 1930
Phoenix, AZ 85004
602-379-2800

Pittsburgh Penguins
Civic Arena
Gate 9
Pittsburgh, PA 15219
412-642-1800

St. Louis Blues
1401 Clark Avenue
St. Louis, MO 63103
314-622-2500

San Jose Sharks
San Jose Arena
525 West Santa Clara Street
San Jose, CA 95113
408-287-7070

Tampa Bay Lighting
Ice Palace
401 Channelside Drive
Tampa, FL 33602
813-229-2658

Toronto Maple Leafs
Maple Leaf Gardens
60 Carlton Street
Toronto, Ontario, Canada
M5B 1L1
416-977-1641

Vancouver Canucks
General Motors Place
800 Griffiths Way
Vancouver, British Columbia, Canada
V6B 6G1
604-899-4600

Washington Capitals
USAir Arena
Landover, MD 20785
301-386-7000

APPENDIX XII
AMERICAN HOCKEY LEAGUE TEAMS

The following is a listing of the teams in the American Hockey League (AHL) provided by that organization. Names, addresses, and telephone numbers of teams are included, in case you would like to contact them to obtain general information, locate internships, and/or to send your résumés for possible jobs.

Remember to check postage rates when sending mail from the United States to Canada.

American Hockey League (AHL)
425 Union Street
West Springfield, MA 01089
413-781-2030

Adirondack Red Wings
1 Civic Center Plaza
Glens Falls, NY 12801
518-798-0366

Albany River Rats
51 South Pearl Street
Albany, NY 12207
518-487-2244

Beast of New Haven
275 South Orange Street
New Haven, CT 06510
203-777-7878

Cincinnati Mighty Ducks
2250 Seymour Avenue
Cincinnati, OH 45212
513-351-3999

Fredericton Canadiens
P.O. Box HABS
Fredericton, New Brunswick, Canada
E3B 4Y2
506-459-4227

Hamilton Bulldogs
85 York Boulevard
Hamilton, Ontario, Canada
L8R 3L4
905-529-8500

Hartford Wolf Pack
196 Trumbull Street
Hartford, CT 06103
860-246-7825

Hershey Bears
P.O. Box 866
Hershey, PA 17033
717-534-3380

Kentucky ThoroughBlades
410 West Vine Street
Lexington, KY 40507
606-259-1996

Lowell Lock Monsters
77 Merrimack Street
Lowell, MA 01852
978-458-7825

Philadelphia Phantoms
The CoreStates Spectrum
1 CoreStates Complex
Philadelphia, PA 19148
215-465-4522

Portland Pirates
85 Free Street
Portland, ME 04101
207-828-4665

Providence Bruins
1 LaSalle Square
Providence, RI 02903
401-273-5000

Rochester Americans
50 South Street
Rochester, NY 14604
716-454-5335

Saint John Flames
P.O. Box 4040, Station B
Saint John, New Brunswick, Canada
E2M 5E6
506-635-2637

Springfield Falcons
P.O. Box 3190
Springfield, MA 01101
413-739-3389

St. John's Maple Leafs
6 Logy Bay Road
St. John's, New Foundland, Canada
A1A 1J3
709-726-1010

Syracuse Crunch
800 South State Street
Syracuse, NY 13202
315-473-4444

Worchester IceCats
303 Main Street
Worchester, MA 01608
508-798-5400

APPENDIX XIII
MAJOR LEAGUE SOCCER

The following is a list of the teams in Major League Soccer (MLS). Names, addresses, and phone numbers are included for each. Use them to obtain general information, to locate internships, and/or to send your résumé for job possibilities.

MAJOR LEAGUE SOCCER
110 East 42nd Street
10th Floor
New York, NY 10017
212-687-1400

EASTERN DIVISION

Columbus Crew
77 East Nationwide Boulevard
Columbus, OH 43215
614-221-2739

D.C. United
13832 Redskin Drive
Herndon, VA 20171
703-478-6600

New England Revolution
Foxboro Stadium
60 Washington Street–Route 1
Foxboro, MA 02035
508-543-0350

N.Y./N.J. MetroStars
One Harmon Plaza
8th Floor
Secaucus, NJ 07094
201-583-7000

Tampa Bay Mutiny
1408 North Westshore Boulevard
Suite 1004
Tampa, FL 33607
813-288-0096

WESTERN DIVISION

Colorado Rapids
555 17th Street
Suite 3350
Denver, CO 80202
303-299-1570

Dallas Burn
2602 McKinney
Suite 200
Dallas, TX 75204
214-979-0303

Kansas City Wizards
706 Broadway Street
Suite 100
Kansas City, MO 64105
861-472-0299

Los Angeles Galaxy
1640 South Sepulveda Boulevard
Suite 114
Los Angeles, CA 90025
310-445-1260

San Jose Clash
1265 El Camino Real
Second Floor
Santa Clara, CA 95050
408-241-9922

APPENDIX XIV
ADDITIONAL PROFESSIONAL
SOCCER LEAGUES

The following is a listing of additional professional soccer leagues in the United States and Canada. Names, addresses, and phone numbers are included for each in case you would like to contact them. Use them to obtain general information, locate internships, and/or to send your résumé for job possibilities.

A-League/USISL
14497 North Dale Mabry
Suite 211
Tampa, FL 33618
813-963-3909

A-LEAGUE

PACIFIC DIVISION

California Jaguars
12 Clay Street
Salinas, CA 93901
408-757-7475

Colorado Foxes
6200 Dahlia Street
Commerce City, CO 80022
303-893-6937

El Paso Patriots
6941 Industrial
El Paso, TX 79915
915-771-6620

Orange County Zodiac
540 North Golden Circle
Suite 212
Santa Ana, CA 92705
714-479-0880

Seattle Sounders
10838 Main Street
Bellevue, WA 98004
206-622-3415

VanCouver 86ers
1126 Douglas Road
Burnaby, British Columbia, Canada
V5C 4Z6
604-299-0086

CENTRAL DIVISION

Atlanta Ruckus
1131 Alpharetta Street
Roswell, GA 30075
770-645-6655

Milwaukee Rampage
Uihlein Soccer Park
7101 West Good Hope Road
Milwaukee, WI 53223
414-358-2655

Minnesota Thunder
1700 150th Avenue NE
Blaine, MN 55449
612-785-3668

Nashville Metros
7115 South Springs Drive
Franklin, TN 37067
615-771-8015

New Orleans Riverboat Gamblers
5690 Eastover Drive
New Orleans, LA 70128
504-241-4400

Orlando Sundogs
One Citrus Bowl Place
Orlando, FL 32805
407-872-0707

ATLANTIC DIVISION

Carolina Dynamo
3517 West Wendover Avenue
Greensboro, NC 27407
910-852-9969

Charleston Battery
4401 Belle Oaks Drive
Suite 450
Charleston, SC 29405
803-740-7787

Hershey Wildcats
100 West Hersheypark Drive
Hershey, PA 17033
717-534-8900

Jacksonville Cyclones
9428 Bay Meadows Road
Suite 175
Jacksonville, FL 32256
904-737-9800

Raleigh Flyers
130 Wind Chime Court
Raleigh, NC 27615
919-848-3063

Richmond Kickers
2320 West Main Street
Richmond, VA 23220
804-644-5425

NORTHEAST DIVISION

Connecticut Wolves
P.O. Box 3196
New Britain, CT 06050
203-223-0710

Long Island Rough Riders
Greater New York Soccer, Inc.
1670 Old Country Road
Suite 227
Plainview, NY 11803
516-756-4425

Montreal Impact
800 Langelier
Suite 104
St. Leonard, Quebec, Canada
H1P 3K2
514-328-3668

Rochester Rhinos
333 North Plymouth Avenue
Rochester, NY 14608
716-454-5425

Toronto Lynx
c/o Hit Pro Soccer, Inc.
55 University Avenue
Suite 506
Toronto, Ontario, Canada
M5J 2H7
416-360-4646

Worcester Wildfire
500 Main Street
Suite 515
Worcester, MA 01608
508-755-7799

USISL "D3"
(Professional League)

WEST DIVISION

Arizona Aztecs
802 North 3rd Avenue
Phoenix, AZ 85003
602-276-2237

Chico Rooks
5 Kingston Circle
Chico, CA 95926
916-343-7665

Hawaii Tsunami
7040 Kamilo Street
Honolulu, HI 96825
808-395-1470

Reno Rattlers
P.O. Box 9179
1299 Uri Court
Incline Village, NV 89452
702-832-2283

Sacramento Scorpions
1601 Fulton Avenue
Suite 11
Sacramento, CA 95825
916-485-7288

San Francisco Bay Seals
120 Magallan Avenue
San Francisco, CA 94116
510-373-9433

Valley Golden Eagles
11305 Goes Street
Sun Valley, CA 91352
714-832-0650

SOUTH CENTRAL DIVISION

Austin Lone Stars
10409 Tweedsmuir Drive
Austin, TX 78750
512-335-0427

Dallas/Ft. Worth Toros
6434 Maple Avenue
Suite 112–7
Dallas, TX 75235
214-654-0544

Houston Hurricanes
1415 North Loop West
Suite 150
Houston, TX 77008
713-862-5425

Tulsa Roughnecks
2214 West Houston
Broken Arrow, OK 74012
918-258-1881

NORTH CENTRAL DIVISION

Chicago Stringers
545 Consumers Avenue
Palatine, IL 60067
847-670-5425

Dublin Xoggs
1812 Barrington Road
Columbus, OH 43221
614-486-6539

Rockford Raptors
8800 East Riverside Boulevard
Loves Park, IL 61111
815-885-1135

NORTHEAST DIVISION

Cape Cod Crusaders
349 Main Street
Hyannis, MA 02601
508-790-4782

Central Jersey Riptide
214 Highway 18
East Brunswick, NJ 08816
908-296-9166

New Jersey Phantoms
One Park Avenue
Hudson, NJ 03051
603-578-5588

Albany Alleycats
1110 Nott Street
Schenectady, NY 12308
518-462-3911

North Jersey Imperials
223 Gates Road
Little Ferry, NJ 07643
201-440-9004

Rhode Island Stingrays
P.O. Box 16251
Rumford, RI 02916
401-351-8455

Vermont Wanderers
Green Mountain Indoor Sports Center
25 New England Drive
Essex Junction, VT 05452
802-878-7740

SOUTH ATLANTIC DIVISION

Charlotte Eagles
2101 Sardis Road North
Suite 201
Charlotte, NC 28227
704-841-8644

Florida Strikers
10360 C–Courtside Lane
Boca Raton, FL 33428
407-479-2637

Mobile Revelers
P.O. Box 851538
Mobile, AL 36685
334-432-4625

Myrtle Beach Seawags
4033 Highway 501 West
Myrtle Beach, SC 29577
803-236-1968

South Carolina Shamrocks
P.O. Box 1923
Spartansburg, SC 29304
803-585-0083

Daytona Tigers
1331 Beville Road
Daytona Beach, FL 32119
904-304-0700

Wilmington Hammerheads
1630 Military Cutoff Road
Wilminton, NC 28403
910-256-0975

MID-ATLANTIC DIVISION

Baltimore Rays
7048 Golden Ring Road
Baltimore, MD 21237
410-682-2222

Delaware Wizards
Peddlers Village
Suite 3A
Christiana, DE 19702
301-738-1305

New Jersey Stallions
3 Mount Prospect Avenue
Clifton, NJ 07013
201-773-2299

Philadelphia Freedom
100 Matsonford Road
Building 2, Suite 300
Radnor, PA 19087
610-971-0401

Reading Rage
2201 Ridgewood Road
#375
Wyomissing, PA 19610
610-375-4405

South Jersey Dragons
12 East Stow Road, Ste. 150
Marlton, NJ 08053
609-567-5748

APPENDIX XV
COLLEGE ATHLETIC CONFERENCES

The following is a listing of many of the college athletic conferences in the country. It was provided by the National Collegiate Athletic Association (NCCA). The names, addresses, and phone numbers are included so that you can call or write for information.

National Collegiate Athletic Association (NCAA)
6201 College Boulevard
Overland Park, KS 66211
913-339-1906

America East
P.O. Box 69
Orono, MA 04473
207-866-2383

Atlantic Coast Conference
P.O. Drawer ACC
Greensboro, NC 27419
910-854-8787

Atlantic 10 Conference
2 Penn Center Plaza
Suite 1410
Philadelphia, PA 19102
215-751-0500

Big East Conference
56 Exchange Terrace
Providence, RI 02903
401-272-9108

Big Sky Conference
P.O. Box 1459
Ogden, UT 84402
801-392-1978

Big South Conference
Winthrop Coliseum
Eden Terrace
Rock Hill, SC 29733
803-817-6340

Big Ten Conference
1500 West Higgins Road
Park Ridge, IL 60068
847-696-1010

Big Twelve Conference
2201 Stemmons Freeway
Dallas, TX 75207
214-742-1212

Big West Conference
2 Corporate Park Suite 206
Irvine, CA 92606
714-261-2525

California Collegiate Athletic Association
40 Via Di Roma
Long Beach, CA 90803
310-985-4051

Capital Athletic Conference
24750 Marva Point Way
Hollywood, MD 20036
301-373-3293

Carolinas-Virginia Athletic Conference
26 Cub Drive
Thomasville, NC 27360
910-884-0482

Centennial Conference
P.O. Box 2003
Franklin & Marshall College
Lancaster, PA 17604
717-399-4463

Central Collegiate Hockey Association
100 South State Street
Ann Arbor, MI 48109
313-764-2590

Central Intercollegiate Athletic Association
P.O. Box 7349
Hampton, VA 23666
804-865-0071

City University of New York Athletic Conference
250 Bedford Park Boulevard
West Lehman College
The Apex
Bronx, NY 10466
718-960-7193

College Conference of Illinois and Wisconsin
Wheaton College
Wheaton, IL 60187
708-752-5167

Collegiate Water Polo Association
MacDonough Hall
U.S. Naval Academy
Annapolis, MD 21402
410-267-3958

Colonial Athletic Association
8625 Patterson Avenue
Richmond, VA 23229
804-754-1616

Commonwealth Coast Conference
Anna Maria College
Sunset Lane
P.O. Box 116
Paxton, MA 01612
508-849-3446

Conference USA
35 East Wacker
Suite 650
Chicago, IL 60601
312-553-0483

Constitution Athletic Conference
Massachusetts Institute of Technology
77 Massachusetts Ave.
Cambridge, MA 02139
617-253-4497

Dixie Intercollegiate Athletic Conference
3101 Elwood Avenue
Richmond, VA 23221
804-358-3543

Eastern College Athletic Conference
P.O. Box 3
Centerville, MA 02632
508-771-5060

Eastern College Football Conference
175 Forest Street
Bentley College
Waltham, MA 02154
617-891-2330

Eastern Intercollegiate Volleyball Association
42 Warren Street
The State University of New Jersey, Rutgers
Newark, NJ 07102
201-688-5474

Eastern Intercollegiate Wrestling Association
P.O. Box 3
Centerville, MA 02632
508-771-6060

Eastern Wrestling League
Lock Haven University
Lock Haven, PA 17745
717-693-2114

Empire Athletic Association
Hartwick College
Oneonta, NY 13820
607-431-4702

Freedom Football Conference
Plymouth State College
Plymouth, NH 03264
603-535-2751

Gateway Football Conference
1000 Union Station
Suite 333
St. Louis MO 63103
314-421-2268

Great Lakes Football Conference
P.O. Box 869
Saint Joseph's College
Rensselear, IN 47978
219-666-6157

Great Lakes Intercollegiate Athletic Conference
3250 West Big Beaver
Suite 300
Troy, MI 48084
810-649-2036

Great Lakes Valley Conference
Pan Am Plaza
201 South Capitol Avenue
Suite 560
Indianapolis, IN 46225
317-237-5636

Great Northeast Athletic Conference River College
420 South Main Street
Nashua, NH 03060
603-888-1311

Gulf South Conference
4 Office Park Circle
Birmingham, AL 35223
205-870-9750

Hockey East Association
Volpe Athletic Complex
Merrimack College
North Andover, MA 01845
508-837-5341

Indiana Collegiate Athletic Conference
903 East Street
North Manchester, IN 46962
219-982-6422

Iowa Intercollegiate Athletic Conference
608 33rd Street
West Des Moines, IA 50265
515-225-3021

Ivy Group
120 Alexander Street
Princeton, NJ 08544
609-258-6426

Lone Star Conference
1221 West Campbell Road
Suite 217
Richardson, TX 75080
214-234-0033

Massachusetts State College Athletic Conference
Salem State College
Salem, MA 01970
506-741-6570

Metro Atlantic Athletic Conference
1090 Armboy Avenue
Edison, NJ 08837
908-225-0202

Michigan Intercollegiate Athletic Association
P.O. Box 643
Hillsdale, MI 49242
517-439-0492

Mid-America Intercollegiate Athletics Association
P.O. Box 508
Maryville, MO 64468
816-582-5665

Mid American Conference
Four SeaGate
Suite 102
Toledo, OH 43604
419-249-7177

Mid-Continent Conference
40 Shuman Boulevard
Suite 118
Naperville, IL 60563
630-416-7580

Mid-Eastern Athletic Conference
102 North Elm Street
Suite 401
Greensboro, NC 27401
910-275-9961

Middle Atlantic States Conference
1010 College Avenue
Lebanon Valley College
Annville, PA 17003
717-867-6395

Midwest Conference
Beloit College
700 College Street
Beloit, WI 53511
608-363-2718

Midwest Intercollegiate Football Conference
3250 West Big Beaver
Suite 300
Troy, MI 48084
810-649-2036

Midwestern Collegiate Conference
201 South Capital Avenue
Suite 500
Indianapolis, IN 46225
317-237-5622

Midwestern Intercollegiate Volleyball Association
Ohio State University
261 Northmoor Place
Columbus, OH 43214
614-262-3290

Minnesota Intercollegiate Athletic Conference
2004 Randolph Avenue
Mail # 4014
College of St. Catherine
St. Paul, MN 55105
612-690-8734

Missouri Valley Conference
1000 St. Louis Union Station
Suite 333
St. Louis, MO 63103
314-421-0339

Mountain Pacific Sports Federation
2 Corporate Park
Suite 206
Irvine, CA 92606
714-261-2525

New England College Wrestling Association
Wesleyan University
Middletown, CT 06459
203-685-2896

New England Collegiate Conference
P.O. Box 1307
Farmington, CT 06034
860-677-1269

New England Football Conference
Framingham State College
100 State Street
Framingham, MA 01701
608-626-4614

New England Small College Athletic Conference
Ferris Athletic Center
Trinity College
Hartford, CT 06106
860-297-2055

New England Women's Eight
Wellesley College
Wellesley, MA 02181
617-283-2001

New Jersey Athletic Conference
Rowan College
201 Mullca Hill Road
Glassboro, NJ 08028
609-256-4888

New York Collegiate Athletic
Conference
3031 Arrowhead Lane
Norristown, PA 19401
610-825-5068

New York State Women's Collegiate
Athletic Association
Union College
Alumni Gym
Schenectady, NY 12308
518-386-6546

North Central Intercollegiate Athletic
Conference
Ramkota Inn
2400 North Louise Avenue
Sioux Falls, SD 57107
605-338-0907

North Coast Athletic Conference
24700 Center Ridge
10
Westlake, OH 44145
216-871-8100

Northeast Conference
900 Route 9
Woodbridge, NJ 07095
908-636-9119

Northeast-10 Conference
P.O. Box 1197
Westfield, MA 01066
413-562-4789

Northern California
Athletic Conference
2551 Garfield Avenue
Carmichael, CA 95608
916-488-4243

Northern Collegiate
Hockey Association
410 South Third Street
River Falls, WI 54022
715-425-3246

Northern Sun Intercollegiate
Conference
6458 City West Parkway
Suite 100
Eden Prairie, MN 55344
612-943-3929

Ohio Athletic Conference
8984 Darrow Road
#2B
P.O. Box 400
Twinsburg, OH 44047
216-963-0444

Ohio Valley Conference
279 Franklin Road
Suite 103
Brentwood, TN 37027
615-371-1698

Old Dominion Athletic Conference
P.O. Box 971
Salem, VA 24153
540-389-7373

Pacific-10-Conference
800 South Broadway
Suite 400
Walnut Creek, CA 94596
510-932-4411

Pacific West Conference
P.O. Box 2002
Billings, MT 59103
408-657-2932

Patriot League
3897 Adler Place
Building C
Suite 310
Bethlehem, PA 18017
610-691-2414

Peach Belt Athletic Conference
P.O. Box 204290
Augusta, GA 30917
706-860-8499

Pennsylvania Athletic Conference
Beaver College
Glenside, PA 19038
215-572-2194

Pennsylvania State Athletic
Conference
105 Zimmerill Building
Lock Haven University
Lock Haven, PA 17745
717-693-2512

Pioneer Football League
1000 Union Station
Suite 333
St. Louis, MO 63103
314-421-2268

President's Athletic Conference
51 West College Street
Waynesburg College
Waynesburg, PA 15370
412-852-3251

Rocky Mountain Athletic Conference
1631 Mesa Avenue
Copper Building-Suite B
Colorado Springs, CO 80906
719-471-0066

St. Louis Intercollegiate Athletic
Conference
700 College Avenue
Blackburn College
Carlinville, IL 62626
217-854-5526

Skyline Conference
King Boulevard
New Jersey Institute of Technology
Newark, NJ 07102
201-596-5727

South Atlantic Conference
McGregor Downs
Suite 201
10601 Johnston Road
Charlotte, NC 28226
704-543-1181

Southeastern Conference
2201 Civic Center Boulevard
Birmingham, AL 35203
205-458-3000

Southern California Intercollegiate
Athletic Conference
1950 Third Street
University of La Verne
La Verne, CA 91750
909-593-3511

Southern Collegiate Athletic
Conference
3338 Gwinnett Plantation Way
Suite A-1
Deluth, GA 30136
770-495-9563

Southern Conference
One West Pack Square
Suite 1508
Asheville, NC 28801
704-255-7872

Southern Intercollegiate
Athletic Conference
P.O. Box 92032
Atlanta, GA 30314
404-659-3380

Southern Conference
8150 Central Expressway
Suite 930
Dallas, TX 75206
214-750-7522

Southwestern Athletic Conference
1500 Sugar Bowl Drive
New Orleans, LA 70112
504-523-7574

State University of New York
Athletic Conference
State University College
Fredonia, NY 14063
716-673-3105

Sun Belt Conference
One Galleria Boulevard
Suite 2115
Metairie, LA 70001
504-834-6600

Sunshine State Conference
7061 Grand National Drive
Suite 138
Orlando, FL 32810
407-248-8460

Trans American Athletic Conference
The Commons
Suite 108-B
3370 Vineville Avenue
Macon, GA 31204
912-474-3394

University Athletic Association
668 Mount Hope Avenue
Rochester, NY 14620
716-273-5881

Upstate Collegiate Athletic Conference
Skidmore College
Saratoga Springs, NY 12866
518-584-5000

West Coast Conference
300 Oyster Point Boulevard
Suite 221
South San Francisco, CA 94080
415-873-8622

West Virginia Intercollegiate Athletic Conference
1422 Main Street
Princeton, WV 24740
304-487-6298

Western Athletic Conference
9250 East Costilla Avenue
Suite 300
Englewood, CO 80112
303-799-9221

Western Collegiate Hockey Association
10 University Drive
170 SPHC
Deluth, MN 55812
218-726-8732

Western Water Polo Association
580 Brambles Way
Orange, CA 92669
714-639-9106

Wisconsin State University Conference
P.O. Box 8010
Madison, WI 53708
608-263-4402

Wisconsin Women's Intercollegiate Athletic Conference
P.O. Box 8010
Madison, WI 53708
608-263-4402

Yankee Conference
University of Richmond
P.O. Box 8
Richmond, VA 23173
804-289-8371

APPENDIX XVI
BOXING AND WRESTLING PROMOTERS AND PROMOTION COMPANIES

The following is a listing of some of the larger boxing and wrestling promoters and promotion companies in the United States. You will notice that most are located in the eastern part of the country. However, the majority of these organizations promote events nationally as well as abroad.

Big Fights
9 East 40th Street
New York, NY 10016
212-532-1717

Houston Boxing Association
72 Heights Boulevard
Houston, TX 77007
713-862-0604

Don King Productions
32 East 69th Street
New York, NY 10021
212-794-1266

Butch Lewis Productions
250 West 57th Street
New York, NY 10107
212-582-4344

Main Events Productions, Inc.
811 Totowa Road
Totowa, NJ 07512
201-389-9000

MSG Productions
Madison Square Garden
New York, NY 10020

Tap Rank Inc.
3980 Howard Hughes Highway
Las Vegas, NV 89109
702-732-2717

Titan Sports
W.W. Federation
1241 East Main Street
Standford, CT 06902
203-352-8600

World Championship Wrestling
C.N.N. Center NW 105366
Atlanta, GA 30303
404-827-2066

APPENDIX XVII
CABLE AND NETWORK TELEVISION SPORTS DEPARTMENTS

The following is a listing of cable and network television sports departments. This list only includes the larger stations. Look in your television guide for information on other stations. Use them to obtain general information, locate internships, and/or to send your résumés for possible jobs.

ABC Sports
47 West 66th Street
13th Floor
New York, NY 10023
212-887-4867

CBC Sports
P.O. Box 500 Station A 5 H 100
Toronto, Ontario, Canada
M5W 1E6
416-205-6523

CBS Sports
51 West 52nd Street
25th Floor
New York, NY 10019
212-975-4321

Classic Sports Network
35 East 21st Street
New York, NY 10010
212-529-8000

CNN Sports
One CNN Center
P.O. Box 105366
Atlanta, GA 30348
404-827-1500

ESPN & ESPN2
ESPN Plaza
Bristol, CT 06010
203-585-2000

Fox Sports
5746 Sunset Boulevard
Sunset Building
Los Angeles, CA 90929
213-856-2128

HBO Sports
1100 Avenue of The Americas
New York, NY 10036
212-512-1066

Madison Square Garden (MSG)
4 Penn Plaza
New York, NY 10001
212-563-8000

NBC Sports
30 Rockefeller Plaza
New York, NY 10020
212-664-4444

Newsport
3 Crossways Park West
Woodbury, NY 11797
516-921-3764

Prime SportsChannel Networks
5251 Gulfton Street
Houston, TX 77081
713-661-0078

Showtime Sports
1633 Broadway
New York, NY 10019
212-708-1600

Sports Channel New York
200 Crossways Park West
Woodbury, NY 11797
516-364-3650

Turner Sports
P.O. Box 105366
Atlanta, GA 30348
404-827-1735

USA Network
1230 Avenue of the Americas
New York, NY 10020
212-408-9100

APPENDIX XVIII
BIBLIOGRAPHY

A. BOOKS

There are thousands of books written on all aspects of the sports industry. The books listed below are separated into general categories. The subject matter of many of the books overlap.

These books can be found in bookstores and libraries. If your local library does not have the ones you want, ask your librarian to order them for you through the Inter-Library Loan System.

This list is designed as a starting point. For other books that might interest you, look in the sports section of bookstores and libraries. You can also check *Books in Print* for other books on the subject. *Books in Print* may be located in the reference section of libraries as well as many bookstores.

AMATEUR ATHLETICS
Vanderveer, Tara, and Ryan, Joan. *Shooting from the Outside: How a Coach and Her Olympic Team Transformed Women's Basketball.* New York: Avon Books, 1997.

BASEBALL
Adair, Robert Kem. *The Physics of Baseball.* New York: Harper-Collins, 1995.

Bakalar, Nick. *The Baseball Fan's Companion: How to Master the Subtleties of the World's Most Complex Team Sport and Learn to Watch the Game Like an Expert.* New York: Macmillan, 1996.

Dickson, Paul. *The Joy of Keeping Score: How Scoring the Game Has Influenced and Enhanced the History of Baseball.* New York: Walker & Co., 1996.

Forker, Dom. *1,001 Baseball Questions Your Friends Can't Answer.* New York: Signet Publications, 1997.

Fox, Stephen R. *Big Leagues: Professional Baseball, Football and Basketbook in National Memory.* New York: Morrow, 1994.

Frommer, Harvey, ed. *The New York Yankee Encyclopedia.* New York: Macmillan, 1997.

Gardner, Robert, and Shortelle, Dennis. *The Forgotten Players: The Story of Black Baseball in America.* New York: Walker and Co., 1993.

Halberstam, David. *Summer of '49.* New York: Avon Books, 1997.

Mandel, Brett. *Minor Players, Major Dreams.* Lincoln, Nebr.: University of Nebraska Press, 1997.

Monteleone, John J., Gola, Mark, and Plunkett, Michael. *The Louisville Slugger Ultimate Book of Hitting.* New York: Henry Holt, 1997.

Orodenker, Richard. *The Writers' Game.* New York: Twayne Publishers, 1996.

Ribowsky, Mark. *A Complete History of the Negro Leagues 1884 to 1955.* New York: Birch Lane Press, 1995.

Seaver, Tom, and Lowenfish, Lee. *The Art of Pitching.* New York: William Morrow & Co., 1994.

Schlossberd, Dan, Shea, Stuart, Tully, Mike, and Bradley, Michael. *1997 Baseball Almanac.* New York: Signet, 1997.

Simpson, Allan, ed. *Baseball America's 1997 Directory: Major and Minor League Names, Addresses, Schedules, Phone and Fax Numbers.* New York: Simon & Schuster, 1997.

Thorn, John, Palmer, Pete, and Gershman, Michael, eds. *Total Baseball: The Official Encyclopedia of Major League Baseball (5th Ed.).* New York: Viking Press, 1997.

BASKETBALL
Carril, Pete, and White, Dan. *The Smart Take from the Strong: The Basketball Philosophy of Pete Carril.* New York: Simon & Schuster, 1997.

Feinstein, John. *A March to Madness: The View from the Floor in the Atlantic Coast Conference.* New York: Little Brown & Company, 1998.

Jordan, Michael. *Hang Time: Days and Dreams with Michael Jordan.* New York: St. Martin's Press, 1993.

Karl, George Matthew, and Yaeger, Dong. *This Game's the Best!: So Why Don't They Quit Screwing with It?* New York: St. Martin's Press, 1997.

Keteyian, Armen, Araton, Harvey, and Dardin, Martin F. *Money Players: Days and Nights Inside the New NBA.* New York: Pocket Books, 1997.

Lee, Spike, and Wiley, Ralph. *The Best Seat in the House: A Basketball Memoir.* New York: Crown, 1997.

Phelps, Digger, and Walters, John. *Basketball for Dummies.* San Mateo, Ca.: IDG Books Worldwide, 1997.

Telander, Rick. *Heaven Is a Playground.* Lincoln, Nebr.: University of Nebraska, 1995.

Wissel, Hall, *Basketball: Steps to Success (Steps to Success Activity).* Champaign, Ill.: Human Kinetics, 1994.

Wooden, John, R., and Jamison, Steve. *Wooden: A Lifetime of Observations and Reflections On and Off the Court.* Contemporary Books: Chicago, 1997.

BOXING
Diamond, Arthur. *Muhammad Ali.* San Diego, Calif.: Lucent Books, 1995.

Frazier, Joe, and Berger, Phil. *Smokin' Joe: The Autobiography of a Heavyweight Champion of the World.* New York: Macmillan, 1996.

Gorn, Elliott J. *Muhammad Ali, The People's Champ.* Urbana, Ill.: University of Illinois Press, 1995.

Hauser, Thomas. *Muhammad Ali: His Life and Times.* New York: Simon & Schuster, 1992.

Walsh, Peter. *Men of Steel: The Lives and Times of Boxing's*

COACHING AND TRAINING

American Sports Education Program. *Coaching Youth Basketball.* Champaign, Ill.: Human Kinetics Pub., 1995.

American Sports Education Program. *Coaching Youth Softball.* Champaign, Ill.: Human Kinetics Pub., 1996.

Arnheim, Daniel D., and Prentice, William E. *Principles of Athletic Training.* Madison, Wisc.: Brown & Benchmark, 1997.

Burroughs, Jeff. *Jeff Burroughs' Little League Instructional Guide/Tips and Techniques for Coaches and Parents from the Coach of the Two-Time World Champs.* Chicago, Ill.: Bonus Books, 1994.

Cluck, Bob, and Cluck, Rob. *How to Hit/How to Pitch: A Complete Self-Coaching System for Winning Baseball.* Chicago, Ill.: Contemporary Books, 1995.

Depel, Jim. *The Baseball Handbook for Coaches and Players.* New York: Macmillan, 1991.

Geist, Bill. *Little League Confidential: One Coach's Completely Unauthorized Tale of Survival.* New York: Dell, 1993.

House, Tom. *The Pitching Edge.* Champaign, Ill.: Human Kinetics Pub., 1994.

Lindsay, Arthur L. *I Can: Coach Ron Brown's Search For Success.* Cross Grand Island, Nebr.: Training Publishers, 1992.

Lynberg, Michael. *Winning!: Great Coaches and Athletes Share Their Secrets of Success.* New York: Doubleday, 1993.

Marcus, Howard. *Basketball Basics: Drills, Techniques, and Strategies for Coaches.* Chicago, Ill.: Contemporary Books, 1991.

McCarthy, John P., Jr. *Youth Basketball: The Guide for Coaches & Parents.* Crozet, Va.: Betterway Publications, 1996.

McIntosh, Ned. *Little League: Drills and Strategies.* Chicago, Ill.: Contemporary Books, 1987.

Murphy, Pat, and Forney, Jeff. *Complete Conditioning for Baseball.* Champaign, Ill.: Human Kinetics Pub., 1997.

Reade, Bob. *Coaching Football Successfully.* Champaign, Ill.: Human Kinetics Pub., 1993.

Wootten, Morgan, and Gilbert, Dave. *Coaching Basketball Successfully.* Champaign, Ill.: Leisure Press, 1991.

COLLEGE SPORTS, RECRUITING & ATHLETIC SCHOLARSHIPS

Athletic Scholarships: A Complete Guide. Cleveland, Ohio: Conway Greene Pub., 1994.

McQuilken, Kim. *The Road to Athletic Scholarship: What Every Student-Athlete, Parent, and Coach Needs to Know.* New York: New York University Press, 1996.

Walsh, Jim, and Trubo, Richard. *Everything You Need to Know About College Sports Recruiting: A Guide for Players.* Kansas City, Mo.: Andrews and McMeel, 1997.

Wilson, Susan M. *Get Yourself a College Sports Scholarship.* New York: Macmillan, 1996.

EQUIPMENT MANAGER

Rudman, Jack. *Track Equipment Maintainer.* Syosset, N.Y.: National Learning Corporation, 1994.

FITNESS

Glover, Bob, Shapard, Jack, and Florence, Shelly-Lynn. *The Runner's Handbook: The Best-Selling Classic Fitness Guide for Beginner and Intermediate Runners.* New York: Penguin, 1996.

Neporent, Liz, and Scholsberg, Suzanne. *Weight Training for Dummies.* San Mateo, Calif.: IDG Books Worldwide, 1997.

Smith, Kathy, and Schlosberg, Suzanne. *Kathy Smith's Fitness Makeover: A 10-Week Guide to Exercise and Nutrition That Will Change Your Life.* New York: Warner Books, 1997.

Van Raalte, Judy L., and Brewer, Britton W. *Exploring Sport and Exercise Psychology.* Washington, D.C.: American Psychological Association, 1996.

FOOTBALL

Bissinger, H. G. *Friday Night Lights: A Town, a Team, and a Dream.* New York: HarperCollins, 1991.

Carroll, Bob, Gershman, Michael, and Neft, David, eds. *Total Football: The Official Encyclopedia of the National Football League.* New York: HarperCollins, 1997.

Golenbock, Peter. *Cowboys Have Always Been My Heroes: The Definitive Oral History of America's Team.* New York: Warner Books, 1997.

Green, Tim. *The Dark Side of the Game: My Life in the NFL.* New York: Warner Books, 1996.

Hawkes, Dwight Dee, ed. *Football's Best Offensive Playbook.* Champaign, Ill.: Human Kinetics Publishers, 1994.

Hickok, Ralph. *The Pro Football Fan's Companion: How to Watch the Game Like an Expert.* New York: Macmillan, 1995.

Hubbard, Steve. *Shark Among Dolphins: Inside Jimmy Johnson's Transformation of the Miami Dolphins.* New York: Ballantine, 1997.

Johnson, Keyshawn, and Smith, Shelley. *Just Give Me the Damn Ball!: The Fast Times and Hard Knocks of an NFL Rookie.* New York: Warner Books, 1997.

LaBlanc, Michael L., and Ruby, Mary K. *Football.* Detroit: Gale Research, 1994.

Maher, Tod, and Gill, Bob, eds. *The Pro Football Encyclopedia: The Complete and Definitive Record of Professional Football.* New York: Macmillan, 1997.

Montana, Joe, and Weiner, Richard. *Joe Montana's Art and Magic of Quarterbacking.* New York: Henry Holt, 1997.

Oriard, Michael. *Reading Football. How the Popular Press Created an American Spectacle.* Chapel Hill, N.C.: University of North Carolina Press, 1993.

Pluto, Terry. *When All the World Was Browns Town: Cleveland's Browns and the Championship Season of '64.* New York: Simon & Schuster, 1997.

Shula, Don, Blanchard, Ken, and Blanchard, Kenneth H. *Everyone's a Coach: You Can Inspire Anyone to Be a Winner.* Grand Rapids, Mich.: Zondervan Pub. House, 1995.

Sugar, Bert, Randolph, ed. *I Hate the Dallas Cowboys: And Who Elected Them America's Team Anyway?* New York: St. Martin's Press, 1997.

GENERAL INTEREST SPORTS BOOKS

DeGeorge, Gail. *The Making of a Blockbuster: How Wayne Huizenga Built a Sports and Entertainment Empire from Trash, Grit, and Videotape.* New York: John Wiley, 1996.

Firestone, Roy, and Ostler, Scott. *Up Close, and in Your Face with the Greats, Near-Greats, and Ingrates of Sports.* New York: Hyperion, 1993.

Goodwin, Doris Kearns. *Wait Till Next Year: A Memoir.* New York: Simon & Schuster, 1997.

Jacobs, Timothy. *100 Athletes Who Shaped Sports History*. San Francisco: Bluewood Books, 1994.

Jackson, Phil, and Delahanty, Hugh. *Sacred Hoops: Spiritual Lessons of a Hardwood Warrior*. New York: Hyperion, 1996.

MacCambridge, Michael. *The Franchise: A History of Sports Illustrated Magazine*. New York: Hyperion, 1997.

Rampersad, Arnold. *Jackie Robinson: A Biography*. New York: Knopf, 1997.

Wiggins, David K. *Glory Bound: Black Athletes in a White America*. Syracuse, N.Y.: Syracuse University Press, 1997.

GOLF

Hurt, Harry, III. *Chasing the Dream: A Mid-Life Quest or Fame and Fortune on the Pro Golf Circuit*. New York: Avon Books, 1997.

Davis, Love. *Every Shot I Take: Lessons Learned About Golf, Life, and a Father's Love*. New York: Simon & Schuster, 1997.

Kite, Tom, and Herskowitz, Mickey. *A Fairway to Heaven: My Lessons from Harvey Penick on Golf and Life*. New York: William Morrow & Co., 1997.

Rotella, Robert J.; Rotella, Dr. Bob, and Cullen, Bob. *Golf Is Not a Game of Perfect*. New York: Simon & Schuster, 1995.

HOCKEY

American Sports Education Program. *Coaching Youth Hockey*. Champaign, Ill.: Human Kinetics Pub., 1995.

Berger, Howard. *On the Road: An Inside View of Life with an NHL Team*. Buffalo, N.Y.: Warwick, 1995.

Chamers, Dave. *Complete Hockey Instruction: Skills and Strategies for Coaches and Players*. Chicago, Ill.: Contemporary Books, 1994.

Fishler, Stan. *Hockey Stars Speak*. Buffalo: Warwick Pub., 1996.

LaBlanc, Michael L., and Ruby, Mary K. *Hockey*. Detroit: Gale Research, 1994.

Ross, Sherry. *Hockey Scouting Report 1997–1998*. New York: Sterling, 1997.

HORSE RACING

Beyer, Andrew. *The Winning Horseplayer: A Revolutionary Approach to Thoroughbred Handicapping and Betting*. Boston: Houghton Mifflin, 1994.

Bolus, Jim. *Derby Dreams*. Gretna, La.: Pelican, 1996.

———. *Derby Magic*. Gretna, La.: Pelican, 1997.

———. *Kentucky Derby Stories*. Gretna, La.: Pelican, 1993.

Krone, Julie, and Richardson, Nancy. *Riding for My Life*. New York: Little Brown, 1995.

Haw, Sarah. *The New Book of the Horse*. New York: Howell Book House, 1993.

Savage, Jeff. *Julie Krone, Unstoppable Jockey*. Minneapolis: Lerner, 1996.

Schwartz, Jane. *Ruffian: Burning from the Start*. New York: Ballantine, 1994.

OFFICIATING

Clegg, Richard, and Thompson, William A. *Modern Sports Officiating: A Practical Guide*. Dubuque, Iowa: WCB Brown & Benchmark, 1993.

Diagram Group. *The Rule Book: The Authoritative Up-to-Date Illustrated Guide to the Regulations History and Object of All Major Sports*. New York: St. Martin's Press, 1987.

Gerlach, Larry R. *The Men in Blue: Conversations with Umpires*. Lincoln, Nebr.: University of Nebraska Press, 1994.

O'Bryant, M. C. *Making It as a Sports Official*. Reston, Va.: National Association for Sport and Physical Education, 1991.

Wagner, Glen, and Eisenberg, Lee, eds. *Rotisserie League Baseball: The Official Rule Book and Draft-Day Guide (1996)*. New York: Little Brown & Company, 1996.

PUBLICITY AND PROMOTION

Carter, David M., *Keeping Score: An Inside Look at Sports Marketing*. Grants Pass, Oreg.: Oasis Press, 1996.

Field, Shelly. *Career Opportunities in Advertising and Public Relations*. New York: Facts On File, 1997.

Johnson, John R. *Promotion for Sport Directors*. Champaign, Ill.: Human Kinetics Pub., 1996.

Pinskey, Raleigh. *You Can Hype Anything: Creative Tactics and Advice for Anyone with a Product, Business or Talent to Promote*. New York: Citadel Press, 1995.

Rein, Irving, Kotler, Philip, and Stoller, Martin. *High Visibility: The Making and Marketing of Professionals into Celebrities*. Lincolnwood, Ill.: NTC Business Books, 1997.

Schlossberg, Howard. *Sports Marketing*. Cambridge, Mass.: Blackwell, 1996.

PHYSICAL EDUCATION

Lumpkin, Angela. *Physical Education and Sport: A Contemporary Introduction*. St. Louis, Mo.: Mosby, 1994.

Swanson, Richard A., Albin, Richard and Spears, Betty Mary. *History of Sport and Physical Education in the United States*. Madison, Wisc.: Brown & Benchmark, 1995.

Wilmore, Jack H., and Costill, David L. *Training for Sport and Activity: The Physiological Basis of the Conditioning Process*. Champaign, Ill.: Human Kinetics Pub., 1993.

Wuest, Deborah A., and Bucher, Charles Augustus. *Foundations of Physical Education and Sport*. St. Louis, Mo.: Mosby, 1991.

RECREATION

Mueller, Pat. *Intramural-Recreational Sports: Programming and Administration*. New York: John Wiley & Sons, 1979.

Mull, Richard, Bayless, Kathryn, and Ross, Craig. *Recreational Sports Programming*. Palm Beach, Fla.: Athletic Institute, 1984.

Zeigler, Earle F., and Campbell, John. *Strategic Market Planning: An Aid to the Evaluation of an Athletic/Recreation Program*. Champaign, Ill.: Stipes Publishing, 1994.

SOCCER

Douglas, Geoffrey. *The Game of Their Lives*. New York: Henry Holt, 1996.

Glanville, Brian. *The Story of the World Cup*. Winchester, Mass.: Faber & Faber, 1993.

Hanna, S. S. *Beyond Winning: Memoir of a Women's Soccer Coach*. Niwot, Colo.: University Press of Colorado, 1996.

Luxbacher, Joseph A., and Klein, Gene. *The Soccer Goalkeeper*. Champaign, Ill.: Human Kinetics Pub., 1992.

Reeves, John A., and Simon, J. Malcolm. *Select Soccer Drills*. Champaign, Ill.: Leisure Press, 1991.

SPORTS ADMINISTRATION

Baim, Dean V. *The Sports Stadium as a Municipal Investment.* Westport, Conn.: Greenwood Press, 1994.

Berlow, Lawrence H. *Sports Ethics: A Reference Handbook.* Santa Barbara, Calif.: ABC-CLIO, 1994.

Berry, Robert C., Gould, William B., and Staudohar, Paul D. *Labor Relations in Professional Sports.* Dover, Mass.: Auburn House Publishing Company, 1986.

Gorman, Jerry, Calhoun, Kirk and Rozin, Skip. *The Name of the Game: The Business of Sports.* New York: John Wiley & Sons, 1994.

Judson, Karen. *Sports and Money: It's a Sellout!* Springfield, N.J.: Enslow, 1995.

Katz, Donald R. *Just Do It: The Nike Spirit in the Corporate World.* New York: Random House, 1994.

Nygaard, Gary, and Boone, Thomas H. *Coaches' Guide to Sports Law.* Champaign, Ill.: Human Kinetics, 1985.

Parkhouse, Bonnie L. *The Management of Sport: Its Foundation and Application.* St. Louis, Mo.: Mosby Year Book, 1991.

Schaaf, Phil. *Sports Marketing: It's Not Just a Game Anymore.* Amherst, N.Y.: Prometheus Books, 1995.

Scully, Gerald W. *The Market Structure of Sports.* Chicago, Ill.: University of Chicago Press, 1995.

Weiss, Ann E. *Money Games: The Business of Sports.* Boston, Mass.: Houghton Mifflin, 1993.

Wilson, Neil. *The Sports Business.* London, England: Piatkus, 1988.

SPORTS JOURNALISM, REPORTING AND COMMUNICATIONS

Anderson, Douglas A. *Contemporary Sports Reporting.* Chicago, Ill.: Nelson-Hall, 1994.

Baker, Aaron, and Boyd, Todd. *Out of Bounds: Sports, Media, and the Politics of Identity.* Bloomington, Ind.: Indiana University Press, 1997.

Bloom, Don. *Confessions of a Sportswriter.* New York: Vantage Press, 1987.

Bender, Gary, and Johnson, Michael L. *Call of the Game: What Really Goes on in the Broadcast Booth.* Chicago: Bonus Books, 1994.

Catsis, John R. *Sports Broadcasting.* Chicago: Nelson-Hall, 1996.

Fischer, Heinz Dietrich. *Sports Journalism at Its Best: Pulitzer Prize-Winning Articles, Cartoons, and Photographs.* Chicago: Nelson-Hall, 1995.

Garrison, Bruce, and Sabljak. *Sports Reporting.* Ames, Iowa: Iowa State University Press, 1993.

Kahn, Roger. *Memories of Summer: When Baseball Was an Art, and Writing About It a Game.* Hyperion: New York, 1997.

Plimpton, George, ed. *The Best American Sports Writing 1997.* Boston: Houghton Mifflin Co., 1997.

SPORTS MEDICINE

Andrews, James R., Clancy, William G., and Whiteside, James A. *On-Field Evaluation and Treatment of Common Athletic Injuries.* St. Louis, Mo.: Mosby, 1997.

Benjamin, Patricia J., and Lamp, Scott P. *Understanding Sports Massage.* Champaign, Ill.: Human Kinetics Pub., 1996.

Martire, Mark E., and Levinsohn, Mark E. *Imaging of Athletic Injuries: A Multimodality Approach.* New York: McGraw-Hill, 1992.

Morgan, Lyle W. *Homeopathic Treatment of Sports Injuries.* Rochester, Vt.: Healing Arts Press, 1988.

Peterson, James A. *American College of Sports Medicine's Health/Fitness Facility Standards and Guidelines.* Champaign, Ill.: Human Kinetics Pub., 1997.

Pettrone, Frank, A. *Athletic Injuries of the Shoulder.* New York: McGraw-Hill, 1995.

Pike, Greg. *Sports Massage for Peak Performance.* New York: HarperPerennial, 1997.

Potparic, O., and Gibson, J. *A Dictionary of Sports Injuries and Disorders.* New York: Parthenon, 1996.

Tippett, Steven R. *Functional Progressions for Sport Rehabilitation.* Champaign, Ill.: Human Kinetics Pub., 1995.

SPORTS NUTRITION

Burke, Ed, and Berning, Jacqueline R. *Training and Nutrition: The Diet and Nutrition Guide for Peak Performance.* Carmel, Ind.: Cooper Publishing Group, 1996.

Kies, Constance. *Sports Nutrition: Minerals and Electrolytes.* Boca Raton, Fla.: CRC Press, 1995.

STATISTICIANS

Rudman, Jack. *Statistician.* Syosset, N.Y.: National Learning Corporation, 1982.

TENNIS

Collins, Bud, and Hollander, Zander, eds. *Bud Collins' Tennis Encyclopedia.* Detroit: Visible Inc. Press, 1997.

Gallwey, Timothy W. *The Inner Game of Tennis.* New York: Random House, 1997.

Gilbert, Brad, and Jamison, Steve. *Winning Ugly: Mental Warfare in Tennis—Lessons from a Master.* New York: Fireside Publications, 1994.

WOMEN & SPORTS

Blais, Madeline. *In These Girls, Hope Is a Muscle.* New York: Warner, 1997.

Birrell, Susan, and Cole, Cheryl L. *Women, Sport, and Culture.* Champaign, Ill.: Human Kinetics Pub., 1994.

Cohen, Greta L. *Women in Sport: Issues and Controversies.* Thousand Oaks, Calif.: Sage Pub., 1993.

Costa, D. Margaret. *Women and Sport: Interdisciplinary Perspectives.* Champaign, Ill.: Human Kinetics Pub., 1994.

Corbett, Sara. *Venus to the Hoop: A Gold-Medal Year in Women's Basketball.* New York: Doubleday, 1997.

Kessler, Lauren. *Full Court Press: A Season in the Life of a Winning Basketball Team and the Women Who Made It Happen.* New York: E.P. Dutton, 1997.

Lieberman-Cline, Nancy, Roberts, Robin, Warneke, Kevin, and Summitt, Pat. *Basketball for Women: Becoming a Complete Player.* Champaign, Ill.: Human Kinetics Pub., 1995.

Sherrow, Victoria. *Encyclopedia of Women and Sports.* Santa Barbara, Calif.: ABC-CLIO, 1996.

WRESTLING

Lewin, Ted. *I Was a Teenage Professional Wrestler.* New York: Hyperion, 1994.

Keith, Art. *Successful Wrestling: Coaches' Guide for Teaching Basic to Advanced Skills.* Champaign, Ill.: Leisure Press, 1989.

B. PERIODICALS

Magazines, newspapers, membership bulletins, and newsletters may be helpful for finding information about a specific job category, locating a job in a specific field, or giving you insight into what certain jobs entail.

As with the books in the previous section, this list should serve as a starting point. There are many periodicals not listed due to space limitations. Periodicals also tend to come and go. Look in your local library or in the newspaper/magazine shops for other periodicals of interest.

ATHLETES

ACC Athlete Magazine
3101 Poplarwood Court
Raleigh, NC 27604

ACC Sports Journal
Denmark Sports
P.O. Box 4323
Chapel Hill, NC 27515

Athletes in Action
P.O. Box 588
Lebanon, OH 45036

AUTO RACING

Area Auto Racing News
P.O. Box 8547
Trenton, NJ 08650

Auto Racing Digest
990 Grove Street
Evanston, IL 60201

BASEBALL

Baseball America
P.O. Box 2089
Durham, NC 27702

Baseball Blue Book, Inc.
P.O. Box 4087
7225 30th Avenue North
St. Petersburg, FL 33743

Baseball Digest
990 Grove Street
Evanston, IL 60201

Baseball Parent
4437 Kingston Pike #2204
Knoxville, TN 37919

Baseball Research Journal
Society for American Baseball
   Research (SABR)
Box 93183
Cleveland, OH 44101

Bullpen
Babe Ruth League, Inc.
P.O. Box 5000
Trenton, NJ 08683

Collegiate Baseball
P.O. Box 50566
Tucson, AZ 85703

Fantasy Baseball
700 East State Street
Iola, WI 54990

Junior League Baseball
America's Youth Baseball Magazine
P.O. Box 9099
Canoga Park, CA 91309

Sporting News Baseball Yearbook
1212 North Lindbergh
St. Louis, MO 63132

Sports Card Collectors Digest
Krause Publications, Inc.
700 East State Street
Iola, WI 54990

Sports Collectors Digest
Krause Publications, Inc.
700 East State Street
Iola, WI 54990

Superstar and Rookie Special
Krause Publications, Inc.
700 East State Street
Iola, WI 54990

USA Today Baseball Weekly
Gannett Company, Inc.
1000 Wilson Boulevard
Arlington, VA 22229

BASKETBALL

Basketball Digest
990 Grove Street
Evanston, IL 60201

Eastern Basketball Magazine
P.O. Box 370
Rochester, MI 48308

Basketball Weekly
17820 East Warren Avenue
Detroit, MI 48224

**Sporting News College Basketball
   Yearbook**
1212 North Lindbergh
St. Louis, MO 63132

**Sporting News Pro Basketball
   Yearbook**
1212 North Lindbergh
St. Louis, MO 63132

The Giants Newsweekly
Pro Publishing, Inc.
P.O. Box 816
Red Bank, NJ 07701

Touchdown Illustrated
Touchdown Publications Inc.
355 Lexington Avenue
New York, NY 10017

BOWLING

Bowling Digest
990 Grove Street
Evanson, IL 60201

BOXING

Boxing Buzz
P.O. Box 26881
Akron, OH 44319

**KO Magazine Superfight Color
   Special No. 1**
P.O. Box 910
Fort Washington, PA 19034

International Boxing Digest
530 Fifth Avenue
Ste. 430
New York, NY 10036

LadyBoxer Magazine
Special Events
P.O. Box 453
Wilksboro, NC 28697

Ring Magazine
130 West 37th Street
New York, NY 10018

COACHING & TRAINING

Coach and Athletic Director
Scholastic Inc.
2931 E. McCarthy
P.O. Box 3710
Jefferson City, MO 65102

Coaching Women's Basketball
4646 B Lawrenceville Highway
Lilburn, GA 30247

MWN Coaching Newsletter
MWN Sports Enterprises Inc.
1235 E East Boulevard
Charlotte, NC 28203

**National Strength and Conditioning
   Association Journal**
251 Capitol Beach Boulevard
P.O. Box 81410
Lincoln, NE 68501

Scholastic Coach
555 Broadway
New York, NY 10003

Scholastic Coach and Athletic Director
Scholastic, Inc.
Jefferson City, MO 65101

CYCLING

Cycling USA
U.S. Cycling Federation
U.S. Olympic Complex
1750 East Boulder Street
Colorado Springs, CO 80909

FITNESS

American Fitness
15250 Ventrura Boulevard
Suite 200
Sherman Oaks, CA 91403

Atlanta Sports and Fitness Magazine
359 East Paces Ferry Road NE
Suite 101
Atlanta, GA 30305

Fit Magazine
1700 Broadway
New York, NY 10019

Fitness and Sports Review
P.O. Box 460429
Escondido, CA 92046

Fitness Diet and Excercise Guide
Family Circle Publications
110 Fifth Avenue
New York, NY 10011

Fitness Magazine
New York Times Magazine Group
5520 Park Avenue
Trumbull, CT 06611

Fitness Management
215 South Highway 101
Suite 110
Solona Beach, CA 92075

Fitness Management's Fitness World
3923 W. 6th Street
4th Floor
Los Angeles, CA 90020

**Journal of Sports and Excercise
   Psychology**
P.O. Box 5076
Champaign, IL 61825

**Maryland Sports, Health & Fitness
   News**
P.O. Box 32684
Baltimore, MD 21282

Men's Fitness
2100 Erwin Street
Woodland Hills, CA 91364

Philly Health & Fitness
150 James Way
Southampton, PA 28966

Shape Magazine
21100 Erwin Street
Woodland Hills, CA 91367

T'ai Chi
P.O. Box 26156
Los Angeles, CA 90026

Women's Sports & Fitness
2025 Pearl Street
Boulder, CO 80302

FOOTBALL

Football Digest
990 Grove Street
Evanston, IL 60201

Football News
8033 N.W. 36th Street
Miami, FL 33152

NETSport Magazine, Inc.
5696 Peachtree Pkwy.
Norcross, GA 30092

Pro Football Weekly
666 Dundee Road
Northbrook, IL 60062

Silver and Black Illustrated—Raiders
American Sports Media
2604 Elmwood Ave., Suite 343
Rochester, NY 14618

**Sporting News College Football
   Yearbook**
1212 North Lindbergh
St. Louis, M 63132

**Washington Pro Football
   Illustrated—Redskins**
American Sports Media
2604 Elmwood, Ave., Suite 343
Rochester, NY 14618

**Shout! The Weekly Newspaper for
   the Buffalo Bills**
American Sports Media
2604 Elmwood Ave., Suite 343
Rochester, NY 14618

Jets Confidential—N.Y. Jets
American Sports Media
2604 Elmwood Avenue
Suite 343
Rochester, NY 14618

GENERAL INTEREST

American Sports
P.O. Box 6100
Rosemead, CA 91770

Black College Sports Review
Winston-Salem Chronicle
617 North Liberty Street
Winston-Salem, NC 27102

Journal of Sport
1010 White Building
Pennsylvania State University
University Park, PA 16802

Journal of Sport and Social Issues
Sage Periodicals Press
2455 Teller Road
Thousand Oaks, CA 91360

Inside Sports
990 Grove Street
Evanston, IL 60201

Sporting News Sports
1212 North Lindbergh
St. Louis, MO 63132

Sport Literate
1623 West Belmont
No. 6 B
Chicago, IL 60657

Sport Magazine
Peterson Publishing
6420 Wilshire Boulevard
Los Angeles, CA 90048

Sports Afield
Hearst Corporation
250 West 55th Street
New York, NY 10019

Sports History Review
1607 N. Market Street
P.O. Box 5076
Champaign, IL 61825

Sports Illustrated
Time Inc.
1675 Broadway
New York, NY 10019

Sports Illustrated for Kids
Time Inc.
1675 Broadway
New York, NY 10019

Sports Tech
121 West 72nd Street
Suite 16D
New York, NY 10023

The Sporting News
1212 North Lindbergh Boulevard
St. Louis, MO 63132

GOLF

golf.com
3426 N. Washington Blvd., Suite 102
Arlington, VA 22201

Golf Digest
5520 Park Avenue
Trumbull, CT 06611

Golf Journal
Far Hills, NJ 07931

Golf Magazine
2 Park Avenue
New York, NY 10016

Golf News Magazine
Poppers
P.O. Box 1040
Rancho Mirage, CA 92770

Golf Shop Operations
5520 Park Avenue
Trumbull, CT 06611

Golf Week
7657 Commerce Center Drive
Orlando, FL 32819

Golf World
5520 Park Avenue
Trumbull, CT 06611

Grounds Maintenance Magazine's
Golf Course Manual
P.O. Box 12901
Overland Park, KS 66212

PGA Magazine
P.O. Box 12458
Palm Beach Gardens
Lake Park, FL 33403

HOCKEY

American Hockey
CBA Service Corp., Inc.
P.O. Box 200
Colorado Springs, CO 80901

Cage Canada
McKay Sports Marketing
P.O. Box 48057
St. Albert, Alberta, Canada
T8N 6J7

Hockey Digest
Century Publishing Company 990
Grove Street
Evanston, IL 60201

Hockey Magazine
1200 North 7th Street
Minneapolis, MN 55411

Hockey Weekly
25042 West Warren Road
Dearborn Heights, MI 48127

Inside Hockey
85 Scarsdale Road
Suite 100
Don Mills, Ontario, Canada
M3B 2R2

HORSE RACING

American Equine Magazine
P.O. Box 116
Plymouth, PA 18651

Daily Racing Form
P.O. Box 47012
Gardena, CA 90247

Hoof Beats
U.S. Trotting Association
750 Michigan Avenue
Columbus, OH 43215

Horse and Horseman
Gallant/Charger Publications, Inc.
Camino Capistrano
Box 2429
Capistrano Beach, CA 92624

Horse Illustrated
P.O. Box 6050
Mission Viejo, CA 92690

National Horseman
14455 North Hayden Road
Suite 208
Scottsdale, AZ 85260

The Record
Horses Publishing Company
21 Greenview Terrace
Carsbad, CA 92009

The Thoroughbred Record
801 Corporate Drive
Lexington, KY 40503

The Thoroughbred Times
801 Corporate Drive
Lexington, KY 40503

MEDIA

Broadcasting
1705 De Salle Street
Washington, DC 20036

Channels
P.O. Box 600
Exeter, NH 03833

Contacts
CAP Communications Associates
35-20 Broadway
Astoria, NY 11106

Media Alerts
Bacon's Inc.
332 South Michigan
Chicago, IL 60604

Media News Keys
40–29 27th Street
Long Island City, NY 11101

Party Line
2 Sutton Place
New York, NY 10022

OFFICIATING

Referee Magazine
P.O. Box 161
Franksville, WI 53126

OLYMPICS

The Olympian
U.S. Olympic Committee
One Olympic Plaza
Colorado Springs, CO 80909

PHYSICAL EDUCATION

Adapted Physical Activity Quarterly
P.O. Box 5076
Champaign, IL 61825

**Journal of Physical Education,
Recreation and Dance**
1900 Association Drive
Reston, VA 22091

**Journal of Teaching in Physical
Education**
P.O. Box 5076
Champaign, IL 61825

PHYSICAL THERAPY

Journal of Hand Therapy
210 South 13th Street
Philadelphia, PA 19107

PUBLIC RELATIONS AND
PUBLICITY

Inside PR
235 West 48th Street
New York, NY 10036

O'Dwyer's PR Service Report
271 Madison Avenue
New York, NY 10016

O'Dwyer's PR Market Place
271 Madison Avenue
New York, NY 10016

Jack O'Dwyer's Newsletter
271 Madison Avenue
New York, NY 10016

PR Reporter
Box 600
Exeter, NH 03833

PR Watch
3313 Gregory Street
Madison, WI 53711

Public Relations Journal
PRSA
33 Irving Place
New York, NY 10003

Public Relations News
1201 Seven Locks Road
Potomac, MD 20854

Public Relations Review
55 Old Post Road
2
Box 1678
Greenwich, CT 06836

RETAIL/WHOLESALE

Sporting Goods Business
SGB Sports Publications
One Penn Plaza
New York, NY 10119

Sporting Goods Dealer
Times Mirror Magazines, Inc.
2 Park Avenue
New York, NY 10016

Sport Shop News
Trade Publishing Company
53 Sterling Road
Trumbull, CT 06611

RUNNING

American Track and Field
Shooting Star Media, Inc.
583 D'Onofrio Drive, Suite 203
Madison, WI 53719

Runners World
Rodale Press
33 E. Minor Street
Emmaus, PA 18098

SKATING

American Skating World
1816 Brownsville Road
Pittsburgh, PA 15210

International Figure Skating
55 Ideal Road
Worcester, MA 01604

SKIING

Snow Country
5520 Park Avenue
Trumbull, CT 06611

Snow Country Business
5520 Park Avenue
Trumbull, CT 06611

SOCCER

Soccer Digest
990 Grove Street
Evanston, IL 60201

Soccer Ink
P.O. Box 20489
Charleston, SC 29413

SOFTBALL

Lets Play Softball
2721 East 42nd Street
Minneapolis, MN 55406

USA Softball Magazine
ASA/USA Softball
2801 NE 50th Street
Oklahoma City, OK 73111

SPORTS BUSINESS & ADMINISTRATION

Athletic Business
1842 Hoffman Street
Madison, WI 53704

Business of Sports
Carew Tower
Suites 442–443
Cincinnati, OH 45202

Sports Business
501 Oakdale Road
North York, Ontario, Canada
M2N 1Q7

SPORTSCASTING

SportsCaster
Liberty Publishing Group
100 East Royal Lane
Suite 250
Irving, Texas 75039

SPORTS MANAGEMENT

Journal of Sports Management
Human Kinetics
Box 5076
Champaign, IL 61825

SPORTS MARKETING

Direct Marketing
Hoke Communications, Inc.
224 Seventh Street
Garden City, NY 11530

The Journal of Marketing
American Marketing Association
250 South Wacker Drive
Chicago, IL 60606

Marketing News
American Marketing Association
250 South Wacker Drive
Chicago, IL 60606

SPORTS MEDICINE

American Journal in Sports Medicine
230 Calvary Street
Waltham, MA 02154

Clinical Journal of Sports Medicine
Lippincott-Raven Publishers
1185 Avenue of the Americas
New York, NY 10036

Clinics in Sports Medicine
W.B. Saunders Co.
The Curtis Center
Philadelphia, PA 19106

International Journal of Sports Biomechanics
P.O. Box 5076
Champaign, IL 61825

Clinical Journal of Sport Medicine
1185 Avenue of the Americas
Mail Stop 3B
New York, NY 10036

Medicine and Science in Sports and Exercise
351 West Camden Street
Baltimore, MD 21201

Operative Techniques in Sports Medicine
W.B. Saunders Co.
The Curtis Center
Philadelphia, PA 19106

SPORTS PSYCHOLOGY

Journal of Sport Psychology
Human Kinetics
1607 North Market Street
Box 5076
Champaign, IL 61825

SPORTS RESEARCH

**Research Quarterly for Exercise
    and Sport**
1900 Association Drive
Reston, VA 22091

SPORTS SOCIOLOGY

Sociology of Sport Journal
Human Kinetics
1607 North Market Street
Box 5076
Champaign, IL 61825

SPORTS TRAVEL

Women's Sports Traveler
101 East 52nd Street
Ninth Floor
New York, NY 10126

TENNIS

Tennis Buyer's Guide
5520 Park Avenue
P.O. Box 0395
Trumbull, CT 06611

Tennis USTA
New York Times Magazine Group
5520 Park Avenue
Trumbull, CT 06611

VOLLEYBALL

Coaching Volleyball
American Volleyball Coaches
  Association
1227 Lake Plaza Drive
Suite B
Colorado Springs, CO 80906

WRESTLING

The American Grappler
P.O. Box 5205
Bloomington, IN 47407

WCW Magazine
G.C. London Publishing Enterprises,
  Inc.
55 Maple Avenue
Rockville Centre, NY 11570

Wrestling USA Magazine
109 Apple House Lane
Missoula, MT 59802

WOMEN'S SPORTS

Full Court Press
Womens Basketball
47 Lafayette Circle Box 346
Lafayette, CA 94549

APPENDIX XIX
GLOSSARY

The following is a list of abbreviations, acronyms, and lingo that will prove helpful to individuals interested in the sports industry. Entries are listed alphabetically.

AAABA	American Amateur Baseball Association
AABC	American Amateur Baseball Congress
AAF	American Advertising Federation
AAHPERD	American Alliance for Health, Physical Education, Recreation and Dance
AARWBA	American Auto Racing Writers and Broadcasters Association
AATACB	American Athletic Trainers Association and Certification Board
AAU	Amateur Athletic Union of the United States
AAU/USA JO	Amateur Athletic Union/U.S.A. Junior Olympics
ABAUSA	Amateur Basketball Association of the United States of America
ABCA	American Baseball Coaches Association
ABO	Affiliated Boards of Officials
AC	Advertising Council
AEMA	Athletic Equipment Managers Association
AFA	American Fitness Association
AFAA	Aerobics and Fitness Association of America
AFB	Association for Fitness in Business
AFCA	American Football Coaches Association
Affiliate	A broadcast station that belongs to a network. For example, WABC in New York and KABC in Los Angeles are both affiliates of the ABC network.
AFM	American Federation of Musicians
AFT	American Federation of Teachers
AFTRA	American Federation of Television and Radio Artists
AGMA	American Guild of Musical Artists
AGTD	Athletic Goods Team Distributors
AGVA	American Guild of Variety Artists
AHAUS	Amateur Hockey Association of the United States
AHCA	American Hockey Coaches Association
AHL	American Hockey League
AI	Athletic Institute
AISA	American Indoor Soccer Association
AJA	American Judges Association
AL	American League

ALB	American Legion Baseball
All Star Game	An exhibition game played annually between the best players in the American League and the National League.
AMA	American Management Association
AMA	American Marketing Association
AMAA	American Medical Athletic Association
Amateur	An athlete who does not receive money for competing in a sport.
American League	One of the professional baseball leagues in the United States.
ANA	Association of National Advertisers, Inc.
APB	Associated Press Broadcasters
APBPA	Association of Professional Ball Players of America
APFC	Association of Physical Fitness Centers
APTA	American Physical Therapy Association
ARF	Advertising Research Foundation
ARFA	American Running and Fitness Association
ARPA	Association of Representatives of Professional Athletes
ASA	Amateur Softball Association of America
ASA	American Sportscasters Association
ASCA	American Swimming Coaches Association
ASTVC	American Society of TV Cameramen
AT	American Turners
ATA	American Tennis Association
ATAS	Academy of Television Arts and Sciences
AWRT	American Women in Radio and Television
AYSO	American Youth Soccer Organization
B & W Glossy	Used by publicists, press agents, and public relations people when putting together press kits. It is an 8 X 10 inch glossy photograph of a client that can be used for reproduction purposes in newspapers or magazines.
B/PAA	Business/Professional Advertising Association

Ballgame	A baseball game.
Ball Park	The area where baseball games are played.
Basket	The hoop in a basketball game.
Batter	The player who is at bat in a baseball game.
BBWAA	Baseball Writers Association of America
Bell	A gong, buzzer, or bell used to indicate the start and finish of a round in boxing.
BHFCBV	Baseball Hall of Fame Committee on Baseball Veterans
Bio	A biography put together by press agents, publicists, public relations people, etc., on a client.
Blow	A punch used in boxing.
BRB	Babe Ruth Baseball
BWA	Boxing Writers Association
BWAA	Bowling Writers Association of America
BWI	Boating Writers International
CABA	Canadian Amateur Boxing Association
CABMA	College Athletic Business Managers Association
CAC	Consolidated Athletic Commission
Campaign (Advertising)	A series of advertisements used to promote and publicize a product or group of products.
Campaign (Public Relations)	A public relations concept used to promote a client.
CBA	Continental Basketball Association
CCA	Collegiate Commissioners Association
CFA	College Football Association
CIAA	Central Intercollegiate Athletic Association
Circulation	The number of copies distributed of a newspaper or magazine.
Combination	Two or more punches used quickly in combination with each other in boxing.
Counter Punch	A boxing blow thrown after one opponent hits another.
Course	Golf course; area where people play golf.
Court	A basketball court; the playing area in basketball.
CPRBLS	Cardiopulmonary resuscitation and basic life support.
CSCA	College Swimming Coaches Association of America
CSIDA	College Sports Information Directors of America
CSL	Cosmopolitan Soccer League
CSS	Center for Sports Sponsorship
Defense Tackle	An athlete in football; one of the positions played in football.
Double-header	Two games played consecutively on the same day.
Draft	A system where teams get to choose athletes from a list of amateur players who want to become professionals.
ECBA	Eastern College Basketball Association
ECHA	Eastern College Hockey Association
ECSA	Eastern College Soccer Association
EIGL	Eastern Intercollegiate Gymnastic League
E-Mail	Mail transmitted electronically via modems and telephone lines
EWABL/AAU	Eastern Women's Amateur Basketball League of the AAU
FCC	Federal Communications Commission
Forward Pass	A play in football.
Foul	An illegal move or an infraction of rules.
FPA	Federation of Professional Athletes
Free Throw	A shot in basketball.
FTA	Fitness Trade Associations
FWAA	Football Writers Association of America
GGAA	Golden Gloves Association of America
GKABL	George Khoury Association of Baseball Leagues
Golden Gloves	The Golden Gloves Association of America sponsors amateur boxing tournament across the country.
Golf Pro	Golf professional.
Group Sales	Ticket sold in blocks to groups of people.
GWAA	Golf Writers Association of America
Halftime	The break after the first half of the game has been played in a football game.
Harness Racing	Horse racing involving horses that pull sulkies.
Heavy Bag	Bag used to develop boxer's punch.
HHI	Harness Horsemen International
HHYF	Harnes Horse Youth Foundation
Hook	A boxing blow
HTA	Harness Tracks of America
Hype	Extensive publicity used to promote people, products, events, etc. Hype is not always true.
IAABO	International Association of Approved Basketball Officials
IABA	International Amateur Boxing Association
IADRS	International Association of Dive Rescue Specialists
IBA	International Baseball Association
IBC	International Boxing Council
IBF	International Boxing Federation
IBHF	International Boxing Hall of Fame

IBRO	International Boxing Research Organization	**Men in Blue**	Umpires
IBWA	International Boxing Writers Association	**Mike**	Microphone
ICAAA	Intercollegiate Association of Amateur Athletes of America	**Minor League**	Professional leagues other than the major leagues.
ICAEO	International Center for Athletic and Educational Opportunities	**MLBBPA**	Major League Baseball Players Association; union representing major league baseball players.
ICF	International Cheerleading Foundation	**MLBPA**	Major League Baseball Players Association
ICNATAS	International Council—National Academy of Television Arts and Sciences	**MLUA**	Major League Umpires Association
ICSF	International Collegiate Sports Foundation	**Mouthpiece**	Used in boxing to protect a fighter's mouth and teeth.
IDEA	International Dance-Exercise Association	**MVP**	Most Valuable Player
		NAB	National Association of Broadcaster
ILPBC	International League of Professional Baseball Clubs	**NAB**	National Association of Broadcasting
		NAB	Newspaper Advertising Bureau
INHL	International Hockey League	**NABC**	National Association of Basketball Coaches of the United States
IPFA	International Physical Fitness Association	**NABET**	National Association of Broadcast Employees and Technicians
IPRA	International Public Relations Association	**NABF**	National Amateur Baseball Federation
		NABF	North American Boxing Federation
ISAA	Intercollegiate Soccer Association of America	**NABR**	National Association of Basketball Referees
ISSP	International Society of Sports Psychology	**NACDA**	National Association of Collegiate Directors of Athletics
ITCA	Intercollegiate Tennis Coaches Association	**NACGC**	National Association of Collegiate Gymnastics Coaches
ITPA	International Trotting and Pacing Association	**NAIA**	National Association of Intercollegiate Athletics
IVBA	International Veteran Boxing Association	**NAJSA**	North American Judges and Stewards Association
Jab	A blow used in boxing	**NALUS**	National Association of Leagues, Umpires and Scorers
JGI	Jockey's Guild, Inc.		
Jockey	The person who rides a horse in a Thoroughbred race.	**NAPBL**	National Association of Professional Baseball Leagues
Judge	An official who scores and judges sporting events.	**NAS**	National Academy of Sports
Jump Shot	A shot in basketball.	**NASCAR**	National Association for Stock Car Auto Racing
KBTI	Knights Boxing Team International		
KO	Knockout. Used to indicate when a boxer is knocked out.	**NASF**	North American Soccer Foundation
		NASGW	National Association of Sporting Goods Wholesalers
LLB	Little League Baseball	**NASLP**	North American Soccer League Players Association
Low Blow	In boxing, an illegal punch delivered below the waist.		
		NASO	National Association of Sports Officials
LPGA	Ladies Professional Golf Association of America	**NASPE**	National Association for Sport and Physical Education
MANA	Manufacturer's Agents National Association	**NATA**	National Athletic Trainers Association
		NATAS	National Academy of Television Arts and Sciences
Market	Refers to a geographical location in television or radio; may refer to a specific size or style of audience market such as small market radio, major market television, etc.	**National League**	A professional baseball league.
		NAYSI	North American Youth Sport Institute
		NBA	National Basketball Association
		NBC	National Baseball Congress

NBPA	National Basketball Players Association	NPPA	National Press Photographers Association
NBPRS	National Black Public Relations Society	NSCA	National Strength and Conditioning Association
NCAA	National Collegiate Athletic Association		
NCBWA	National Collegiate Baseball Writers Association	NSCAA	National Soccer Coaches Association of America
NCFA	National Collegiate Football Association	NSGA	National Sporting Goods Association
NCSA	National Club Sports Association	NSL	National Soccer League
NDA	National Dance Association	NSPBA	National Semi-Professional Baseball Association
NDEITA	National Dance-Exercise Instructor's Training Association		
NEA	National Education Association	NSSA	National Sportscasters and Sportswriters Association
NEJA	National Entertainment Journalists Association	NVBA	National Veterans Boxers Association
NESRA	National Employee Services and Recreation Association	NWBW	National Women Bowling Writers Association
Net	The Internet	NWCA	National Wrestling Coaches Association
Network	A group of TV or radio stations affiliated and interconnected for simultaneous broadcast of the same programming.	NYSCA	National Youth Sports Coaches Association
		OBUD	Office for Baseball Umpire Development
Neutral Corners	Corners of a boxing ring that are not used during rest periods between rounds.	Official	A referee or judge of an athletic game.
		OFPCP	Organization of Fitness and Personal Care Professionals
NFF	National Fitness Foundation	Olympics	Games and tournaments held every four years for amateur events in a variety of sports.
NFICA	National Federation Interscholastic Coaches Association		
NFIOA	National Federation Interscholastic Officials Association	On-line	Connected to the Internet
NFL	National Football League	Out of Bounds	Out of the playing area.
NFLPA	National Football League Players Association	Overtime	Extra time needed to complete a game.
		P.E.	Physical Education
NFPW	National Federation of Press Women	PR	Public Relations
NFSHSA	National Federation of State High School Associations	PAC	Public Affairs Council
		Pacers	Horses trained to pace instead of gallop.
NFT	National Federation of Teachers	PB	Pony Baseball
NGJA	National Gymnastics Judges Association	PBWAA	Professional Basketball Writers Association of America
NHL	National Hockey League		
NHLPA	National Hockey League Player's Association	PFATS	Professional Football Athletic Trainers Society
NHSACA	National High School Athletic Coaches Association	PFRA	Professional Football Referees Association
NIRSA	National Intramural-Recreational Sports Association	PFRA	Professional Football Researchers Association
NISCA	National Interscholastic Swimming Coaches Association of America	PFWA	Professional Football Writers of America
NISOA	National Intercollegiate Soccer Officials Association	PGA	Professional Golfers Association of America
NJCAA	National Junior College Athletic Association	PHWA	Professional Hockey Writers' Association
NL	National League of Professional Baseball Clubs	Pitcher	The athlete who throws or pitches the ball in baseball.
NLC	National Lifeguard Championships	Play Ball	Begin playing the game or restart game.
NLCAA	National Little College Athletic Association	PMAA	Promotion Marketing Association of America
NPC	National Press Club	PPA	Professional Photographers of America

Press Kit	A promotion kit containing publicity, photographs, and other promotional materials used by publicists, press agents, and public relations people to help publicize a client.
Pro	Professional
Pro	Professional Athlete
Professional	An athlete who receives compensation for competing in sporting events.
Promo	Promotion
PRSA	Public Relations Society of America
PRSSA	Public Relations Student Society of America
PSIA	Professional Ski Instructors of America
Purse (Boxing)	The amount of money a boxer is paid for fighting.
Purse (Racing)	An amount of money a horse earns if it wins.
PWF	Pop Warners Football
RAB	Radio and Advertising Bureau
Rate Card	A card listing rates for space or time and providing mechanical requirements for advertisements.
Ref.	Referee
Retail Sports Store	A Store in which consumers buys sports equipment or products.
RTNDA	Radio Television News Directors Association
SABR	Society for American Baseball Research
SAG	Screen Actors Guild
Scale	Minimum wages that can be paid to a union member.
Search the Net	Look for information on the Internet
SEG	Screen Extras Guild
SF	Sports Foundation
SGAA	Sporting Goods Agents Association
SGMA	Sporting Goods Manufacturers Association
Shoot	Throw a basketball.
Shortstop	A defensive player in baseball.
Site	Web site
Stats	Statistics
STD	Sports Therapy Division
Surf the Net	Going on-line, visiting various sites on the Internet.
TAC/USA	The Athletics Congress of the U.S.A.
Tennis Pro	Tennis professional
Thoroughbred	Breed of horse.
Trades	Magazines and newspapers that deal with specific industries.
Trotters	Horses trained to trot instead of gallop.
Ump.	Umpire

Umpire	Official who enforces the rules of a game.
USAA	United States Athletes Association
USAABF	U.S.A. Amateur Boxing Federation
USAFHA	U.S.A. Field Hockey Association
USAIGC	United States Association of Independent Gymnastics Clubs
USAWF	United States Amateur Wrestling Foundation
USBF	United States Baseball Federation
USBF	United States Boxing Federation
USBWA	United States Basketball Writers Association
USCCCA	United States Cross Country Coaches Association
USGF	United States Gymnastics Federation
USHWA	United States Harness Writers' Association
USL	United Soccer League
USLA	United States Lifesaving Association
USS	United States Swimming, Inc.
USSA	United States Ski Association
USSA	United States Sports Academy
USSCA	U.S. Ski Coaches Association
USSF	United States Soccer Federation
USSF	United States Swimming Foundation
USSWA	United States Ski Writers Association
USTA	United States Trotting Association
USWTCA	United States Women's Track Coaches Association
USYSA	United States Youth Soccer Association
WABA	Women's American Basketball Association
WBA	World Boxing Association
WBC	World Boxing Council
WBCA	Women's Basketball Coaches Association
WBF	World Boxing Federation
WBO	World Boxing Organization
Web	The World Wide Web
Web site	A place on the World Wide Web
WEPR	Women Executives in Public Relations
WIC	Women In Communications, Inc.
WIS	Women In Soccer
WNBA	Women's National Basketball Association
WSF	Women's Sports Foundation
WWSRA	Western Winter Sports Representatives Association
WWW	World Wide Web

INDEX

CAREER OPPORTUNITIES
IN THE SPORTS INDUSTRY

Second Edition ◆ by Shelly Field

Whether you're a student or a professional ready for a career change, you'll find in this invaluable book everything you need to know to start an exciting career in sports or change the direction of your current career.

Career Opportunities in the Sports Industry is the most comprehensive and up-to-date guide to this challenging and diverse field. This second edition has been revised to provide the latest information on salaries, opportunities for minorities and women, and using the Internet in your job search. In it you'll also find indispensable and realistic information on more than 70 specific jobs such as:

PROFESSIONAL ATHLETES
Professional Baseball Player
Professional Basketball Player
Professional Boxer
Professional Football Player

SPORTS JOURNALISM
Sportscaster/Television
Sports Photographer
Sports Writer

WHOLESALING AND RETAILING
Manufacturer's Representative/Sporting
    Goods or Equipment Company
Store Manager

SPORTS MEDICINE
Athletic Trainer
Physical Therapist

PROFESSIONAL SPORTS TEAMS
Professional Scout
Professional Sports Team Publicist
Team General Manager
Ticket Manager

SPORTS BUSINESS AND ADMINISTRATION
Professional Sports Agent
Sports Industry Publicist
Sports Information Director/College

COACHING AND EDUCATION
Athletic Director
High School Coach
Physical Education Teacher/Secondary School

RACING
Jockey
Racetrack Announcer
Racing Secretary

BOXING AND WRESTLING
Boxing Trainer
Matchmaker
Professional Boxing Judge
Professional Wrestling Referee

OFFICIATING SPORTS TEAMS
Pro Football Referee
Umpire/Amateur-Scholastic Baseball
Umpire/Pro Baseball

RECREATION AND FITNESS
Aerobics Instructor
Golf Pro
Health Club Manager
Lifeguard
Personal Trainer

For each position detailed, you'll find a *Career Profile* presenting an overview of the salient features of the job (duties, alternate titles, salary range, employment and advancement prospects, and prerequisites); a *Career Ladder* illustrating frequent routes to and from the position described; and a comprehensive text pointing out special skills, education, training and various associations relevant to each job. Also included are an index for fast, easy reference, as well as recently updated appendixes with listings of major trade periodicals and books, trade organizations and associations, and relevant educational institutions.

Shelly Field is the owner of The Shelly Field Organization, a public relations and management firm specializing in celebrity clients in the music, sports and entertainment industries. Field is a career consultant to educational institutions, employment agencies, corporations, libraries, women's groups and individuals. She frequently lectures on empowerment and various career-oriented subjects. Field is also the author of *Career Opportunities in Advertising and Public Relations*, *Career Opportunities in Theater and the Performing Arts*, *Career Opportunities in the Music Industry*, *Career Opportunities in Health Care* and numerous other career-counseling guides.

ISBN 0-8160-3795-7

Cover design by Amy Beth Gonzalez
Printed in the United States of America

$18.95 U.S.
$26.95 Can.

9 780816 037957